Shocking Tales
From
Victorian Portsmouth

Convict in Chains on Public Works

Shocking Tales
From
Victorian Portsmouth

Paul Newell

Moyhill Publishing

© Copyright 2018 Paul Newell.

All rights reserved. This book, or any portion thereof, may not be reproduced or used in any manner whatsoever without the express written permission of the author except for the use of brief quotations in a book review.
The moral right of the author has been asserted.

First Published in 2018 by Moyhill Publishing.
ISBN 9781905597819.

A CIP catalogue record for this book is available from the British Library.

Printed and bound in Great Britain by Marston Book Services Ltd, Oxfordshire

Transcripts and Images have been created by myself with thanks to
the The British Newspaper archive (www.britishnewspaperarchive.co.uk),
or from my own private collection.

Cover photograph by Charlotte Newell.
I would also like to acknowledge the unknown artist who created the mural which I have used on the front cover. This mural is located on a wall behind what was the Portsea Island Union, St. Mary's Road.

Book Design and Production by *Moyhill* Publishing.
Cover Design by Moyhill Publishing.

The papers used in this book were produced in an environmentally friendly way from sustainable forests.

Moyhill Publishing,
1965 Davenport House, 261 Bolton Rd, Bury, Gtr. Manchester BL8 2NZ. UK

This book is dedicated

To my family and generations to come.

Contents

INTRODUCTION	1
1838 – HIDDEN IN HER APRON	2
1840 – DREADFUL FIRE AT SOUTHWICK HOUSE	2
1844 – MELANCHOLY ACCIDENT AT PORTSMOUTH	2
1847 – A MISERABLE STATE OF AFFAIRS	2
1848 – MURDER OF A CONVICT KEEPER	3
1850 – INSUBORDINATION ON THE HULKS	5
1851 – CONVICT PRISON AT PORTSMOUTH	6
1852 – SENTENCE OF DEATH AT THE YARDARM	6
1854 – CONVICTS BREAKING UP THE "YORK" HULK	7
1855 – AN EXPLOSION IN PORTSMOUTH DOCKYARD	7
1856 – THE MURDER OF DR HOPE BY A CONVICT	8
1856 – COURT MARTIAL OF A DESERTER	11
1858 – A MAIDEN LADY BURNT TO DEATH	11
1860 – ACCIDENT WITH A BAYONET	12
1863 – CORPORAL PUNISHMENT FOR GARROTTERS	12
1864 – CASE OF CHILD STEALING FROM A PORTSMOUTH WORKHOUSE	13
1865 – THE PORTSEA MURDER	14
1865 – CURIOUS SUICIDE BY SWORD	16
1866 – TALES FROM THE PORTSMOUTH POLICE COURT PART 1	16
1867 – CRUEL TREATMENT OF A BOY ON BOARD THE SHIP MEGAERA	18
1867 – FATAL ACCIDENT OF A CHILD AT PORTSEA	20
1867 – CONVICT LIFE IN A PORTSMOUTH PRISON	22
1867 – WOULDN'T PAY A COPPER!	29
1869 – DISCOVERY OF HIDDEN PROPERTY	29
1869 – TALES FROM THE PORTSMOUTH POLICE COURT PART 2	29
1869 – SHOCKING SUICIDE OF AN ARTILLERYMAN AT HILSEA	33
1869 – SHUGARO DAUGHTER ASSAULT	34
1870 – DEATH OF A RECLUSE AT LANDPORT	34
1870 – ATTEMPTED MURDER AND SUICIDE	36
1872 – CASES OF SUDDEN DEATH AT SOUTHSEA	36
1872 – TALES FROM THE PORTSMOUTH POLICE COURT PART 3	37
1873 – LOSS OF A DOG	40
1873 – THE SHOCKING CASE OF POISONING AT PORTSMOUTH	41
1874 – TERRIBLE ACCIDENT ON THE RAMPARTS	45
1874 – PRISON DISCIPLINE	48
1875 – A NOTORIOUS CAREER	50
1876 – STEALING TROUSERS, BOOTS AND A COAT	51
1877 – PROSECUTIONS BY THE SCHOOL BOARD	51
1878 – THE MURDEROUS ASSAULT UPON A CONSTABLE AT COSHAM	52
1879 – THE CHARGE OF MANSLAUGHTER AT PORTSEA	53
1879 – THE ADMIRALTY AND NAVAL LUNATICS	53
1879 – SUDDEN DEATH OF A CHILD AT LANDPORT	53
1879 – THE CHARGE OF ATTEMPTING TO SHOOT A SON AT MILTON	54
1879 – AN EXTRAORDINARY SHOOTING CASE	55
1879 – THE SINGULAR CASE OF DROWNING IN PORTSMOUTH HARBOUR	55
1879 – FATAL FIRE AT CRASSWELL STREET	56

Contents

1880 – A BURIAL SCANDAL AT PORTSMOUTH.	56
1880 – THE PUNISHMENT OF A BRUTE.	57
1881 – THE ALLEGED DEATH FROM VIOLET POWDER AT LANDPORT.	57
1881 – MAN GORED BY A BULLOCK.	60
1881 – THE FATAL TRAMWAY ACCIDENT AT HILSEA.	60
1881 – CHILDREN AT LUNATIC ASYLUMS.	62
1881 – A PORTSMOUTH GHOST STORY.	62
1882 – A PORTSMOUTH PLAGUE SPOT. SHOCKING REVELATIONS.	63
1882 – FATAL PURSUIT OF A LUNATIC.	64
1882 – FALSE TEETH: CHOKED OR DROWNED?	66
1883 – HORSE MANURE ACCIDENT.	66
1883 – SUPPRESSING THE TRAMPS.	66
1884 – FATAL ACCIDENT AT THE PUBLIC BATHS.	66
1884 – FALL OF A BUILDING – INJURY TO CONVICTS.	68
1884 – A LUNATIC'S VIEWS OF SOUTHSEA.	68
1884 – INQUEST AT THE PORTSMOUTH LUNATIC ASYLUM.	69
1884 – FIGHT ON BOARD A MAN-OF-WAR.	70
1885 – A CHILD BURNT TO DEATH.	71
1885 – CONVICTION OF A SOUTHSEA RESIDENT.	71
1885 – THE FATAL ACCIDENT AT PORTSMOUTH DOCKYARD.	72
1885 – A FATAL MEAL.	73
1885 – SUICIDE IN DORSET STREET.	73
1886 – ATTACK ON PRISON WARDERS.	73
1886 – ATTEMPTED SUICIDE WITH A REVOLVER.	73
1886 – KILLED ON TRAMWAY.	74
1886 – AN ELEPHANT AT LARGE.	74
1886 – THE FATAL ACCIDENT AT THE LANDPORT RAILWAY STATION.	74
1888 – MILITARY AFFRAY AT PORTSMOUTH.	75
1888 – FRIENDSHIP AND FATE.	76
1889 – DEATH FROM HYDROPHOBIA.	77
1890 – A LUNATIC AT LARGE IN PORTSMOUTH.	78
1891 – A PORTSMOUTH CHARACTER IN COURT.	79
1891 – AT THE CORONER'S COURT.	79
1891 – SHOCKING MURDER AT STAMSHAW.	79
1891 – SERIOUS FIRE AT PORTSMOUTH.	86
1891 – BROTHEL KEEPING.	87
1891 – SAD DEATH OF A DIVER.	88
1891 – "TIPTOE JOHNNY" GOES TO PRISON.	88
1892 – A FATAL FRACTURE.	89
1892 – A HORRIBLE DISCOVERY AT HILSEA.	89
1892 – THEFT AND DESERTION.	90
1892 – A MARINE ARTILLERYMAN KILLED AT COSHAM.	90
1893 – THE PORTSMOUTH TRAGEDY. THE CASE OF ADA URRY.	92
1893 – THE COPPER STREET FIRE.	117
1893 – POINT DROWNING CASE.	123
1893 – MYSTERIOUS OCCURRENCE AT SOUTHSEA.	123
1893 – A SHOCKING AFFAIR AT SOUTHSEA.	124
1893 – DEATH FROM ALCOHOLISM AT BUCKLAND.	124

Contents

1893 – THE SCENE ON SOUTHSEA ESPLANADE.	124
1893 – DROWNED IN DESERTING.	126
1894 – THE TALE OF THE TEA LEAVES.	127
1894 – OUTRAGE AND SUICIDE NEAR PORTSMOUTH.	127
1894 – PORTSMOUTH FOOTBALL FATALITY.	127
1894 – DARING ROBBERY IN SOUTHSEA.	128
1894 – ANOTHER HUMAN OSTRICH – DEATH AT THE MILTON ASYLUM.	129
1894 – RESCUED FROM THE MOAT AT HILSEA.	130
1894 – THE ALLEGED KIDNAPPING OF A PORTSMOUTH BOY.	130
1894 – A RUNAWAY HORSE.	131
1895 – AFTER THE CRAB TEA WAS OVER.	131
1895 – STARVING A FAMILY. SAD CASE AT LANDPORT.	131
1895 – ALLEGED BRUTAL ASSAULT.	132
1895 – A DEFIANT HAWKER.	133
1895 – A QUESTION OF AGE.	133
1895 – SHOPKEEPERS AT VARIANCE.	133
1895 – ATTEMPTED SUICIDE. RESCUE AT PORTSEA.	133
1896 – THE CHILD MURDER NEAR PORTSMOUTH.	134
1898 – AN UNNATURAL FATHER.	134
1897 – SUDDEN DEATH AT COSHAM.	135
1897 – A SIAMESE SAILOR'S SOVEREIGN.	135
1897 – THREE SUDDEN DEATHS.	136
1898 – FINED FOR ASSISTING DESERTERS.	136
1898 – HILSEA BARRACKS POISONING.	137
1899 – A VALUABLE STAMP ALBUM. CURIOUS CASE AT PORTSMOUTH.	137
1899 – ALL THROUGH POVERTY.	138
1899 – ROUGHS AT SOUTHSEA.	138
1899 – THE DESERTER AND THE SCARECROW.	138
1899 – DEATH OF A KINGSTON NONOGENARIAN.	138
1899 – "MONTE CARLO DAMSELS."	139
1899 – A LUNATIC'S SUICIDE. EXCITING SCENE AT MILTON ASYLUM.	139
1899 – SIDELIGHTS ON CONVICT LIFE.	141
1900 – EXTRAORDINARY CASE OF FRAUD ON A PORTSMOUTH TRADESMAN.	147
1900 – MURDER BY HYPNOTISM.	147
1900 – A BIG FIRE AT PORTSEA.	148

INTRODUCTION

Victorian Portsmouth – home of Her Majesty's Navy – a city of contrast, from the affluent multi-roomed houses of Southsea, the garrisons and Dockyard, to the slums of Portsea. Life could be vibrant, when the eyes of the world were upon the city during Fleet Reviews and other such occasions, but beneath this pageantry festered a desperate class, bereft of the niceties of their neighbours along the seafront. Despite improvements to basic amenities such as sanitation and lighting, the poor and destitute suffered greatly. As a result of this, notorious areas of Portsea, such as White's Row, became a denizen of vice and murder and the criminal fraternity thrived in the densely packed streets and courtyards. Many of these areas no longer exist in their original form.

Rich pickings then for the sensational and shocking style of journalistic reporting which was so prevalent at the time. In the absence of modern day, readily available, news coverage, the local press was the only source of information and they held their audience captive with their graphic descriptions of tales of woe and the scandalous, darker side of city life.

Tales of "lunatics," kidnapping, murder, drunkenness and debauchery to name but a few, gripped the public, desperate for the next chapter or the latest update from the Coroner or Magistrates' Courts. Alongside these, tales from the Workhouse or Asylum highlighted the plight of those at the mercy of the system. The Press left little to the imagination and were not afraid to describe the misery and gruesome occurrences in great detail, as the more sensational it was, the more papers were sold.

A classic example of this is The Illustrated Police News, famously known for its front page sketches of the Whitechapel "Jack the Ripper" Murders. They were deliberately shocking to capture the imagination of the readers. Some of the illustrations in this book are taken from the front pages of this publication and suitably bring to life certain stories.

The stories are deliberately transcribed as they appeared when first published and in as many cases as possible I have endeavoured to find a natural conclusion to each story so as not to leave the reader wondering what happened next. Not all the tales are of woe and suffering, indeed in some of the police court sessions there are a few light-hearted moments to show the Magistrates had a sense of humour.

As well as the newspaper reports I have tried to illustrate what life was like for those who were punished for their crimes. Hard labour meant just that and the treadmill inside Kingston prison was put to constant use no matter what the age of the felon. It was not unusual to see children as young as ten sentenced for petty crimes such as stealing fruit.

Being Portsmouth born and bred, I have found the research as fascinating as those reading the stories over a hundred years ago, and I hope that you gain an insight into the darker side of Victorian Portsmouth and try to "enjoy" what is to follow.

So come with me and step back over a century in time and don't loiter in any dark alleys along the way!

1838 – HIDDEN IN HER APRON.

Jane Sweetman, 31, for stealing a piece of calico, was sentenced to two months' imprisonment. She deliberately put the article under her apron while the owner was serving her with a yard or two of tape.

1840 – DREADFUL FIRE AT SOUTHWICK HOUSE.

On Monday, intelligence reached the various fire insurance offices in the metropolis of a most disastrous conflagration that occurred on Saturday morning, and occasioned the total destruction of Southwick House, the seat of Thomas Thistlethwayte, Esq., situated in Southwick Park, Portsdown Hill, near Portsmouth. From the particulars received it appears that the fire originated in the kitchen, through, it is supposed, some imperfection in the flues, with which the mansion was heated, and was discovered about half past four o'clock in the morning by some labourers who were going to work in the park. The family and the domestics were at the time fast asleep. They were instantly aroused, and fortunately escaped without injury. So rapid was the work of destruction that within an hour the beautiful building presented one sheet of fire, and in another hour the massive roof had fallen in, and the building was completely gutted. An express was sent off to Portsmouth for assistance, and in the course of a short time two engines arrived with a strong detachment of the 58th Regiment, but unfortunately too late to be of any service. The fire was got wholly under control by eight o'clock. The loss of property is estimated at £20,000, £13,000 of which is insured in the Sun Fire Office.

1844 – MELANCHOLY ACCIDENT AT PORTSMOUTH.

A fatal accident took place at Portsmouth on Monday afternoon, on the King's Bastion. As the Artillerymen were reloading one of the guns, which is supposed to have hung fire, the charge went off, and blew one of them to pieces and the other was so horribly mutilated that he died soon afterwards. The guns upon this Bastion are 32 pounders, and there are only four of them. Consequently, to fire a royal salute requires each gun to be loaded five times and one six. It is usual to use the worm to clear out the gun every second charge, and it is supposed some fire had remained in the chamber. The names of the unfortunate men are Alexander Miller and Michael Walker, between 25 and 27 years of age. Miller was blown into fragments, and Walker had his thigh broken, his arm blown off into the moat, and his body otherwise disfigured. The remnants of the victims were conveyed instantly to the hospital of the Royal Marine Barracks. Only five guns had been fired when the awful catastrophe occurred. They instantly ceased firing. An inquest was held on the bodies of the unfortunate men on Tuesday, when the above circumstances were given in evidence, and the Jury returned a verdict of Accidental death.

1847 – A MISERABLE STATE OF AFFAIRS.

At Winchester Assizes on March 6. Mary Ann Beveridge was charged with the wilful murder of Thomas Beveridge, her male child, of the age of 13 months. Mr. Poulden was counsel for the prosecution. The prisoner was undefended; but the learned judge thought she should have the benefit of counsel's assistance, and Mr. Missing, therefore, volunteered to defend her.

The facts of this case are very simple, but extremely painful. The Prisoner was 39 years of age. She had been blind for seven years, and was the mother of several children. Her husband was a man of extremely profligate habits, generally to be found in beer houses, and taking up with a woman of the name of Bunter. This course of life entailed great misery on his family; their meals for a length of time were reduced to bread and water, and the mind of the prisoner, the wife of this inhuman, unkind brute, became affected. She had this infant in her arms. It was 13 month's old. She still continued to suckle it, because, as she stated, if she weaned it, she was fearful it must die for want of proper nourishment. She was a kind mother, but was always tearful that she could not procure for her children the simple food that was necessary for their existence.

The father heeded this not, he continued on his habits, and left his blind wife to get on the best way she could. Shortly after the birth of the deceased she became evidently mad for a time, but had become better. She was frequently complaining of her head, and did so particularly in the afternoon of the 22nd of January. Soon afterwards she told her eldest girl, 15 years old, to fetch her father from a public house, where she expected he was spending his hours and his money. Obeying her mother's order, the girl went to the public house, and there saw her father drinking with the woman whose company he seemed to prefer to that of his unhappy and unfortunate blind wife. The girl, having fulfilled her errand, returned to her home of misery, and told her mother that her father would be home directly. The mother told her to go again, she did so, received a similar message and again returned home. Her mother then had her bonnet on her head, and was standing on the stairs, but not seeing the baby in her arms as usual, the girl asked her mother where he was. The mother said he was asleep, and she then told the girl she wanted to fetch a policeman for that brazen Bunter, and she must go to the police station.

The girl, accustomed to attend to the wants of her mother, in consequence of her blindness, led her to the police station. Having arrived there, the mother said, "I am come to give myself up as a murderer. I have murdered my child." This did not create much alarm in the girl's mind, and she told the constable that he must not take any notice what her mother said, for she was out of her mind. The mother, however, persisted in her story. The officer asked her where the child was. She said she had hung it upstairs behind the door in her house. The policeman hurried away to the prisoner's house, and, in an upstairs room, he discovered the child on the floor with a handkerchief tied around its neck. A surgeon was called, in, and he stated that the death of the child had been occasioned by strangulation.

The Jury acquitted the prisoner on the grounds of insanity. She was in a miserable state during the trial.

1848 – MURDER OF A CONVICT KEEPER.

Considerable sensation was excited in Portsmouth Dockyard on Saturday morning last, in consequence of a report being circulated through the above establishment, that one of the convicts had made a violent and murderous attack on his keeper, and had inflicted such serious injuries on him that he was not expected to survive them. This, on further inquiry, was ascertained to be true, the unfortunate victim of the savage attack being James O'Connor, a convict guard belonging to the *York* prison ship in this harbour, and the murderer, William Alter, a convict working under his directions in the loft over the rigging house.

The unfortunate man, it appears, had excited the animosity of Alter, in consequence of his having reported him to the Captain of the ship for misconduct, and so deadly was the revenge sought for that he watched an opportunity, when his back was turned, to strike him a blow in the back of the head which fractured his skull, following this by a second blow when on the floor. The workmen employed in the building immediately rendered their assistance, and the sufferer was conveyed to the surgery in the Dockyard, thence to the *Briton* convict hospital ship, lying alongside the *York*, and there being no room for his reception there, he was taken to his residence at the Star Inn, Gosport, where he occupied a room.

Dr. Gay Shute was in immediate attendance upon the sufferer, and every possible assistance was rendered him in his condition, which was however hopeless, an extensive fracture of the skull rendering his recovery exceedingly improbable; he lingered until 10 o'clock on Sunday evening, when death terminated his sufferings.

The prisoner Alter, immediately after the commission of the act, was conveyed to the hulk and placed in a solitary cell, to await the result.

On Monday afternoon a highly respectable Jury was empanelled at the top of the Star Inn, Gosport, by the County Coroner, Charles Bear Longcroft, esq., to investigate the circumstances connected with the fatal affair.

There were present in the inquest room during the inquiry Captain Barrow, the Superintendent, and Mr. Meatyard, the chief mate of the *York* and Captain Bennison, of the *Sterling Castle*, prison ships, and a great many of the inhabitants.

The Coroner having made application to the authorities in whose charge the prisoner then remained, to permit him to be present to hear the evidence adduced against him he was brought from the hulk, and seated at the end of the table, handcuffed and heavily ironed. He is a well-built man, about the ordinary height, but of determined and sullen aspect. He was convicted at Hertford, in July last, of highway robbery, attended with a violent assault on the person, and cast for death, which sentence, however was commuted to transportation for life. He had previously been convicted of housebreaking and sentenced to seven years transportation, which term he served on board the *Warrior* hulk, at Woolwich. He was received on board the *York* on the 13th May last, and during the time he has been there his conduct has been of the most refractory nature. He is only 25 years of age.

The Jury, after being sworn, proceeded to view the body of the deceased, and on their return to the inquest room, the following evidence was received:

Richard Smith was sworn and deposed. "I am a seaman rigger, and on last Saturday morning, about half past 11 o'clock, I was over the rigging house in the Dockyard; the deceased James O'Connor, a convict guard, was in the passage on the same floor, and adjoining where I was, in charge of some convicts, among whom was the prisoner William Alter. I had occasion to come halfway down the loft for a "sampson post," and while picking it up I heard a blow struck, and on looking round saw the deceased fall on the floor. Alter was near him and I saw the mallet, now produced, over his shoulder, about to strike a second blow, which he did as the deceased was on the floor; this second blow was on the face.

I immediately went round to the deceased's assistance in company with two others, and we found him insensible; he never spoke in my presence; he had a violent blow over the eyes on the forehead, from which he was bleeding. The deceased was removed to the surgery in the Dockyard, and afterwards to his residence at Gosport. I heard the prisoner say, "I told him I'd cook his goose, and now I have done it." The mallet now produced I am certain was the one used by the prisoner; there was no other there. I identify the body I have today seen as that of O'Connor."

Charles Gregory, being sworn, deposed. "I am a sail-maker in the Dockyard. I have known the deceased some months; I was in the rigging-loft on Saturday morning, saw O'Connor there, and conversed with him; shortly after which I heard two heavy blows. I was attending there to see that the convicts did their work properly. The blows proceeded from the spot where O'Connor was, I immediately proceeded to the place, and there saw O'Connor lying on his back on the floor, bleeding from the nose and mouth; his lip was cut in two, and he was insensible. Shortly after, Alter was walking away from him, and the other convicts remained where the deceased lay. I afterwards saw the mallet, now produced, with blood upon it, which has been in my custody ever since."

Thomas Mantel Pettit was sworn, and deposed. "I am a convict keeper of the *York* hulk. When I was on board I had charge of Alter, with other convicts. On last Monday morning, about nine o'clock, I heard Alter say, when on board, confined in a solitary cell for refusing to go out to work with O'Connor, "that if the Captain didn't shift him from going to work with O'Connor, he should do something for him" (O'Connor.) Alter afterwards went to work, I don't know on what day. On Saturday last, about twelve o'clock, I received him on board, being told that he had knocked O'Connor down. I locked him up in a solitary cell, when he said to a fellow-prisoner, in a solitary cell opposite, "that he had done for one _____ ." The other prisoner asked him who that was, when he said that it was O'Connor; "I gave the _____ a blow on the head and knocked him down, he then turned up his eyes, and I gave the _____ another blow on the face, and knocked his nose flat in his face." He also said, "I saw the old Devil standing round when I killed him." [While the witness was giving this part of his evidence, the prisoner, who evinced the utmost unconcern and indifference, burst out into a loud laugh, to the astonishment of all present.]

The witness continued. "Alter also said to his fellow-prisoner "I told you I would do it, and I looked for an opportunity all the morning before I could get one, and I was an hour before I could find anything to do it with: at last I found a mallet, and that I killed him with;" I (witness) was about 10 feet from him when he said this; and he could not see me, but I heard what he said most distinctly. The other prisoner was about five feet and the other side of the passage. I said nothing to induce him to say what he did."

On the Coroner reading over the evidence of this witness to the prisoner, he said he had stated falsely, he never said any such words and wished three of his fellow-prisoners to be brought up to disprove it. This, of course, was not acceded to.

James William Williamson was next sworn, and deposed. "I am a guard on board the *York*, hulk, and was called up to assist in putting Alter into a solitary cell on Saturday morning. I stood on the ladder with the last witness after the prisoner was put into the cell. I heard every word that Alter said, and it is the same as that stated by the last witness. After Pettet had gone up to report to the Captain what the prisoner had said, I heard Alter say, "Harry (addressing his fellow-prisoner) where shall I be topped." He replied "At Winchester." Alter then said "I shan't make a fine speech on the scaffold." One of his fellow-prisoners replied, "Yes, and remember us in it; bring us up at the trial, and we will swear that O'Connor was always upon you." Another prisoner said, "Yes, he is always upon you." There were two prisoners in cells opposite, and one beside him."

Mr. Gay Shute, surgeon, deposed. "About two o'clock on Saturday last, I received a message to attend the deceased at the Star Inn, Gosport, and went immediately, and found O'Connor with his face covered with blood, a tremendous wound on the upper lip, and bleeding profusely. I observed another wound on the upper part of the nose, and detected the bones of the nose in a state of comminution, and the integument very pulpy. The eyes were obscured from observation, swollen to the greatest extent, and the patient insensible. I suggested remedies on general principles, which such wounds indicated, and these were continually adopted. In the evening I requested a consultation, which was held on Sunday morning. At two o'clock on that day he was more tranquil; at three o'clock he became comatose. At six I saw him again, when be was under the influence of delirium. I then considered it a lost case. At 10 o'clock he died in my presence. There was a wound at the back of the head, with a portion of bone denuded of its membrane. I attributed this wound to the probability of a fall by his own gravitation presuming from the extensive injury over the whole face that such might have been the effect. This morning, by authority of the Coroner, I made a post mortem examination of the head of the deceased. On exposing the brain, there was sufficient extravasation of blood on its surface to account satisfactorily for the cause of his death, confirmed by the result of minute examination of two distinct surfaces, one turgid from high inflammation, the other part divested of it. The skull being now empty, I found the portion of bone mentioned as denuded, was the commencement only of a terrible fracture of the skull, extending nearly to its base. The cause of the death of the deceased is fracture of the skull producing inflammation and extravasation of blood on the surface of the brain, under the *dura mater*. I have seen the mallet now produced, and such an instrument would cause the injuries to the head I have described. I do not think a fall, unless from a considerable height would have caused such injuries."

The Coroner now read over the evidence to the Jury, during the reading of which, the prisoner, to the utter surprise of all present, again burst out into a loud laugh, evincing the most hardened deportment. The evidence being clear and satisfactory against the prisoner as having caused the death of the deceased, the Jury, without hesitation returned a verdict of "Wilful Murder against William Alter."

The Coroner forthwith made out his committal to Winchester to take his trial at the ensuing assizes, and he was handed over to the custody of Inspector Martin, by whom be was removed the following morning to Winchester gaol. The deceased, who was an excellent officer, has left a widow and one child. He was only 28 years of age. The Jury very kindly handed over their usual fee to the poor widow. Alter has a mother and sisters living at Great Gallavey, near Grantham, Lincolnshire, to whom the sad intelligence that the son and brother had become a murderer was communicated by the Chaplain of the prison-ship.

William Alter, convicted at the last assizes for the murder at Portsmouth Dockyard of O'Connor, was executed on Wednesday at Winchester. A few minutes before nine o'clock he was led to the place of execution, amidst a large concourse of people, who, it is gratifying to observe, maintained a generally decent behaviour. He continued praying whilst the executioner prepared him for the fatal moment, and died instantly. The wretched man was born of decent parents in Lincolnshire. He was sentenced to be transported for seven years for housebreaking, and after being released at the expiration of half his time, for good conduct, he enlisted for a soldier, and having deserted and become destitute, he then committed a highway robbery, for which he was sentenced to be transported for life, and was placed on board the *York* hulk in Portsmouth harbour, where, by his own account, from being very bad in disposition he became much worse, and eventually resolved on murdering the man for whose death his own life was taken.

1850 – INSUBORDINATION ON THE HULKS.

A somewhat serious case of insubordination has occurred on board one of the convict hulks in Portsmouth harbour. A telegraphic despatch from the Admiral Superintendent of the Dockyard at Portsmouth was received at the Admiralty on Monday forenoon, announcing that the convicts on board the *Stirling Castle*, moored near the entrance of the harbour of Portsmouth, had been in a state of insubordination during the whole of Friday night, which still continued. Sir George Grey immediately despatched Mr. Voules, superintendent of convicts, to Portsmouth, to investigate the circumstances attending this proceeding, happily infrequent. The convicts on board that hulk are amongst the most unruly of the able-bodied portion of those condemned to various terms of transportation, who are placed there to undergo the preparatory stage of their disciplined labour before they are selected for transmission across the seas, and the complement on board is from 400 to 500. This *emuete* was followed by one on board the *York*, on Monday, when the convicts refused to go to work, and commenced with the legs of their stools to batter the bulkheads, and to use all sorts of abusive language to their keepers; but the officer who had charge of the ship promptly seized two of the ringleaders. One of these men received two dozen lashes, and he then asked for a glass of water, which on being given to him, he told the officer he did not care, and that he might flog away; his request was complied with, and he was ordered to receive two dozen lashes more, when he altered his tone and begged off. This prompt and decisive conduct on the part of the superintendent crushed in its bud the insubordination on board the *York*. The *emeute* on board the *Stirling Castle* was put to an end on Monday evening by the superintendent of the ship flogging several of the ringleaders. On Tuesday morning several boats' mates, with a guard of Marines, went on board, and further punishment was administered; altogether about a dozen of the convicts were flogged, the most hardened fellows receiving about three dozen lashes; the others will be detained in solitary confinement and be more heavily ironed, being in number about sixty.

1851 – CONVICT PRISON AT PORTSMOUTH.

A large convict prison, designed as a substitute for the present mode of locating convicts on board hulks in the harbour, is now being completed at Portsmouth. At its commencement, the inhabitants of the borough manifested much opposition and repugnance at the location of a large number of convicts on shore, and in the midst of a dense population but this opposition has since subsided, although much of the repugnance remains, and the Home Office has proceeded with the rapid erection of the building.

The prison is situated at the south-east boundary wall of the dockyard, with which it will have means of egress and ingress for the convicts employed in that establishment; the site of the building being that formerly occupied by the Old Laboratory. It is constructed to accommodate about 1,000 prisoners; and the object of this substitution of a prison for hulks is understood to be the necessity for exercising a large amount of discipline and authority over the convicts than is possible on board ship. The arrangements on board the latter do not prevent communications being carried on between the inmates of the different cells; consequently very serious organisations and *emeutes* have frequently arisen, and which required a strong military force to quell.

In the new prison each convict will be completely and effectually separated from all communications of any kind with his fellow prisoners, whilst any one of them inclined to be refractory will be under the complete control of the officers, and so be subjected to the requisite punishment without hindrance or annoyance from others. The cells being well ventilated, and every other regard being paid to good sanitary arrangements, the prisoners will certainly be free from the unhealthy influences inseparable from living on board confined and damp hulks.

The above are the alleged reasons for this change in convict location, but by some it is believed to be only the commencement of a comprehensive plan for meeting the difficulties arising from the objections of the colonists to convict's being sent amongst them, by establishing a series of convict prisons or "homes," as they have been called throughout this country, for retaining felons in.

The plan of the new building comprises an east and west wing, between which are situated kitchens, cooking, washing, and other domestic offices. To the north of these is a chapel, and to the east the residences of the governor, chaplain, and other officers. The whole of the buildings are of brick, and are surrounded by lofty walls. The walls of each wing are roofed over with slates, having a range of skylights on each side. Down the entire centre of each wing is a spacious corridor, having the prisoners' cells on either side and opening into it; the west wing is 292 feet long, the east wing 286 feet, both being thirty-six feet wide. There are four tiers of cells, each cell seven feet by four, and seven feet in height; on both sides of the corridor. All of the cells are fitted with a desk, for writing or reading, a seat, hammock, and shelves. The divisions between the cells are of a very simple and, both as far as space and cost are concerned, of a very economical character, being formed of plates of strong "corrugated" iron. The ceiling of the under cell and the floor of that above it are at once formed of a plate of stout slate.

The upper tier of cells open on to light iron galleries, reached by flights of stairs of the same material. Some of the cells are supplied with light by glazed openings in the wall, whilst others derive it from the corridor. Warm air is forced into the corridors from proper apparatus, finding its way into the cells, and expelling any foul air that may be generated through apertures provided for the purpose. In addition to these cells there are forty punishment cells in course of construction, each ten feet by six, and nine feet in height.

The contractors for the entire building are Messrs. Piper, of London, and the work has been carried on under the direction of Colonel Jebb, the Home Office Inspector of Prisons. The immediate superintendence of the building has been confided to Mr. C. J. Woolcott, the government clerk of the works. It has been constructed with great rapidity, not having been six months in course of erection; and by the 1st of October it is expected that the larger wing will be occupied by prisoners.

1852 – SENTENCE OF DEATH AT THE YARDARM.

A court-martial, consisting of Rear-Admiral Prescott, C.B., President, Captain Chads, C.B., of the *Excellent*, Captain Talbot, of the *Meander*; Captain Scott, of the *Neptune*; Captain Robinson, of the *Arrogant*; Capt. Giffard, of the *Termagant*; Captain Gordon, of the *Encounter*; Captain Matson, of the *Highflyer*, and Mr. G. L. Greetham. Deputy Judge Advocate of the Fleet, assembled on board the *Victory* on Thursday morning, to try William Alexander Williams, alias William Bigg, a gunner in the R.M. Artillery detachment, serving on board H.M.S. *Dauntless*, on the following charge:— "For having on the morning of the 31st of July, the *Dauntless* then being at sea, assaulted and struck Mr. Joseph Oliver, the Gunner of the said ship, who was on duty at the time."

Captain Halsted prosecuted for the Admiralty. Mr. Oliver deposed that he was on duty on the main deck about 10 o'clock in the forenoon of the day named in the charge, standing with his back towards the breech of the 8th gun on the starboard side of the ship, and speaking to the Paymaster's steward, when the prisoner struck him under his right ear. The prisoner was at the time in irons, for having on a former occasion, used abusive and improper language towards Mr. Oliver whilst then also on duty. The witness said he felt the effects of the blow for a fortnight afterwards.

Richard Platt, the Paymaster's steward, above referred to, deposed to having seen the blow struck by the prisoner, and that no provocation whatever was given by Mr. Oliver, This witness was cross examined by the prisoner, who asked him if Mr. Oliver did not tread upon his irons, to which witness replied, "No."

Captain Halsted was sworn by the court, for the purpose of explaining how the prisoner came to be in irons on the day of the commission of the crime laid in the charge. He said the prisoner being in irons on the of 31st July, was in consequence of a charge, preferred against him, and investigated before him, (Capt. Halsted) having made use of most violent and mutinous language to Mr. Oliver when in the discharge of his duty. On investigating Mr. Oliver's complaint, the impression on his (Capt. Halsted's) mind, was that Mr. Oliver had conducted himself with great calmness and forbearance, and had simply fulfilled his duty, he having the care or charge of the main deck.

There was a sentinel watching over the prisoner at the time he committed the assault, but it was found at the moment the blow was struck he, (the sentinel) had his back turned to the prisoner, and therefore did not see the blow given, consequently he was not brought forward on the prosecution as a witness.

The Prisoner did not cross-examine Capt. Halsted. This being the whole of the evidence in support of the charge the prisoner was called upon for his defence. He said he had none to make. Thereupon the Court offered him time to prepare a defence, and seek the assistance of the Judge Advocate, but he declined to avail himself of the advantage volunteered. He said, however, "All I hope is that, if the court find me guilty, you will take into consideration the length of time I have been in confinement with both feet in irons, and placed in that part of the ship by which I was degraded in the eyes of my officers, which was far worse punishment than the confinement itself. I have no one to call in my favour, but this is a certificate of former good conduct," (handing in a general certificate of character from Captains of the different ships he had been in). The court was then cleared for deliberation, and remained closed for about an hour, at the expiration of which time it was re-opened when the Judge Advocate pronounced that the court found the charge fully proved, and adjudged the prisoner to suffer death by being hanged by the neck till he was dead, at such time as shall please the Lords Commissioners of the Admiralty.

1854 – CONVICTS BREAKING UP THE "YORK" HULK.

Transportation being no longer a sentence of punishment, convict labour now engages the attention of Government, not only as regards the disposal of it, but as a system which national works may be constructed, with advantage to public finance. The most arduous work is accomplished by these unfortunate men, in all weather, and at all times, night as well as by day; and, during the preparations for war at Portsmouth Dockyard, these convicts have been employed breaking up the York Hulk, by torch light.

It is worthy of remark that frequently these men are employed upon various works, and often of that nature from which free labour would shrink; and volunteers can always be obtained for any service where hard labour is essential.

Such conduct on the part of men who are looked upon as the most abandoned reckless characters, seems certainly to offer great hopes that the reformatory system, under which they are now so happily placed, will be attended with most beneficial results; and that, if any care and interest is taken in them after their discharge from prison, many of them will become useful and respectable members of society.

1855 – AN EXPLOSION IN PORTSMOUTH DOCKYARD.

An explosion of gas occurred on Saturday night in this dockyard, in the police station, at an entrance where the steam factory labourers have egress and regress, abutting upon the new buildings. A strong smell of gas had been prevalent since Friday night, which could not be accounted for. It appeared, however, to be very strong under the flooring of the building used as the police station, in which the members of the force just relieved (at nine o'clock) were engaged in taking their suppers. It is said that one of these turned the exposed light of his lantern on in searching out the

Convicts breaking up 'The York' hulk by torchlight, in Portsmouth Harbour.

chief spot of the effluvium, whereupon the explosion instantly ensued. The sound of the explosion resembled the discharge of a piece of ordnance as large as a 32 pounder. The building was immediately shattered to a wreck, and the roof, in its descent, buried all beneath at the time, about ten persons, all of whom were more or less injured, and were borne to Haslar Hospital as soon as extricated. Their names are Strout, inspector, both legs broken; Thomas Ripley, sergeant, seriously wounded; Constables W. Helms, Henry Neville, and Miller, seriously injured; James Giles, arm and leg broken; James Wassell, thigh broken; Thomas Sydenham, leg broken; Daniel Palmer, wounded in the face and eye.

1856 – THE MURDER OF DR HOPE BY A CONVICT.

On Friday morning was committed in Portsmouth harbour, one of those cold-blooded murders, which have lately become so frequent in this country, but from which, until now, Portsmouth has happily been exempt.

The victim was Mr. Charles William Hope, assistant surgeon of the invalid convict establishment at this port, aged about 42, and unmarried. He was a general favourite amongst the convicts under his charge, for many of whom he had interceded with the Governor when they were in disgrace.

The murderer is a convict named Thomas Jones, who was transported for 7 years, in July, 1853, at Kingston-upon-Hull, for stealing a gold watch-chain. The only inducement for him to commit the deed of violence, appears to have been the doctor removing him from the lower deck, which appeared to be the place appropriated for those who were in the worst state of health, and where they enjoyed many comforts and privileges, which a removal into "a class," as it is termed, took away from them.

On Thursday morning Jones was removed into a class, by Mr. Hope's orders; but on the Friday, he again appeared before him to be examined, expressing his wish to be placed on the lower deck again. This Mr. Hope declined to do, and shortly afterwards the villain gave him the fatal blow which caused his death. Mr. Hope did not appear at first to know that he had been struck by any weapon, the scarf and neck-tie round his neck apparently keeping the wound from bleeding; but on his reaching the deck, he felt faint; and on the scarf being removed much blood flowed from the wound, and he shortly afterwards expired.

Not content with one victim, the villain, on the Infirmary Warder apprehending him, endeavoured to stab him, and he also threatened to serve the Chief-Warder in the same way.

The instrument used by Jones has not yet been found; but a piece of razor fitted to a bit of wood, had been seen in his possession previously, by another convict.

The inquest on the body of the deceased was held on Friday afternoon, on board the *Stirling Castle*, before W. Swainson, Esq., Admiralty Coroner, and a Jury composed of inhabitants of Gosport, of whom the Rev. A. Ewing was selected to be the foreman. The Jury having been sworn, they proceeded to view the body of the deceased, after which the Coroner proceeded to call the witnesses.

William Charles, who being sworn, deposed: I am the infirmary warder of the convict invalid establishment in Portsmouth harbour; I knew the deceased, Charles Wm. Hope; he was assistant surgeon of the invalid convict establishment, and resided on board the *Britain*, hospital ship; I identify the body the Jury have viewed as that of Mr. Hope; the duties of Mr. Hope called him on board both ships this morning, a few minutes before 8 o'clock, the prisoner Thomas Jones (124 C), convict, confined on board the *Stirling Castle*, went to the surgery, and asked Mr. Hope to examine his chest; deceased told Jones to undress, and he would examine him; he did so, and Mr. Hope sounded him. Jones then asked the deceased if he meant to send him to the lower deck; he replied, "No, I do not see any occasion for it at present, we are very full on the lower deck; if I see any change in you for the worse, I will send you either to the lower deck, or to the *Britain*." Jones then began to put on his clothes, saying, "Very well Mr. Hope," the deceased, was then about leaving, when Jones snatched up his clothes, and ran out before him, putting his clothes on the form, outside the galley door.

The deceased returned to the surgery to see another man, and on again coming out, I saw the prisoner Jones catch Mr. Hope round the neck with his left hand, and with his right hand strike him, apparently in his face. I was as this time about two yards from the deceased. I stepped forward and caught hold of Jones, and drawing him away from the deceased, threw him down. Mr. Hope then ran away round the galley; he did not call out that he was hurt, and there was no appearance of blood from him to attract attention.

When I seized hold of the prisoner, he struck me on the left side, and my two coats, I have since ascertained, are cut through, as if with some sharp instrument. The prisoner then made his way towards the galley door, saying he wanted to see Mr. Williams (the chief warder). I stood opposite to him to prevent his going, when he said, "I don't want to hurt you, Mr. Charles; I want to see Mr. Williams."

He made a step towards the galley door, to go towards the upper deck, and I stopped him. I was three or four minutes with the prisoner, another officer (Mr. Meader) being with us. I told Mr. Meader to take charge of him, whilst I went to seek Mr. Williams. Not finding Mr. Williams in the cabin, I went on the quarter-deck. Passing by the governor's office door, I saw Mr. Hope lying down in the office. A convict, George Mitchell, was leaning over him, apparently about to staunch the blood, which was flowing fast from deceased's neck and mouth. Mitchell said to me, "Mr. Hope has fell down in a fit, and is bleeding." I then untied his neckerchief and took it off, when I found that he had received a wound in his throat. I sent immediately for Mr. Keeling, who came about 10 minutes afterwards. When I saw Mr. Hope, he was gasping; he continued in this state for about five minutes, when he appeared to be dead.

Yesterday morning Mr. Hope discharged the prisoner from the lower deck to a class; this change would cause the prisoner to receive a change of diet, and to sleep in a hammock, instead of on a bedstead. I now recollect that about five minutes before the blow was struck, the prisoner Thomas Jones, said to the deceased, "You and Mr. Williams are conniving together to do me serious injury." Mr. Hope interrupted him, and told him not to believe anything of the sort, Mr. Williams had not even mentioned it to him. He also said to Mr. Hope, that he would not be slow poisoned or slow murdered, I don't remember which expression he used.

William Header, being sworn, deposed: I am an assistant-warder on board the *Stirling Castle*. This morning about 10 minutes after 8 o'clock, on coming into the gallery of the chapel, I saw the prisoner Thomas Jones on the deck, Mr. Charles having hold of his collar. I took hold of him and lifted him up, and in consequence of instructions I received from Mr. Charles, I took charge of him. Mr. Charles then told me I was not to let him out of the chapel. Whilst I had charge of him the prisoner enquired for Mr. Hope. Mr. Charles told him he was gone for Mr. Williams, and would be back again directly. I detained him for about 10 minutes in the chapel, when I received orders to lock him up. Previous to locking him up in the refractory cell, I searched the prisoner. I found nothing on him but a comb and handkerchief. I searched him in the usual way, not having received any information of what he had done; there is a closet in the cell in which he was confined, through which a knife could be thrown. I did not observe any blood upon the prisoner's hands. I afterwards stripped the prisoner, but could not find any instrument, but did not examine his clothes to see if any blood was there. I have also examined the passages where he was, and through which he passed, but could find no instrument.

The prisoners are not allowed to have knives except at meals, and the officer in charge would know if one was then missing. He would have had no opportunity of throwing the knife overboard, after I had charge of him in the chapel. After I had locked the prisoner up in the cell, after stripping him, I went on the quarter-deck, and reported having done so. I received from Mr. Williams a pair of handcuffs, and went down to put them on the prisoner. Mr. Williams followed me. The prisoner Jones then said, "If 1 could get at you, I would serve you the same, you b____ villain, mark my word, there's a person waiting for you in this place." With that I locked the door and left him.

Scott, deposed: I am the principal warder on board the *Stirling Castle*; about 10 minutes past 8 this morning, Mr. Hope came up the after-ladder on the quarter-deck, where I was standing. I walked towards him to take a key which I was in the habit of receiving from him. He said in a very loud voice, and agitated manner, "Mr. Scott, I have been struck." I said, "Struck, by whom, sir?" He said, "That man Jones." I said, "Are you hurt, sir?" He said, "Let me sit down."

I led him by the arm into the governor's office, and placed him on a chair. I ran out on the quarter-deck to call Mr. Charles. The convict George Mitchell was cleaning windows at the time. I returned to the office immediately, Mitchell was then entering the office, and said," Mr. Hope has fallen down, sir." I moved the chair, and laid hold of Mr. Hope to lift him up. I removed the scarf from off his neck, when I saw the blood issuing from a wound in the neck of the deceased. With the assistance of Mr. Charles and Mr. Prescott, I moved him outside the office door. Mr. Charles called for some lint and brandy, and the former was applied to the wound. He did not speak, and appeared to be dead in five or six minutes.

The Coroner then adjourned the inquest until Monday next, to allow for a further search being made for the weapon which was used by Jones.

INQUEST RECONVENED.

The inquest on the body of the late Assistant-Surgeon Hope, of the convict establishment at Portsmouth, who was murdered on Friday morning last, was resumed on Monday, on board the *Stirling Castle* hulk, by Mr. Swainson, the Admiralty Coroner, when further testimony was adduced to show the vindictiveness of the prisoner towards the deceased, and also towards Mr. Williams, the chief warder, and Mr. Bowler, the surgeon of the convict establishment, both of whom the prisoner expressed his regret at not having "finished" also, as then, he said, he should have been happy.

The Rev. J. K. Walpole, chaplain of the establishment, deposed that the prisoner had told him he had resolved, on the night before the accomplishment of his premeditated purpose, that he would give Mr. Hope another chance for his life, alluding to his desire to be examined again by the deceased touching an alleged complaint which required the treatment of cupping, and which deceased would not certify the necessity for doing. The prisoner, being thus disappointed in his object of being restored to the invalid deck, said to the chaplain, "I did it without pang."

A convict named Haynes, No. 716, deposed to the prisoner having had a part of a razor, set into a small wooden handle, about his person for some weeks, on the pretext of using it at work in the oakum-house. The prisoner interrupted this witness in his testimony, and stated to the Jury that he had had two of these knives or razors in his possession, and, in fact, a third, and that he had been in the hulk about 10 months, and had never been searched once. The truth of this statement seems to be doubtful, for it is the custom of the convict service to search all prisoners on leaving the oakum-house whenever they are employed therein.

The prisoner was on Monday placed before the Jury, between two warders, in the gallery of the chapel, and asked several questions, imputing cruelty and oppression on the part of the deceased and other officers towards him; but the evidence did not support his accusations. He said "the razor" could yet be produced, and it was on the lower deck, and he hoped the Jury would hear his statement of the treatment he had received, which was the "cause" of his murdering (for he made no disguise or equivocation about having done so) Mr. Hope.

After hearing the evidence of Mr. Kealey, surgeon, of Gosport, who deposed to the death of the deceased having been caused by the wound in the throat, which had penetrated to the spine and severed the jugular vein, the Jury returned a verdict of "Wilful murder" against the prisoner Jones, who was removed to Winchester Gaol to await his trial. The prisoner seems rather a superior or intellectual, than a forbidding or ferocious looking man, and appeared as cool and collected throughout the whole proceedings as if he were at his commonest avocations.

The murderer of Dr. Hope, convict-surgeon at Portsmouth, Thomas Jones, underwent the extreme sentence of the law at Winchester on Saturday. Before he died he repented of his crime, acknowledged the justice of his sentence and sought the aid of religion to support him in the prospect of an ignominious death. From his condemned cell he sent the following letter:

"To the friends and relatives of the late Dr. Hope. It is quite impossible for me to express feelings of deep sorrow and shame with which I reflect on the wicked deed of mine which has deprived you of one so near and dear to you. I feel I cannot depart this life without this expression of my sorrow, even though it may be suspected, or spurned, as I deserve it should be; but as it will be too late when this reaches you to ask you to forgive me, I can only entertain the hope that your Christian charity would have afforded me that comfort if there had been an opportunity. "May you be found on the day of judgment amongst those who shall be saved." – Thomas Jones.

The parties to whom this was addressed believing in its sincerity, and compassionating the unhappy writer, sent a reply which consoled him in his last agonies. He partook of the Holy Sacrament on the day previous to his execution. He met his death with firmness, but without bravado, and the drop fell as he prayed to God through the Saviour of mankind to sustain and receive his soul.

1856 – COURT MARTIAL OF A DESERTER.

A court martial, consisting of among others, Rear-Admiral the Hon. Sir R. S. Dundas, K.C.B, Commander of the Baltic Fleet, and Mr. W. J. Hellyer, Deputy-Judge Advocate of the Fleet, assembled on Tuesday on the flagship *Victory* at Portsmouth, to try Henry Duncan, Acting Assistant Engineer of the second class, belonging to Her Majesty's ship *Cressy*, for having deserted, or having absented himself without leave from that ship on the 12th February last, and for not returning until taken back into custody on the 25th.

It appeared by the evidence of Commander John Seccombe that the prisoner was sent ashore on the day in question, (when the ship was lying in the Downs), to take the chief engineer's expense book to that officer, who was then sick in Deal Naval Hospital, Commander Seccombe strictly enjoining him to use despatch and to return to the *Cressy* the same day, as he was the only engineer they had to depend upon in the event of weighing or the engines being started. The prisoner did not go near his chief, but left the books at a public house in Deal, (The New Inn), and made off to Dover to visit his brother with whom he took a trip to France in the *Queen* mail packet, of which his brother is the engineer.

From Calais, the prisoner was off to London to finish his "spree," when he was apprehended about forty miles from Deal, and sent as a deserter to the flagship *Waterloo*, at Sheerness, whence he was forwarded to the *Cressy* to be dealt with as the Lords of the Admiralty might direct.

The prisoner had nothing to say in defence, but put in certificates of good character from the mercantile firms where he learnt his craft, and he called on Commander Seccombe to speak as to his knowledge of his conduct during the three months he had been on board the *Cressy*. This testimony was very favourable to him.

The Court, after a very long deliberation, pronounced the charge proved, except in that part relative to the prisoner's apprehension on the road on the 18th February, which they had no direct evidence to prove; and he was sentenced to be mulcted of all pay and allowances due to him, to be reduced to the grade of a third class assistant engineer, and to be disqualified for promotion to a higher grade for the term of one year.

1858 – A MAIDEN LADY BURNT TO DEATH.

A melancholy circumstance occurred in the pretty, quiet town of Cosham, on Tuesday, the 19th inst., which has caused a considerable sensation, and resulted in the death of the unfortunate lady who was the subject of the accident.

It appears that two elderly maiden ladies named Farley, have been living together for some time at East Cosham. They were in comfortable circumstances, but lived very retired, keeping no servant. They were somewhat eccentric in habit, their neighbours knew little about them, and they were in a great measure isolated from society.

About six weeks back the unfortunate deceased exhibited most unequivocal signs of aberration of the mind. She called upon some of the inhabitants at Cosham, expressing her fears for the safety of certain persons' lives, and behaved so wildly that Mr. Baker, druggist, thought it to be his duty to inform Sir Lucius Curtis, a country magistrate residing on the spot, of the state of mind of the deceased. Sir Lucius sent word to the parish officers, who unfortunately did not see the necessity for their interference.

On the morning of the above named day, a next-door neighbour saw smoke arising from the back of the house of the deceased. She went immediately to ascertain from whence the smoke proceeded; she found Miss Farley lying on her back upon the stones, enveloped in flames. A bucket of water was immediately thrown over the sufferer, while the friendly neighbour rushed into the house, from which volumes of smoke were issuing. She found a Bible and Prayer book on the carpet smouldering; she extinguished the fire. By this time Mr. Wildey, surgeon, had arrived. Upon examination, it was found that Miss Farley was much burnt about the body, but not sufficiently so to cause death. Her wounds were dressed, but the deceased tore off the bandages, saying she was not in pain; they were again replaced, and she was put to bed. All seemed to be going on well until Wednesday evening, when violent pains came on, which drew the most fearful shrieks from the unhappy sufferer until half past 10 o'clock when she expired.

About one hour before she died the pain subsided, and she informed the medical man that on Tuesday "a spirit came to her, and told her that if she burned a certain passage in the New Testament she would see a miracle. She did as commanded, but the spirit then said she had not read it sufficiently, and set fire to her."

On the Thursday afternoon an inquest was held on the body at the George Hotel, before Mr. Longcroft, Coroner for the county, when the Jury, a very respectable one, brought in a verdict to the effect "that the deceased was of unsound mind, and that death was occasioned by the conjoint effect of the burning and the shock given to the system."

1860 – ACCIDENT WITH A BAYONET.

At Portsdown Hill on Thursday last, a lad named Chapman, residing in Butcher Street, Portsea, who is a member of the Royal Artillery Corps, met with an accident by cutting the calf of his leg with a sword bayonet. It appeared that while he and several comrades were returning to the Hill from Wymering, he pulled a bugler's bayonet from its sheath and while brandishing it about he let it fall and by some means or other while in the act of stepping, the point of the weapon which fell upwards, ripped up his trousers, and inflicted a wound on the calf of his leg, about 3 inches in length, and half an inch in depth. Mr. Garrington, jun., Surgeon, sewed up the wound shortly afterwards, and the unfortunate youth was then conveyed to his home. We are happy to hear that the wound is healing and that the lad will shortly be enabled to resume his daily calling.

1863 – CORPORAL PUNISHMENT FOR GARROTTERS.

In the House of Commons, on Wednesday, Mr. Adderley moved the second reading of the Security from Violence Bill, declaring the object of the instrument to be the fitting punishment of garrotters.

We are exceedingly glad to find that notwithstanding government opposition the second reading of the Bill was carried by a majority of 63, as the fact indicates the strong desire of our legislators at once to end, by a strong hand, the abominable practice of ruffians who, to use Mr. Adderley's words, "can only be deterred from commission of crime by forcible appeals to their fear of physical pain."

But not alone to garrotters would we extend the benefit of the Act, there are other brutal fellows up for criminal offences, upon whose hearts not all the kindness of mistaken philanthropists can produce the faintest impression, but upon whose backs the lash would do a positive service since it would restrain the recipients of the scourging from indulging in violence. There are men to whom penal servitude for life would be no punishment, but to whom the terrors of the lash would prove wholesome lessons —men who would sneak through a life of confinement, not too severely dealt by and well fed, apparently contentedly, yet ever on the watch for indulgence in their brutal passions.

These fellows know that they cannot be punished much more severely, according to the law as it now stands, but introduce a Bill for flogging incorrigible criminals, and we are satisfied that the records of crime would soon exhibit marked improvement. The honest indignation of Colonel North, who could not understand "why Hon. members should be mealy mouthed about flogging a set of ruffians," we admire. The gallant Colonel referred to the case tried at the Hampshire Assizes and published in last week's issue of the *Portsmouth Times*, of Lewis Francis, the convict who was indicted for maliciously wounding with intent to murder George Dean, one of the warders of the Convict Prison, in the Dockyard, on the 19th December and instanced the folly of imprisonment without flogging in his case.

Thrice had this deep-dyed ruffian attacked and nearly murdered warders before his attack upon Dean, receiving after each of his murderous essays a sentence for a fresh term of penal servitude, but the effect of these sentences upon him, as punishment, was nil. Again for his last ferocious exploit he was sentenced last week to 20 years' penal servitude, for which, we believe, the fellow cares no more than had he received a sentence for only 20 weeks' incarceration. We maintain that such villains as the convict Francis and the more successful wretch Preedy, another convict, indicted at the Crown Court, Dorchester, on Tuesday, for the murder of Charles Evans, another convict warder, at Portland, on the 8th September last, ought not to receive that consideration at the hands of justice which mercy for the erring prompts.

The semblances of men like these have little human nature left; they have become brutalized and require to be dealt with judicious harshness to prevent them from doing harm. Every indication of ferocious violence exhibited by convicts should be followed by a certain number of lashes. The cure would be infallible. There was one observation made by Colonel North, however, in reference to the convict Francis, and the authorities here, which calls for correction.

The indignant Colonel remarked, "What is the use of passing such sentences (penal servitude) upon such a blackguard as that? Better put up the triangles and flog him on the spot, and all his fellow prisoners who aided or abetted him in his murderous assaults. If the Governor of Portsmouth gaol had the power of doing that but would not use it, he was a wretched old woman for his lenity."

Now the Governor of Portsmouth gaol, as generally understood, has nothing at all to do with convict prisoners, therefore the gallant Colonel's observations do not apply to him. Evidently the Governor of the Convict Prison at Portsea is the individual to whom Colonel North referred, but we are by no means sure that it is in the power of this official to administer the lash without due trial of a mutinous and murderously inclined prisoner. We are inclined to think no such power is vested in the Governor, and the comparison made by the Hon. member, uncomplimentary and un-parliamentary as it is, may be passed over. The duties of the Governor of a convict establishment are onerous, and before the lash is resorted to remedy for ruffianism extreme, at penal stations, the hands of the prison officials must be considerably strengthened. It will not do to stir up the passions of a horde of half brutalized men without possessing the power and the means for promptly suppressing revolt.

Let the Governors of our Convict Prisons feel assured of their exact powers, of strong support, and they would doubtless act up to the letter of the law, if not, as there is remedy for every evil under the sun, doubtless one could be found applicable to a Prison Governor disinclined to maintain strict prison discipline.

1864 – CASE OF CHILD STEALING FROM A PORTSMOUTH WORKHOUSE.

On the 11th October inst. application was made to the matron of the Portsea Island Union by a respectable-looking woman for a wet nurse. The applicant (who was apparently about 35 years of age, 5 feet 7 inches high, of fresh complexion, with dark hair and eyes, dressed in a black silk drawn bonnet, with feathers and flowers, black woollen shawl, and black merino dress) informed the matron that she had been sent by her mistress, the lady of "Sir John Creamer," whose residence was Salisbury, but who was then lodging at Southsea, to procure the services of a wet nurse for a lady residing in London. The matron recommended a woman named Hannah Turton, who is about 30 years of age, and who had given birth to a female child in the union on the 11th of October. The applicant then left, but called again the following day, stating that she had received a telegram from London directing her to alter the arrangements, and to take Turton's child up to London, with the view of its being brought up by hand there. The mother of the child raised no objection to the suggestion, and at the latter end of last week the female in question called again at the union, and the mother and the child were driven away in a cab. On arriving at the Portsmouth Railway station the mother was told that when she reached the Waterloo station she would find a carriage waiting to receive her, and that she would be able to identify the same by the gold lace on the servants' hats. She was also told that she would be driven to Peckham House, the residence of Sir John Creamer's brother. The mother, believing in the truth of this representation, and that her child would be taken to Southsea, gave up her infant to the woman who had brought her from the union. The mother accordingly left by train, and the supposed servant went away with the child. On the arrival of the train at Waterloo station, the deluded mother looked in vain for the carriage and the "servants with the gold lace." She was driven in a cab to 44 Peckham House, when she discovered it was not a private residence at all, but a lunatic asylum; but nothing was of course known of "Sir John Creamer." The Portsmouth police are actively engaged investigating this strange case, but up to the present have not been successful in tracing either the woman or the child.

A few days since we published the particulars of a case of child stealing from the Portsmouth workhouse under circumstances of an extraordinary character, and on Thursday last Sergeant Poole, a detective officer belonging to the Portsmouth force, received information which induced him to proceed to East Cowes, in the Isle of Wight. He went to Cambridge House, and found the missing child in bed with a female named Mary Ann Flucks, aged 27 years, who it appears is the wife of a labourer, and had charge of the house in question. On being interrogated about the child, the woman declared it was her own, and that she had been delivered of it on the 5th of November. She then called her mother, Sarah Fry, who said she was present and assisted her daughter in her confinement. Poole took both mother and daughter into custody and brought them to Portsmouth, and yesterday they were placed at the bar before the mayor and full bench of Magistrates. Hannah Turton, the mother of the child, on being shown the infant immediately recognised it, and appeared overjoyed at its recovery. She said that on the 11th of October the prisoner Flucks called the union and engaged her as wet-nurse to "Lady Creamer" at a salary of 15l. a year, stating that the family were at the present time residing at "Peckham House," London. After consulting the matron, she agreed to accept the offer made by Flucks. A few days afterwards she called at the union in a cab, and brought some clothes, which she put on the child. Flucks and the mother and child then got into the cab and were driven to the railway station, when Flucks induced the mother to leave by train for London, and took charge of the child, saying she would follow with it in a day or so. On reaching London, Turton found she had been duped, and nothing was heard of the child till Thursday last, when Poole recovered it in the manner above stated. It appears that the father of the child is a marine artilleryman, at present serving in Canada, and Turton is a very respectable-looking and prepossessing young woman. Flucks (whose husband is undergoing a short term of imprisonment for assault on a police officer) has, it is stated, been carrying on an intrigue with a married man, and the supposition is that the child was stolen for the purpose of being palmed off as the result of such intrigue, with the view of extorting money from him to prevent exposure. The prisoners were remanded till Tuesday next.

At the Borough Quarter Sessions at Portsmouth, on Saturday, Mary Ann Flucks, 27, was indicted for feloniously taking away by fraud a female child named Emily Eleanor Turton, of the age of 27 days, with intent to deprive Hannah Turton, its mother, of the possession of the said child, on the 7th of November; and Sarah Fry, 62, her mother, charged with aiding and abetting in the commission of the offence. The circumstances of the case were of a most extraordinary character, and the greatest interest was manifested, the court being densely crowded. The evidence was very voluminous, but the facts may be briefly stated as follows:

The prosecutrix, a single woman, was confined of a female child at the Portsea Island Workhouse on the 11th of October. On the 4th November the prisoner Flucks called at the union and was introduced to the prosecutrix, whom she told that her mistress required a wet nurse, and would give 15l. a year and what was required for the baby. Prosecutrix accepted those terms, and it was arranged that Flucks should call for her at the union on the Monday afternoon. She, however, called on the Saturday, and stated that she had come to alter the arrangement, as her mistress had received a telegram; she therefore wished to know if she would go to London and leave her child at Southsea. Prosecutrix assented to this arrangement, and it was fixed that she should leave for London on Monday morning, the prisoner telling her she was to pack her clothes to take to Salisbury. Flucks accordingly called at the union Monday morning, and prosecutrix and her baby went with her in a cab to the railway station. Prisoner paid the fare, and told prosecutrix she would get to Lady Creamers,' at Peckham House, about five o'clock, ready for tea. She added that the servants, wearing gold lace, would be waiting at the Waterloo station with the carriage for her.

On her arrival she failed to discover either servants with gold lace or the carriage, and taking a cab, she proceeded to Peckham House, which she found to be lunatic asylum. She went to a magistrate, and the workhouse authorities at Portsmouth being communicated with, prosecutrix was sent back to the union. Nothing was heard of the prisoner or the baby until 21st of November, when prosecutrix went with Sergeant Poole, of the Portsmouth police, to Cambridge House, East Cowes, and found the prisoner Flucks in bed with the baby. Fry told Poole that she was present at her daughter's confinement, but afterwards said, "I will tell you the truth; my daughter went away Thursday, and brought the child back Monday."

Mr. Julian Slight, the surgeon of the Portsmouth borough gaol, distinctly proved that the prisoner Flucks had never had a child at all.

When the prisoners were called upon for their defence, Flucks asserted that it was her child, and said it was hard to give it up into the hands of a single woman, more especially when they daily and hourly hear of women destroying their infants.

The Recorder having briefly summed up, the Jury found both prisoners guilty.

The Recorder, in passing sentence, told the prisoner Flucks that she had been found guilty of a very cruel act, as far as the woman Turton was concerned, and the sentence of the Court was that she be imprisoned and kept to hard labour for six calendar months. Addressing the other prisoner, the Recorder said she had undoubtedly had a very strong temptation to do what she had done, in endeavouring to screen her daughter from the punishment which was certain to follow her, and the sentence upon her was that she be imprisoned for three calendar months.

On being removed from the dock the prisoner Flucks burst out crying, and said. "I shall see my child again, I shall."

1865 – THE PORTSEA MURDER.

A murder of a most savage character was committed in Montague Street, Landport, at an early hour on Monday morning. At a quarter past six information was given at Landport police station that a woman named Clements, the wife of Charles Clements, a stoker belonging to H.M.S. *Diadem,* was lying dead at her residence, and that she had been cruelly murdered there being marks of violence on her throat, which appeared to have been bitten by some person. The features were much discoloured and the skin had been literally torn from the throat. Dr. Bentham was immediately sent for, and after examining the body externally, pronounced that life had been extinct for some hours.

On making inquiries, the police succeeded in finding out that on the previous evening the deceased woman had been drinking at a low beer shop in Greetham Street, kept by a man named Wyatt, in company with three privates of the 26th Regiment (Cameronians). They left the house about eleven o'clock, and one of the soldiers, named Hughes, went home with the deceased. The locality in question is a very low one, and is principally occupied by women of the most depraved character. What occurred during the night is unknown; but it is stated that at an early hour on Monday morning loud screams were heard proceeding from the house of the deceased, but as disturbances are of frequent occurrence in that part not the slightest notice was taken of them, and nothing more was thought of the matter until the discovery that the woman had been murdered was made by Mary Harris, a neighbour, who has charge of two little children belonging to the deceased.

Hughes was apprehended on Monday morning by Mr. Superintendent Barber and Detectives Campion and Poole, at the Clarence Barracks, Portsmouth. He was in the guard room, where he was confined for having broken his leave. He was at once taken to the Portsmouth police station. He is an Irishman, and about 20 years of age; and, on being told the serious nature of the charge against him, he did not appear in the least concerned.

At Winchester assizes on Saturday the 15th inst, John Hughes was indicted for the wilful murder of Maria Clements, at Portsea, on the 4th of June. It appeared from the evidence that the prisoner was a private soldier in the 26th Regiment of Foot, quartered at Cambridge barracks at Portsea. The deceased woman, Maria Clements, was the wife of Chas. Clements, a stoker belonging to the *Diadem*, lying in the harbour. Mr. and Mrs. Clements lived at Montagu Street, Portsea, but Clements' duty frequently detained him on board his ship. On Sunday the 4th of June, in the afternoon, the prisoner and two of his comrades, Parker and O'Neil left the barracks and went to the Queen's Head public house which was near Montagu Street. Mrs. Clements went into the public house, accompanied by her two children. She ordered a pint of beer, and then sat down in a chair by the prisoner, with whom she got into conversation about Ireland. The prisoner took her eldest child on his knee. After Mrs. Clements had drunk her pint of beer she ordered two quarts of beer for the soldiers, and they all partook of it.

The time arrived for the soldiers to return to barracks, and Parker tried to persuade the prisoner to go with him to the barracks, but he said he should stay out with the woman. All the party then went to the bar and had some more beer. The prisoner endeavoured to induce Mrs. Clements to go home. He took one of the children in his arms, and led the other to the door of the Clements' house. He put the children down on the step of the door and returned to the public house, and again begged the woman to come home. The landlady said, "What have you to do with the woman? She is a married woman." The prisoner said, "She is a 'towny' (of the same town) of mine, and I want to see her safe home." He then went and fetched the children back again to the public house, and eventually the prisoner and the woman and her children went to Clements' house. She tried to open the door but could not, and she went to the house of one Mr. Davis and asked him to come and open the door for her. The prisoner, however, followed her and said he had opened the door, and then the prisoner, Mrs. Clements, and the children went into the house and shut the door. This was about a quarter past 9 o'clock.

The next morning about 6 o'clock the deceased's eldest child, about five years of age, was heard crying outside the door, "Oh my mother, my poor mother!" She was quite naked. Mrs. Harris, a neighbour, went into the house, and found Mrs. Clements lying on her back on the floor with her clothes up round her waist, quite dead, cold, and stiff. She was without shoes or stockings. Upon examining the body there were five distinct marks of teeth on her face and neck. The death of the woman, in the opinion of the surgeon, was caused by one of these bites, which took effect upon the windpipe, producing suffocation.

The prisoner was not at barracks all that night, and did not return there till 20 minutes before 7 the next morning. Inquiries were made. The husband of the deceased had been on board his ship all night. The prisoner was taken into custody, and in his pockets two stockings were found which Clements at first said had belonged to his wife; he knew them because she had a very short foot, and was in the habit when she bought stockings of cutting off part of the feet; but upon further examination he found they were not hers.

When before the Magistrates the prisoner said he had left the woman at the door of her house, had then gone to another public house, and then to another house, where he remained all night and did not return to barracks until after 6 in the morning. The prisoner was found guilty, and sentenced to be hanged.

1865 – CURIOUS SUICIDE BY SWORD.

The Portsmouth Coroner and Jury were on Thursday engaged for some hours in the investigation of an extraordinary case of suicide. It appears that Mr. A. E. Baker, statuary, of Cottage Grove. Southsea, has been for some time in a very depressed state of mind owing to his pecuniary embarrassments. On Tuesday he was defeated by some legal proceedings in London, and became so melancholy that he was watched by his relatives, and, on the advice of Mr. Knight, a surgeon, the razors, etc. were kept out of his reach. On Wednesday he was watched by his sister-in-law, but, unobserved, he managed to obtain possession of his sword (he was a member of the yeomanry corps), and, having placed the hilt on the ground, pressed his body on to the point. The sister-in-law was alarmed hearing a noise like the falling of the sheath, and on going into the room saw Mr. Baker trying to press the sword into his breast A desperate struggle took place between them, during which both fell together on the floor. The sword was ultimately wrested from Mr. Baker's grasp, but his injuries were such that he died a few hours later. The Jury found that he was Temporarily Insane.

1866 – TALES FROM THE PORTSMOUTH POLICE COURT PART 1

CAUTION TO BOYS.
Thomas Payne, 11, John Honey, 11, and Edward Fennell, 12, for stealing four gallons of potatoes from a field in St. Mary's Road, the property of Mr. Salisbury, were fined 10s. each, including costs, and in default sentenced to five days' imprisonment with hard labour.

ALLEGED ROBBERY BY AN UNFORTUNATE.
Mary Lucas, a respectably-dressed unfortunate was charged with stealing a ring, the property of Mr. Dennis. The prosecutor was staying at the Fountain Hotel, High Street, and about 12 o'clock on Tuesday night was smoking a cigar on the balcony, when the prisoner and another girl went by. They stopped and entered into conversation with him, during which the prisoner's companion remarked "That's a nice ring you have; will you allow me to look at it?" The prosecutor took the ring off his finger and gave it to her to look at. She returned it, and as he was about to put it on his finger again the prisoner snatched it from him and ran down the street. The other girl said she would go and fetch her back, and ran in the direction taken by the prisoner, but, according to her account, she met a fellow with whom she was acquainted and gave up the pursuit. The prosecutor gave information to a police constable, and about two hours afterwards the prisoner was apprehended in the Sun public house, on the Parade, where she lodged. The prisoner said she had no intention of keeping the ring, and that she merely took it for a "lark" because the prosecutor owed her some money. The Magistrates did not believe the prisoner intended to steal the ring, and therefore discharged her.

DRUNK AND DISORDERLY.
Sarah Jackman, the wife of a painter, pleaded guilty to being drunk and disorderly in Russell Street, at nine o'clock the previous night, and was fined 15s., including costs, which she paid, Captain Maitland telling her that if she came there again she would be imprisoned without the option of paying a fine.—Amy Campbell, an unfortunate, who has been several times previously convicted and only came out of gaol about a week since, was sentenced to 21 days imprisonment with hard labour for a similar offence in Queen Street at quarter to 12 o'clock on Saturday night, Mr. Carter remarking that if she was brought again an information of a different sort would be laid against her, by which she would liable to three mouths' imprisonment.

A MENDICANT.
John McDonald, an old man, was sentenced to seven days' imprisonment with hard labour for begging in Wish Street on Saturday.

APPLE THEFT.
Samuel Lassiter, aged 10 years, was charged with stealing half-a-gallon of apples from a garden at Fratton, the property of Mr. K. F. Jolliffe. Mr. Jolliffe, jun., said that prisoner's parents had been to him about it, and he did not wish to press the charge. The Clerk: Then he'll come and rob your garden again. (Laughter). Prisoner was then discharged, and handed over to his mother, who was advised to correct him.

DISORDERLY BOYS.
Daniel Hart, alias *Shugaro*, 15 years of age, was charged with wilfully breaking a window in Messum's Court, the property of George James. It appeared that the prisoner and five other boys had been about the streets halloaing and making a great noise all the night, and at quarter to three this morning the prosecutor was roused out

of his bed by two of his windows being broken. He got up and saw the prisoner and the others and told them if they did not go away he would come out to them. He then went out and ran after them and could only catch the prisoner, whom he gave into custody. The Magistrates discharged the prisoner, the evidence not being sufficient to convict.

AN OLD CASE.
John Hammond was brought up on suspicion of stealing five hams, the property of Mr. Green, of Church Road. The hams had been stolen eleven months ago, and as they had now been consumed, and there was no chance of proving the case, the prisoner was discharged.

STEALING WOOD.
Richard Stone, alias Churchill, was charged with stealing seven pieces of wood, the property of George Hyde, of Arundel Street. About twenty minutes past five o'clock this morning P.S. Buxey saw the prisoner take the wood from outside the prosecutor's timber-yard, and he then took him into custody. Some of the wood had since been identified as belonging to the prosecutor. Prisoner said the wood was his own and he brought it from home. Prisoner's brother-in law was called, and said the prisoner was not responsible for his actions, but the Magistrates convicted him, and sentenced him to seven days' imprisonment with hard labour.

SHOP ROBBERY.
John Leppy, an old man, was charged with stealing a piece of bacon, value 1s. 0d., the property of Richard Pearce, grocer, of 56, St. Mary's Street. It appeared that the prisoner, who is a customer of the prosecutor's, went into the shop at a quarter past eight on Saturday night and made a small purchase, and about five or ten minutes after he had left the bacon was missed. Information was given to P.S. Hales, who apprehended the prisoner, and found bacon in the lining of his coat. He first said he had no bacon, and afterwards said, "I bought it, and gave 8d. for it." He was sentenced to seven days' imprisonment with hard labour.

A DISORDERLY UNFORTUNATE.
Louisa Ford, an unfortunate, who has been once previously convicted, pleaded guilty to a charge of being drunk and disorderly, in Smith's Lane, Portsea, at nine o'clock on the previous evening. She said if the bench would forgive her she would go into a reformatory, but Mr. Stigant said they could not rely on her promises as she had been leniently dealt with on the former occasion under similar promise. He sentenced her to five days' imprisonment with hard labour, and hoped that during that time she would make the necessary arrangements to carry out her intention.

NEGLECTING HIS WIFE AND FAMILY.
John Atkinson, shoemaker, on bail from the previous day, having been apprehended on a warrant on a charge of neglecting his wife and family whereby they had become chargeable to the parish, was sentenced to 21 days' imprisonment with hard labour, in default of paying £1 2s. 6d., the amount paid by the guardians, and 4s. 6d. costs. Mr. Nance told him that at the expiration of that period he would still be liable for any amount the guardians might have paid to his family.

SHOCKING SUICIDE OF A COLOUR SERGEANT.
An inquest was held on Wednesday at the Queens Hotel, Brockhurst, before E. Hoskins Esq., Coroner, on the body of Alexander Herd, a colour sergeant belonging to the 11th Depot Battalion aged about 38 years. The deceased was an orderly room clerk at Fort Grange. He was of a cheerful disposition until about a week ago, since which he had not appeared cheerful and had not attended constantly to his duties as before. He had been drinking for the last week. On Tuesday morning about quarter past six, James Moffett, a platelayer in the employ of the London and South-Western Railway Company, was going about his rounds, and when just above Ann's Hill found the body of the deceased lying on his stomach, in the grip or watercourse, partially concealed from view by the "grip."

One hand was firmly grasping the metal underneath and the other hand appeared as if it had hold of the metal; the cap was under one of the arms and the stock near the other arm. The body was not on the line at five o'clock on Monday afternoon, and between that time and the finding of the body two trains had passed up the line, one at a quarter past five and the other at 35 minutes past six. When the body was found the head was severed from the body and lying just inside the metals, the face being perfectly clear and no sign of any marks whatever upon it.

On Monday the deceased went to the Queen's Head, which is only a short distance from where the body was found. He appeared very melancholy and almost crazy. He left the house about a quarter past six, and instead of going in the direction of the Fort he went down towards Ann's Hill. He told the landlady that the time was very long when one was waiting for something. He said he was absent and did not like to go into the Fort till dark, and was afraid the colonel was very strict and there would be no chance for him. He said he had been in the service 17 years and a sergeant ten years, and that he was a married man.

The Jury returned a verdict of "Suicide while in an unsound state of mind."

1867 – CRUEL TREATMENT OF A BOY ON BOARD THE SHIP MEGAERA.

On Monday morning, Captain James Simpson, of her Majesty's ship *Megaera*, appeared upon an adjourned summons at the police court, Portsmouth to answer the charge of assaulting Charles Wallis, of Plymouth, a boy twelve years of age, in the harbour of Portsmouth, on the 11th of April.

The case excited a good deal of interest, and the court and its approaches were densely crowded. The Magistrates on the bench were the Mayor (E. Emanuel, Esq.), S. P. Pratt, E. M. Wells, W. E. Garrington, P. White, and R. Marion, Esqs., and Captains M'Coy and Maitland.

Mr. Cousins, solicitor, of Portsea, appeared on behalf of the prosecution; and Mr. Joyce, of the Home Circuit (instructed by Mr. Swainson, solicitor, of Portsmouth), defended Captain Simpson, who was allowed to be seated by the side of his counsel. The complainant, Charles Wallis, a delicate boy, whose appearance exited much commiseration in court, said: I believe I am thirteen years of age. I reside with my father at Plymouth and my mother is dead. My father is a paviour. On Wednesday, the 10th of April, I went on board the ship *Megaera* to take some things off to the ship. I helped a waterman to take some boxes on board. The cook's mate asked me to peel some potatoes. I did so. It took me about half an hour. The cook's mate gave me some grub for doing so. (A laugh.) After I had eaten the food one of the men told me the vessel was getting underway. I went to the corporal and told him I did not know the ship was going. The corporal went away from me. I then saw the captain, and did not hear him say anything, but I was placed under the ladder on the upper deck aft. This was not long after the ship sailed, but I cannot tell what time it was. I was kept under the ladder until twelve, I think, at night. I was then taken

CRUEL TREATMENT OF A BOY ON BOARD THE SHIP MAGÆRA.

on to the second deck, and kept there from twelve to four. I was under the charge of a sentry all the time. At four o'clock I was taken up to the top deck again. I was kept there until the ship came to Portsmouth. I was under the ladder, and was in charge of a sentry all the time. The ship arrived in Portsmouth about ten o'clock. I did not lie down while on the upper deck, as the water kept coming over, but between decks I lay down on a sail, where they keep the men in irons. I had nothing to eat except a piece of biscuit the sentry gave me and he told me not to let anyone see it.

On arriving at Portsmouth the captain called me, and said, "If you don't tell the truth you shall be flogged." The captain was at one side of the ship, and I was on the other, where the corporal took up the rope. I told the captain I took something on board, and the cook asked me to peel some potatoes, and while I was peeling them the ship got underway. That is the case. I did not stow myself away on board. I did not wish to come to Portsmouth. I wish I had never got into the boat. (A laugh.) The captain told the corporal to flog me. The corporal took up a rope, and began flogging me. The flogging was outside my clothes, but the corporal tucked up my jacket. The captain saw the corporal could not hold me by himself, and called the master-at-arms, who held my right arm, the corporal having hold of my left; while the blows were being struck the captain said, "Go on." The corporal then sent me on shore in a waterman's boat. I was landed at Portsea. I had no money or food with me. The waterman sent a boy to show me where the relieving officer lived, and I have been in the union ever since. A man came to me when I was peeling potatoes, and said, "It's time you were off, for the visitors are going." The man also said, "The visitors are nearly all gone." The reason I remained was that I was trying to get a bit of biscuit. Before the ship was underway I saw that all the visitors had left. The captain said he would flog me if I did not answer the question as to how I got on board. I forget whether I answered or not.

Mr. Bloxam, surgeon, of the Parade, Portsmouth, was examined as to the nature of the injuries the complainant had received. He found a mass of black and blue bruises on the back, extending 10 inches, the width being six inches. The flogging the boy had received must have been excessive, and a continuation of stripes.

Another witness, a Customs' officer, said he saw the boy flogged in Captain Simpson's presence, with a three inch rope. One of the ship's corporals was flogging him, and another man was holding his right wrist. The flogging lasted three minutes. It was very severe, and he never saw such flogging in his life, (Hisses.)

Mr. Joyce addressed the bench, and admitted that his client had been guilty of a common assault, although in a moral sense he had not been guilty of an offence at all. The fact was, that Captain Simpson thought that correcting the boy and sending him on shore would do him much more good than having him taken before a magistrate.

Witnesses were then called for the defendant, who proved that the boy must have concealed himself on board, and that his statement that he wished to be put on shore was untrue. It was denied that he was kept without food, but it was admitted that he was flogged on his declining to tell the captain the truth as to how he came on board.

Thomas Yamblin, the ship's corporal, said he flogged the boy. It was not a severe flogging. He gave him about two dozen stripes – (hisses) – and was about five minutes in administering them.

The bench then retired, and after an absence of forty minutes returned into court. The Mayor said: Captain Simpson, the Magistrates have given your case due consideration, and have decided that it is a case which they cannot deal summarily with, and have determined upon sending it for trial to the quarter sessions. (Loud applause, which was instantly suppressed.) The case occupied upwards of seven hours. The bench consented to take bail, and the required sureties having been entered into, Captain Simpson left the court.

At the Portsmouth Quarter Sessions on Saturday Captain James Simpson, of Her Majesty's ship Megaera, surrendered to take his trial for having unlawfully assaulted a boy named Charles Wallis, on the 11th of April. The indictment contained four counts. The first charged the defendant with having wilfully and maliciously inflicted grievous bodily harm on Charles Wallis; the second charged a false imprisonment; the third was for having caused actual bodily harm; and the fourth was for common assault.

Mr. Besley, of the Home Circuit (specially retained), and Mr. Bullen appeared on behalf of the Society for the Protection of Women and Children, for the prosecution, and Mr. Gunner, of the Western Circuit for the defendant. The facts of this case have already appeared at length in this journal, and it is therefore only necessary briefly to recapitulate them. The gist of the evidence is, therefore, as follows:

On the 10th of April the boy Wallis, who said he was about 14 years of age, went on board the *Megaera*, with a waterman, the ship was lying in Plymouth Sound, and remained on board until she got under way; by accident, as was alleged by the prosecution; by design, alleged by the defence. On the arrival of the ship at Portsmouth Captain Simpson insisted upon the boy telling the truth as to the circumstances of his being brought away from Plymouth in the ship, and the boy said he told the truth when he told Captain Simpson that he did not hear the visitors being warned to leave the vessel, and did not know that she was actually underway until she had got outside Plymouth Breakwater. However, the captain did not believe this statement, and when the ship had been moored in Portsmouth harbour he ordered the boy to be flogged with a rope's end. The ship's corporal appears to have performed that duty very vigorously with a rope one inch in diameter; for when the boy was sent ashore and examined by Mr. H. Bloxam, surgeon, of Portsmouth, the lower part of his person, particularly the thigh, was found to indicate, by discolouration, the severity of the punishment which he had received. The result was that some of the townspeople took compassion on him, and hence this prosecution.

Mr. Gunner, for the defendant, did not deny that an assault had been committed, but he denied that the flogging was as severe as had been alleged. He said he should call two Magistrates of the borough who examined the boy on the same day that Mr. Bloxam did, and that they would tell the Jury that, though they could perceive marks of discolouration, those marks were scarcely visible; and should also call officers of the navy, who would swear that Captain Simpson had served under them, and that he had always conducted the ship with care and discretion. He thought, then, that if the Jury did not give Captain Simpson a verdict of absolute acquittal, they would, at all events, not convict him on any other count than that of common assault.

Several witnesses were then examined on behalf of the defendant, including Mr. W. G. Chambers and Mr. P. White, justices, who deposed that, although there were discoloured marks which showed that the boy had been flogged, there was no abrasion of the skin. Vice-Admiral Sir Lewis Tobias Jones, K.C.B., deposed that he had known the defendant when, as lieutenant, he was doing duty in the Black Sea, and he was then of an extremely considerate disposition, kind to all people under him, and that had been his character ever since.

Captain Beckford said that, as senior lieutenant of the Princess Royal, of which witness was the commander when that ship was in the Black Sea, there was nothing like harshness in the defendant's conduct.

Mr. Gunner then summed up the evidence for the defence, and contended that there was no reason why the boy should not have been landed had he been so disposed; that the flogging was not unnecessarily severe, and that the defendant could only be convicted of common assault.

Mr. Besley replied, and the Recorder (Mr. Poulden), in summing up said that, although there was no justification for the assault, he thought there was a total absence of malice; and he did not believe that grievous bodily harm had been sustained. Beyond the heedlessness, the thoughtlessness, and carelessness with which Captain Simpson had acted, it appeared to the Recorder that nothing serious could be imputed to him. The count in the indictment referring to false imprisonment was withdrawn.

The Jury found a verdict of guilty on the other three counts. The Recorder, in addressing the defendant, said he disagreed with the verdict; but, although he did not think it necessary to inflict a degrading punishment, he was bound to pass a severe pecuniary one.

The sentence was that the defendant pay a fine of £100, and that he be imprisoned until the same paid. An application was made for the costs of the prosecution, but it was refused.

1867 – FATAL ACCIDENT OF A CHILD AT PORTSEA.

On Monday evening an inquest was held at the Anglesea Arms, Queen Street, Portsea, and thence by adjournment at the Sessions room, before W. H. Garrington Esq., Coroner, on the body of Louisa Peatey, a child aged six years, who was run over on Saturday in Pud's Lane by a carter, named Francis Woods, in the employ of Mr. Stephen Burrell, of Fareham. The facts of the case may be elicited from the following evidence.

Sarah Peatey deposed: I am the wife of Stephen William Peatey, sawyer, and reside at No. 5, Pud's Lane, Portsea. The body which the Coroner and Jury have viewed in my presence is that of my late daughter, Louisa Peatey, aged six years. She went out of doors about four o'clock on Saturday afternoon to play in the street. She had asked my permission to play with another child in the street, which I granted. There was a hand truck, which my son had been using, standing on the opposite side of the lane, at the back of Mr. Cavander's store. One of the wheels was in the gutter and the body of it on the pavement.

About five minutes after she went out of doors, my attention was attracted by something heavy, which appeared to be a waggon or a cart coming through Pud's Lane from St. James's Street, towards Hay Street. In consequence of hearing that I went towards the front door, and when I got there I saw a horse and cart going at a quick walking pace. It was a half-tilted cart, so that I could not see the driver. I was apprehensive that in a narrow road the cart would injure the truck, and I called out twice loudly to the driver. No notice was taken, but directly after I saw the wheel of the cart strike the truck and turn it over on the pavement. I was not then aware that my child was there, but as the cart proceeded onward I saw her lying on the pavement with her head lying in the gutter. I ran over, lifted her up, and took her into the house. Blood was issuing from her mouth and from a wound in the right side of her head. I think she breathed after I raised her from the ground, but she died almost immediately.

By Mr. Wallis (who appeared for Woods, who was present) The truck was standing on the left hand side on coming from St. James's Street, and the cart was proceeding from St. James's Street to Hay Street. The handles of the truck were in the opposite direction to that in which the cart was coming. If the deceased had been between the handles of the truck the view of a person in the cart would have been intercepted. When I called out the wheel of the cart was in the act of striking the truck, and the words I made use of were "Hoy! Mind the truck."

Edward Maker deposed: I reside at No. 1, Green's Court, Hay Street, and I am a sawyer. The house in which I live is exactly opposite Pud' Lane, and a window in it commands an entire view of that lane. On Saturday afternoon last, at a little after four o'clock, I was standing at this window, when I saw a hand truck standing in the position as described by the last witness. There were two or three children at the head of the truck, and the deceased and a little boy between the shafts. I saw a horse and cart standing near the middle of the lane for nearly an hour before this time. When I saw the children in the situation I described I noticed the horse and cart move on and proceed towards my residence. The man was sitting in the front of the cart driving the horse, and as the cart was passing the truck I saw the wheel catch the head of it, which had the effect of dragging it a short distance, and then it overturned on to the pavement. The deceased was thrown down by the shafts of the truck, and fell with her head in the gutter, while the cart was in the act of passing, and the wheel of the cart went over it. I went immediately to the spot, but the child had been removed indoors. I saw blood issuing from the head of the deceased. I went into the house and saw the child lying on the mat quite dead. I afterwards proceeded towards home, when I saw the policeman stop the horse. The driver had jumped down, when I heard him say, "I have not hurt the child." The brother of the deceased had previously said to him, "You have killed my sister." The policeman then took the driver into custody. He was the worse for drink and I do not think was fit to drive a horse. When the accident happened the horse was not going at an improper pace.

By Mr. Wallis: The driver was sitting outside with his feet on the foot-board. I only saw one man. The roadway is paved with stones, and so is the gutter. From my knowledge of driving I know that when a wheel is in a gutter of this description and where the road is narrow it is apt to cling to the gutter. The roadway is about seven feet wide. When the deceased's brother told the driver he had killed his sister he appeared to be unaware of what had happened. I thought the driver was drunk because he staggered when he took hold of the horse's head. I cannot describe any act on the driver's part arising from his being drunk.

Tom Hulbert deposed: I am a police constable of this borough and on Saturday afternoon at four o'clock I was on duty in Queen's Street, Portsea, and on passing the end of Hay Street, I saw a horse and cart driven by Francis Woods from Pud's Lane into Hay Street, and in doing so he drove the horse on to the pavement on the opposite side. I then turned down the street towards the horse, and saw a boy take hold of the horse's head and heard him say to the driver, "Stop, you have killed my sister." He would not stop but struck at the boy with his whip. I took hold of the horse's head and said to the driver, "You are not fit to drive this horse." I did not see anybody else in the cart.

When I stopped the cart I saw the driver rocking about like a drunken man. I said to him, "You had better get down, you heard what the boy said." He replied, "I have not hurt her." When he got down he staggered about. I took him to the house where the deceased was lying in the passage and said to him, "See what you have done, you have rode over a child," to which he replied, "I have not hurt her." I then took him, and the horse and cart to Portsea police station, where I charged him with being drunk and having driven over a child. He said, "I am not drunk, I have only had three pints of beer."

The width of the road was eight feet, and allowing a foot for the overhanging of truck, I should think there was seven feet clear. If the off wheel of the cart had been in the gutter there would have been five inches to spare between the near wheel and the truck. I am of the opinion that Francis Woods was not in a fit state to drive a horse and cart.

By Mr. Wallis: I think he knew what had occurred. He was going at a very fast walking pace, and I therefore think he knew what had occurred. I did not see him rock about before I stopped the horse. The horse's forefeet were both on the pavement, and its head was close to the shutters. I measured the cart from the box of the near wheel to the tier of the off wheel, and found it to be 6ft. 7 inches. I will not swear that it is not seven feet from box to box.

Dr. J.W. Cousins deposed: I have today made a post mortem examination of the body of the deceased. There was an irregular lacerated wound of the scalp on the right side, exposing the skull. The right ear was considerably lacerated. The right side of the head was extensively depressed, and the skull driven in over a large space. There was also a considerable depression of the left ear. There was also two slight contusions on the left arm and right shoulder. The scalp was found detached from the right half of the skull. The skull was extensively fractured, extending through the base, where there was a considerable amount of extravasated blood. The injuries which I have described are such as would have been caused by the passage of a heavy body over the head.

James John Dore deposed: I am a mariner, and reside at Fareham. I know Francis Woods, as a carter, in the employ of Stephen Burrell, of Fareham. I accompanied him to Portsmouth on Saturday last and arrived here at about eleven or twelve o'clock. We stopped at several places coming down. More than three of these stoppages were at public houses. Being an invalid, I did not get out of the cart, and so I could not see whether Woods had anything to drink. After the cart was unloaded we went to the railway station, and from thence to Pud's Lane. Woods went into a private house and remained there for a quarter of an hour. He sat on the front of the cart with his legs outside. He was quite sober. We then went down Pud's Lane. I did not feel the cart strike against anything, nor did I hear anyone call out. Not very long afterwards a boy came and said, "Stop the cart, a young 'un is rode over," and he stopped the cart directly, and got down like a sober man.

By Mr. Wallis: I have been ill for some time past, and have been paralysed. I came down to Portsmouth to get fresh air. I know Woods is a steady man, and that he has been in Mr. Burrell's employ for several years. The load consisted of sacks of oats, and when we stopped he delivered them at different places. He did this as a sober man. I had not the least idea that a child had been rode over until the policeman stopped the horse.

Henry Pearce deposed: I am a police constable of this borough, and I was on duty at the Portsea police station on Saturday afternoon when Hulbert gave Woods into my custody for having ridden over a child. I had him in custody in the reserve room for three quarters of an hour, and during that time he frequently got up and staggered about. He was drunk and was not capable.

Cross-examined: He seemed very much excited when he was in my custody, and the fact of being taken into custody and being charged with so serious a crime was enough to make him shake.

The Coroner, in summing up, remarked that the case was very simple in its character. It was perfectly clear that the death of Louisa Peatey was caused by her being rode over by a cart; but the question was how did this come about? It was also clear that the cart was being driven by Francis Woods, and it was alleged by three witnesses that he was in a state of intoxication.

On the other hand there was the evidence of a man who had been with Woods all the morning, and who stated that he had not had anything to drink. The question which the Jury had to consider was whether they were able from the evidence to judge that the death of the child was purely accidental, and that the condition of the driver had nothing to do with it, or whether the driver was in such a state of intoxication as to be unable to manage the horse. He (the Coroner) need hardly tell them that if the latter were their opinion the man Woods ought to be placed on trial for a very serious offence.

Manslaughter had been described as "where one doing an unlawful act, not felonious, or tending to bloodshed, or doing lawful act, without proper caution, killed another undesignedly." This case came under the latter clause of the quotation, and if they believed that the man did a lawful act, as driving along a lane without proper caution, and the death of this child was the result, they ought to return a verdict of manslaughter; but if they believed that proper care had been used, and that the state of the driver in no way contributed to the death, it would clearly not be manslaughter.

The Jury retired, and after an absence of twenty minutes returned into court. The Coroner: Mr. Foreman, have you agreed upon your verdict? The Foreman; Yes, sir, we have. The Coroner: Then what is it?

The Foreman: The Jury are of a unanimous opinion that it was an "Accidental death."

Woods was brought up at the police court on Monday before Captain McCoy and G. Gillman, Esq., charged with the manslaughter of Louisa Peatey. Mr. Wallis appeared for the prisoner, who was remanded till Wednesday.

He was, however, again brought up on Tuesday before the Mayor (E. Emanuel, Esq.), and J. Scale and G. Curtis, jun., Esqs., when it was stated that after the result of the inquest on the previous evening, it was not proposed to proceed further with the case.

The Mayor said that in his opinion the parents of children were almost as much to blame as drivers, for allowing them to run about the street. He expected that someday or other he should brought up for manslaughter. (Laughter.) He discharged the prisoner.

1867 – CONVICT LIFE IN A PORTSMOUTH PRISON.

We take the following interesting personal narrative, (slightly abridged) of convict life in Portsmouth prison from a capital article in Chambers' Journal, entitled "Twenty Years' Penal Servitude":-

I can scarcely remember the first few days after my sentence; I woke up, as it were, in Millbank Prison. I awoke, to the tortures of my punishment. Oh those weary days; the tread-mill, the grinding-mill, the oakum-picking, the ceaseless routine of labour, the eternal silence. They soon affected my constitution, and by the recommendation of the doctor, I was sent to another prison, where the work was outdoors. Hitherto, I had been separated from all association; but in the prison I was going to, I was to work in company with a gang. Strange to say, I preferred separate confinement. I hated the thought of associating with thieves and pickpockets – I, a gentleman, with refined and honourable feelings – I, who would not wrong a child, to have to herd with the scum of society! I felt it bitterly, for I did not look on my own crime as morally wrong; illegal, I know it was, and I know the law cannot make distinctions.

By the time I got to Portsmouth prison, the numb feeling which I had after my sentence was wearing off. I was beginning to observe things more closely, and, alas daily to feel them more keenly. I shall never forget the journey by rail in a third-class carriage, with eleven others, handcuffed together, with a heavy bright chain drawn through rings in our horrid bracelets. I sat quite silent; the rest, probably hardened wretches, were willing enough to converse, which they did at every opportunity when they could escape the sharp eyes of the warders. At last the train stopped, and we got out amongst the crowd of passengers; we saw the kind greetings of meeting friends, and the happy faces around us. I hoped that I should not be recognised at this station, where many a time I had stepped out of a first-class carriage to spend a season at Southsea. But now what a change, I was now a felon, chained and handcuffed! As the people gazed on us, I fancied I was particularly stared at, and that everyone knew my story. It was only fancy. My dearest friend could not have recognised me in my convict's dress. A van took us to the prison, and as I heard the ponderous gates bolted and barred behind me, I felt sick at heart, and mentally prayed for death to take me. The recollection of this past so oppresses me, that, as I write, I feel as if I could scarce proceed further with my relation. However, for the sake of all who read this story, I will show the horrors of my punishment, as a warning against temptation to go astray.

Immediately on our reception inside Portsmouth prison, we were marched, still handcuffed and chained, into a small yard, where we were placed in a row, and our irons removed; our names were then called over, and we were then told to stand to 'attention.' In a few minutes the doctor appeared, and examined us to see if we carried any contagious disorder with us. I suppose we were all right, for none of us were detained, but were marched at once into a long passage, on one side of which was a blank wall with a stove, and on the other, cells with a door and a barred gate at each. Here we found complete suits of clothing, which we were told to put on; but before doing so, after removing the clothes we already wore, we were stripped and subjected to a most minute examination; our mouths, and even under our tongues, were examined. This over, we dressed in our new suits, and were then taken away to the cells. Having had our mid-day meal, we were again mustered, and marched off to another yard, where we listened to the articles and rules of the prison read aloud by the governor. On our way to and fro through the prison, I observed that several of my companions were well known to the warders and they, my companions, appeared to take a pride in showing themselves to be acquainted with the localities and the routine. After the governor had finished with as, we were again marched off for the doctor's inspection. This inspection was also very minute, and not made by the same medical officer. He inquired into our previous state of health and general history; name, age, and occupation were noted down, as well as height and weight, which were taken by an attendant warder. I answered every question (they were put as humanely as possible) truthfully, except when asked what was my, "previous occupation." I answered 'a labourer.' I could see by the doctor's expression that he guessed I held a higher position, but he said nothing, and entered what I told him in his register.

We had not yet done with inspections. Being dismissed by the doctor, we were taken before the

chief warder; when again in a complete state of nudity, we were rigorously examined, every mark or mole, natural or artificial, was noted; our eyes, hair, speech, in fact everything that would serve to identify us, was copied in a book. This, at length, was finished, and I was thankful to hear a fellow prisoner say that it was the last ceremony of the kind, adding: 'I ought to know, for this is the third time I went through 'em." We then were returned to our cells, ready to enter on the ordinary routine of the prison the following morning.

To save repetition, I will detail as shortly as possible the rules that governed my daily life.

The prison is divided into four halls, distinguished respectively as A, B, C, and D halls; and their occupants are divided into four classes, called respectively first, second, third, and probation classes. Each class occupies as far as numbers can be accommodated, a distinct hall, the first class, which is also the highest, belongs to D hall, the second to C, the third to B, and the probation to A. These classes are formed on the principle of time and good conduct. The probation class being dependent on time, all prisoners on first admission are placed in it for a certain period, their promotion altogether depending on themselves. Good conduct is estimated by there being no reports against them, and by their assiduity at their work. A man who is fortunate enough never to have had a report against him during the whole period of his gradations, is entitled to certain privileges during the latter part of his imprisonment. Such cases are very rare for often a report is made for an imaginary fault and the officer reporting is generally believed rather than the prisoner. These reports are made to the governor, who sits every day to judge and adjudicate. First offences, if not heinous, are generally 'admonished' but a repetition of an offence, no matter how trivial, is always punished. In awarding punishment, the powers of the governor are limited to solitary confinement in a cell, light or dark, on bread and water, and with or without bodily restraint for three days. In cases where the governor thinks that this punishment is not adequate to the offence he reports the prisoner to the director, who at his periodical visit examines into the case, the witnesses being sworn. The director has in his power to award corporal punishment to the extent of thirty six lashes and solitary confinement in irons for six months with punishment diet.

The incentives held out to good conduct are the class privileges, of which not the least is the improved diet, and the remission of sentence on ticket-of-leave. Formerly, when first penal servitude took the place of transportation beyond the sea, this remission was very much a matter of chance as to its extent; but latterly, by a system of marks, which are allotted by fixed rules, the period of remission is determined accurately, and is known perfectly well to the prisoner.

The rule for remission of sentence is this: Three-fourths of the sentence have been undergone; and if at that period the prisoner has earned the full number of marks, he is set free on ticket-of-leave; but if not, he must remain until he has done so. The marks are obtained by labour, at seven or eight a day, according to his capability and earnestness; but whether he works or not, as in illness or under prison punishment, he is accredited with six marks a day. But he is liable at any time to lose, in punishment, any or all the marks previously earned, and also to be degraded to any stage or class. The maximum daily number that can be earned is eight, and the minimum number awarded is six.

The labour at Portsmouth is, in a general way, what is known as navvies' work, the prisoners being employed in and about the dockyard, a small party being sent to Southsea Common, and formerly to Gosport. The hours for labour differ, of course, at different seasons of the year; but, in a general way, the day is divided as follows: First bell rings to get up at a quarter past five, from which hour until six o'clock the prisoners are employed washing, cleaning out cells, and making-up beds. Breakfast at six o'clock, forty minutes being allowed. Directly after breakfast comes chapel service, which occupies half an hour, after which they proceed to labour; in winter, a little later. Dinner is at noon, for which meal seventy minutes are allowed, and then labour again, until six o'clock in summer, and four o'clock in winter. Prayers, a supper, school, and making-down beds, take up the rest of the day, until eight o'clock, when lights are put out, and the prisoners are locked up for the night.

At three different periods of the day-namely, six a.m., noon, and on return from labour, the medical officer attends at the dispensary, to prescribe for out-patients and casual sick.

Besides the 'ordinary labour,' there is 'light labour,' which consists in picking oakum, and is carried on indoors. Only those prisoners are thus employed who are unfit for ordinary labour, on medical grounds; A few words on the meals, and I think I shall have put the reader in possession of a general idea of prison life. The dietary is classed under four heads-namely, for hard labour, for light labour, penal class diet, and punishment diet. The first two are respectively for those working at hard and light labour; the third is given to prisoners on prison punishment for a protracted time; the fourth, which is only bread and water, is given only to those whose prison punishment does not extend beyond three days.

The dietary for convicts at hard labour is: breakfast of bread and cocoa. Dinner-Sunday, bread and cheese; Monday and Saturday, stewed beef and potatoes; Tuesday and Friday, beef, soup, and potatoes; Wednesday, mutton and potatoes; Thursday, suet pudding, and potatoes.

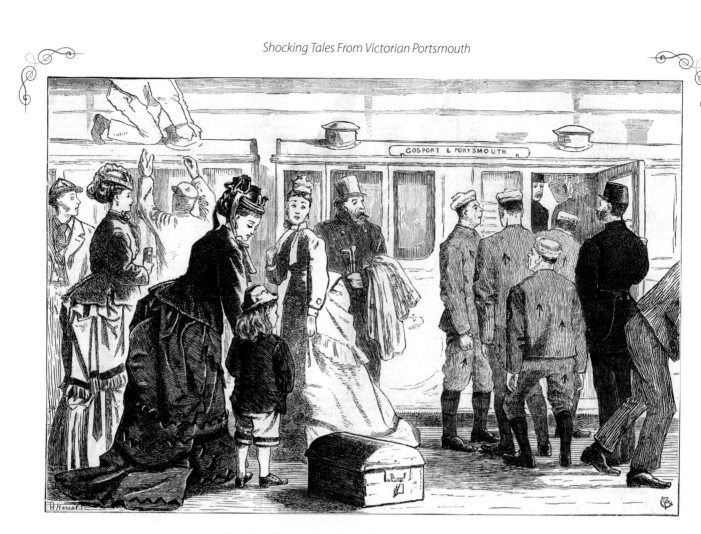

Convicts leaving York Road station for Portsmouth

Reception of Convicts at Portsmouth Prison

Supper-gruel. With each meal bread is given amounting altogether to nearly a pound and a half daily. Those who are engaged in light labour have the same diet in every respect, except quantity, which is reduced by about one-fourth.

The penal class diet consists of milk, porridge and bread for breakfast and supper, and dinner of bread and potatoes. In all cases water *ad libitum*.

I had been accustomed to early rising at Millbank, and I was already awake when the great bell clanged a quarter past five; and found the morning routine pretty much the same: the same rattling of innumerable locks and banging of iron doors, the same sharp orders in sharp tones and the same dreary sombre look of the surroundings; the same half-cold feed – I cannot call it breakfast, the same stereotyped, cold chapel service. Then the parade, and then (new to me) the marching out to work.

The morning was raw and cold, and the place which we worked on exposed to the cold sea-breeze. I was placed with a gang who were levelling a piece of ground; and my part was to wheel the barrows full of clay from one spot to another. At first I did not mind this much; but soon the unaccustomed strain began to tell on my arms and back, and before evening I was ready to drop with fatigue. This barrow work I found was detested almost more than any sort of labour, and various expedients are made use of by the prisoners to get out of it; sickness feigned and induced being the commonest. Indeed, almost every day someone or other of the prisoners desired to be brought before the medical officer with feigned illness. If they do not succeed in deceiving the doctor, they are sent out and punished. Inducing illness is also very common amongst a low class of prisoners – especially London

Dinner Time. Convicts coming in from the Works, Portsmouth

pickpockets. The most effectual way of insuring their admission to the infirmary they find is by making sores on their legs. To do this, they scrape their shins with a bit of slate or broken bottle, and to the abrasion thus formed they apply a paste, which is composed of lime, soap, and soda, all which are articles they can easily obtain. As a result of such malpractices, I have seen sores of a most serious nature, entailing confinement to bed for several months. Of course, if found out in these misdemeanours, they are punished; but they are very cunning, and always pretend that they are the result of an accident. Often, too, they take advantage of a real accident, such as a brick or stone scraping the leg; and on this wound, which is seen to be accidental, they carry out their designs.

During the first week of my work, I thought each day that I should be really sick, and have to give in. How I envied some of my fellow-prisoners, to whose hard hands and brawny arms the work that was almost killing me seemed like play! I thought then, and I think now, that it is not fair to put a gentleman to the same work as a labourer, their crimes being equal, for the crimes being equal the punishment should be equal-and that cannot be the case where a man, who has perhaps never carried a heavier weight than a gun all his life, is put at the same labour as a man who is accustomed to it from boyhood.

My previous healthy life, and well-nourished and good constitution, however, stood the trial; in a short time, as my muscles grew hard and accustomed to the work, I began to find it not so fatiguing; and before 12 months had elapsed, I was as good a workman as any navvy. During all this time, I had not one report against me for idleness; but an officer, who, I fancy, never liked me, reported me for having a penny in my possession. I picked up this unfortunate penny whilst at work, and without caring for nor thinking about it, I put it in my pocket. For this crime, I was only admonished; but was told that a repetition of the offence would be followed by bread and water and close confinement. This little incident awoke to bitterness my half-resigned feelings. I felt what a mere automaton I was; never to move without being told; speech and action no longer my own; it was horrible. The eternal presence of a keeper fretted me also beyond anything. If I had to proceed from one part of the prison to the other, although surrounded by high walls, I could not stir a step without a warder close to me.

I had been about twelve months in prison since I left Millbank, when a conspiracy broke out among a number of the prisoners. I believe it was a question about food. I know that some of the officers were assaulted, and one seriously injured. It was quelled, however, without difficulty; and the ringleaders, seven in number, were sentenced to undergo corporal punishment in the presence of the rest of the prisoners.

I had never seen corporal punishment administered, and I felt a sort of horror at being forced to witness it. I applied to the governor to be allowed to be absent, but he would not hear of it. The punishment was to take place at ten o'clock in the morning, so, at half past nine, we were mustered in a hollow square, in one of the large yards. As I stood there, looking at the preparations, I felt a cold shiver run through me. The bright steel triangle with its straps stood in the centre, and near it were two stalwart men, with their coats off, and the horrible cats in their hands. A dead silence reigned through the place. The warders, at regular intervals, stood in front of the prisoners with their staves in their hands; and a party of the prison guard stood near the triangle with bayonets fixed. At last, the silence was broken by the unlocking of a gate the governor, medical officer, and chief warder entered the square; and, in a few minutes, the prisoner was marched in between two warders. On approaching the place of punishment, he was told to halt. The governor then read aloud his offence and sentence, and desired him to strip. The unfortunate wretch looked very pale whilst taking off his upper garments, which alone were removed. A band of stiff canvas was then tied round his waist, and another round his neck; his feet were stretched apart, and strapped to the base of the triangle; and his hands, fastened together, were drawn above his head, and the punishment began. With deliberate strokes, applied with the whole force of a strong man's arm, the knotted cords descended on the victim's bare shoulders; each stroke was deliberately counted, the executer of the sentence smoothing and disentangling the cords each time; and thus the unfortunate wretch received three dozen. His white skin was soon a mass of purple, blue, and red wales. But all through this dreadful punishment he never uttered a cry, and when let free, walked away without showing the slightest appearance of suffering, we had to stand and watch the whole number going through this revolting punishment. Some took it bravely – some screamed as if for their very life; only one man fainted. Among the spectators, however, many fainted, whilst others cheered those who showed courage and did not cry out. This was the first and, I am thankful to say, last, exhibition of the sort at which I had to be present, as an order was issued shortly afterwards that corporal punishment was to be administered in private. Besides their flogging, four of the culprits on this occasion, were sentenced to close confinement on punishment diet for six months, and the others to wear a party coloured dress and cross irons for the same period.

Year after year passed on without any change-the same dreary monotony, the ever conscious feeling of being watched. Even our holidays, of which there were three in the year, were no relaxation. To be sure, we did not work, but we spent the weary hours in our lonely cells. During all this time, I never thought of escape. It never entered my head, although there were several attempts made, and one or two successful ones. It is astonishing how old housebreakers often succeed with the most insignificant means in making an escape. I know one instance where a thick iron bar was cut through with a saw made of a watch spring. How the saw itself was made, I do not know; for prisoners manage both to preserve money and to traffic with labourers outside. An escape was always a break in the routine of our life, as, on such occurrences, all the prisoners were taken in from work, the warders being needed to scour the country in search of the runaway. On such a day as Sunday, our time was spent in our cells, except two hours exercise, which we took walking two and two in the yards. I had been about ten years in prison, when one day I caught cold from a severe wetting. At first, I tried to work it off, but it grew worse, and I had to apply to the doctor, who sent me into the infirmary. Here I was well treated indeed; but I felt the want of kind and friendly voices, which are so comforting in sickness. My affection proved to be inflammation of the lungs, and I did not leave the hospital for more than six a weeks. I was then discharged to light labour, and shortly afterwards taken into the prison as a cleaner. This was a great relief, as the work was not so monotonous or so laborious. The part of the prison to which I was attached was called the Separate Cells; these were rows of cells in which prisoners were confined for petty offences committed in the prison, such as fighting, stealing food, being found in possession of tobacco, and such like. A misdemeanour is very easily made out against a prisoner; an ugly look, a quick reply, an impatient manner, even silence itself is construed into an offence; there is really no way of guarding against being reported. I was brought up one day before the governor for not informing the warder of the misconduct of another prisoner. In my defence, I said that I was a prisoner myself, and that I could not be answerable for anyone else's crimes. This was called insolence; and I was told that, were it not for my previous good conduct, I should be punished on that account, and I was desired to give some other plea in justification of what was termed my connivance; so, with shame, I pleaded fear of violence from the delinquent. This was accepted, though it was not likely that I, one of the strongest men in the prison; perhaps the strongest, should be in bodily fear of a miserable sneak, which was the character of the prisoner I should have informed against.

The crime he had committed was stealing bread, which he effected thus. Every day, at dinner hour, before the bell rings, it was part of my duty to bring round a loaf of bread and a tin of water, and leave them outside the cell door of each prisoner in separate confinement. The officer coming round shortly afterwards, opened the doors, and handed each mess in. The prisoner in question, on several occasions, had stolen bread thus placed. He used, when his cell was opened by an officer which he always managed, by some excuse or other to have done before the loaves were deposited outside, to insert a loop made of the thong of his shoe into the hole of the lock, just as the officer shut the door: these doors shut with a spring lock, and could be double-locked, in fact, always were, as a rule, but not generally before the serving of the meals. The loop thus inserted caught on the bolt, which could thus be pressed back. Waiting until the officer's back was turned, this thief would open his door, rush out in the landing, and seize three or four loaves, always leaving untouched those next to his cell; then retreating, and shutting his cell door, he ate them as fast as possible. This trick went on continually, until the unlucky day that I saw him steal no less than six loaves; unfortunately, a warder saw him also, and reported me as an accomplice, because I did not give information.

I had been about three years at indoor work as cleaner, when I caught a severe cold, with some attendant fever, which laid me up for three weeks, and left me a good deal debilitated. To recruit my health, the doctor recommended me to be sent to work on Southsea Common. I was not sorry for the change; but, at the same time, it was like opening an old sore, for on this very common I had often rode and walked, one amongst the crowd of seaside visitors. I had often watched, from windows in Clarence Terrace, the convicts at work, and expressed my want of pity for those outcasts of society. I recollected, now that I was there myself, how I had, one evening, compared them with the paupers, and said they were much better off. I had been at work on the common for about twelve months, when one day I was informed that I was to be made 'a special;' that meant that I had special privileges, of which the greatest was, that I could work without an attendant warder. I could go by myself from one part of the prison to the other, and even be outside the walls, about the officers' quarters, unattended. These privileges are only granted to those who have borne a good character, and who are also near the end of their term of imprisonment. As a breach of trust would entail undergoing the entire sentence, no 'special' would attempt to escape. Whilst at my work about the yards, I used often to see Roupell, who had been in this prison about eighteen months, but whom I had never seen before; besides him, there were also at the time several of superior birth in prison, but I did not know their names. At last, the day came on which I was to be discharged.

1867 – WOULDN'T PAY A COPPER!

Margaret Shugaro, alias Gage, was charged with using abusive language towards Mr. William Brown. The complainant is the proprietor of the South of England Music Hall; and at eleven o'clock on Sunday night the defendant was making use of very disgraceful language, and he went to a police constable to have her removed. Her conduct was, generally speaking, so disgraceful and disgusting as to be a nuisance to the whole neighbourhood, and he (complainant) was generally awoken about three or four times a week, at three or four o'clock in the morning, in consequence of her dissolute habits.

The defendant denied the assault, and, amidst some amusement, stated that she was the best woman in Portsmouth, although she had been before their worships upon a good many occasions. She had paid 850l. for fines, and if she wanted a drop of beer, and paid for it, what business was that of Mr. Brown's, or anybody else? She liked a drop of beer, certainly, but then, she paid for it. (Laughter.)

The Magistrates fined her 40s. and 9s. costs, or two months' imprisonment.

Defendant: Let that stop till the others come on. I've got some more. (Laughter.)

The Clerk: Oh, no. Are you going to pay?

Defendant: How much?

The Clerk: 49s.

The defendant (throwing the money on the table)- Well, I'll pay that.

Mr. William Brown was then charged with using abusive language towards Margaret Shugaro, but there was no foundation for the allegation, and the information was dismissed.

There was a second information against the woman for assaulting Ann Winter, the wife of the landlord of the "Jolly Brewers," in Armoury Lane. This was clearly proved, and she was fined 5l., including costs, or two months' imprisonment with hard labour.

Jonathan Winter, the husband of the previous complainant, was charged with assaulting Shugaro, but this information was dismissed.

Shugaro said she wouldn't pay a copper. She wanted to go below for a month or two, and as for the Magistrates, they could all go to ___ for what she cared. There was no "justice in that house." She became so violent at the close of the case that she was removed by force.

1869 – DISCOVERY OF HIDDEN PROPERTY.

On Tuesday morning, as two lads named Henry Williams, and William Saunders were looking for birds' nests, on the Portsmouth ramparts at the back of Colewort Barracks, one of them thrust his arm up a galley-hole, and in doing so found a collar-box in which were two gold Albert chains, twenty gold finger-rings, and twenty-three gold earrings, all new. The boys took the property to the father of Saunders, who with them proceeded to the police station. The property is supposed to be part of the proceeds of a burglary effected at the house of Mr. Prior, a jeweller, living at Hanover Street, Portsea, whose premises were entered on the night of the 9th of September, 1868, and on which occasion one hundred and thirty gold finger-rings, twenty-eight gold earrings, and eleven gold chains were stolen. A seaman named Smith was tried for that robbery before the borough recorder, Mr. Sergeant Cox, at the last Michaelmas quarter sessions for Portsmouth, and sentenced to ten years' penal servitude.

1869 – TALES FROM THE PORTSMOUTH POLICE COURT PART 2

Before W. R. Garrington and E. Emanuel, Esq., and Capt. Hodgkinson.

DRUNK AND RIOTOUS.

Francis Goodwin, a private in the 99th Regiment, was charged with being drunk and riotous. P.C. Carter stated that soon after six o'clock the previous evening he was in Commercial Road, and found the defendant there drunk and creating a disturbance, and as he would not go away, he was taken into custody. The defendant pleaded guilty, but was discharged with a caution, as this was his first offence.

MARGARET GAGE AGAIN.

Margaret Shigaro, alias Gage, was once more charged with being drunk. P.S. Aylward stated that about half past nine the previous evening he was on duty in St. Mary's Street, when he was applied to go into Warblington Street. He did so and found the defendant drunk, He did not advise her to go away, but took her into custody, as there had been so many complaints about her. Mr. Greetham: I suppose it is just after pension day. Aylward: I believe so, sir.

Defendant said she had been out in the afternoon and met some sailors and marines, who wanted some beer. She had some with them and got a drop too much. Mr. Emanuel: Do you recollect that when you were last brought up before me you promised not to get drunk again and that I recommended you to go to Plymouth, thinking that a change of residence would do you good? Defendant: Yes, sir, I recollect. Mr. Garrington said defendant had somewhat reformed of late. Mr. Emmanuel said the Magistrates were inclined to deal leniently with her, and he would take her promise not to get drunk again. Defendant: I will not indeed, sir. Mr. Greetham, to defendant: I think you had better take the pledge again. The Magistrates ordered her to pay 8s. and 7s. costs, with the alternative of five days, imprisonment.

A BAD BOY.

William Edney, a little fellow only eight years of age, was charged with stealing 2d from the till at the "Harp" beer house, Church Path, Landport, the property of George Shipp. Mrs. Peachy Biggs, a married woman, daughter of the prosecutor, stated that on the previous afternoon the prisoner came to the bar and, asked for a drink of water. Her cousin went to get it, and while she was gone she (witness) heard a chink of money, and ran into the bar, when she saw prisoner taking the money out of the till. When he saw her he ran out, and she followed him but could not overtake him. He was subsequently apprehended by the police.

The mother of the boy, in answer to the Magistrates, said her husband was a stoker in the navy. The boy was a very bad one, and she could not do anything with him. She sent him to church and to school, but he would not go. The Magistrates expressed their regret at seeing a boy so young before them upon such a charge, and said they could not help thinking that if he had been properly looked after he could have been kept from committing crimes of this description. He would be imprisoned for seven days and would receive a birching at the discretion of the governor.

SUSPICIOUS PERSONS.

James Austin, 23, and James Williams, 22, labourers, were charged with being in Hanover Street, Portsea, with intent to commit a felony. The last-named prisoner pleaded guilty. The wife of Mr. Charles Prior, a watchmaker and jeweller carrying on business in Hanover Street, stated that at a quarter past nine o'clock the previous night she was in the shop with her daughter, when she heard a "thump, thump, thump" at the plate glass window. She ran out and saw two men run away. She, with her daughter, followed them into Queen Street calling out "Stop thief," and as they could not keep up to them they called to a boy, who pursued them. She could not swear to the prisoner Austin.

George Stares, the boy in question, said he saw two men run by him, and from what the last witness said he pursued them down Daniel Street and into Cumberland Street, where he lost sight of them. He could not swear to the prisoners faces, but the two men he went after were dressed similarly to the prisoner.

P.C. Harvey said that from information he received between nine and ten o'clock the previous evening he went in search of the prisoners, and apprehended them about eleven o'clock in Queen Street, near the end of White's Row. He took them through Hanover Street, and when opposite the prosecutor's shop told them they would be charged with loitering in the street with intent to commit a felony, they having attempted to break the window of Mr. Prior's shop. They made no reply to the charge. When at the station he searched them, but found nothing on them. They were together at the end of White's Row when he apprehended them.

Mr. Emanuel said it was quite clear that the prisoners' intention was to break the window and steal the prosecutor's goods. This case was the first here under the "Criminal Justice Act," which said that it was not necessary to show that the offence had really been committed but only the intent. The sentence upon each of the prisoners was that they be imprisoned and kept to hard labour for the space of three calendar months, and he advised them to leave the town when they came out of gaol, for they would be continually watched by the police as habitual criminals.

A BOY CHARGED WITH ROBBING HIS FATHER.

Henry Quinn, a boy eleven years of age, was placed at the bar on a charge of having stolen half-a-crown from his father, a merchant seaman. Mr. Garrington asked the prosecutor whether he could not find some means of chastising his child without bringing him to that court to be sentenced to a term of imprisonment, the result of which would be that he would mix with others who would probably make him worse than he was.

The prosecutor said he should like to know how he was to punish him. He (prisoner) had stolen a shilling before, and had frequently stolen pence. Upon this occasion his mother had given him the half-crown to get some bread on Friday afternoon, and he remained away until Tuesday, and spent the money. Mr. Garrington asked whether the prosecutor meant to go on with the case, or whether he wished the prisoner to be discharged. Prosecutor: I don't care which way it is. Mr. Garrington: Do I understand you to say that you are indifferent as to what is done with your son? Prosecutor: Yes. Mr. Garrington: Well, then, all I can say is your answer is a most disgusting and disgraceful one.

Mr. Emanuel said he supposed the child had never seen a bible. Did the prosecutor or his wife make him go to church or school? Prisoner's mother: He will not go. He has been sent to school, but has left to look for some work. In answer to Mr. Emanuel and Mr. Garrington, prisoner said he did not know why he took the money. He bought food with it, but might have had some if he had gone home. While he was away he slept in some houses which were in course of erection, opposite where his father and mother lived.

The Prosecutor ultimately decided not to go on with the case, and the prisoner was discharged with a very strong caution as to his future conduct; the Magistrates, at the same time, telling the prosecutor that they did not think the boy was properly looked after.

ALLEGED ROBBERY FROM THE PERSON.

George Julian Payne and Isaac Ransom, two youths of about 19, described as tailors, were brought up on remand, charged with stealing a pair of boots, a knife, and 2l. 1s., from the person of Joseph Bond, a Marine. P.C. Coldrey said he apprehended the prisoners in Oyster Street on Sunday morning on the charge of having robbed a Marine, who was lying insensibly drunk on the ramparts. He asked for a remand on Monday in order that enquiries might be made on the case. This had been done; but nothing had been elicited. A knife was found on one of the prisoners which had been sold to a Marine by an assistant to Mr. Snow, of the Hard, on Saturday evening. The prosecutor was not now present, although he had been warned to appear and prosecute. Hodgkinson said the Magistrates thought the circumstances looked very suspicious against the prisoners, and it was lucky for them the prosecutor did not appear. They would be discharged and he cautioned them that if they came before the court again this affair would be remembered against them.

EMBEZZLEMENT.

William Henry Haddon, a lad of 17 years of age, was charged, on remand, with embezzling the sums of 2l. 10s. 6d and 1l. 0s. 3d., the monies of James John Killpartrick, baker, grocer, and tea dealer, of Lake Road.

From the evidence adduced it appeared that the prisoner was in the prosecutor's employ about one year and nine months, his duty being to take out bread to the customers, and to account for all monies he received when he returned home. One of the customers was a Mr. Akaster, of Queen's Road, Buckland, and the bill owing by that gentleman for bread and flour amounted to 2l. 10s. 9d. according to the prisoner's account. That money had not been received.

Mrs. Gillham, of Brunswick Road, was also a customer, and had bread and flour to the extent of 11l. 0s. 3d. The prisoner had not accounted for this money. Prosecutor had frequently asked the prisoner whether these customers had paid yet, and lying, he said they had not, and he (prosecutor) consequently kept sending in bills.

Mr. James Akaster, a gunner in the navy, deposed to having paid the amount named to the prisoner. Mrs. Ruth Gillham, wife of a schoolmaster, also proved paying the prisoner every day when the bread and flour were delivered. She owed the prosecutor nothing.

P.C. Fiford stated that when he took the prisoner into custody in Lake Road on Monday morning he (prisoner) admitted having received the monies, and said he had given it to his mother, who had promised to pay it back. The prosecutor stated that these defalcations extended from July last up to Saturday. The prisoner pleaded guilty, and said he had lent some to his mother; he had lost some, and had spent what he had left. His father was a carpenter. His mother knew where he got the money from.

The prosecutor strongly recommended the prisoner to mercy, on the ground that the prisoner, who had received no education, had been led away by others. Dr. Miller said the offence was a very serious one, and but for the recommendation so kindly made by the prosecutor, the Magistrates would have given him a very severe punishment. As it was, he would be imprisoned and kept to hard labour for three months.

SUSPICION OF FELONY.

Ellen Cox, 32, a married woman, was brought up on a remand charged on suspicion of being concerned in stealing a quantity of wearing apparel from No. 5, Sidney Place, Landport, the property of Edward Baker. There was also a charge against the prisoner for being concerned in stealing a pair of boots from No.1, Hawke Street, the property of George Martin. Inspector Poole stated that he had found a quantity of stolen property at the prisoner's lodgings. The property had been identified, but he was not prepared to go on with the case, and he therefore asked for a remand till Monday, and that the prisoner should be given up to the county police should an application be made. Applications were granted.

ASSAULT BY A BARGEMAN.

Robert Tewkesbury, a bargeman, was charged with assaulting Jane Reed, a single woman, on the 9th. The complainant stated that on the day in question she was going upstairs in her mother's house, in West Street, Southsea, when the defendant, who lodged in the same house, abused her and knocked her down on two chairs. He hurt her very much. The complainant's sister-in-law confirmed this. The defendant said he never laid a finger on the complainant, and called a woman with whom he lived, who bore out his statement. The Magistrates believed the offence clearly made out, and ordered the defendant to pay 1s., including costs, or be imprisoned for seven days, with hard labour.

HEAVY PUNISHMENT.

Samuel Rooke, a middle-aged man, having the appearance of a labourer, was brought up in custody, charged with assaulting P.C. Morgan in the execution of his duties. The complainant stated that on the previous evening, at about half past nine, he was on duty in Curtis Terrace, Landport, when he saw the defendant, who was drunk, and using bad language to a woman who was with him. He (the complainant) advised him to go away, and, as he refused to do so, he took him into custody, when defendant became very violent and kicked him several times about the legs. The assistance of two policemen and a man had to be obtained to take the defendant to the cells. The statement was corroborated by the evidence of P.C. Reed.

In answer to the charge, the defendant said he had had a little drop of drink and was quarrelling with his wife. He was very sorry. Mr. Marvin said the prisoner was well known at that Court. These assaults on the police were becoming very numerous, and the Magistrates were determined to put them down as far as possible by the infliction of heavy punishments. In this case the prisoner would be sent to gaol for three months, during which time he would be kept to hard labour, and the Magistrates hoped the sentence would be a warning to him and that he would not come before the Court again. The prisoner, who seemed somewhat surprised at the sentence, was removed below.

DRUNKENESS OF AN EX-SOLDIER.

A discharged soldier from the 69th regiment, was charged with being drunk. P.C. Bidgood was on duty in East Street at half past five o'clock the previous evening, when he found the defendant there too drunk to be able to take care of himself. He then took him into custody. The prisoner pleaded guilty, and in answer to the Magistrates said his regiment had only just returned from India, and he had got his travel warrant for Ireland. Mr. Emanuel asked the defendant whether, if the Magistrates suspended judgment, he would promise not to get drunk again between this and Sunday, the day upon which he would have to leave the town according to his warrant. Defendant made the necessary promise and judgment was suspended for a week.

A STOLEN RING.

Ernest Louis Baker, a seaman, serving on board H.M.S *Monarch*, was placed at the bar charged with having stolen a gold ring, value two guineas, the property of Mr. Francis Elliott, a lieutenant on board the ship. The evidence taken, it appeared that between about the 7th or 13th of September the *Monarch* was in a gale in the Bay of Biscay, when by some means or other the prosecutor lost the ring from his finger. Search was made for it immediately it was missed, and the impression was that it had fallen overboard. Nothing further was heard of it until Thursday afternoon, when the prisoner entered the shop of Mr. Joseph George Whitcombe, at the corner of Warblington Street, Portsmouth, and offered the ring in pledge. As Mr. Whitcombe perceived that the ring was of one which few persons in the prisoner's position in life wore, his suspicions became aroused, and he told the prisoner that there was something about the matter which made him suspicious. Prisoner replied that he had a sister in London, who was servant to a gentleman there, and she had sent it to him (prisoner) as a present. This being to Mr. Whitcombe's mind a very improbable story he sent for the police, and P.C. Dibbin took the prisoner into custody on the charge of stealing the ring. Prisoner then made no reply. Prisoner pleaded not guilty, and, after being cautioned in the usual way, said a boy belonging to the ship had given him the ring to pledge. At first he would not do so, thinking that it was not all right, but subsequently went to Mr. Whitcombe's shop, where he was apprehended. He was then fully committed to take on his trial at the ensuing quarter sessions to be held next Friday.

JUVENILE DELINQUENTS.

George Compton, Edward Lipshaw, Edward Davis, and Henry Taylor, all boys under twelve years of age, appeared on summonses obtained by P.C. Toomer, who charged them with cruelty in the ill-treating of a horse by throwing stones at it for a quarter of an hour. The informant stated that about half past two o'clock on Sunday afternoon last, he was standing at the door of his cottage in Queen's Road field, at Buckland, when he saw the four defendants and another boy throwing stones at a horse which was attached to a chain about ten yards long, on some building land on the property of Mr. Sergeant Gaselee. He went indoors and put on his uniform, and then went behind them and caught them.

The horse was much hurt, some of the stones which struck him being as big as his (Toomer's) fist. This was a common occurrence on a Sunday afternoon. The whole of the defendants addressed the Magistrates, and said they were setting a trap to catch some birds when the horse ran after them and bit one of them on the cheek, when they threw some stones at it.

P.C. Toomer, in answer to the bench, said the land was marked out for building purposes, and the defendants had no right to be there at all.

Mr. Emanuel said some boys were becoming a very great nuisance in the borough on Sundays. It was only on the previous Sunday that he was on the Common, and saw several boys overturn a waggon used for the conveyance of earth, and conduct themselves very badly. He went after them himself, but they were too sharp for him.

The Magistrates did not wish to send such young children to prison, and he hoped their parents would take care that they were never brought up at that court again. They would each have to pay 4s. 6d., including the costs. The fines were paid.

1869 – SHOCKING SUICIDE OF AN ARTILLERYMAN AT HILSEA.

Mr. Edward Hoskins, the county Coroner, held an inquest at the "King's Head" public house, at Hilsea on Monday evening to enquire into the circumstances attending the death of Joseph Merry, a gunner in the 11th Brigade Royal Horse Artillery. The first witness examined was James O'Reilly, a gunner in the 11th Brigade Royal Artillery, who said he had known the deceased about six years. He (deceased) was a gunner when witness first knew him, and he had risen from that rank to that of bombardier. He was reduced from the rank of bombardier a week since because he misconducted himself.

Witness last saw the deceased alive about half past nine o'clock in the barrack-room where the sub-division to which the deceased belonged was quartered. Witness was on duty in the room as cook, and deceased came in and said he was going on guard and that he wanted a carbine and "buffs," and witness pointed to some belonging to Gunner Kearney, which deceased took. The carbine was not then loaded, but the ammunition pouch was attached to the "buffs." Witness asked him why he did not take the sword, but as that was worn by Kearney at church parade the deceased said he would come back for it, at the same time leaving the room. There was always ammunition kept in the pouch of the "buffs."

There was nothing peculiar in the deceased's manner or appearance. He appeared in his usual spirits, but was not in his proper uniform to go on guards. About a quarter of an hour afterwards witness heard that the deceased had shot himself and he at once went to a water closet attached to the married quarters; but at that time he saw nothing of him, and had not since seen anything of him until he saw his body that (Monday) morning. Witness had not noticed that the deceased had given way to drink, nor was he aware of any circumstance beyond having been reduced from the position which he formerly held likely to upset his mind.

Thomas Hutchisson, another gunner in the same brigade, also knew the deceased, but had no intimate acquaintance with him. Witness last saw the deceased about half past nine o'clock on Sunday morning going towards the water closets in the barracks from his own quarters. He then had no arms with him, nor was there any in the closet, which witness had left about five minutes previously. Witness went out of sight of the closet, and about ten minutes afterwards he heard a rambling noise proceeding from the closet. Gunner Atkins, who was passing at the time directed the attention of witness to the closet, the door of which was latched, and on approaching it Hutchisson saw that blood and brains were issuing underneath.

Witness opened the door and saw the deceased sitting on the closet with the carbine between his legs, and his left hand on the barrel and the right on the trigger-guard. The carbine had been discharged, and the deceased was quite dead. When deceased passed witness he said "It's a nice morning after yesterday's rain" to which witness replied, "Yes." He was then in his shirt sleeves. Dr. George Park, assistant surgeon attached to the 11th Brigade Royal Artillery, had known the deceased for some little time, but he had not been under his charge, nor did he believe him to be a man of weak intellect. Witness was called out of church on Sunday morning by the sergeant-major, whom he accompanied immediately to the water closet, where he found the deceased in a sitting posture with a carbine between his legs, grasping the barrel about six or eight inches from the muzzle with the left hand, and his right hand just near the trigger. The muzzle was close to the throat near the right side. There was a large wound on the top of the head, the scalp being completely blown away, and a great part of the brain was protruding and blood was flowing.

From its appearance witness believed that it was a recently inflicted injury, and he afterwards found that the piece was discharged under the right side of the throat, and that death must have been instantaneous. From the position of the deceased and the nature of the wounds, witness thought it was impossible for anyone but himself to have inflicted the injury. Witness was afterwards shown a bullet, and to this was a portion of a human skull attached.

A Juror asked if it were known whether the deceased suffered from any disease during his service in India; which would have a tendency to affect his reason? Park, after having referred to the medical history sheet of the brigade, said that deceased twice suffered from fever, but that neither attack was of a long duration. Dr. Park added that the ammunition pouch was examined in his presence, and that one charge was gone. The next witness examined was Ann Merry, the widow of the deceased, whose weak and prostrate condition rendered it necessary for her to be supported as she approached from an adjoining room to that in which the enquiry was conducted. She sobbed bitterly, and frequently pressed her closed hands across her forehead as though suffering from some temporary aberration of intellect, when she would suddenly exclaim, "Let me see him. Do let me see him. Poor fellow. Why did I come here to tell all his faults?"

The Coroner, by dint of soothing expressions of sympathy, succeeded in occasionally getting an answer to one of his many questions. She said that the age of her late husband was 37. He had been very much distressed lately, and witness thought that was in consequence of his being reduced. The deceased had been drinking a great deal lately. He had had fever twice in India, and witness had heard him say frequently that he never felt so well since. At times he was very desponding, when he would say he should never do any good for himself, and at other times he was very cheerful.

Witness last saw the deceased at half past nine on Sunday morning, and he then said something about going on guard. He left the room without saying a word, and did not return afterwards. The deceased was not then dressed in his uniform. Early the same morning the deceased got up and went to the stables, from which he returned in about an hour and a half. Once after the deceased was reduced he told witness that when he was in the barrack-room undergoing punishment he had a feeling come over him that he must get up and get the carbine, but that someone came into the room and aroused him, when he was lying on his bed-irons in a state of perspiration.

Witness thought she heard the deceased upon one occasion say something about using a carbine after he came home from punishment within the past week. Witness did not think the deceased had breakfast when he returned from the stable. He said he had done an hour and a-half's work there, and as he did not feel well he should lie down again for half an hour. The deceased, when he got up, watched witness in a peculiar manner, but as she was very ill she did not like to ask him if anything were the matter with him.

Witness also said that she and the deceased did not quarrel, and that the only disputes which ever took place between them had reference to the money she supplied him with. On Saturday evening the deceased assisted her to clean her place, and he then asked for 4d. to go to the canteen to see two marines with whom he was friendly. She offered him 2d. only, but as he pressed for 4d. she gave it to him, and when he returned from the canteen he was slightly under the influence of drink.

This was the whole of the evidence taken, and at the close the Coroner summed up, and pointed out that there could be little doubt that the deceased shot himself, and the only question, therefore, would be as to the state of his mind at the time. After a brief consultation, the Jury returned a verdict to the effect that the deceased committed suicide when in an unsound state of mind.

1869 – SHUGARO DAUGHTER ASSAULT.

Mary Ann Smith, daughter of the notorious Margaret Shugaro, alias Gage, was charged with assaulting Ada Palmer, wife of a marine. The complainant stated that just before twelve o'clock on the previous Tuesday night she was coming from the Golden Bell public house with two other young women, and as they got to Mrs. Shugaro's door, in St. Mary's Street, a young woman named Elizabeth Hunt came out and knocked one of the young women down. She (complainant) remonstrated, when the defendant came out and struck her, and knocked her down. After this, the defendant asked her if she wanted any more, and she (complainant) said, "No," when defendant again struck her on the side of the face and over the eye. The blow over the eye was a very violent one, and caused the blood to flow copiously. [The complainant here exhibited a pocket handkerchief, which appeared to have been perfectly saturated with blood.]

A witness was called who was with the complainant, and she corroborated her (complainant's) statement. Defendant, in answer to the charge, said the complainant and her witness together with another young woman, were "pitching into Liz. Hunt," and she came out to take her part.

The Magistrates considered the offence proved, and fined defendant 15s., including costs, or, in default of payment, 14 days' hard labour.

Defendant: "I can pay, but I won't, so that she shan't have her 3s. 6d. for the summons. When I come out I'll pay you out." She was cautioned that if she repeated these threats the sentence would be altered, and she was removed below.

1870 – DEATH OF A RECLUSE AT LANDPORT.

On Monday evening the Coroner (W. H. Garrington, Esq.,) held an inquest at the Duke of Wellington Tavern, Russell Street, on the body of Henry Webb, aged 50 years, who had lived in a private house in Russell Street in a very reclusive state for some time past, and who was found dead in his house on Saturday evening. The mode of living pursued by the deceased, together with other circumstances connected with his life and also with his death, will be best gathered from the following evidence.

William James Webb, a joiner in the dockyard, residing at 67, Fleet Street, Southsea, identified the body viewed as that of his brother, who was 50 years of age. He was formerly a watchmaker in Barrack Street, Portsmouth, but had not been in business for the last 18 years. He went there to reside with his mother, and had lived in the same house since her death, which took place five years ago. At this period he began to exhibit what witness believed to be signs of insanity, principally on religious subjects, and, with the consent of the other members of his family, witness caused him to be examined by three different medical gentlemen, but they all declined to sign a certificate of lunacy, so as to remove him to an asylum.

At his mother's death the property left by his father became divisible between the deceased, witness, and another brother—John Webb, but the deceased would not sign a release for the executor's satisfaction, and never received his share. The executor, his brother John, and witness, under legal advice, determined to allow the deceased 10s. per week for his sustenance, and witness laid it out with deceased's sanction. He supplied deceased with dinner from his own table every day, and whenever he wanted it witness sent him coffee, sugar, tobacco, and anything else he wanted.

He also always had pocket money when he asked for it. Rather more than a year ago witness took the deceased home to his house, as he was ill, and he remained there for seven months. Witness wished him to continue there, but he wanted to get back to his house, where he had accumulated a large amount of rubbish, and left witness. The deceased was in the habit of picking up pieces of paper and sticks in the streets, which he took home, and after his death a cart-load of these things and other rubbish was removed into the yard and burnt. Since the deceased left witness the latter had frequently called to see him, but deceased had refused to admit him into the house.

Deceased was dirty in his habits, and amongst his singularities he would walk to Cosham, Fareham, or Gosport to be shaved, saying that he liked to circulate the money. On Friday, witness sent his daughter as usual with the deceased's dinner, but she brought it back again, as he was not at home. Witness had no suspicion of anything unusual having occurred, and did not send again until the next day, when the dinner was brought back again. Deceased would not have dinner until six or seven o'clock in the evening, and when witness' daughter returned and told witness that she could not make her uncle hear, witness went and tried to gain admission. Failing to do so, witness' son and a man living next door got over the wall of the back garden and opened the shutters. Witness then removed a pane of glass from the window of the back sitting room, and on opening it saw the deceased lying on his back with his feet towards the fireplace and his head near the door.

Being near the police station, witness went and gave information of what he had seen and a constable on duty there accompanied him back, and they entered the room together. The deceased was partly dressed. The front of the shirt was open showing his neck and chest, and his trousers undone. There was a basin full of coffee standing outside the fender, but no bread and butter or any other eatable. There were both bread and butter in a cupboard in this room. There was no implements by which the deceased could have done injury to himself, nor any cup, glass, bottle, or powder paper in the room, giving rise to the suspicion that he had been poisoned. Witness had since, with two police officers', searched the clothes of the deceased, but found nothing. The police also took possession of a carpet-bag and a tin hat box. They had not opened them, as the keys had not been found, but witness knew the latter was the place in which the deceased was in the habit of keeping a number of watches which witness saw about two years ago. There had not been a thorough search of the house yet.

At present nothing had been found, but what witness had stated, and he did not believe there was any money secreted. The house belonged to the deceased. Witness and his mother paid the rates and taxes for him. The deceased's life was not, to the best of his belief insured, and he did not think he had left a will.

By the Jury: He last saw deceased alive about a month ago in the street. He did not speak to him. They were on friendly terms. There was no person resident in the house but the deceased. His meals were almost always sent ready cooked. The deceased was a Wesleyan Methodist, and attended chapel regularly on Sundays and week days. He could not assign any reason for the deceased's eccentricities. He never had any injury to his head, nor any severe illness likely to injure his faculties. The deceased was singular from his boyhood. No member of the family had ever exhibited similar symptoms.

P.C. John Edward Purse said he was passing through Russell Street on Friday afternoon, about half past one o'clock, when he saw the deceased open the front door and enter his house. The children in the neighbourhood were in the habit of annoying and vexing the deceased. He went with the last witness on Saturday evening and saw the body washed and the house cleaned up. The former was very dirty and covered with vermin and the latter was in a deplorable state of dirt, some of the rooms being filled with pieces of paper and sticks and other rubbish. There was a good amount of furniture in the house, and in the drawers a large quantity of linen and two new suits of clothes. There was no appearance of any struggle. The house was fastened from within.

Acting P.S. Henry Savage said that on Saturday morning, about ten minutes after two o'clock, he was on duty in Russell Street, and standing on the pavement on the west side of the street, opposite the deceased's residence, when he heard a noise like somebody gasping loudly in the front bedroom. He went over and then heard a man apparently muttering to himself close to the window, and he then appeared to walk across the room, and proceed towards the back of the house. There was no light in the room. Witness heard nothing more. He could not say positively that it was the deceased he heard talking, but he had no doubt in his mind about it. As soon as he heard of the death of the deceased he reported the circumstance to the inspector.

Mr. Walter Hardin, surgeon, said he had that day, by an order of the Coroner, made a post mortem examination of the body of Henry Webb, assisted by Mr. Samuel Bentham, surgeon. There were no marks of violence upon it. The deceased was a man of spare habit of body, but there did not appear any want of nutrition. On opening the chest witness found the whole of its contents in a state of violent inflammation. The pericardium contained about a wine glass full of serous fluid in which flakes of lymph were floating, and the two surfaces to a great extent adhered to each other. Nearly the whole of both lungs showed signs of acute inflammation. On both sides of the pleural membrane were adhesions of an old date, and others of recent formation. The remainder of the organs were in a healthy condition.

The stomach contained a considerable quantity of food. As the result of his examination, he was of the opinion that the deceased died from natural causes and that his death resulted from pleuropneumonia, or violent inflammation of the lungs and other organs contained in the chest. The disease had not probably existed many days.

The Coroner, in summing up, remarked on the singularity of the coincidence that a man should live in such a reclusive condition in a populous thoroughfare like Russell Street.

The Jury returned a verdict in accordance with the medical testimony.

1870 – ATTEMPTED MURDER AND SUICIDE.

A shocking affair occurred at Portsea on Saturday morning. About a week previously a young woman named Julia Ward, twenty years of age, belonging to the "unfortunate" class met with a respectably-dressed man, with whom she had not been previously acquainted, and they remained in company together, proceeding eventually to the female's lodgings in Hawke Street, Portsea. Between nine and ten o'clock on Saturday morning the report of firearms was heard, and immediately afterwards the young woman, who was dressed, ran down stairs; having been shot in the abdomen by her companion. On the arrival of the police they found the man lying on his side on the bed partially dressed, with a wound in the neck, and a five-chamber revolver lying on a chair alongside. The man had first shot the woman and then, it is thought, lay down on the bed and attempted to take his own life.

Between £6 and £7 and a silver watch were found upon him, and he had spent a considerable sum during the week. They were both removed to the Portsmouth, Portsea, and Gosport Hospital, and on Saturday evening; it was deemed advisable to take the declaration of the woman, which was done in the presence of the assistant clerk to the borough Magistrates. The police have instituted inquires, and it is believed that the man is a brewer's clerk from Uckfield, Sussex. The unfortunate woman, who is a native of Southampton, remains in a dangerous condition, but that of the man is considered less precarious.

1872 – CASES OF SUDDEN DEATH AT SOUTHSEA.

The Borough Coroner (W. H. Garrington, Esq.) held an inquest on Saturday evening, at "Wilson House," Havelock Park, Southsea, on the body of Hannah Brown. It appeared that the deceased, who was 46 years of age, was the wife of an army pensioner, and had been for two months past in the employ of Miss Hobbs, of "Wilson House," as cook. In June last, while on a visit to her daughter, the deceased was attacked with a fit, which lasted upwards of half an hour, during the continuance of which she foamed at the mouth. She had never complained since, and appeared to her fellow-servant, Caroline Harrison, in good health. She remarked, however, on Friday morning, that she had a cold, but attended to her work during the whole of the day, and at ten o'clock she went to bed.

At a quarter past one o'clock on the following morning the deceased aroused Harrison, and said she felt sick. She attempted to sit up in bed, but rolled out on to the floor in a fit, striking her temple against the dressing table. Assistance was obtained, and soon afterwards deceased recovered, and went to bed again. At six o'clock, on going into her room, Harrison saw her sit up in bed, and suddenly fall out, and roll on to the floor a second time, where she expired in a few minutes.

Mr. Burford Norman, surgeon, stated that he was called to see the deceased on the morning in question, and from her appearance thought she died from an epileptic fit, produced by natural causes. A verdict was returned accordingly.

The Coroner held a second inquest on Monday at the "Granada Arms" touching the death of Thomas Ellwood, aged 63 years, who died from heart disease. The deceased was a retired grocer, residing at No. 1, Beech Place, Waverley Road, Southsea, and from the evidence of Martha Harwood, who had been in his service for the past 12 years as housekeeper, it appeared that he had been in the enjoyment of good health. At half past nine o'clock on Friday evening he went to bed, and Harwood last saw him alive at four o'clock on Saturday morning, when she went into his room to make up his fire. He was awake, and conversed with her. At six o'clock, on again going into his room, she found him dead in bed. Dr. Axford was called, but his services were of no avail. He was of the opinion that death resulted from disease of the heart, and a verdict was returned in accordance with this testimony.

On Tuesday afternoon Mr. Garrington held a third inquest, at the "Osborne Arms," on the body of Elizabeth Breedon. From the evidence in this case it appears that the deceased was 72 years of age, and the wife of a gentleman residing in Osborne Terrace, Southsea. She had always enjoyed good health, and her husband had no idea that she was labouring under any disease. On Monday she appeared in her usual health, and ate her meals heartily, but at three o'clock she complained of feeling faint, and her husband, becoming alarmed, sent for Dr. Norman. That gentleman attended as quickly as possible, and on his arrival found the deceased on the side of the bed, supported by her husband, dead. The body presented more than the usual pallor of death. He had made inquiries, and had heard the evidence of the previous witness, and from these facts, combined with the appearances of the body, he believed death to have resulted from the bursting of an internal aneurism, arising from natural causes. A verdict to this effect was recorded.

1872 – TALES FROM THE PORTSMOUTH POLICE COURT PART 3

DRUNKENESS.

Louisa Ford was charged by P. C. Brading with being drunk and incapable in St. George's Square, at a quarter to 10 o'clock, on the previous night. She pleaded guilty, and having nothing to say in defence, was ordered to pay a fine of 9s. 6d., including costs; or in default, seven days' imprisonment. Capt. McCoy said if she came there again she would be committed for trial, and no doubt be sentenced to a long term of imprisonment.

DARING ROBBERY.

George Thomas Gue, an old man, a 65 years of age, was charged with breaking a pane of glass, and abstracting. From the shop window of Mr. James Hamilton, jeweller, of the High Street, a silver watch, gold necklet, and a locket, of the, total value of 11l. 10s., the property of that gentleman. John Wheeler, a warder in the borough prison, stated that about a quarter past seven o'clock on the previous evening he was passing through High Street, and hearing a smash of glass he looked round and saw the prisoner taking his hand from Mr. Hamilton's window (a pane of glass in which was broken) and run away. Witness pursued him and caught him in the middle of the street, and conveyed him towards the police station. On the way they met P. C. Hart, and from the prisoner's right hand they took a piece of rag, in which was wrapped a stone, and from the left hand the watch, chain, and locket attached. P. C. Hart deposed to receiving the prisoner into custody from the last witness, and conveying him to the police station, where he was charged with the offence, to which he replied, "Did I steal all that?" Mr. Henry Gardner, assistant to Mr. Hamilton, was in the shop on the previous evening, and hearing a smash of glass he went into the street where he saw the prisoner running into the road, pursued by Wheeler. The damage done to the window was 8l., a large pane being broken from top to bottom. The usual caution was read to the prisoner, after which he was committed for trial at the ensuing sessions.

FELONY CASES.

John Witchelo was charged with stealing a purse, a gold chain, a gold ring, some pawn tickets, and 30s., the property of Mr. W. Mann, of Cross Street, Portsea. The case was remanded till Thursday, for the witnesses who live at Brighton to appear, the prisoner having, it was alleged, pledged some of the stolen articles at that town.

Jacob Curtis and Louisa Sarah Keanett were charged with stealing some boys' cloth cuttings, the property of Mr. W. Marshall. Mr. H. Ford, who appeared for the prosecutor, asked for a remand till Thursday, which was granted.

STEALING LADDERS.

Percy Rommey, a young man, was charged with stealing two ladders, value 30s., the property of Mr. Clarke. The prosecutor, who is a draper, living at Portland Street, Portsea, said he hired the prisoner, who is a painter, to do some work on his premises in October last. The job lasted about ten weeks; and, after its completion, the prosecutor missed the ladders. He had seen the prisoner a dozen times since, and he had promised to bring them back, but he had never done so. On Thursday last the prosecutor ascertained that the prisoner had sold the ladders, and he (the prosecutor) went to the man to whom they had been sold, and identified them as his property. On the evening of the same day he saw the prisoner, who said he would return the ladders, and he (the prosecutor) said "That will do."

At this stage of the case the Magistrates retired, and on their return into court, Captain McCoy said himself and a colleague had retired in order to consider the latter part of the prosecutor's statement, as to his saying "That will do," after he knew that the prisoner had sold the ladders. They thought that the prosecutor had acted very improperly, and that no Jury in the world would convict in such a case. The prisoner would, therefore, be discharged.

SMUGGLING TOBACCO.

James Fawcett, a seaman, pleaded guilty to the charge of shipping 1lb. 14ozs. of unmanufactured tobacco. The duty was 6s. 7d., the value 1s. 6d., and the costs 5s. He was discharged on paying 13s. 1d. Henry Brown, another seaman, pleaded guilty to a similar offence, the tobacco being the same quantity, and the defendant was also discharged on paying 13s. 1d. Seizures took place on the Flathouse Wharf.

SEIZURE OF BAD MEAT.

Thomas Warren, a butcher, carrying on business in Arundel Street, Landport, was summoned by Mr. Superintendent Barber, the Inspector of businesses, for having a fore quarter of beef, two breasts of veal, a piece of bacon, 21 pieces of beef, and 7lbs. weight of sausage on his premises, such meat being unfit for humans' food, the same being exposed for sale and for the use of man.

Mr. H. Ford, who appeared for the defendant, admitted that the meat mentioned in the information was unfit for food, with the exception of the fore quarter of beef, and said that his defence would explain how the bad meat came to be in the slaughter house. Mr. Superintendent Barber then stated that he called at the defendant's premises on the 2nd inst. He found in the slaughter house a fore quarter of beef; it was very poor, not a sign of any fat upon it, and it was sticky and slimy, the animal having suffered from some disease. There were two breasts of veal, which were mildewed, one piece of bacon very much decayed, and very offensive.

In different parts of the slaughter house, he found 21 pieces of corn-beef, some of which was decayed, and the smell of which was very offensive. Six or eight pounds of stale sausage meat was also hanging up. The defendant manufactured sausages for sale. On a bench he found some meat which filled a bushel-basket and which was about to be made into faggots. Amongst the meat, which was covered with sage and onions, were pieces of entrails, some lumps of congealed blood, cold potatoes, and greens. The smell was as offensive as anything he ever smelt in his life, and the place was so filthy that he was unable to stay there but a few minutes at a time. The whole of the meat was taken to the Landport police station, where it was examined by a magistrate and declared unfit for human food. The meat was then buried.

By Mr. Ford: Two constables were sent to the slaughter house at five o'clock, and I followed them. In moving the meat the articles were kept separately, the beef being put on the top. Mr. Warren said very little indeed. He had never been in court before. P.C. Kelloway said he went into the defendant's slaughter house on the 2nd inst., and having seized some bad meat he sent for the Superintendent. In answer to Mr. Ford, the witness said the defendant's boy said that some of the meat which was lying on the bench was to be boiled for the pigs, and some of the other meat was to be made into faggots.

Mr. J. Gregory, veterinary surgeon stated that he was called to see the meat mentioned in the information, and found the fore quarter of beef in a flabby condition, which arose from the beast having had an inflammation of the lungs. The piece of bacon looked "very dirty," and of the 21 pieces of beef a great deal of it was decomposed. The sausages were very bad. Some of the seized meat was, in his opinion, fit for food. Mr. Ford: I should think the quarter had been killed more than 48 hours, and when killed I think it was diseased. In defence Mr. Ford said that his client had been carrying on business for 19 years in Arundel Street, and no complaint of this kind had ever been brought against him during the whole of that time. He called attention to a circumstance (which he said was a remarkable one) in the evidence of Mr. Barber, who said that the shop through which he had to pass was full of meat exposed for sale, and that out of the whole quantity so exposed none was unfit for food. It was only in the slaughter house where the meat which was said to smell offensive was placed, and he contended that there was no proof whatever that this meat in the slaughter house was intended for sale.

The meat, in fact, was intended to be prepared for his client's pigs, and the reason why such a large quantity had accumulated was that he had had no pigs for some time, and consequently the meat with which he was accustomed to feed them had gradually grown in the bulk. In conclusion, he hoped the Bench would not convict the defendant on the fact that diseased meat had been found in his possession.

William Fudge stated that he was in the employ of the defendant, and on the afternoon when the police came into the slaughter house he was present. The quarter of beef had been hanging up since ten o'clock that morning, and it had not been exposed for sale, neither were the bacon and veal intended for sale. The sausages had been in the shop, but were brought back into the slaughter house as unfit for food. His master was in the habit of keeping pigs, but for six weeks previously had had none, and on the day before the visit of the police 12 pigs were brought, and were in the sty when the officers arrived. He (witness) had received orders to boil the whole of the diseased meat seized by the police on Monday, but had not done so.

Mr. Barber: Do you mean to tell the Magistrates that Mr. Warren feeds his pigs on salt beef? Witness: Yes. – Mr. Barber: Would you like to eat any of the meat which was seized? Witness: I should not like to eat the beef. I wouldn't mind one of the faggots though. In reply to Mr. Cousins, he said that the fore quarters of beef was for the purpose of making sausages.

This concluded the case, and the Magistrates retired from court. On returning after an absence of five minutes, Captain McCoy asked Mr. Gregory if it were customary to feed pigs on salt meat. Mr. Gregory said it was not, for if they did it extensively it would poison them. The Bench again retired, and were absent for 20 minutes. Mr. McCoy then said that they had given the case their best consideration, and did not hesitate to say they had very grave doubts whether or not they should not impose a penalty for each piece of meat, which they had power to do. Of the fore quarter of beef they had not the slightest doubt, and on this point they convicted him, and thought that, taking the whole of the circumstances into consideration, they should inflict the full penalty. He would, therefore, be fined £20 including the costs, or in default of payment, two months' imprisonment with hard labour. The defendant at once paid the money, and left the court.

A BRUTAL FELLOW.

Thomas Baker was summoned for assaulting Elizabeth Winter, to which he pleaded not guilty. Mr. H. Ford prosecuted, and characterised the assault as a most unprovoked one, and asked the Bench to deal with it as an aggravated case. The complainant stated that she was the wife of John Winter. On Monday evening she was coming from North End towards Landport in company with two or three men and women. When near Kingston Cross, the defendant, whom she had never seen before, rushed upon them and struck one of the men named House, twice. She then put her hand on his shoulder and remonstrated with him, and he struck her in the eye, knocking her senseless. No one had given him any provocation. Richard Shaw, who was in company with the complainant, corroborated her statement.

Mrs. House, who formed another of the party, also corroborated. In defence, the defendant said that he owed a grudge to the man, and when striking him the complainant got in the way, and the blow she received was accidental. George Dent corroborated this version of the affair. The Bench considered the case proved, and committed the defendant for 21 days' without the option of paying a fine.

A DISORDERLY SOLDIER.

Soldier Michael Swan, a private in the 4th Regiment, was charged with being drunk and disorderly in Bishop Street, Portsea, at half past 11 o'clock last night. P.C. Coles said the prisoner was making a great disturbance, and flourishing his belt in a threatening manner. The officer was obliged to take him into custody, as he would not desist making a disturbance. He was fined 20s., including costs, or, in default, 14 days' imprisonment. The prisoner's sergeant paid the money.

INCORRIGIBLE FEMALES.

Elizabeth Steele, alias Evans, a prostitute, was charged with being drunk and disorderly on Friday. At ten o'clock on the night in question, P.C. Sprake found the prisoner in Queen Street, Portsea, making a great disturbance. She was drunk, and having an altercation with another woman, who was trying to get her home. She refused to go away, and the officer took her into custody. There was a crowd of persons round the prisoner, who was using very bad language. A previous conviction, having been proved against her, she was ordered to be kept in prison until the next Quarter Sessions (Friday next), to be dealt with by the Recorder as an incorrigible person.

Ann Evans, another prostitute, was charged with a similar offence. P.C. Hard said that about six o'clock on the evening of Wednesday he was on duty in Commercial Road, Landport, when he saw the prisoner, who was drunk and creating a disturbance. She refused to go away, and he took her into custody. He was, however, obliged to have assistance. A previous conviction having been proved against the prisoner, she was also ordered to be dealt with at the Quarter Sessions as an incorrigible person.

THREATENING LANGUAGE.

Robert Rawlinson, a dealer, was summoned by Ann Chittenden, the wife of a sailor belonging to the *Orontes*, for using threatening language to her on the 10th inst. Mr. G. H. King appeared for the complainant, and Mr. Feltham represented the defendant. Mr. King, in opening the case, said the defendant was under the impression that the house in which the complainant lived – No. 10, Cressy Place, Landport, belonged to him, and on several occasions he had threatened and assaulted her. He (Mr. King) submitted that, after the Magistrates had heard the evidence, they would consider that the defendant had committed a most aggravated assault on the poor woman, whose husband was away at sea. The complainant then stated that on the 30th of March the defendant called upon her and said she must prepare herself to pay him some money for the rent. She answered that if he had any claim on the property he must take it to the court and have it settled in a legal way. He called again in the evening of the same day and pushed her off the sofa, and then knelt on her. He said to her "If you do not go out of the house I will do for you." In consequence of his threats she and her children had been compelled to sleep out of the house.

In cross-examination, the complainant said she had not had any beer with the defendant since the assault. Some conversation took place between the legal gentlemen and the Magistrates as to the jurisdiction of the court to try the case, Mr. Feltham contending that, as it was a question of title, the case should be heard in a civil court, and Mr. King arguing that so far as the threatening language and the assault were concerned, the case ought to proceed. The Magistrates decided to hear the case, and requested the parties to confine themselves to the threatening language mentioned in the information.

A woman, who lives next door to the complainant, was called to corroborate the complainant's statement. This witness said that she was standing outside her door on the evening in question when she heard the complainant crying for mercy. She went to her and saw the defendant knock the complainant down several times. Witness expostulated with him, whereupon the defendant told her to go out of the house, and then struck her. The witness further stated that she had heard the defendant use threatening language on that and other occasions. Mr. King said that was his case.

Mr. Feltham said he would bring witnesses who would deny that the assault was committed. If, however, the defendant had pushed the complainant off the sofa, he was only using necessary force in trying to eject her from the house, which he considered he was entitled to. He then called James Hoare, who said that on the 8th of March he went with the defendant to the complainant's house. They remained outside, and he heard the defendant ask for the rent, and the complainant said "I'll be -— if I pay it." Cross-examined by Mr. King: I was not there at eight o'clock (the time of the alleged assault.) John Young said he went with the defendant and the last witness to No, 10, Cressy Place, on the night in question. The defendant asked permission to enter the house, but the complainant said her husband was away, and that she would not allow him in. No assault was committed; neither did the defendant say he would have the house down about her ears. Cross-examined: The defendant asked me to go with him to take charge of some furniture. It was between five and six o'clock. The complainant used no abusive language to him. If he had I should have heard it.

Mr. Feltham said that the threatening language was alleged to have been used on the 6th of April, but no witnesses had been called who mentioned that date. Mr. Feltham then called a man who said he went with the defendant to the complainant's house at 8 o'clock on the 6th March. The defendant did not enter the house. There was a mob of persons inside, and they appeared to be drunk. Indeed, there seemed to be a fine old jubilee going on. The Magistrates said they had heard enough of the case, and they had decided that the complaint had not been established.

1873 – LOSS OF A DOG.

The plaintiff is a carter, and defendant was formerly a clerk of works at the school being erected for the School Board in Flying Bull Lane. The claim was 10l., for damage sustained by the plaintiff through the defendant killing a dog. Mr. King appeared for plaintiff, and Mr. Douglas Ford for the defendant.

The plaintiff's case was that on the 6th of May the dog was in the charge of John Fowler, a lad in his employ, in Flying Bull Lane, and by him defendant was seen to take the dog up twice by the skin of its back, which he placed upon a stack of bricks. Upon attempting to repeat it a third time the dog bit the defendant through the nose, and afterwards went and laid down quietly. The defendant then threw a brick at the dog, and was seen by Ellen Watts to continue the ill-usage by throwing flint stones, finally killing it with a short iron bar.

Sergeant-Major Steele, the senior instructor at the Military Gymnasium, had offered the plaintiff 5l. for the dog, which was a bull terrier, and believed it to be worth 7l. or 8l.

In reply to Mr. Ford, the last witness stated that men of experience and fanciers differed materially in the valuation of dogs. Ugliness was a beauty in bull-terriers. It was contended for the defence that on the defendant dropping a pencil the dog picked it up, and defendant afterwards whistled the dog to him, when the animal flew at the defendant, and seized him by the nose. The cruelty was denied, but the actual killing was admitted.

In justification for the act fears of hydrophobia resulting were urged. The Judge: "There is no foundation for such an idea as that." Two witnesses, named Boxall and Lewis, were called on defendant's behalf, the former of whom spoke to defendant being too far from a stack of bricks to have placed the dog on it, and to seeing the defendant throw part of a brick at the animal, but that it did not hurt it; and the latter witness deposed that the dog formerly belonged to his father, and that he had sold it for 5s. The value of the dog, at the outside, was 10s. or 15s., as it was not a thoroughbred animal.

Judgement was given for 7l., to be paid in instalments of 1l., a month.

1873 – THE SHOCKING CASE OF POISONING AT PORTSMOUTH.

On Thursday afternoon an inquest was held at the Hospital at Landport, before W. H. Garrington, Esq., on the body of Henry Charles Horner, an errand-boy in the employ of Mr. Lewis, chemist, of the High Street, who was poisoned under circumstances reported in our impression of Saturday last. Mr. R. W. Ford (with Mr. Douglas Ford) attended to watch the case on behalf of Mr. Lewis.

The Coroner said he was very pleased to see Mr. Ford. He only wished the legal gentlemen attended his court more frequently. He did not know why they did not, whether it were because they had not there an opportunity of airing their eloquence. The Coroner, in opening the proceedings, said the case into which they had met to enquire was one of a very painful character, alleged to be a death from taking poison. Since he had been Coroner, now for several years, this was the first case he had had either of accidental or homicidal poisoning. The only cases had been suicidal poison, of which, in a large town like this, there were sure to be a number.

Having stated the facts as reported to him by the police, the Coroner said it was unfortunate for Mr. Lewis that such a circumstance as this should have taken place in the early part of his career in Portsmouth; though if it were proved he was in no way blameable, he (the Coroner) hoped it would, as it should, have no prejudicial effect on his future prospects. He was pleased to see the servant present, and congratulated her that she had been more fortunate than the poor boy.

The Jury (of whom Mr. Rattenbury was foreman) having viewed the body.

William James Horner, wheelwright, of 13, Melbourne Street, Southsea, identified it as that of his son, who was 15 years of age last birthday, and was employed as errand-boy to Mr. Lewis.

In reply to Mr. Ford, the witness said his son had been about three months in the employ of Mr. Pasmore, of whom Mr. Lewis took the business, and before the latter arrived.

Sarah Witt, domestic servant in the employ of Mr. Lewis, said on Monday or Tuesday of last week the deceased brought into the kitchen a paper marked "Corn-flour," which had been opened, and some of the contents had gone. He said Mr. Lewis had told him to throw it away. The packet remained in the kitchen till Friday. That morning, a little after nine o'clock, the deceased mixed the corn-flour in a tea-cup with water, and asked witness to boil it for him. She did so. She then poured some into a cup for him, mixing some milk and sugar with it, and reserved the remainder for herself. She thought he did not have more than three teaspoonfuls. He complained that it was very hot.

The Coroner: Did he mean that it was hot from boiling, or that it was hot in the taste? Witness: Hot in the taste. I said it was too. I then threw the remainder away directly. Coroner: Before you felt ill? Witness said she did. She went upstairs, and began to feel sick. Not more than ten minutes elapsed before she was sick. The Coroner: Did you feel a burning sensation in the mouth and throat? Witness said she felt it was rather hot as she took the flour. After she was sick, she was not relieved, but felt very ill. She was sick several times. On going downstairs into the kitchen, she met the deceased on the stairs, who said he had been sick in the drug-room. She did not think there was anything wrong, but thought the flour must have been stale. She was very faint, sick several times, and had pains in her throat and stomach.

Mrs. Lewis came in the kitchen to her, and was followed by Mr. Lewis, who administered something to her to make her sick. The pain and heat subsided towards evening, but she was very thirsty during the day. She had felt no inconvenience since except that her throat was sore for a day or two, she had breakings-out, and felt weak. Coroner: Did you see Horner afterwards? Witness: No. I have not seen him since I met him on the stairs, and he said he had been sick.

In reply to the Jury, the witness said the deceased told her he intended to take the corn-flour home. The Foreman: You see a whole family was imperilled by the boy's disobedience. Coroner: Yes. You will draw your own conclusions from that. Foreman thought the girl had given her evidence in a very satisfactory manner. The Coroner concurred. The father of the deceased also said he was satisfied with the girl's evidence. In reply to Mr. Ford, the witness said the packet the deceased brought into the kitchen was exactly like the one which was produced, except that one corner was open, and a little had gone. The paper, too, looked dirty. Mr. Lewis kept his drugs in a room upstairs.

Mr. Ford: Mr. and Mrs. Lewis were very kind to you, I believe? Witness: Yes, very. Mr. Ford: And they sent for a doctor? Witness: Yes. In reply to the father of the deceased, the witness said the lad had free access to the drug-room. Mr. John Phillip Lewis, a registered chemist and druggist, of 84, High Street, said, under the advice of Mr. Ford, he tendered himself as a witness. The Coroner said he was bound to give the legal caution, that Mr. Lewis was not bound to answer any question which he thought might tend to criminate himself. Mr. Lewis said he desired to give evidence. Mr. Ford said Mr. Lewis had nothing to conceal, and was willing to produce any person in his house to give evidence.

The witness said he succeeded Mr. Pasmore in the business in November last, and took his stock. About nine on the evening of Saturday week, after the shutters were up, his wife and he fancied they heard a rat behind the drawers. They took out one of the drawers, and in the space between it and the counter they saw a paper packet. He removed it, and it appeared to be a packet of "Chapman and Co.'s Entire Wheat Flour," a little torn at the end, as he supposed by the rats. The Coroner: Are you infested by rats? Witness: Yes, in the cellar. The Coroner: What did you do with it? Witness: I placed it on the floor behind the counter, where it remained till the following Monday morning. The Coroner: What was done with it then? Witness: I gave it to the boy, and told him to throw it away into the dirt-cask. The Coroner: Had you any reason for telling him to throw it away? Witness: I thought it was dirty, stale, and unsaleable. The Coroner: You had no suspicion at that time that it contained poison? Witness: No. I did not open the packet, which had a thick coating of dust on it. The Coroner: You did not know it was reserved in the kitchen? Witness: No. I heard nothing of it till Friday, the 20th. I was in the shop serving a customer, when the boy asked to be allowed to go out on the walls, as he often had done before. I went out of the shop, and saw the servant, Sarah Witt, who complained that she felt sick. Shortly afterwards Mrs. Lewis informed me that the girl was very ill. I went into the kitchen, and saw her, and as she appeared very faint, I fetched some sal volatile, which seemed to revive her. I pressed her as to what she had been taking, when she said she and "Arthur" (meaning the boy) had eaten some of the corn-flour he had brought from the shop.

I gave her a strong emetic (ipecacuanha and warm water), and then ran out in search of the boy. I did not find him, but sent another boy (who knew the neighbourhood) after him, and he was brought into the shop in a few minutes. He was carried in, as he could not walk. I administered a similar emetic to him; but he was able to swallow only a very small quantity, if any. The Coroner: Was he convulsed, or did he twitch? Witness: His hands were rather black, and he seemed drawn up; but he did not go off into a convulsive fit. We sent to the police station. Two policemen came, and they took the boy in a cab to the hospital. In the meantime Mrs. Lewis had sent out for Mr. Murrell, surgeon. The Coroner: What became of the packet? Witness: It was thrown into the dust-cask; and a man calling every morning, it was taken away. I did not see it after I gave it to the boy to throw away.

The girl Witt here, in reply to the Coroner, said she threw the packet away unopened as soon as she was sick. The man came directly afterwards, and took it away. The Coroner: I hope the man would not think he had got a prize. It would be just the thing a poor man might like to get hold of. Mr. Lewis said he had made enquiries of the man, who said it was put into the ship, and it might have gone to Fareham.

A Juror said there was no proof at present that this packet contained poison. It had not been analysed. The Coroner: It is impossible to analyse the packet, because it has been removed, and it is my object to show that by the questions I am putting, you must draw your own conclusions. Here are two persons taken suddenly ill after partaking of the packet. Have you any idea how the packet came where it was found? Witness: No. I only suppose my predecessor must have placed it there. The Coroner: You did not? Witness: No. The Coroner: Nor any person in your house that you are aware of? Witness: No. The Coroner: Where do you keep your arsenic? Witness: It is locked up in the cellar, and I have the key. The deceased could not get access to it. The Coroner: Had you been selling any of these poisons about this time? Witness: I have not sold any arsenic since I have been in business here. We register all the sales of poisons.

In reply to the Jury, the witness said his stock of corn-flour was kept in the window, and not near where this packet was found. The packet did not appear to have been emptied and re-filled. In reply to Mr. Ford, the witness said he had been a chemist and druggist about 14 years. He had always endeavoured to exercise great care with regard to poisons. When he took over Mr. Pasmore's stock, he believed there was a quantity of corn-flour; but it had been sold, and he had had several quantities since. He had never had occasion to search behind the drawer, and he had never seen the packet before. Until the servant told him she had taken some of the flour, he supposed the packet had been thrown away, in accordance with his directions. Mr. Ford: Can you suggest any source from which poison could have been obtained by the boy or girl except from this packet? Witness: No. After this event, I wrote to Mr. Pasmore, asking if he recollected placing a packet of Chapman's Wheat Flour, with arsenic mixed with it, behind the counter; and I have received the following letter from Mr. Pasmore:

"Exeter, June 22, 1878.

Dear Sir, In reply to yours, I beg to say I have no recollection ever placing a packet of Chapman's Flour behind the drawers. I remember some 12 months since or more, the rats being behind the drawers, some arsenic mixed with flour was placed there, and after a short time taking all away which was not eaten. I regret to hear of the accident, but hope the patients will soon be well again.

Yours truly, G. Pasmore.

P.S. I should be glad to hear how they get on."

Mr. Ford: The deceased was a very good boy? Witness: Yes. Mr. Ford: And he has always said he has been treated kindly? Witness: Yes.

Mr. William Royston Pike, surgeon, acting as house-surgeon at the Hospital during the absence of Mr. Madeley, said soon after ten o'clock on Friday last the deceased was admitted into the Hospital. He was in a state of collapse, and only partially sensible. He said he had taken some poison in corn-flour. Witness administered an emetic at once, and the deceased vomited immediately, and freely. He was put to bed, and soon afterwards he had a slight attack of convulsive spasms with great restlessness. Hot baths with other remedies were applied. The honorary medical officer of the week saw the deceased the same morning. Severe bilious vomiting set in, but no purging. He seemed to get slightly better, though he had a certain amount of delirium occasionally.

On Monday the sickness returned, with diarrhoea, and other symptoms indicating inflammation of the alimentary canal. Delirium also came on. In the evening he was much worse, and witness sent for his parents. He died about noon on Tuesday. Witness had made a post mortem examination of the body, assisted by Mr. George Turner, Medical Officer of Health for the borough. He found a large amount of inflammation of the lining coat of the large intestines and of the stomach. The other organs appeared healthy. The first vomit, was not saved, as it was not in any vessel; but he analysed some of the subsequent bile, and could find no trace of arsenic. He had not had time to analyse the contents of the stomach. The symptoms during life and the appearances after death led him to believe that death was caused by taking some irritant poison, probably arsenic, into the stomach, causing inflammation of the stomach and bowels. The symptoms and appearances were consistent with arsenical poisoning; but he could not say they were not caused by some other irritant poison.

The Coroner said he should have been glad if he could ascertain whether the symptoms were referable to arsenic; and he read the evidence of the servant girl as to her symptoms. The witness said he could only express his opinion that the poison was most probably arsenic. The Coroner said he was thinking it might be necessary to state in the verdict the precise poison which was the cause of death. After some consideration, he thought he had better adjourn the inquest, in order that Mr. Pike might have time to make an analysis of the contents of the stomach, without which the case would not be complete. Mr. Pike had given his evidence exceedingly fairly, and they ought not to press him to go further than he felt able. If arsenic were detected, of course they would be able to say that death was caused by taking arsenic.

A Juror called attention to the fact that the packet had not been entirely opened, but that the poison was inside. He suggested whether the latter might not have been introduced at the manufactory.

The Coroner said of course it was possible, but there would be a combination of unusual circumstances in connection with that. For instance, there would be the fact that, so far as they were aware, it was introduced into no other packet but this; then, that the particular packet should have been placed where it was found, &c. His opinion was that the packet was placed behind the drawers to kill the rats, and that Mr. Pasmore was mistaken when he said it was all removed. It was possible that a slight opening was made in the packet, and the arsenic put in. After some further conversation, it was agreed that the enquiry should be adjourned till Wednesday evening next.

On the enquiry being resumed on Wednesday, the Coroner stated he had a certificate setting forth that one of the Jury was ill and unable to leave his bed. There however, more than the legal number on the Jury so they could proceed without him.

Mr. William Royston Pike, surgeon, said since the adjournment of the inquest, he had made an examination of a small quantity of contents of the intestines, and an organic analysis of the stomach, liver, and intestines. In the stomach and intestines, and contents of the latter, he found no traces of arsenic; but the organic analysis of liver afforded abundant evidence of the cause of death.

Arsenic had undoubtedly been taken and absorbed into the system. Examination by the microscope also showed numerous crystals of arseneous acid in the liver. He was not assisted by anyone in the analysis; but the crystals had been seen by the house-surgeon, Dr. Wilson, and others. He had no hesitation in saying from the symptoms before death, the appearances after death, the post mortem examination, and the analysis, that death arose from taking white arsenic, or arseneous acid.

The father of the deceased asked if the Coroner thought it necessary to examine Mr. Pasmore. The Coroner thought nothing hung on his testimony, and that he would not be justified in putting the borough to the expense of sending for him from Exeter. It was not likely Mr. Pasmore put the parcel where it was found purposely to poison the deceased; and if he came, he would not be bound to answer any questions. He (the Coroner) thought they might assume that this packet was part of the one put behind the drawers, while Mr. Pasmore had the business; but he could have no *animus*, and could not see into futurity. This was one of those unfortunate events which did sometimes occur. The father: If you are satisfied, then so am I. The Coroner: I am satisfied; and I am anxious that you and the public should be.

Charles Colson, an errand-boy in the employ of Mr. Hard, draper, of the High Street, said he was intimate with the deceased. On Friday, the 20th ult., he met him on the Parade about twenty minutes past ten. He was going towards the walls, and he told witness he had been very sick, and still felt so. Witness suggested he had been eating something which had disagreed with him. He said he had not eaten anything that morning. They then parted. About a quarter of an hour or twenty minutes afterwards he saw Mr. Lewis, who enquired if he had seen the deceased, and asked him to go in search of him. He went on the ramparts, and there found Horner lying on the ground on his back. He was lying still. Witness spoke to him, and the deceased told him he could not get up, as he was so weak.

There was no appearance on the ground or on his clothes that he had vomited. Witness helped him to rise, and with his assistance and that of another boy, the deceased was able to get to his master's shop. He did not say anything about having taken anything. He was not sick on the way.

Witness waited with the deceased till he was taken away in a cab, and then went and told his mother what had occurred. The Coroner said the witness had acted very feelingly and judiciously. In reply to Mr. Ford, who again attended on behalf of Mr. Lewis, the witness said the deceased had not said anything about having disobeyed his master's orders.

This concluded the evidence.

The Coroner, in summing up, said they had now arrived nearly at the conclusion of this painful case, and there were two points for the consideration of the Jury. First, what was the cause of the death of the deceased; secondly, whether anybody were blameable for what took place. With regard to the first point, they had the evidence of a fellow sufferer, the servant maid who partook of some of this packet of corn-flour, and who was attacked in a similar manner (but not so severely) to the deceased. These two persons were in perfect health until they partook of a small quantity of what was supposed to be corn-flour brought from the shop, two or three days before. While partaking of it, each made some remark as to there being something nasty in it. They then separated; and shortly afterwards, the servant was sick. In coming downstairs she met the deceased, who said he also had been sick. The girl became worse, was kindly attended by Mrs. Lewis, who called Mr. Lewis; and he, having made enquiries, found she had partaken of the corn-flour. Judiciously and promptly, he administered an emetic, which caused her to vomit.

The poor boy, less fortunate, supposing if he got into the air it would do him good, asked his master for and obtained permission to go on to the walls. On his way there he was met by the last witness whom he told that he had been sick. After he had been absent some time, Mr. Lewis began to be anxious, and went out to search for him; but having been only a few months in the place, he was not sufficiently conversant with the walls to find the deceased, and he sent the last witness in search of him. The deceased was found, taken back to Mr. Lewis's shop, and the police very properly recommended his removal to the Hospital.

Mr. Pike's evidence was to the effect that the boy was, on his arrival, in a state of collapse, but that he gave him an emetic (as Mr. Lewis had attempted to do), which made him very sick, and so soon that it was impossible to catch what was vomited. The contents of the stomach, therefore, were not analysed; but from the symptoms and the after-death appearance, Mr. Pike was pretty certain that death was caused by some irritant poison, though, with a caution which was commendable, he refused to be led so far as to say it was the result of arsenical poison.

In the interim, however, he had made the necessary analysis, which had unmistakably shown the presence of arsenic in the liver, where it was generally found when taken and absorbed into the system. There could not, therefore, be a doubt that death was caused by arsenic or arseneous acid. But the next point was how the arsenic came where it was found. Mr. Lewis told them that on the Saturday preceding this occurrence he heard a noise behind a drawer which he attributed to a rat, knowing the house was infested by them. He opened one of the drawers, and found a packet of corn-flour, not quite full, for at the upper edge there was a little slit, as if it had been opened. The packet was covered with dust, as if it had been there a long time. Mr. Lewis did not put it with the other packets of corn-flour, which were kept in the window, but on the floor behind the counter, and he kept it there till the Monday morning, when he gave it to the boy, directing him to throw it into the dirt-tub. Instead of doing so, however, the poor boy, was, unfortunately, disobedient, took it down to the kitchen, and placed it on the dresser, stating what his master, had said. The Jury, therefore, had not merely the evidence of Mr. Lewis that he told his boy to throw it away, but the statement of the boy himself. The packet remained till the Friday, when it was opened by the boy, who took some of the contents, put it into a, tea-cup, and requested the servant to prepare it. She did so, adding some milk and sugar after boiling it, giving the greater portion, to the boy, and reserving some for herself. Both were taken ill, as he had already stated.

At the last meeting a letter from Mr. Pasmore was read, the purport of which was that about twelve months ago he placed some arsenic mixed with flour in the back of the drawers, but in a few of days the whole, with the exception of that consumed by the rats, was removed. There could be no doubt that there was arsenic in the packet of corn-flour found. Whether, as feasibly suggested by Mr. Ford, a little were merely put on the top, or whether it were mixed throughout, was immaterial. (He might say, in parenthesis, that none of the contents of the packet had been saved; for when the girl was seized with sickness, she immediately throw it away, and when Mr. Lewis enquired about it, he ascertained that it had been taken away, probably to Fareham.)

The theory was that Mr. Pasmore had made a mistake, and that the whole of the poison was not removed, as he supposed. It so was very easy after the event to say Mr. Pasmore did not remove all he put there; but no doubt he thought he had to done so. He could have no interest in placing the packet there; and if it had been left, it must have been an act of forgetfulness. When he heard of this occurrence, he would doubtless be very sorry, leading, as it had done, to so dreadful a result.

With regard to Mr. Lewis, he told them he was totally unaware that any poisonous matter was behind the drawer; that since he had been here, he had not placed any there, or caused any to be placed there; that when he took it out he had not the slightest idea it contained poison; but that he directed it to be thrown away because he thought it was stale and unsaleable.

On these facts the Jury would say whether any criminal negligence were attributable to anyone, or whether it were a pure accident. There was no doubt the poor little boy had been disobedient, and that had he thrown the packet away, as directed, this would not have happened. He had forfeited his life for this trivial act of disobedience, and one could not but regret that one so young should have perished in so dreadful a manner. That, however, was not a question for the Jury; but was blame attributable to anyone.

After a few minutes' deliberation (during which the room had been cleared), the Foreman (Mr. J. Rattenbury) said the verdict of the Jury was that the deceased was accidentally poisoned by taking arsenic. They were unanimous in expressing their thanks to Mr. Lewis for his kind and humane conduct, and his efforts to save the lives of those who had, unfortunately, partaken of the corn-flour. The Coroner: And with regard to any blame? The Foreman: We think there was no blame at all attributable to him. The Coroner said the Jury had unanimously agreed to this addendum to their verdict, that not only was no blame attributable to Mr. Lewis, but that he was much to be commended for the promptitude and discretion with which he treated the symptoms of the servant, whereby, under Providence, he was probably the means of saving her life; and had the deceased been subjected to similar treatment, in all probability he would still have been living. But that did not detract from the conduct of Mr. Lewis; and he had his (the Coroner's) best wishes that this occurrence might have no unfavourable effect on his prospects here, but that his conduct, when brought prominently before the public, might rather have a good effect.

He was also sure the parents had the sympathy of everyone in the loss they had sustained. The deceased seemed to have been a well conducted boy. Mr. Ford: Mr. Lewis wishes me to say he was a very good boy indeed. He is also very grateful for the observations of the Coroner and the Jury. The Coroner said they were due, and he was very glad to have been able to make them. He advised Mr. Lewis to have a thorough search at the back of the drawers, to see if there were any more packets. Mr. Lewis said he had already done so.

A Juror suggested that a good cat should be kept in the house. The Coroner said when he was more accustomed to handling drugs, he invariably tore off the direction on any white medicine, if it were in the least obliterated, so as to run no risk. Most of these poisons were white, and the number had of late much increased. A Juror said a cat would remedy all this. His house was swarmed with vermin when he went to it, but he soon got rid of them. The Coroner said it was not all cats that would attack a rat. Another Juror suggested the use of the "Vermin Killer;" but the Coroner said they were frequently hearing of accidents, and that all these preparations were dangerous. The Jury having signed the inquisition, the proceedings terminated.

1874 – TERRIBLE ACCIDENT ON THE RAMPARTS.

An inquiry into the circumstances concerning the means by which Alfred Scott, a lad of eight years (whose parents live at 25, Durham Street, St. James's

Road, Southsea), was killed at the Platform Saluting Battery on Monday evening last, took place before the Borough Coroner (W. H. Garrington, Esq.), on Wednesday afternoon, at the Volunteer Artillery Drill Shed, on the Governor's Green.

The Jury (of whom Mr. W.B. Daish was foreman) having been sworn, the Coroner said that since he had hold of his office he did not recollect so painful a case as the one which was presented to them that afternoon. Most of them, he supposed, had either heard or read the account of the accident and, as the facts would be fully brought out in the evidence, he should not indulge in any sensational remarks. After hearing the witnesses, they (the Jury), in their judicial capacity, would say whether they were of the opinion that the occurrence was entirely accidental, or whether anyone was censurable or answerable for what had happened; and he (the Coroner) was sure that in a case of that kind he need not bespeak their earnest attention.

The Coroner and Jury then proceeded to view the body of the deceased, which was lying in the room adjoining that in which the inquiry was held. The remains of the little fellow, as he lay enshrouded in pure white wadding in his small coffin, presented a sad spectacle, the upper parts being greatly scorched, and a portion of the cheek torn in the region of the mouth. The spot where the accident occurred was next visited, and details in connection with the leading and discharge of the gun were explained by the Master Gunner of the Royal Artillery.

On the return to the Drill Shed, the first witness called was Nathaniel Scott, the father of the deceased, a joiner in the Steam Reserve, who identified the body as that of his son. Coroner: Do you know anything of his leaving home? – Witness: No. I met him when coming from Landport about six o'clock, and beckoned him to come into the house; but, instead of doing so, he must have gone around another way. Do you know whether he went by himself? – He did. Was he in the habit of coming so far by himself? – I think not.

Samuel Scott, 18 years of age, the brother of the deceased, deposed that on Monday evening he (witness) went to bathe at the "hot walls" with some companions, and after doing so he saw the deceased climbing up the parapet near the saluting battery. Coroner: Did you tell him you were going to bathe? – No, sir. When had you seen your brother? – I met him in Grosvenor Street after my father had requested him to go home. When you saw your brother on the walls, what did you do? – I wished to take him home with me; but when he saw me he ran away, round by the gun. Then, in order to avoid you, he ran in front of the gun as it was being fired at sunset? – Yes. – How far was he from the muzzle of the gun? – About five yards. What was the result of the firing of the gun? – He was knocked down on the top of the bank, and I went to him. He was not coming up the slope then? – No. Are you are quite sure that he was not knocked down the slope or against the wall? – Yes. When you got to him, did he speak or move? – He was on his knees and arms, and looked up at me, but he did not speak. Did he appear to you to be injured? – Yes. He was hurt in the face, which was bleeding. I wiped the blood away. Did anyone come to you? – The man who had fired the gun was going away home, and I ran and told him that he had killed my brother. Whom did you leave with your brother? – Some other boys. I then went towards home to tell my mother what had occurred; but meeting a policeman at the bottom of the steps in Green Row, I returned to the platform with him. Was he dead when he was removed here? – Yes, sir. Who brought him here? – I don't know, as I went away. You saw the two artillerymen who fired the gun? – Yes, sir. Were they looking in the direction of your brother? – No. Where were you when the gun fired? – Behind the man who pulled the tube string. When you told the artilleryman what had occurred, did he seem aware of it or surprised? – He did not know that my brother had been hurt, but he coloured up red. He did not continue to walk away after you had spoken to him? – He went with me to where my brother was lying. When the gun was fired, where did the artilleryman appear to be looking? – At the hole in the gun in which the tube is put. Did you see any other artilleryman or hear any order given? – No, sir. Have you ever been there before when the gun was fired? – Yes, once. When was that? – Last week. What did you do when the gun was fired? – Put my hands to my ears. I mean did you and the other boys search for any tubes or anything? – No, sir. By Mr. Chestle (one of the Jurymen):- It took me about four or five minutes to get to my brother after I saw him from the beach. I got upon the walls by climbing over the "bunny" and pointed wall.

Frank James, of 13, Hawks Street, Portsea, a cab-driver, deposed that he was on the King's Bastion about a quarter after eight on Monday evening, where he saw a bombardier and two gunners of the 21st Brigade of the Royal Artillery. The pin for firing at sunset was loaded by the gunners, and he saw that the gun had been depressed and elevated. The Coroner: Where was the bombardier? – On his knees, watching the clock. When the friction tube was placed in the gun, what did you see? – The gunner held the lanyard in his hand at the right side of the rear of the gun. Then, as he stood, he was looking across the gun. He was watching the bombardier for the word of command. Then neither were looking in the direction of the muzzle of the guns? – No. So that a boy passing could not have been seen. – No. Where was the third man? – On the opposite side of the gun. What was he doing? -Looking to his front. And he could have seen anyone? – Yes. Did you see the deceased? – No.

Were there any other children there? – I should think there were thirty or forty children of both sexes there. They were standing on either side of the gun, and I heard the bombardier warn them to get back as the gun was about to be fired off. He drove some of them away, and one he pulled by the ear. One of the boys said, "I would as soon sit on the gun when she is fired as not." Were you told what had occurred? – Yes, immediately afterwards. I went back with the gunner, and rendered assistance. Where was the deceased then? – He was lying on the parapet on his side, about twelve feet from the muzzle of the gun. Was he dead then? – No, his mouth moved, and he gasped. Before, however, we could get him across the green to the drill shed he had ceased to live. He was conveyed thither on a stretcher obtained from the guard-house. In what direction was the deceased lying when you first saw him? – His head was lying towards the Southsea Pier, to the left of the muzzle of the gun. When the bombardier and gunner were brought back did they exhibit sympathy, or were they indifferent? – The bombardier appeared to be much frightened and down-hearted. Did these men appear to be performing their duty in a quiet and orderly manner? – Yes, Does it not seem strange that they did not see the boy after the accident? – Well the smoke hung about a great deal. Was the gun sponged out after it had been fired -No, sir. It never is. And do you consider the accident purely accidental? – Yes, I consider there was no negligence whatever.

The Coroner said he had three or four other witnesses in attendance who could be called. There were the two gunners, and the master gunner could, if the Jury desired, give them an account how the duties in connection with the gun were performed. He (the Coroner), however, rather preferred having the testimony of an independent witness like James than those actually concerned in the matter. If they liked to have the depositions taken they could; but he should leave it to them to determine. The Jury intimated that they wished to have the bombardier who was in charge on Monday evening to be examined.

Bombardier William Henry Smith was then called, and having been cautioned by the Coroner that he need answer no questions which might tend to incriminate himself, he stated that he had no hesitation in giving testimony. On Monday evening witness was on guard at the Gunwharf Barracks, and it was his duty to attend at the firing of the sunset gun on the saluting battery. The two gunners, whose duty it was to attend to perform the manual labour came from the Point Barracks, and were posted specially for service on the Kings Bastion. Gunner Warby loaded the gun just as witness arrived, with a cartridge composed of 2lbs. of large-grain powder, deposited in a rough silk bag. Gunner Anderson was the look-out man.

Witness, was watching the church clock from the battery, and when the time got within half-a-minute of the fixed period for the sunset, (8.16), witness called out "Ready." The tube was then inserted, and witness saw that the gunner was in his right position.

The Coroner: Then, at the proper time, you gave the word to fire, and the gun went off? – Yes. – You were not aware that anybody had been hurt? – No. But you went away to re-join your guard? – Yes. How far had you got when you were called back? – I had gone about twelve paces, when Gunner Anderson told me that an accident had occurred to a little boy. Where was the deceased when you got back? – He was lying on his back on the parapet about four or five yards from the muzzle of the gun, near the edge of the slope. Some of the people who had congregated there told me that he had pulled up from the exterior slope of the battery. Do you know who it was told you that? – No. I was very much excited and I cannot tell. Was the duty which you went to see executed with care? – Quite in the usual way. When you came onto the battery were there any children there? -Yes, and I sent them away. Some of the boys answered that they should like to stand on the top of the gun when it was fired. Have you been on duty there before? – Very often. And have you known that it is a place where children congregate? – Yes. Merely for the fun of seeing and hearing the gun go off, or for the purpose of getting possession of the empty friction tubes? – For both, sir. There is quite a scramble for the tube sometimes. I should like to remark that it is not part of my duty to keep the children back, although I have done and would do so. Do you use a wad of any kind in loading the gun for sunset? – No, sir; nothing but the bag of powder. Do you think the deceased must have been coming up the slope? – Yes. If he had been in front he would have been blown to pieces. If he had been on the slope, the gun being elevated, would not the charge have gone over his head? – No; I think not. The powder greatly expands after leaving the muzzle. We must have seen him if he had been on the parapet. No one supposes that he was standing passively in front.

The brother states that he was on the parapet; but you think that he must have been on the slope. Was the deceased dead when you got back? – Nearly so. By a Juror: As near as I can imagine, the distance from the muzzle of the gun to the edge of the slope is about five yards. If the deceased had been nine yards away, probably he would not have been injured. A Juror observed that if the deceased had been on the slope he must have gone to the front.

Coroner: Well, the bombardier only tells you what he was told. It is possible that the deceased might have been coming up from the slope, and the brother in the excitement might not have known it.

Mr. Frederic Crossly, surgeon, of St. Mary's Street, deposed that by accident he happened to be in the drill shed when the deceased was brought in on Monday evening, between eight and nine o'clock. He was then dead. Coroner: What did you find on examination? – The whole of the face, neck, and chest were scorched and blackened as if by an explosion of gunpowder. The cheek was split through at the mouth about an inch in length, but I did not detect any fracture of the bones either of the face or chest. What do you think was the cause of death? – The shock caused by the explosion.

The Coroner said after the prolonged enquiry and the attention which the Jury had paid to the evidence it would not be necessary to detain them for a lengthened time in order to go over the whole case. There was a little discrepancy between the evidence of the brother of the deceased and that of Bombardier Smith; and although they would have observed that the latter was a man of intelligence, and had given his evidence with apparent truthfulness, one spoke to a fact, whilst the other only gave his testimony as an opinion. He (the Coroner) rather leant to the opinion that what the boy had stated was correct, because it was quite evident that the deceased must have received the effects of a large amount of the explosion. He thought that he must have been fairly in front of the gun, and that he ran into that position just in the same lamentable way as they found children sometimes run from the pavement in front of horses. The only thing that had not been explained was the position of the man Anderson, the second gunner who was there at the time; but he might have been looking along the gun, or for ships (which was a portion of his allotted duty).

Of course if he had seen anyone in front of the gun, he would have told his companion to refrain from firing, and have removed the person; but they (the Jury) could easily perceive that if a number of children were standing around the gun, one might easily shoot out from the rest and imperil his or her life. Even if that were so, and the man Anderson saw it, he might not have had time to stop the deceased; but it would be for them (the Jury) to say whether the deceased came by his death through the shock produced by the explosion, and whether blame was attributable to any person. If so, they would have to say who that person was, and the degree of their culpability, whether merely censurable or of a higher nature. They must all of them regard it as a very dreadful case, and with him (the Coroner) commiserate the parents, who deserved their sympathy. The only satisfactory thing about it was that the shock caused instantaneous death, and, therefore, that there was no very prolonged suffering.

The Jury immediately returned a verdict that the deceased had been accidentally killed, and that no blame was attributable to anyone.

1874 – PRISON DISCIPLINE.

The laying of the foundation of the New Borough Gaol, on Thursday, renders opportune a few remarks on modern prison discipline and the effects which it has upon the criminal population. We desire all the more to call attention to this question because many of the speakers at the luncheon were disposed to treat the subject of the treatment of criminals from the philanthropic standpoint, forgetful of the fact that the application of philanthropic principles has not proved a great success.

Though far from satisfied with the stationary results of the present system, we are not of those who take a desponding view of things. In point of fact, there are unquestionable signs of amendment. There is a fashion in crime as in other things, and Mr. Sergeant Cox has pointed out, in his essay on the Principles of Punishment, that there is among the criminal class a strong tendency to imitation, insomuch that any crime which is greatly talked about forthwith becomes the mode. The present fashion appears to run strongly in the direction of wife-beating and violent assaults. But the enormity of these offences must not blind us to the fact that they are for the most part confined to certain well-defined areas, or induce us to devote our attention to them alone, to the exclusion of every other species of crime.

In Portsmouth, there has been a steady decrease in the number of commitments since 1860. In that year the total number of culprits sent to prison was 1,030, while last year, notwithstanding the increase which has taken place in the population during the interval, the total was 914. Nor is this gratifying improvement confined to Portsmouth as it appears that from the Judicial Statistics which have just been published that there has been a very perceptible decrease in crime throughout the country.

As compared with 1870, there was last year a decrease of 12.9 per cent in the number of indictable offences, and the decrease has, with the exception of 1868, gone on regularly since 1866. It is true that the number of cases summarily dealt with in 1873 show an apparent increase of 7.8 per cent on the previous year; but the total increase is more than accounted for by an augmentation in the commitments for drunkenness,.

With the exception of offences against the person, a reduction has taken place in all classes of crime; and it furthermore appears that there has been a considerable decrease in the number of professional criminals, and that, while there has been a slight increase in the sentences to imprisonment and reformatories, the returns of sentences to death and penal servitude show a perceptible falling off.

All this is very gratifying as far as it goes, since it proves that serious crimes are becoming less frequent, and that the ominous totals are made up to a very large extent of the offences which could be adequately dealt with by fines or the requirement of sureties. But the most unsatisfactory features connected with our criminal administration is the number of re-commitments. There is a class of habitual and professional rascals for whom our gaols possess no terrors; and in order to meet the requirements of these we wish that the opening of our new Gaol could be celebrated by an experiment in prison discipline.

The prisons at the beginning of the century were described by Sydney Smith as large public seminaries maintained at the expense of the country, for the encouragement of profligacy and vice, and for providing a proper succession of housebreakers, profligates, and thieves. They were schools conducted without the smallest degree of partiality or favour, there being no man, however mean his birth or obscure his situation who could not easily procure admission to them. The moment, we are assured, any young person evinced the slightest propensity for these pursuits, he was provided with food, clothing, and lodging, and put to his studies under the most accomplished cut-throats the country could supply. We have since rectified many of these abuses by a system of classification – a classification which will be further perfected in our new gaol; but it is evident that we have not succeeded yet either in reforming our gaol birds or in inoculating them with a wholesome dread of prison, and it is therefore impossible to resist the conclusion that our existing prison discipline is a costly failure.

What diminution there has been has taken place altogether apart from our system of pains and penalties and may be sufficiently accounted for by a drying-up of the criminal supply. Or, to put the thing in another way, the decrease is as the result of prevention rather than cure. And we are convinced that it is only by devoting our attention to the affluents that the stream of crime can be arrested. Benevolence and all the customary appliances are, we fear, lost upon those who have become habituated to the atmosphere of a gaol. Mercy appears to be thrown away upon a prisoner who has been previously convicted.

As the Rev. Mr. Jones, the Ordinary of Newgate, has observed, humanity should be exercised rather for the protection of those who keep the law than for those who break it; for, in nine cases out of ten, "it is choice, and not necessity, that leads to crime."

The object of criminal discipline, consequently, should be almost exclusively directed to deter the culprit from again offending, and, by the example of his suffering, to deter others from offending in the same way. Now a gaol should be a place of punishment from which men recoil with horror; a place of real suffering, at once painful to the memory, and terrible to the imagination; a place of detention the recollection of which would induce the habitual criminal to prefer busiest labour to making its acquaintance a second time. Of course we cannot torture a prisoner with bad air and bad food, or allow disease and neglect to work their will, as in the sad unreformed days. At the same time it must be remembered our gaols are frequently more comfortable and desirable residences than the ordinary home of the culprit. There is no crowding in them; and when we consider that the buildings are spacious, clean, and perfectly ventilated and warmed and that inmates are well fed and clothed, it will be seen that the advantages on the side of the prisons are not inconsiderable.

The means, therefore, which remain to us of making detention in them as far as possible disagreeable, without injury to the health or minds of the inmates, ought not to be lost sight of. The *Quarterly Review* once indulged in an elaborate argument to prove that incorrigible thieves and irreclaimable burglars ought to be imprisoned for life, we shut up lunatics for life, it observed, because they are dangerous to society so why should we liberate confirmed and habitual criminals who are infinitely more dangerous? Such men, it was contended, have forfeited all claim to personal liberty, and their repeated convictions have proved them to be a constant source of danger to society. And, having ceased to banish them, the only remedy which suggested itself to the mind of the reviewer was continuous incarceration, with compulsory productive labour.

This is simply the language of despair, and we have not yet reached that stage. Lunatics are kept in perpetual confinement as a necessary result of their condition. They cannot be permitted to be at large, and they are not amenable to punishment. What else can be done with them beyond keeping them in durance? But as regards habitual criminals, if we can by any means keep them out of gaol the end in view would be gained just as much as if they were not permitted to leave it.

It has been recently suggested, with the object of increasing the deterrent effects of punishment, that the judges should have power to sentence culprits to longer terms of imprisonment, with the addition of flogging in certain cases. Habitual offenders have no claims upon our consideration. But the question of expediency arises; for however long they may be

1876 – STEALING TROUSERS, BOOTS AND A COAT.

George Beech, a private of the 64th Regiment was charged with stealing a pair of trousers of the value 6s, 6d., the property of Messrs. Chalcraft and Son. The prosecutors are outfitters living at 17 Russell Street, Southsea, and the trousers in question were pinned to a bar outside the shop on Saturday night.

About half past nine o'clock, Mr. Chalcroft junior saw the prisoner run away up Percy Street, then having the trousers under his arm, and just at that moment, Sergeant Harvey happened to be near the police station and caught the prisoner. He became very violent, and assistance had to be obtained to get him inside the station after his having attempted to strike Mr. Chalcroft.

It appeared that the man had been drinking, but was sober enough to know what he was doing. The prisoner admitted the theft, but excused his conduct on the grounds that he had had "a drop of beer." He was sentenced to six weeks imprisonment with hard labour.

Enoch Shore, another private in the 64th Regiment, was charged with having stolen a pair of men's boots belonging to Edward Hanham, boot and shoe dealer, of 27 Russell Street, Southsea. At a quarter after ten on Saturday night the boots were hanging at the doorway of the prosecutor's shop, when George Hollis, an assistant, saw the prisoner pull them by force from the nail.

Hollis overtook the prisoner when he exclaimed, "Let me go," and struck Hollis across the forehead with the boots, which were pelted and nailed and worth 8s 6d.

P.C. Voller took the man into custody in Commercial Road, but he made no reply when charged with the theft. There was a second charge against the prisoner of having stolen a coat worth 18s., the property of Messrs. Chalcraft the prosecutors in the last case. When apprehended for the robbery of the boots the coat was being worn by the prisoner over his uniform, and was identified by Mr. Chalcraft junior, it having been seen hanging safely outside the shop about an hour previously.

The prisoner, who pleaded for mercy owing to having "drunk hard," lately was sentenced to two months hard labour on the first charge and to one month's hard labour on the second. The Magistrates said they had passed a heavier sentence in this case than in the last owing to the prisoner having used violence against the prosecutor.

1877 – PROSECUTIONS BY THE SCHOOL BOARD.

James Carr, of Armoury Lane, Portsmouth, was summoned for not having sent his child of seven years regularly to school during the week ending the 4th inst. The attendance had been but seven out of forty school openings. A fine of 5s, was imposed.

Alfred White, of 71, Sussex Street Landport, was summoned in respect of a girl of ten years, who had been absent from school altogether and, in his absence, the defendant was fined, 5s., or five days imprisonment.

David Pegg, cork cutter, of High Street Portsmouth, was fined 5s., or five days' imprisonment, for neglecting the education of his boy of twelve years, who had attended but 21 times out of 40.

John Ayling, of Parker's Place. Marylebone, a bargeman, was also fined 5s., or five day's imprisonment, for not sending his girl of ten years to school.

Edward Moore, a dealer, of 2, Beck Street, Portsea, whose step-son of ten years had attended school but three times out of forty; and Reuben Fryer, labourer and pensioner, of Green's Court, Hay Street, Portsea, in respect of a boy of eleven years, were each fined 5s., or five days imprisonment.

Mary Kemp, a widow of Carpenter's Place, St. James's Street, Portsea, in respect of her son of eleven years, who had attended 22 out of 40 school openings, was allowed a fortnight to make matters better.

Eliza Hudson, of Havant Street, was summoned to show cause why an attendance order should not be made upon her to secure the attendance of John Hudson, twelve years of age, at some efficient school. An order for attendance at the Kent Street school was made.

Mary Webster, of Nelson's Court, was also charged upon a similar information with regard to her boy of seven years, and was ordered to see that he attended the public school in Pembroke Road, Portsmouth.

James Compton, twelve years of age, of Cosham Street, Landport, who was brought up on remand from the Workhouse on a charge of having wandered in a destitute state in North Street, Landport, on the 7th inst., was discharged, the Magistrates being of the opinion that the circumstances did not come within any of the sections of the Act of Parliament, the boy having a home.

Elizabeth Leary, 13, charged under similar circumstances of wandering, having no home, was ordered to be sent to the St. Mary's Home for Catholic Girls at Torrington Lodge, Eltham, Kent, until she attained the age of 16 years.

1878 – THE MURDEROUS ASSAULT UPON A CONSTABLE AT COSHAM.

On Monday at the Fareham Petty Sessions, before Frank Bradshaw, Esq., and Captain Turner, John Kelly, a desperate looking fellow, was charged on remand with having maliciously wounded P.C. Vincent Gregory, with intent to do him grievous bodily harm, on the 11th of May.

The prisoner, who gave the age of 22, but appeared much older, was brought handcuffed into the Court, and remained so during the whole proceedings, occasionally casting a savage glance towards his accuser.

The constable (who appeared in the witness-box with his face still bound) stated that he was stationed at Cosham, and at a quarter to seven on the morning of the 11th instant he was on duty in the parish of Wymering, when he saw the prisoner come from the direction of Portsmouth. Suspecting that he was a deserter, witness stopped him and asked him how long he had been out of the Army, to which he replied, "I have not been in the Army, but I belonged to the Kent Militia and have bought myself out." Witness told him that he did not believe it, but suspected he was a deserter from the Army, and upon that the prisoner ran away.

Witness pursued and caught him, charged him with being a deserter, and took hold of his arm. While leading him up the main street of Cosham the prisoner said, "You have got me right; I am a deserter and you will get 1l. for me." Directly afterwards, the prisoner turned upon him all of a sudden, and dealt him three blows upon the face with the knife produced [an ordinary clasp pocket knife] with all his force. One of the blows was in the forehead, a second close under the right eye, and the third lower down the cheek. The blood flowed freely over his (witness's) face and coat, and some went upon the prisoner's face.

Witness held the prisoner until George Ripley came to his assistance, and the handcuffs were put upon him after he had been thrown to the ground. After the prisoner had got upon his feet subsequently he said "You _____, it was a good job you got some civilian to help you or I would have murdered you, for that was what I intended to do. You_____, I would have cut your daylights out, or I would have cut your _____ head off but what I would have made my escape."

He (prisoner) afterwards said "I don't care a ____ now you have caught me; I may as well tell, for you will find it all out. I belonged to the Royal Artillery at Aldershot, and was confined there awaiting a court-martial. There are 38 offences against me, for which I expected I should get seven years, but I made my escape, beating the provosts and the whole lot of them. I have belonged to fourteen different corps, but this morning I deserted from the 66th Regt. at Portsmouth. I have been convicted of burglary and knocking the police about."

On the way to the police station at Fareham by railway the prisoner added, "You _____, the only thing I am sorry for is that I have not killed you, for that was what I meant to do." After witness was stabbed he went to Mr. Baker's, chemist at Cosham, as he was unable to stop the bleeding, and there the wounds were strapped up; and afterwards he went to Mr. Barnard, of Fareham, the divisional police surgeon who examined the wounds and dressed them. Witness was still under Mr. Barnard's care. Being asked if he had anything upon which to question the witness, the prisoner carelessly said "No; I've got nothing to ask him. It's no use to ask anything."

George Ripley, a labourer living at the "King and Queen" public house at Cosham, deposed that on Saturday morning, the 11th inst., about a quarter to seven, he saw the constable apprehend the prisoner, and when they had got to the top of the street the prisoner turned round sharply, took his knife out of his left hand jacket pocket, and "dagged" at the constable back-handed three times with his left hand. Witness saw the blood begin to flow, and he then jumped off the footpath and went to the constable's assistance, took hold of the prisoner by the collar of his coat, and together they got him upon the ground, where the constable put the handcuffs upon his wrists. The prisoner told the constable that it was a good job for him there was a civilian there or he would have "mortally injured" him, making use of a vile expression.

Mr. William Barnard, surgeon, of Fareham, stated that as he saw Gregory at his surgery on the morning of the 11th instant, and the right side of his face was covered with sticking plaster. He removed a portion of that, and found that blood was oozing from two wounds, one on his temple and the other on the cheek. He dressed both wounds again, but did not remove the plaster from the wound under the eye, as it had been put on very well and the bleeding had ceased, The two wounds upon the forehead and under the eye were not dangerous in themselves, but were so in consequence of their contiguity to other parts and the fear that erysipelas might ensue. The wounds were such as might have been caused by the knife produced, and upon one blade there was still what appeared to be blood. He now considered that the injured man Gregory was quite out of danger.

The prisoner declined making any statement, and was committed to take his trial at the next Winchester Assizes. He was afterwards formally charged with being a deserter from the Army, and he admitted the offence.

At the Hampshire Assizes on 6th July, John Kelly, alias John Duffey, 22, a labourer, pleaded guilty to having feloniously and maliciously wounded Vincent Gregory, with intent to do him grievous bodily harm at Cosham, on the 11th of May. The prisoner, a powerful and vicious looking fellow had positively broken a considerable quantity of the solid masonry of the cell in which he was confined at Fareham, and was so violent that he had to be chained hand and foot while being examined before the Magistrates. He had deserted from several regiments, and when apprehended he was awaiting trial by general court-martial for nearly 30 offences.

The learned Judge, who commented strongly on the prisoner's conduct, sentenced him to be kept in penal servitude for seven years, and at the expiration of that time to be kept under police surveillance for a further term of seven years.

1879 – THE CHARGE OF MANSLAUGHTER AT PORTSEA.

At the Winchester assizes yesterday, Edward McKenzie, 20, stoker, serving on board the *Asia*, and Rose Amelia McKenzie. 19, his wife, were indicted, both on the Coroner's warrant and upon the committal by the Magistrates, for the manslaughter of Eliza McKenzie, at Portsea. Mr. Charles Matthews, instructed by Mr. George Whitehall, appeared for the prosecution, and the prisoners were undefended by counsel.

His Lordship said it seemed to him that the case was one of a very doubtful aspect. There were some fourteen witnesses, and many of them deposed to the same facts in the main, although some of them differed to some of the minor details. He suggested, therefore, that Mr. Matthews should, if the prisoners did not offer any objection, call one or two witnesses as to the facts. He made this suggestion because he thought everything would turn upon the question as to what was the exact character of the injuries the deceased received, and how far they were connected with her death.

After one or two witnesses had been called the doctor might be put into the witness box, and if he traced the death to injuries at the hands of the prisoners or either of them then the details might be gone into at greater length by calling the whole of the witnesses!.

Mr. Matthews having assented to this and the prisoners having no objection, John McKenzie, the husband of the deceased, was then called. He said that on the 10th December the deceased complained of having been struck, and he noticed a lump on her head. She kept to her bed each day afterwards, but came down as usual in the evening. On taking her up a cup of tea on the morning of the 13th he found her dead. Mrs. Margaret Barnes, Catherine McKenzie and a seaman named Mursell said that they did not see the female prisoner strike the deceased, or bump her head on the ground. The foreman of the Jury here intimated that they had agreed that the prisoners were not guilty, and they were subsequently discharged. On reaching the Landport Railway Station the male prisoner was re-apprehended by P.S. Marks, of the Metropolitan Police, and conveyed to his ship.

1879 – THE ADMIRALTY AND NAVAL LUNATICS.

There is reason to believe that the Lords of the Admiralty have slightly modified their instructions with reference to throwing the expense of the treatment or removal of the naval lunatics upon the parishes in which their hospitals happen by chance to be situated. It is now stated that it is merely those of the insane whose insanity can be proved not to be traceable to anything which may have happened to them on board ship. We doubt, however, whether this will prove very satisfactory' to the Alverstoke Guardians or to the ratepayers of that unlucky parish.

1879 – SUDDEN DEATH OF A CHILD AT LANDPORT.

An inquest was held yesterday at the Royal Oak, Lake Road, Landport, by the Coroner (W. H, Garrington, Esq,), on the body of Edwin Steel, aged seven months. The Coroner, in opening the inquiry, said that in consequence of the child being an illegitimate one he had instructed Dr. Knott to make a thorough examination as to the cause of death of the child.

Ellen Louisa Steel said she was a single woman and lived at 48, Kilmiston Street, Lake Road. The deceased was her child, and had been perfectly healthy since its birth. The child was not weaned, but had been frequently fed on bread and milk, as well as from the breast. The deceased had been fed from the breast at half past four on Wednesday, and again at 11 o'clock at night, at the time the witness went to bed. Witness's sister slept with her, and the child slept between them. The child appeared perfectly well on the previous evening. When witness awoke, about six, she found the child lying almost on its face. The left side of the body was discoloured, and the tongue somewhat protruded between the and it was reported that no one could be seen. Witness, with the assistance of the leading stoker, then mustered the hands, and the deceased was found to be missing. Upon examination it was found that the hammock of the deceased had not been unlashed, and it was therefore supposed that the deceased had not slept in it. He ought to have been asleep in his hammock like the others. From enquiries which the witness had made he believed the deceased could not swim, because if he had been able to, he could have kept above water a short time until assistance arrived. The Coroner having summed up, the Jury returned a verdict of "Found drowned, there not being sufficient evidence to show how the deceased came into the water."

1879 – FATAL FIRE AT CRASSWELL STREET.

About twenty minutes to seven o'clock last night, the neighbours opposite No. 60, Crasswell Street, saw a blaze in the bedroom of the house, which was occupied by Isabella Murphy and her daughter. The fire was first seen by a woman named Drake, who lives in Temple Street. The neighbours then ran in and extinguished the flames with a few buckets of water. Isabella Murphy, who is a widow, aged 66, had gone to lie down in her bed, leaving a paraffin lamp on a small table adjoining the bed. The lamp was evidently upset, it was afterwards found on the floor. The bed clothes and the garments worn by the woman had become ignited. She was taken out of the house by a butcher named Triggs, assisted by other neighbours. The police came up at the time with the hose and reel and steam fire engine, but their services were not required. Seeing that the woman was badly injured, the police sent for Dr. J.P. Way, who attended at once and ordered her removal to the Hospital where she was conveyed on a stretcher, but unfortunately her injuries were so serious that she died shortly afterwards.

1880 – A BURIAL SCANDAL AT PORTSMOUTH.

The burial of paupers is a subject which is unhappily prolific of scandals. Hitherto Guardians of the Portsea Island Union have conducted this branch of their business in a manner which has met with general approval. An event has, however, just occurred which would imply that the absence of complaints has been due rather to luck than to good management. The event which we are about to describe implies the existence of an extraordinary amount of laxness in the payment of the last rites to the bodies of the paupers of Portsmouth Union district. The occurrence itself has been made public property through the energetic action taken by a well-known tradesman of Portsea, who, with his wife, chanced to be in the cemetery at the time, and who were the unwilling witnesses of what occurred.

As they were arranging some flowers at a grave, they saw a kind of four-wheeled truck being dragged along spasmodically by four paupers, who ultimately stopped by the side of an open grave. They then drew a coffin from the inner recesses of their curious truck, and laid it on the ground preparatory to lowering it into the grave. The tradesman hastened to them and asked them what they had got, and they said it was a lunatic from Milton. He asked them if they were going to bury him like a dog. They replied that they were going to the Workhouse for another, and that a minister (the grave was dug on the unconsecrated side) would attend at half past two o'clock (it was then little more than half past eleven) to bury the two bodies at once.

This programme they carried out to the letter. They barbarously and unfeelingly left the body of the lunatic lying exposed in the cemetery, unguarded and untended to in any way, whilst they slowly and gently and spasmodically, as when they entered, dragged their truck from the cemetery to the Workhouse and back again with another ghastly burden. At the time mentioned a minister attended, and the ashes of the two poor wretched mortals were then buried with Christian rites; there was, however, no chapel service. No official from either the Workhouse or the Asylum was present to control the movements of the paupers, who could do precisely what they liked and as they liked, and thus the body was left to take care of itself in the open air. We believe the Committee of Visitors have written for an explanation to the Burial Board, but they will scarcely be allowed thus to shift their responsibility on to other shoulders, for it is clearly their duty to see that a patient is properly buried, whilst it is also the clear duty of the Board of Guardians to send an officer with a detachment of paupers who are employed upon such a responsible duty as that of conveying bodies for internment. It is thus a scandal which reflects upon the management of no less than three of our public boards. We absolve the minister from blame, for all probability he was quite unaware of the corpse which was exposed in the cemetery, waiting, waiting, waiting for his services.

1880 – THE PUNISHMENT OF A BRUTE.

That William Burrows is occasionally a brute—although, perhaps, not a brute beast—is undeniable after the evidence of his disgraceful conduct, which was published yesterday, together with a record of his been sentenced to four months' hard labour in consequence for said conduct. It appears that Burrows, savage though he be, has for seven years been living on terms of the most familiar intimacy with a woman, who, throughout that period, has slaved for him in the manner that the wives of labouring men have to slave. During that time she has cooked for him, stitched for him, scrubbed for him, and cared for his comfort and the gratification of his whims and caprices from early morn till late at night.

In return for all this devotion she has received blows and contumely— worse than blows and contumely, for when she has been lying, in all her helplessness, at the ruffian's feet, he has raised his cowardly iron-studded hoof, and kicked her on the head and on other portions of her body. On a previous occasion on which he indulged his brutal instincts by a similar amusement he was rewarded with three months' hard labour, and yesterday the Magistrates' sentenced him to four; but what guarantee is there that the latter punishment will be any more efficacious than the former has been?

A creature who is so great a disgrace to humanity can only be reached in one way, and that is through the infliction of pain upon his own hulking carcase. The law has lately been beneficially altered to meet the case of married women, who can, in extreme cases, be ordered by the Magistrates a judicial separation, during the course of which the husband, although deprived of all marital rights, has still to support his wife and children. In the present case, owing to circumstances which were not divulged, the laws of the country had never sanctioned the union, the woman had simply made a free and unconditional gift of her life to a wretched being who was incapable of estimating its value.

By acting thus she placed herself beyond the pale of any law but that which deals with cases of aggravated assault. Now it cannot be denied that the woman sustained grievous bodily harm, and yet the ruffian who inflicted the damage has received no severer punishment than would have been awarded to him had he ill-treated a horse. Let us turn to the statute books and see what the law lays down as the punishment to be inflicted in cases of aggravated assault. By the Act 24 and 25 Vie. c 100 it is declared expedient to make further provisions for the punishment of aggravated assaults, and it is therefore enacted that "if any person shall unlawfully and maliciously, by any means, wound any person so as to endanger the life of such person, or so as thereby to inflict upon such person any grievous bodily harm, every such offender being convicted thereof shall be liable to be sentenced to penal servitude for life, or for the term of three years, or to be imprisoned with or without hard labour in any common prison for any term not exceeding two years; and if a male to be once, twice thrice publicly privately whipped in addition to such imprisonment if the Court shall think "fit."

The only conclusion, therefore, at which we can arrive is, that the case was, by the Bench, merely considered as one common assault. This conclusion would, however, scarcely have been arrived at if a well-known and influential citizen had been treated in the street, as the poor woman, whose troubles are the subject of this article, was treated in her mother's house by the very individual from whom she had the right to expect protection and assistance.

1881 – THE ALLEGED DEATH FROM VIOLET POWDER AT LANDPORT.

The adjourned inquiry into the circumstances as attending the death of an unnamed female infant of Henry Williams, the keeper of the "Dial" Tavern, Crasswell Street, Landport, was resumed on Wednesday at that house, before W. H. Garrington, Esq., Coroner. At the first sitting of the Court on the 8th inst. it was shown that the child was born on the 18th, and a few days subsequently betrayed uneasiness from the peeling of the skin on the neck below the chin and on the buttocks, after the formation of blisters about the size of a shilling.

Dr. James Green, of Brandon House, Mile End, Landport, was consulted on the 28th ult., and it had being suggested to him by the mother that the condition of the skin was produced by violet powder, the packet of which bore the name of Hovenden's, and which had been purchased at the premises of Timothy White, in Commercial Road, Landport, the use of the powder was discontinued, but death resulted on the 3rd inst., the whole of the skin of the child having peeled. The statement of Dr. Green was to the effect that the death of the deceased was due to the extensive inflammation of the skin produced by impure violet powder and an adjournment was made so that the latter might be analysed.

At the second sitting on Wednesday Mr. R.W. Ford, solicitor, appeared on behalf of Mr. Timothy White and Mr. Wild (of the firm of Messrs. Wild, Brown, and Wild, of London) represented Messrs. Hovenden and Co., wholesale perfumers, of London. Dr. James Green was recalled, and he stated that since the last inquiry he had had his attention called by Dr. Pavy to an article in the *Medical Times and Gazette* of December 5th, 1874, upon the subject of pemphigus in new-born children, the symptoms of which were there described, and so closely resembled by the appearances of the deceased child that he felt bound to ask leave to amend the evidence he gave at the last inquiry, "that he was of the opinion that the inflammation of the skin was produced by the application of impure violet powder," and he felt bound to attribute the cause of death to pemphigus.

The newspaper article referred to was produced and read by the Coroner in open Court. In cross-examination by Mr. Wild, the witness said he knew Dr. Pavy, and any opinion he might give should be worthy of the highest consideration, as he was a gentleman of great experience. Before the inquest, or when he (witness) sent the powder to be analysed, he had an idea that it contained arsenic, but at the time of giving evidence he knew to the contrary but was under the impression that it contained plaster of Paris which would cause irritation of the skin in a recently born child. Dr. Sykes had analysed the violet powder, and had communicated to him the result. He did so not think that sulphate of lime would be sufficiently powerful to produce vesication of the skin. He (witness) believed that sulphate of lime was a neutral substance, but he had had no experience of its use, either internally or externally.

Any directions for the preparation of violet powder were not in the *British Pharmacopeia*, and he could not say in what way it was made. He knew little or nothing about the composition of violet powder. He entirely withdrew the opinion he had expressed that the death of the deceased was produced by the application of impure violet.

By Mr. R.W. Ford: Violet powder was supposed to be powdered orris root, starch, and a little essential oil. It might, and did, consist of other articles. It might consist of powdered alabaster. In his opinion the deceased child died of acute pemphigus, but the ordinary description of acute pemphigus as described in the usual text books adopted by the profession, did not tally with the symptoms as shown in the case of the deceased child, and were it not for the article referred to he should not have adopted the opinion expressed. The deceased child might have died from the disease in question if no powder had been used. The use of the powder in his opinion now, was not the cause of death. Violet powder was largely used all over the kingdom for infants.

By Mr. Williams: The child died from pemphigus, but it was the first case of that severe kind that he had ever seen. Dr. Walter John Sykes, the public analyst for Portsmouth, deposed that about a fortnight previously the father of the deceased child brought him the packet produced, which was in a cardboard box. He analysed the contents of the box, in which there was about a quarter of an ounce. Part of that he analysed qualitatively, and he found it to contain sulphate of lime. The remaining portion he examined carefully and found it to contain 63 per cent of crystallised sulphate of lime.

Witness had never heard of any ill effects from the use of violet powder, except in a case occurring some time ago where the powder contained arsenic. He could not say whether sulphate of lime would cause pemphigus, or any violent inflammation of the skin, or whether it would cause any other effects. He had had no experience on the subject.

By the Jury: Maize starch was the other ingredient in the violet powder examined by him and there was a small amount of perfume. In reply to Mr. Wild, the witness said that 44.49 was the percentage of ash or mineral matter in the violet powder, and about the same amount of dry sulphate of lime. He was bound to concur in the opinion that day expressed by Dr. Green as to the cause of death. That was the first sample of violet powder he had ever analysed. He had no knowledge of the general composition of violet powder, and was, therefore, not prepared to answer the question as to the composition of the violet powder of commerce. He was not prepared to say that sulphate of lime would cause any ill effects to the skin.

By Mr. Ford: There was a decided difference between lime salts and sulphate of lime. He would rather use starch powder than sulphate of lime. Plaster of Paris was sulphate of lime, but sulphate of lime need not necessarily be plaster of Paris. He had no reason to suppose that the use of sulphate of lime on the skin of a young, recently washed, and not properly dried child would have any effect whatever. He had no reason to believe that the powder used in the present case was an irritant in any way.

Elizabeth Short, who had been a domestic servant in the employ of the deceased's mother, said she recollected being sent by Mrs. Williams to buy a packet of violet powder from Mr. Timothy White's. It was before Christmas, about four or five months ago. That was the only packet she had ever bought for her mistress. The box was similar to that produced. It was kept on the top shelf of the kitchen dresser. It was put into another box, a round wooden one, which had a puff in it. It was used every night for the children, and after using it on the two younger children the skin of the lower parts of their bodies peeled off. Her mistress at first attributed it to the soap, and she did not assign any other cause. The powder was used from the time she bought it until she left. What she had described did not spread, but was confined to the lower parts of the bodies of the children.

She asked for a box of the best violet powder. After the powder was used at night, the children complained of pain. The skin was cracked and was very red. The powder was used for three or four months. The places were redder and more raw at the last part of the time. The children nor her master or mistress did not suffer from any eruptions of the skin.

By Mr. Wild: The children were not chapped before the violet powder was used. She did not know why the violet powder was used, except that it was used to dry the children after washing.

By Mr. Ford: The other children were three or two years of age. The mother usually washed them. She now thought that the sores were caused by the violet powder. She first came to think so when Mrs. Williams told her she thought it was so. The powder was commenced to be used directly after it was bought. Sometimes carbolic soap and sometimes the ordinary yellow soap was used. If she (witness) heard a doctor say the soreness was not caused by the powder, she should still think it was.

Mr. Frederick Lovenden, called and examined by Mr. Wild, deposed that he resided at Thurlow Park Road, West Dulwich, and carried on business in partnership with his two brothers as wholesale perfumers and general dealers. One of the articles manufactured by them was violet powder, and they manufactured that which had been the subject of analysis. Their powder was made from one receipt, which they had used for nearly forty years, and he (witness) had been acquainted with it about 29 years. The powder in question was made from that receipt. They sold from ten to twenty tons per year, which was distributed all over the world.

They used 21 percent of terra alba and 75 percent of Indian corn starch, with a little orris powder and perfume. During the 29 years referred to, the witness had never heard a complaint about the preparation. He (witness) had a family of young children, and the powder was used for them. Sulphate of lime was a neutral, harmless substance. It was not an irritant; if it were, they should not, for the sake of their commercial reputation, use it. Less than two years ago they contemplated altering the ingredients, but on full consideration they determined to adhere to the old receipt.

Terra alba was better than starch in many respects. Terra Alba was sulphate of lime. The name "violet powder" did not apply to the composition of the article. There were no recognised formulas. Each manufacturer made after its own receipt, and theirs was much sought after. Terra alba was now a recognised and legalised constituent of violet powder. To his (Witness') knowledge, in many cases violet powder was made of sulphate of lime and a perfume; and if obliged to use one or other of the ingredients alone, he should prefer sulphate of lime to starch for the reasons given.

By Mr. Ford: Mr. Timothy White was a customer of theirs, and they had supplied him with the violet powder then in question. They had supplied it in boxes like the one then produced, which had one of their labels upon it.

By the foreman: Starch powder was used with the sulphate of lime, as he thought the admixture was superior to either article alone.

Dr. Frederick William Pavy, residing at 35 Grosvenor Street, London, deposed that he was physician to and lecturer on the practice of medicine at Guy's Hospital. In reply to questions by Mr. Wild, the witness said he had had a description of the case of the deceased child given to him by Dr. Green, and he had also interrogated the mother and nurse. He was of the opinion, in accordance with that which had been expressed by Dr. Green that day, that the child died from acute pemphigus, a disease which in the form presented by the deceased was of rare occurrence, and only imperfectly or rather confusedly described in ordinary textbooks, and was only briefly described in scattered medical writings.

He was of the opinion that the application of the violet powder had nothing to do with the production of the affliction of which the infant died. He considered that terra alba, or native sulphate of lime, was a harmless neutral substance devoid of irritating properties. He considered it might be admixed with starch in a violet powder without the slightest danger. Hovenden's violet powder had been in his (witness) household for many years and had been sent for especially by Mrs. Pavy.

In reply to Mr. Wild, Dr. Green deposed that he received on the previous Thursday from Dr. Pavy some terra alba and also a packet of Hovenden's violet powder. He also purchased, unknown to those manufacturers, a packet of violet powder at their establishment. At that time he was unknown to them, and they to him. He found the terra alba to be a pure crystallised sulphate of lime, very finely ground. It was a neutral, inert substance, free from anything injurious. Crystallised sulphate of lime, when finely ground, had no action on the unbroken skin, and not on the broken skin when not finely ground. Plaster of Paris, on the contrary, would irritate a chafed skin, in consequence of its powerful affinity for water. There was no plaster of Paris in any of the powders he had submitted to analysis, and he never met with plaster of Paris being mixed with violet powder. Witness found the violet powder given to him by Dr. Pavy contained 21 percent of terra alba, precisely similar in its appearance and the size of its particles under the microscope as in that of the pure terra alba also given to him by Dr. Pavy. The other ingredients were a minute quantity of orris root and scent, the rest being pure maize starch. The terra alba was finely divided, and not in a state to produce irritation. Witness found the powder quite free from all injurious ingredients. In the packet which he had purchased himself he found 27 percent of terra alba, and in all other respects it was similar to that handed to him by Dr. Pavy. There were no standard formula for the manufacture of violet powder.

Mr. Ford: There was no plaster of Paris whatever in any of the specimens from Messrs. Hovenden's establishment which he had examined. By Mr. Williams: Witness said he bought the packet of violet powder from Messrs. Hovenden's on the 14th instant. Mr. Williams remarked that he had sent all over the town to get a packet of powder like that used on the deceased child, and could not obtain it. There had been plenty of time since the death to manufacture several tons of the powder. Mr. Ford said such an observation was most improper.

The nurse, Mrs. Craven, who gave evidence on the first occasion was recalled by Mr. Williams' request, but she could only repeat what she had before stated. The Coroner said there was no imputation at all upon the witness. The Coroner then summarised the case, and remarked that he could not conceive anything more creditable or honourable than the manner in which Dr. Green had behaved in having, on further consideration of the matter, withdrawn his first opinion as given at the opening of the inquiry. Few men indeed would have so acted, but his conduct commended itself to him, and he was sure that it would also to every honest mind. The principal point, however, which the Jury would have to determine, was whether the application of the violet powder had or had not anything to do with the death of the deceased. The Jury then returned a verdict of "Death from natural causes."

1881 – MAN GORED BY A BULLOCK.

About half past six o'clock last evening a bullock, the property of Mr. Body, butcher of High Street, was brought by a drover named Garnett, from Chichester by train to Portsmouth. It was turned out of the truck on to the railway companies' cattle dock by Garnett, and was being driven by him into Blackfriars Road, Southsea, when it turned back into the dock and jumped off on to the railway line. It ran across to the passenger station, amongst the carriages, and jumped up on to the horse dock, accompanied by two others.

The railway companies' inspector ran for the keys, intending to open the gates for Garnett to take the cattle into Bow Street. While he was away the beast that had first jumped off the cattle dock, ran up the line under Somers Road and Fratton bridges to Fratton coal yard, where it got out on to the open country.

An effort would then seem to have been made to drive him back again through the streets towards the railway station as he arrived near the Crystal Palace public house, where he knocked down Mr. John Brown, fishmonger, of Queen Street, Portsea, inflicting a horrible wound on the back of his head. He was immediately placed in a cab and conveyed to the hospital, where he has since expired. The sad occurrence, as may be guessed, created a profound impression in the locality.

1881 – THE FATAL TRAMWAY ACCIDENT AT HILSEA.

On Thursday an inquiry as to the death of David Dealler, 21 years of age, a bricklayer, of 172 Wingfield Street, Landport, took place before W.H. Garrington Esq., Coroner, at the Board room at the Hospital at Landport.

The Coroner, in opening the proceedings, said that the case was one which required the very careful attention of the Jury, and he was sure it would receive it at their hands, because it would no doubt prove to be one of those instances where the statements would be very conflicting. He therefore bespoke their very close attention, so that when they came to return a verdict they might, if blame were attachable to anybody be enabled to place that blame upon the right parties.

The family of the deceased were represented by Mr. A. S. Blake, Solicitor of Portsea, and the proceedings were watched on behalf of the Fareham District Highway Board by Mr. A. Driver, their clerk. The latter suggested that it would be better if an adjournment were made for a legal gentleman to represent the Board, but the Coroner said that he thought Mr. Driver would most likely be able to deal with the evidence. If, however, anything should arise which would require the assistance of a legal gentleman, they could consider an adjournment.

John Richard Rogers, a mariner of 170, Wingfield Street, Landport, stated that the deceased was his brother-in-law and about half past two on Monday the deceased, witness and his wife, and two young women left their home in a hired cart for a drive. They drove as far as Westbourne where they partook of tea, and about half past seven they left for home, the deceased driving. The horse was quiet, and nothing occurred until they reached Hilsea at half past nine. The night was very dark, and they carried no lamps. The Coroner: Was the deceased sober? – Witness: Yes, he was sober. Coroner: And that you say positively? – Witness: Yes. The Coroner: When you reached Hilsea what occurred?

Witness said that when they got to the barracks they noticed a tram car coming in the opposite direction, but before it reached them by the side of the barrack wall the deceased drew the horse to the left to avoid a collision, when the wheel came upon a heap of stones which was lying at the eastern side. By that means the cart was overturned, and all five of the occupants were thrown out.

The Coroner: Was anybody but the deceased seriously injured? Witness replied in the negative. The Coroner: Then the tram car had nothing to a do with the accident? Witness said he thought not. The tram car was by their side when the cart was overturned and he did not see the deceased again until the car had passed and the deceased was picked up by some other persons and carried in a van to the Hospital. At the spot where the accident occurred there were no lamps, and it was so dark that it was impossible for the deceased to see the heap of stones. By the Jury: The deceased had been in the habit of driving. The distance from the edge of the heap of stones to the metal of the tramway was 6ft. 2in., but there was no lamp placed upon the stones. The width of the cart was 5ft. 2in. By Mr. Blake: Witness on the following morning saw the mark on the heap of stones where the wheel had been, and from there (which was the centre of the heap) to the edge of the tram rails was 8ft. 6in. The height of the heap of stones was from 2ft. 6in. to 2ft. 9in. In reply to Mr. Driver, witness said he heard no one suggest that the cart should stop until the tram car had passed. The car was going slowly. Witness was not aware that the traffic in the Road was carried on on the opposite side to that where the stones were lying.

Albert Hatchard, corn factor, living in Sultan Road, deposed that he was driving a light van in the same direction as the deceased was going, but being acquainted with the road and that stones were lying there, he (witness) passed to the other side of the tram car, while the deceased, who was in front of him, kept to his proper side. The deceased was going at a pace just beyond a walk. There was, in his opinion, not sufficient room for a vehicle to pass between the stones and the car. Witness was satisfied that an accident would occur, and on drawing his horse up, directly after the car had passed, he saw the deceased lying with his legs across the tramway metal and a large pool of blood between the metals. The driver of the car sounded his whistle, and no doubt the overturning of the cart threw the deceased beneath the wheels. Both wheels of the car passed over the deceased's legs. The car was going slowly and was almost at a standstill. Witness afterwards conveyed the deceased in his van to the Hospital.

The Coroner: As an independent witness from what should you consider the accident arose? – Witness: From the heap of stones being in an improper place. By Mr. Driver: The tramway metals are not in the centre of the road, but on the eastern side. By the Jury: Had the stones been away there would have been plenty of room for the deceased, but on the side on which he (witness) drove there was room for two vehicles to pass each other. The Coroner: Do you consider the highway is in a proper state for traffic? Witness said he did not, on account of the roughness of the road and the heaps of stones. He did not consider that the tramway ought to have been opened until the rubbish had been cleared away and the road made straight. The Coroner: Had the stones been placed there by the tramway people? – Mr. Driver said he believed they had come from the excavations of the tramway, and had not been cleared away. Mr. Blake: The Fareham Highway Board have removed the heap back to the wall since the accident. The stones occupied altogether upwards of 11 feet of the road. He wished a witness to be called as to that fact.

John David Dealler, a boiler maker, of Chatham Dockyard, and a brother of the deceased, deposed that that morning he had measured the road at Hilsea where the accident occurred, and the distance from the barrack wall to the tramway metals was 16ft. 6in. On Tuesday he saw the men of the Fareham Highway Board throwing the stones back. Mr. Driver: The intention is to clear the refuse away from the roads, upon which the rubbish is everywhere. In fact the line is hardly completed now.

Mr. Claude Clarke Claremont, the house surgeon at the Hospital, deposed that he received the deceased when brought to that institution on the previous Monday night, shortly before eleven o'clock. The deceased was then in a very faint condition (apparently from the loss of blood and nervous shock) and was pale, and he had a compound comminuted fracture of both bones of the right leg. The wound in the integuments was about four inches in length, and through that the upper end of the larger bone protruded. The left lower extremity was extensively bruised through the lower half of the thigh and upper part of the leg, and behind the knee joint there was a wound large enough to admit the thumb, which communicated with a fracture of both bones. A consultation of the honorary medical staff was called, and the deceased's right leg was amputated beneath the knee two hours subsequently. He afterwards complained of a pain in the chest and although he partially rallied he sank again, and death ensued shortly before ten o'clock on Tuesday morning. Witness attributed death to the shock to the system which the deceased had received. In reply to Mr. Blake, witness said it was the unanimous decision of the medical staff who were present that the amputation was absolutely necessary.

The Coroner then summed up, and said there could be no doubt that the death of the deceased, a young man who he understood was to have been married next Sunday, had arisen from the accident. He was very glad, however, that it had turned out that the Tramway

Company were in no way responsible, because anyone who was in the habit of travelling on the line could say that the services of the tramway cars were exceedingly well conducted, and that the drivers and conductors were sober and careful men. There could, therefore, be no imputation upon them in that respect; but it was quite another question whether the line ought to have been opened so soon as it was, and before the roadway was cleared for the ordinary traffic. He supposed, however, that it was opened under some kind of authority. With regard to the heap of stones, they had no evidence to show who placed them on the road, and Mr. Driver seemed to repudiate that the Highway Board were responsible, the stones having, as he said, been left there from the excavations made by the tramway employees. If, however, the Jury thought that the accident did arise from the stones, they might say so without inculpating anybody, but he had no doubt Mr. Blake would take means to ascertain who was really responsible.

The Jury deliberated privately, and then returned a verdict of "Accidental Death, arising from the negligence of the Fareham Highway Board in not keeping the road clear for traffic." The Coroner said he was bound to take the verdict, the latter portion of which, he supposed, was intended as a rider for there was no evidence before them to inculpate the Highway Board.

A Juror: We consider that the Highway Board are guilty of having caused the man's death.

1881 – CHILDREN AT LUNATIC ASYLUMS.

The Portsea Island Board of Guardians at their meeting on Wednesday last, discussed the cases of the poor idiot children who are undergoing treatment in the Lunatic Asylum, and it transpired that they had entered into correspondence with the secretary of the Western Counties Idiot Asylum at Starcross, near Exeter, with the object of ascertaining whether the children could not be received and treated in that institution. Some such change is urgently needed. The interior of adult pauper lunatic wards, even by the exercise of the greatest possible care on the part of attendants, cannot be made in any degree a suitable place for children. In a large institution like that at Milton, children's wards are impracticable, and consequently both boys and girls are perforce subjected to the danger of being morally contaminated by habitual intercourse with the diseased, and, in too many cases, brutalized intellects of their own sex. Thus they are beset with a very palpable danger on the one hand, whilst on the other there is an absence of the countervailing influence of education.

Not alone would children at Milton grow up without a persistent effort to impart to them such a smattering of information as their intellects were capable of imbibing and profiting by, but they are subject to a specific danger which in many cases must inevitably lead to very serious results. There cannot be a question as to the desirability of sending young children of both sexes to such an establishment as that at Starcross, and no peddling question of a few pence per week should be permitted to stand in the way of the mental and moral elevation of the poor little helpless ones for whose welfare the Guardians are, in their corporate capacity, as responsible as they are, in their individual capacity, for the members of their own families. As if, however, to clench the matter, it would appear that the Starcross people charge only 12s. per week for the education and treatment for idiot children, whilst 13s. 1d. is charged for little else than their safe custody at Milton. Thus, by effecting change which is rendered necessary by every dictate of humanity, the Guardians would relieve the rates to the extent of a shilling and penny per week per child. Under these circumstances, they surely will not any longer incur the responsibility of permitting the little girls and boys to remain shut up with the adult lunatics in the borough asylum.

1881 – A PORTSMOUTH GHOST STORY.

For the past few weeks the Sultan public house, next door to the Prince's Theatre, Lake Road, has been closed, the tenant having left. On Wednesday, by some unexplained means, a story got wind that the place was haunted, and that a ghost was frequently to be seen at the windows. This was further circulated yesterday, with the result that hundreds of people came to see the spiritual visitor, and judging by what has occurred today, the crowd may reasonably be expected to be immensely increased tonight. One of the numerous tales afloat was to the effect that a man and woman, with their throats cut from ear to ear, were found in the cellar. There was, however, no foundation whatever for this and the other absurd stories, which have evidently been concocted by some imaginative or weak-minded individual.

1882 – A PORTSMOUTH PLAGUE SPOT. SHOCKING REVELATIONS.

In our issue of Saturday last we reported an application made to the Borough Bench by Mr. R. W. Ford, under the Industrial Schools Acts of 1866 and 1860, for the removal of certain children from the evil surroundings in which they were brought up to the Portsmouth and South Hants Industrial School at Purbrook. A similar application was made to Captain McCoy and J. Griffin, Esq., on Wednesday last. In this case, however, Mr. Ford said the circumstances were of a much more painful character than those which came before the Court on the last occasion. That the action taken by the Magistrates last week had been of benefit, he himself could testify. It had caused many of the people regarding whom action had been taken to see what the powers of the statute were, and to get rid of their children from the haunts of vice and immorality in which they were reared.

With regard to the present case, it was scarcely possible that such a state of things could have existed in any civilised place. The case he alluded to was that of a woman named Eliza Perryman, a widow, living at 2, Ward's Court, Marylebone, and who had five children – two boys and three girls. Two of those girls would be brought before the Bench that day. The place in which these persons lived was a perfect den, for house or home it could not be called. The mother was not fit even to be brought into a court of justice, for she was almost destitute of clothing. One broken chair and an old table constituted the entire furniture of the house.

Notwithstanding all that, prostitution was carried on there by women who also lived in a state of filth and wretchedness past description. Under such a state of things a state which it was a painful tax to the feelings and to the mind to describe the most merciful and the kindest act, not only for them, but for their mother also, would be to separate the children from her and send them to a school where they would be educated and kindly treated; treated, at all events, as human beings.

The ages of the children who would be brought before the Bench were six and nine years respectively. There was another girl about twelve years of age, but he did not intend to make any application regarding her. He believed the attention of the parish officers had been called to that case. The poor thing was half demented, and would, he had no doubt, be removed to the hospital of the Poor House. He would now have the children brought before the Bench, and the facts of the case given in. The children were accordingly brought to the solicitors' table. They were both of them unusually diminutive for their ages. Both were very emaciated and sickly-looking, and throughout the whole of the proceedings they never for a moment exhibited any of those feelings of wonderment, animation, or interest which might have been expected from children of their age.

Thomas Toomor, agent of the Portsmouth and South Hants Industrial School, Purbrook, sworn, said the older of the children was named Maria Perryman, and her age was nine years. – Mr. Griffin: What! that child is nine years of age? – Mr. Ford: Yes, sir, the result of such bringing up – Witness, continuing, said the other child was aged five, and was named Mary. Both of the children were perfectly naked when he saw them at the house but he had procured the things they now wore in order that they might be brought before the Magistrates. He first visited the house on Friday. He then saw the mother, with three of her children, downstairs. The fourth one, aged eleven last birthday, was in the room above. He insisted upon seeing her, and she was accordingly brought down to him. She was without the slightest covering, and had more the appearance of an ape than of a human being. The only articles of furniture in the house were one table and one chair. The place was in a most filthy condition. The house comprised two small rooms, one downstairs and one above. He had several times to return to the open air, the place was so offensive. The house was used as a brothel.

Three registered prostitutes lived there at night. There was no such thing as a bed or bedstead. Half of an old basket was used to sit on. He told the mother that the children could not be allowed to remain in that state. She said she could not alter it. In answer to further questions, she openly stated that she maintained the children by what the women who used her house for the purposes of their calling brought her. He thereupon communicated with the parish authorities. On Tuesday night he again went to the house, between twelve and one o'clock. Upstairs he found Mrs. Perryman and her four children lying together in one corner. A thin partition separated them from a prostitute. In another corner there was a second woman of ill-fame. In the coal-hole downstairs there was another woman, who, to keep herself from the ground, had made a bed of bottles, old tins and brickbats. Mr. Ford said there were other details, which the least said about the better, perhaps.

Mr. Inspector Jones, of the Metropolitan Police, was called next – Magistrates' Clerk: Is this house a brothel? – Witness: Yes. – The Magistrate's Clerk, addressing the Bench, said that was really the only question of which proof was required. The Magistrates agreed to remand the children to the Workhouse for a week pending arrangements being made for their reception into the Industrial School. It was explained to Mr. Ford that the Bench preferred to send the children to the Union, as they would be properly taken care of and kindly treated there.

1882 – FATAL PURSUIT OF A LUNATIC.

The accident having befallen John James Biddlecombe, one of the detectives of the Portsmouth Borough Police Force, while in pursuit of a lunatic named Page on the 29th ult., terminated fatally on Saturday morning. The circumstances as detailed at the inquest which was held before the Coroner (W. H. Garrington, Esq.), at the Boardroom at the Hospital on Monday afternoon, are as follows:

The proceedings were watched on behalf of the police by Chief-Inspector Gibbs.

Mr. Silas Ford, an Inspector in the Borough Police Force, having identified the body, stated that on Monday the 29th of May, he was in charge of the Police Station at Southsea, and about half past ten on that night he was applied to by Mr. Stephens, one of the relieving officers of the borough for assistance in the removal of a wandering lunatic, who was about the streets to the Portsea Island Workhouse. Biddlecombe, who was standing near, volunteered to assist. The deceased was 42 years of age, and had been about fourteen years in the force, in which he bore a very high character.

By the Jury: The deceased was on duty, as the detectives' duties were never finished, but still the deceased himself volunteered. Witness had another man at the station, and he would have gone with the lunatic had not the deceased willingly offered to go.

Mr. James Stephens deposed that he was the relieving officer of the Southsea district in the Portsea Island Union, and at twenty minutes after ten on the night in question he was requested to go to the police station to see a man who was there in the custody of a policeman. Two women were also there, and they told him that a man had been wandering for two or three days and that earlier that evening he had been knocked down by a horse and cab. Believing that the man was of unsound mind he suggested to him whether the Hospital at the Workhouse would not be the most fitting place for him, and he assented to go.

The Coroner: Did the man prove to be a lunatic, or was it only the effects of drink? – Witness said the man was certified on the following day to be a lunatic, and was removed to the Asylum where he still remained. A cab was procured, and the deceased accompanied him towards the Union, on the road to which he (witness) stopped at his own house, 249 Somers Road, to tell his wife (one of his children being ill) that he should probably not be back for an hour. He had been indoors about five minutes, and while on the way back to the cab he was met by the lad who had been driving and was told that the lunatic had escaped and had gone away over the railway bridge. He immediately ran in the direction pointed out, and having got to the centre of the road leading to Sydenham Terrace he found the deceased lying upon the road.

He (witness) asked him what was the matter, and the deceased, replied, "My leg is broken; take me to the Hospital as quickly as you can." He did not say how it had happened but with assistance witness got him into the cab, which was driven at once to the Hospital, where he was attended to immediately. One of the Jurors, (Mr. Layton), asked whether the Lunacy Commissioners had any powers to call upon the police for such duties. The Coroner said that had nothing whatever to do with the matter before them. The Relieving Officer was applied to, and he very properly sought the assistance of the police, which assistance was voluntarily given. In reply to questions, witness said the lunatic presented no symptoms of violence whatever. Had the man been certified by a medical man as a dangerous lunatic, he should never have left him for a moment, but he did consider it consistent with his duty to leave him, as he was quiet and he had the assistance of the constable at the cab. Mr. Layton, in the course of further questions, put it to the Coroner what his opinion was. The Coroner said the Jury would have themselves to argue the question, but if they asked his private opinion, he should say that the possession of a certificate would not lessen the responsibility of the Relieving Officer.

Arthur Shine, the lad who was in charge of the cab at the time the accident occurred, said that three or four minutes after Mr. Stephens had left the cab the lunatic opened the door on the other side of the vehicle and ran to the Fratton side of the Somers Road railway bridge. The deceased at once pursued him, and after he had informed Mr. Stephens what had taken place he (witness) ran across the bridge, and when he came up to the deceased he told witness not to touch him as he had broken his back, by falling down.

Mr. Constantine Cecil Claremont, the acting house surgeon at the Hospital, deposed that he saw the deceased on his admission at the Hospital on the night of the previous Monday, and on examining him he found that he had sustained a simple oblique fracture of the right thigh bone. He appeared to suffer a good deal of pain, but went on well until about midday on Thursday, when he became somewhat delirious and removed his splints, and later on he had to be restrained to prevent him injuring himself. He continued to be violent for the ensuing twenty four hours, then signs of exhaustion appeared, and weakness continued increasing until death ensued about ten o'clock on Sunday morning. The deceased had told witness that in running he must have fallen over a stone with his leg under him.

The Coroner then summed up the case, and he remarked that there could be no doubt that everything possible had been done for the deceased at the Hospital; he knew it was so years ago, when he was one of the Honorary Medical Officers, and he was sure it had by no means deteriorated since. The deceased's mental worry probably had a good deal to do with his after condition, but delirium was likely to occur from any local injury. They were not there to say a word about Mr. Stephens, but one could naturally feel that at having a child ill he would be anxious to say where he was going; but even if Mr. Stephens were wrong, they had nothing to do with that. The Board of Guardians were his employers, and they would leave them to investigate the facts so far as the relieving officer was concerned. A gratifying circumstance connected with the deceased, as he had just been informed by Mr. Gibbs, was that the deceased's comrades had been with him constantly since the accident, he never having been left for an instant without one of them being in attendance.

The Jury returned a verdict of "Accidental death," and they added a rider to the effect that they were unanimously of the opinion that no blame was attachable to Mr. Stephens as in the course of natural events they believed that anyone would have acted in the same way. They also intimated their desire to award their fees to the deceased's widow, owing to her distressed condition with a large family.

The fees amounted to 8s. 8d., and the Coroner made up the sum to a sovereign to head the list. Several of the Jurors also gave additional donations of 6s., the Coroner expressing a hope that the good deed thus commenced would result in substantial benefit to the widow and family. Altogether the sum collected in the room amounted to 2l. 19s. 6d.

At the meeting of the Urban Sanitary Authority yesterday, the Mayor said they had all no doubt heard of the unfortunate death of Constable Biddlecombe, and he was sure he was expressing the opinion of all the Council when he said that the widow and orphans had their entire sympathy. The subject of affording some relief to the family would be considered by the Watch Committee. The large family which the deceased officer had would shortly be increased, and he felt sure that when he suggested a public subscription on behalf of the widow and orphans, there would, if the idea was carried out, be fresh subscribers than the members of the Council.

Alderman Pink said he had no doubt the Watch Committee would do as much as was possible for the family of the deceased. The Mayor had thought that if a subscription list were opened for the purpose of assisting those left unprovided for, there would be found numerous persons willing to subscribe to so deserving an object. He therefore asked the Press kindly to notice that subscriptions would be gladly received by either the Town Clerk or himself (Alderman Pink).

The constable had really lost his life in the public service, and for 14 years had served the borough faithfully and well. Mr. Moorhead said he was struck with the unprecedented character of the matter. Mr. Kennedy said that if it was an unprecedented thing it certainly was most meritorious on the part of the Mayor and Alderman Pink in having the courage to bring the subject forward. Mr. Ward said the constable had fallen as much in the service of his countrymen as any soldier, and he therefore thought that a point should be strained so as to give as much as possible from the public funds. It was said that nothing could be given out of the superannuation fund, but the officer in question had paid into that fund for fourteen years, and surely no injustice could be done to anyone by a payment from that account being made to the widow. The matter was then dropped.

Last night, at the monthly meeting of the Watch Committee, the case was discussed, and it was unanimously resolved to grant the widow of the deceased a twelvemonth's pay (78l odd), subject to the approval of the Council at its next meeting. It was further agreed that the whole of the Watch Committee form themselves into a Relief Committee (with the addition of the Chief Constable to their number) for the purpose of raising subscriptions. The Mayor headed the list with 5l., and collecting cards are to be issued to each member of the Committee and the Force. Should anyone desirous of subscribing not be called upon, the Town Clerk or any member of the Corporation will gladly receive their donations. In Committee a feeling was expressed that there should be a fund established to meet such cases of emergency but it was pointed out also that the circumstances of a constable belonging to the Force losing his life in the execution of his duty was so very rare an occurrence, that when such a case did happen sufficient interest ought to be manifested by the general public to meet all reasonable requirements. The last fatal casualty to a borough policeman took place ten or twelve years ago, when an officer named Winn was thrown from the box of a cab owing to the wheels "skidding" in the old line of tram rails from the Station to Southsea Pier, and sustained a fracture of the skull.

1882 – FALSE TEETH: CHOKED OR DROWNED?

An inquest was held at Portsmouth on May 31st on the body of Mr. John Forbes who had been residing at Southsea for eighteen months, and who was drowned from a bathing machine on Southsea beach the previous day. The deceased was a magistrate for the county of Glamorganshire, and was seventy two years age. On Tuesday he bathed off Southsea beach, and was found shortly afterwards lying on his face in the water. On his being examined it was ascertained that his false teeth had been displaced and had blocked the windpipe, accelerating his death, which was caused by drowning. The Jury returned a verdict of accidental death. It is very probable that the shock caused by diving or plunging into the cold water had induced deep inspiration; that then the false teeth had become impacted in the opened glottis, thus preceding, and in fact causing, the drowning.

1883 – HORSE MANURE ACCIDENT.

George Bevis, of 3, North Place, Mary Street, Fratton, was this morning admitted to the Portsmouth Hospital suffering from a wound in the leg caused by a manure fork. He was standing on a cart laden with manure, when the horse started; he fell, and the fork stuck into his leg. He was detained at the hospital for treatment.

1883 – SUPPRESSING THE TRAMPS.

The Clerk to the Portsea Island Board of Guardians was able to communicate some pleasing intelligence at the last meeting of that body. Until quite recently the tramp nuisance was very seriously felt at Portsmouth, and, possibly through being treated too kindly, those who once paid the ward a visit continued to make it their temporary home at frequent periods.

In order to put a stop to this growing evil it was resolved to build tramp wards on a new principle, providing for the solitary housing of the applicants for shelter. At the same time it is right to say that Parliament rendered very material assistance to the same end passing the law known as the Casual Poor Act. Not merely Portsmouth, but everywhere throughout the country, the effect has been marvellous, and it is eminently satisfactory to know that the reform has been obtained without the exercise of any unseemly harshness. At their first visit it seems that tramps get their night's lodging, but the next day before getting their breakfast or being permitted to leave have to perform an allotted task. Should they like their quarters, breakfast, and work so much as to return within a month they may be detained over two days and kept on the principle that he who will not work neither shall he eat.

As work is, however, the most disagreeable dose that can be given to a true specimen of the nomadic tribe, a very effectual remedy has been provided by the Act against their habitual return to the same Union. The value of the remedy may be best seen in the fact that whereas during the first nine months of 1882 the number of casuals at the Portsea Workhouse was 2,917; the number for the same period this year was but 1,634, the average length of the latter's stay being likewise less than that of their predecessors. Here there is a distinct gain, not only to Portsmouth but to the country, for this great diminution of the number of tramps, observable elsewhere also, must indicate that there are fewer of the wandering fraternity than was the case a year or two ago, and it may be expected that as their ancient "privileges" are curtailed so will there be a further return to honest manly labour.

1884 – FATAL ACCIDENT AT THE PUBLIC BATHS.

On Thursday an inquest on the body of Horace Smith, who was drowned on Wednesday at the Corporation Baths in Park Road, Landport, was held at the White Swan Hotel, Commercial Road, before the Coroner (T. A. Bramsdon, Esq.) Messrs. W. Ward, R. F. Foster, and T. E. Fulijames, members of the Baths Committee, were present during the inquiry.

Thomas Robinson, one of the Jurors who had been summoned, refused to appear, and sent a message by the Constable that the Coroner might summon him to the County Court, as he was too old to serve on Juries and could not leave his business. The Coroner said he had never met a case of more determined insolence, and he was only sorry that he was prevented from imposing a fine by reason of Robinson's name not being on the burgess list.

Edmund Smith, the father of the deceased, living at 72, Kingston Road, Buckland, said the deceased was 16 years old, and was a shipwright apprentice in Portsmouth Dockyard. The deceased could not swim, and he was not subject to fits.

Arthur George Gourd, a lad of 14 years, living at 89, Binstead Road, Buckland, stated that he saw the deceased on the previous night at the Public Baths, when he (deceased) was standing on the steps at the deep end of the bath. Witness was standing on the spring-board, and he asked the deceased if he could swim. He replied that he could a little, and that he was going to get to the chain at the other side of the bath. The deceased then went into the water, and when he got beneath the spring-board he jumped up and tried to take hold of the board, but he failed and went down. Witness told some who were in the bath what had happened and one lad searched about, and they informed the caretaker, who searched over one half of the bath, and ultimately found the deceased under the wooden steps at the deepest end of the bath.

The Coroner asked the witness if he knew whether the deceased was aware of the depth of the bath. – Witness said he did not know whether the deceased knew or not. The Coroner: You knew yourself? – Witness: Yes. The Coroner: You say deceased was swimming a little? – Witness: Yes.

A Juror: How long was it before the caretaker came? – Witness: It might have been five minutes or more. The Coroner: The witness has said that he came directly. A Juror: Were there any adults in the bath? – Witness: There were one or two. Witness subsequently explained that the deceased did take hold of the spring-board, but let it go again. The witness, in reply to other questions, said that the deceased did not appear to be diving, nor did he look ill.

William James Norley, the superintendent at the baths, deposed that at the time the occurrence took place, (half past eight), he was in the passage leading from the bath, lighting a gas jet. He heard someone calling out that there was a man under the water, and he immediately commenced to remove his clothes. The last witness, who was standing on the spring-board, informed him that a man had gone down, and that he hadn't seen him rise again. Witness afterwards thoroughly searched the bath by diving, and ultimately found him under the steps already named. With assistance, the body was got to the edge of the bath, where the usual means of restoration and artificial respiration were resorted to. Witness never saw the deceased breathe, and he believed he was dead when got out.

Drs. Hann and Maybury attended, and subsequently they pronounced him dead. The Coroner: How long were you absent from the bath room? – Witness: Not half a minute. The Coroner: Are there any indications placed anywhere showing which is the deep end of the bath? – Witness said there were in large letters. The deepest water was seven feet. The steps were kept down by large stones on the lower step, and two stones were swung on the sides.

The Coroner: So that the steps do not swing in any way? – Witness: They do not. The Coroner: How many people were in the bath? – Witness: Not more than five. The Coroner: There was not any undue noise? – Witness: No. In reply to a Juror, the witness said that when he ultimately found the body he had to give it a good pull before he could free it from the steps. He did not, however, know whether it was the grasp of the step as of a drowning man or whether the head or legs were between the steps. Replying to other Jurors, the witness said he was not a minute undressing.

The stoker and a lad (the ticket taker) were in the bath room. There was supposed to be only one attendant in the bath room at one time. Witness had sometimes been called to for assistance, but generally in a joke. He did not regard the complaint of last night as a joke, but was determined to see the affair out. By Mr. H. P. Foster: There was no current which could carry a non-swimmer under the steps. It was only two or three minutes before Dr. Hann was present.

A witness named Bradley, who was verbally examined, said that the deceased could scarcely swim at all. He knew that the deceased was aware which was the deep end of the bath. Everything possible was done to restore the deceased.

Dr. H. F. Hann, of Commercial Road, said that when called he attended immediately, at the baths at a quarter before nine. In his opinion the deceased was then quite dead, as having examined the heart, he found no action whatever. A quarter of an hour was occupied in giving artificial respiration.

The Coroner: From what do you think death arose? – Witness: Asphyxia from drowning. The Coroner: Was there anything to lead you to suppose that the deceased had a fit while in the water? – Witness said there was not. By Mr. W. Ward: I think there must have been some other primary cause for death than drowning, although that was the secondary cause. Mr. W. Ward said it was important for the interests of the bath that the matter should be thoroughly sifted. The Coroner said he was quite willing to adjourn the inquiry for the purposes of a post mortem examination.

The question of the steps arose, and Mr. Ward said he should immediately move in committee that wirework should be placed at the sides to prevent any recurrence of such an event. Mr. Foster: Dr. Hann said that every step was being taken by the attendants when he arrived to restore animation.

The Coroner, after the Jury had determined not to adjourn, proceeded to sum up, and said that though the circumstances of the case were very painful, the only thing that could be done would be to that which might prevent a second event of death from accidental drowning, and added that care should be taken to always have the attendant in the bath room.

Mr. Ward said that regulation was now invariably carried out.

as usual. The damage is extensive, and probably the remaining arch will have to be pulled down. The prison authorities refuse the names of the injured, but probably their friends will be communicated with, and informed of the facts and nature of the injuries.

1884 – FALL OF A BUILDING – INJURY TO CONVICTS.

A portion of the new cavalry barracks at Portsmouth, now in course of construction by convict labour, collapsed yesterday morning, burying a number of workmen in the ruins. At first it was feared a great loss of life had occurred, but it is now believed, that although numbers were injured, none of the men were killed on the spot. It appears that a long seven-span archway connecting the men's quarters with those of the officers' was being fitted with girders prior to concrete being laid on, when five of the arches, without warning, suddenly collapsed. Thirty convicts, who were working on the upper portion, were carried down among the ruins. Assistance was immediately at hand, and the unfortunate men were extricated, and after the worst cases had been attended to on the spot, were conveyed to the prison infirmary, where they are now receiving every care. One man had his leg shockingly mangled. The remainder of the convicts employed on the building, some two hundred, were at once marched back to the gaol. The news of the accident created great alarm in the town. It is known that before the occurrence, a crack in one of the arches was observed, but the work proceeded

1884 – A LUNATIC'S VIEWS OF SOUTHSEA.

After a long residence in London, without a day out of it for seven years, I joined a party of more than a dozen for a few weeks at Southsea in October, 1884. My companions were two retired officers in the Army, a stockbroker, a lawyer, and others of various professions. We were located on the South Parade – a pleasant spot, facing the sea, and opposite the Isle of Wight.

To a man who had spent forty years of official life in the National Library it was a change to find himself by "the wide and open sea." Portsmouth is a lively place, full of soldiers and sailors, and always something amusing going on. The air is bracing and invigorating, and you may drink in health at every inspiration. The two piers at either side of Southsea are pleasant promenades, where you may see some of the Southsea beauties.

The barrack accommodation is large, handsome, and comfortable; the Dockyard such as it should be for a nation that is "Mistress of the World." The bathing arrangements are admirable, and to a swimmer all that can be desired. You got into deep water at once, and can launch out into the deep. The churches are numerous, and, for the most part, well attended; and there are places of worship connected with all denominations. There is an "Assembly Room" for balls and concerts, and a new "Theatre Royal." A certain lady of attractive characteristics (Jenny Hill), called "Vital Spark," is a chief favourite with the men. As all our party were enforced bachelors for a time, some of the more tinderish of our number feared to trust themselves to a sight of Jenny Hill, lest the "Vital Spark" should be too inflammable, and cause an explosion.

The hotels, taverns, and other places of refreshment are to be found in almost every street; and at one buffet, near the north pier, the writer met with one of the prettiest barmaids, a class of young people he is particularly fond of.

SERIOUS ACCIDENT TO CONVICTS – PORTSMOUTH.

Some fine women are to be seen promenading on the piers when the bands are playing. The ladies of the demi-monde are numerous, a circumstance not to be wondered at in a town where there are so many sailors and soldiers. It is most true that "wheresoever the carcass is there will the eagles be gathered together."

The walks and excursions at Southsea are very attractive. "The Common," a long stretch of greensward, is mostly occupied by the military, who are trained here and at other places in all the modern improvements in military solstice. The Royal Marine Artillery are a splendid corps, and England may well be proud of such a body of men, always prepared to take the field in any emergency. Other regiments of brave fellows are to be seen to perfection at Southsea and the neighbourhood.

All the London newspapers can be obtained almost as early as they can be had in town, and the various reading-rooms are well supplied with the magazines and periodicals of the day.

Reviews of the military take place frequently, and there is ample open ground all round Portsmouth for the most extensive operations.

Well, this is the place where invalids in mind and body were sent down for a change, and it is certainly a very great change to the very monotony of a private asylum. Our "attendants" were pleasant and agreeable people. The gentleman in charge of us is a very intelligent fellow, and his wife is as pretty and compassionable a woman as is anywhere to be met with. One of the others is a good cornet player, and the other has been a soldier, chiefly abroad, for 12 years.

One of these gentlemen, or the lady just referred to, accompanied us in all our walks, so that there should be a certain amount of surveillance observed. The matron of the Institution with which we are connected, a lady of middle age, was one of the party, and acted as hostess to us. These two women were the only members of the opposite sex that we came in immediate contact with, but it makes it more like home, where some of us hoped to be sent on our return to London.

It was my intention to have dwelt a little upon insanity and the present Lunacy Laws, but I have spent many months in the preparation of a work I hope to publish shortly, under the title of "Memories and Mysteries of Madness," where this awful visitation of God is discussed from various points of view.

In the meanwhile I am trying as much as possible to forget that I am a lunatic, and to obtain as much of pleasure and healthful enjoyment as a man can do under the circumstances.

1884 – INQUEST AT THE PORTSMOUTH LUNATIC ASYLUM.

The Portsmouth Coroner (T. A. Bramsdon, Esq.) held an inquest at the Borough Lunatic Asylum yesterday, touching the death of John Long, aged 33, late a patient at the Institution. In opening the proceedings the Coroner remarked that the deceased was a single man, and was admitted into the Asylum from the Workhouse at Chelsea. He had only been in the Asylum about twelve days, when he died, somewhat suddenly. He (the Coroner) had instructed the Medical Superintendent to make a post mortem examination and this revealed the fact that the deceased had sustained a fractured rib.

This injury would not of course have been produced without violence of some kind, and he mentioned the fact simply to show the Jury the nature of the evidence which would be adduced, and that on seeing the body they might satisfy themselves whether it presented any bruises or other external mark of injury. Dr. Brand would also show them the apartment in which the deceased lived during the time he had been at the Asylum.

The Jury, having viewed the body and apartment in question, Dr. William Charles Bland the Medical Superintendent at the Asylum, formerly identified the body, and further stated that the deceased had been admitted to the Institution on 13th November last, from the parish of St Lukes, Chelsea. He produced the order for his reception. Witness saw him on the evening of his admission and on the 20th. He examined the deceased for the purpose of sending a certificate to the Lunacy Commissioners but he was so excited that the examination was of an imperfect character. Deceased was feeble, but he did not notice any mark of violence or that the deceased had sustained a fractured rib.

Deceased was irrelevant and incoherent in his conversation, and his mental condition was such that he could not feel pain. He was suffering from acute mania, and when he first came in he was placed in what was called the acute ward where there were other patients. On the 13th, witness was told by the attendant that the deceased had a bad leg, and he directed that he should be kept in bed so that he might examine it. On the following morning witness found him very restless and excited, and he had thrown his bed and bedding about the place. His leg was extensively diseased, the result of syphilis, and witness directed the course of treatment to be pursued.

Witness then ordered him to be taken to an adjoining room, the door of which was padded, and subsequently visited him about twice a day. He was always excited and restless, and witness considered his recovery doubtful. Witness saw him last alive about half past six o'clock on

Tuesday evening last, when he was in the same condition, and witness saw nothing to lead him to suppose that deceased would die shortly.

On Wednesday, witness made a post mortem examination and on opening the body found the seventh rib broken, but the periosteum was intact so that the broken ends were not free to rub against the lungs or tissues. There was a slight discolouration of the skin, and there were also some reddish spots over the fracture. The discolouration was, however, superficial and he was of the opinion that the fracture was caused within the last fortnight. It was possible that the injury might have been sustained before his arrival at the Asylum, but it was more probable that it was done after his admission.

In the day ward there were chairs and tables against which deceased could have fallen, but there was nothing of that character in the room in which he slept. It was reported in Medical Science that the bones of lunatics and idiots were more brittle than those of other persons. He did not think the fracture could have been caused by deceased's falling on the floor, but it could have been produced by a blow from a person's fist, or by any direct pressure. Deceased never made any complaint to witness in regard to his treatment. The night attendant would see deceased once every hour, and the electric register showed that he carried out his duty on Tuesday. Four attendants regularly attended deceased during the time he was in the Asylum, and he had always found them to be kind to the patients. Deceased was not likely to provoke or quarrel with the attendants, and witness would not consider him a dangerous lunatic, although he was stated to be so on the paper attached to the order for his removal from Chelsea.

On examination of the internal organs he found them for the most part to be healthy, but the aorta showed commencing disease. In his opinion death arose from collapse brought on by constant maniacal excitement. Death was not in any way accelerated by the fracture he had spoken of, and it was perfectly clear to him that death was entirely due to natural causes.

Thomas Weeks, an attendant, stated that on the 13th of November, he received deceased into the Asylum from Dr. Neal, the medical officer, and took him into the acute ward where he stayed that day. He slept in a single room in the gallery, but on the 15th was transferred to the epileptic gallery, where he occupied a room with a padded door. Witness had charge of him every day, and deceased never met with an accident to his knowledge. Deceased was a most inoffensive man, and he did not consider him to be a dangerous lunatic. He had never struck deceased, neither did he know any other attendant who had, and he could not in any way account for the fracture which deceased had sustained.

By the Jury: On the 13th, deceased fell down while on his way from the reception room to the ward. He attributed his fall to weakness. Deceased fell on his left side and witness at once picked him up. He could not have sustained injury on that occasion, although he fell on the stone paving of the corridor.

John Swan, an attendant, said he first saw deceased on the 15th when he was transferred from the acute to the epileptic ward. He had had charge of him since, and at no time while he was with him did deceased meet with an accident. He could not in any way account for the fracture of deceased's rib, and he had never seen deceased struck or knelt upon.

Edward Alfred Harding, attendant and George Field, night watchman gave similar evidence, the latter adding that when he last saw deceased alive he appeared to be as well as usual.

The Borough Coroner did his utmost to get at the truth of the matter, and he received every assistance from the medical authorities alike of the Asylum and of the Chelsea Workhouse, from whence the deceased had been removed, but without any definite result. It is morally certain that when the patient was admitted into the Asylum none of his bones were broken, and there is no reason to suppose that he inflicted any injuries upon himself, because in all such cases the attendants are very prompt to make the fact known.

The only palliating circumstance in the case is that the injury did not contribute to the patient's death. Both physically and mentally he was in a desperate condition when admitted to the Institution, and death would have ensued had no rib been broken. Still, the Jury did quite right in adding to their formal verdict of "Death from natural causes," a rider to the effect that in their opinion the deceased had not received satisfactory treatment at the hands of someone in whose charge he was. Further point was given to this rider by the Coroner, who told the attendants that "gross neglect, perhaps something worse," had marked the treatment of the deceased, and that it was quite clear one of the attendants had not told all he knew with reference to the affair. Alike for the credit of the Institution and for the clearance of two of the attendants themselves it is desirable that the mystery which at present attaches to this affair should be cleared up.

1884 – FIGHT ON BOARD A MAN-OF-WAR.

For some time past the marines and bluejackets on board the *Duke of Wellington* Flagship at Portsmouth have had an ill-defined grievance against one another, and a day or two ago the irritating wrangles ended in a free fight, in which some forty or fifty belligerents were engaged.

The marines took to their belts in the fashion common to the more obstreperous members of that corps, but as the sailors were armed only with their fists they were not long in seeking for other weapons of an offensive character, and broom handles being the most readily available the fight created a great stir on the ship. The combatants were, however, soon placed under arrest, and they were subsequently brought before Captain P. H. Colomb, who convicted a large proportion of them, and sentenced them to punishments varying from forty two days' imprisonment to seven days' cells. The Flagship has for a long period been free from these squabbles.

1885 – A CHILD BURNT TO DEATH.

Yesterday the Portsmouth Coroner (T. A. Bramsdon, Esq.) held an inquest at the Portsmouth Hospital, Fitzherbert Street, Landport, on the body of John Ernest Munday, aged two years and three months, the son of a stoker in the Navy. The evidence adduced showed that Mrs. Munday, deceased's mother, was a domestic servant, and the child lived with his grandmother, Mrs. Mary Holden, at 3, Marys Row, Southsea. On Tuesday morning the latter placed the child in a low chair and left him by the side of the fire, round which was a large guard, while she went into the back yard. As she was re-entering the house she noticed smoke coming out of the back door, and found the deceased sitting on the hearth rug with his night-dress in flames. The fire was extinguished, and flour was applied to the wounds, and the deceased was then taken to the Hospital. When admitted he was in a dying state, and expired at 11 a.m. from exhaustion. Evidence was given that the grandmother took great care of the child, and that the accident was caused by his poking a piece of stick in the fire.

The Jury found a verdict of accidental death.

1885 – CONVICTION OF A SOUTHSEA RESIDENT.

Samuel Poole, 65, coal agent, of Southsea, was charged with indecency on the 7th inst., by wilfully exposing himself on Southsea Beach to a female who was unknown. Two information's were laid, one by Henry Crusoe, the pier master at the South Parade Pier, and the other P.C. Baker, one being under the Vagrancy Act, and the other under the Towns Police Clauses Act, the second being for a simple exposure. Mr. G. Feltham appeared for the prisoner.

Crusoe stated that between eleven and twelve o'clock on the day named he was at work at the end of the pier, when his attention was drawn by a visitor to the prisoner, who was sitting on the steps of a bathing machine, which was some 14 feet or 16 feet from the edge of the water, and wilfully exposing himself to the view of children and the persons upon the pier. William Austin, a porter at the pier, gave corroborative evidence, and said that the prisoner's conduct continued for half an hour.

Mr. William Cook, a visitor at present residing at Waverley Lodge, St. Simon's Road, and William Watson, a commissioned boatman of the Coastguard, also corroborated, the former stating that he saw the prisoner, and the latter affirming that a lady had made a complaint to him of the prisoner's conduct. Mr. Feltham raised a point of law as to the beach being a public place, inasmuch as the Crown were the owners of the soil and could take it and build over it if they chose, but the Magistrates ruled against him.

There were two other informations against the prisoner for similar conduct on the 9th inst., the exposure being distinctly witnessed to by William Watson, coastguard man, who viewed the prisoner through a telescope, and P.C. Baker, who watched the prisoner and saw the offence twice repeated as people were passing.

Mr. Feltham, in addressing the Magistrates on behalf of the prisoner, pointed out that the prisoner was suffering from a personal affliction, and he urged

FREE FIGHT ON BOARD A MAN OF WAR.

the Bench to give him the benefit of the doubt which must exist in their minds.

The Magistrates, after a long deliberation, announced that with regard the two informations under the Vagrancy Act they considered the evidence too doubtful to convict upon it, and they therefore gave the prisoner the benefit of the doubt and dismissed him; but with regard to the two informations under the Towns Police Clauses Act, they convicted the prisoner and sentenced him to 14 days on each charge, 28 days in all, without hard labour.

1885 – THE FATAL ACCIDENT AT PORTSMOUTH DOCKYARD.

Yesterday afternoon the County Coroner (E. Goble Esq.) held an inquest at the Royal Naval Hospital, Haslar, on the body of William Rogers, aged 27 years, late a skilled labourer employed in Portsmouth Dockyard, who was killed while at work on Tuesday morning. Mr. Graham Harvey (Messrs. Harvey and Harvey) watched the case on behalf of the Admiralty. The evidence adduced showed that deceased was a married man and lived at 40, Stone Street, Buckland. On Tuesday morning at half past seven o'clock, deceased went with a fitter named James Steel, of 5, Charlton Park Terrace, Powerscourt Road. Buckland, to draw some stores from a cabin on a flat erected starboard side of H.M.S. *Camperdown*, and was returning on board that vessel, when he slipped off the staging and fell into the dock, a distance of 37 feet. Deceased was carrying two candles and a ball of cotton waste, and was perfectly sober. There was no handrail on the side of the stage nearest the ship, and Steel expressed opinion that but for its absence the accident could not have occurred. George Edward Warden, shipwright, of 15 St. Cuthbert Road, Kingston, deposed to seeing the deceased in the act of falling. He first struck a projecting piece of timber called a spall, and then fell with a sickening thud into the dock below. The prow from which deceased fell had no handrail when he was on it at 11 o'clock the same morning. The rail had been missing for several days.

The Coroner here remarked that many cases of accidental death are from sheer negligence, and it would be for the Jury now to consider whether there was any culpable negligence on the part of those in authority on board the *Camperdown*. Witness Warden, in reply to the Coroner, said that he considered the staging and prows to be under the charge of the foreman of the ship (Mr. Lemmon)

William Madge of Pains Road, Southsea, leading man of fitters in the Dockyard, said that deceased formed one of a party of 25 men working under witness. He was a very steady man and a teetotaller. Witness then proceeded to explain the position of the various platforms outside the ship, and said that had both handrails been attached to the stage from which the deceased fell the accident could not have occurred. He did not know who had immediate charge of the stages outside the ship, but they would be under the supervision of the foreman. He saw the deceased fall from the side of the stage, but witnessed no skylarking or anything of the kind.

Surgeon Alfred Page, R.N. of Haslar Hospital, said that deceased was received in a dying state shortly before nine o'clock on Tuesday. Witness remained with him up to the time of his death, which took place at 10 minutes to ten.

On examining deceased he found bruises on his head and excoriations on other parts of the body. A post mortem examination showed that the skull was fractured, and the base of the brain lacerated. His internal organs were bruised, and several blood vessels were ruptured. The room was then cleared for a few minutes while the Coroner discussed with the Jury the desirability of adjourning the case in order that further evidence might be brought before them with regard to the supervision of the staging.

On the reopening of the Court, the Coroner, in summing up, said that in the death of the deceased a valuable life had been sacrificed through carelessness and it would be for them to consider whether there was any culpable negligence on the part of the person who had the supervision of the staging. After the evidence which had been adduced, he went on to say that witness Warden had sworn that the foreman of the ship had charge of the prow from which Rogers fell. His opinion was, to speak, backed by the evidence of Mr. Madge, and it was for the Jury to consider whether the negligence shown was attended with such culpability as to justify them in returning a verdict of manslaughter.

He felt great sympathy towards the deceased's widow and two children, and in as much as the evidence clearly showed that his death was entirely due to the gross carelessness on the part of Dockyard officials, he thought that something should be done for them by the Government. He should be very glad to forward anything they might have to say in regard to this matter to the proper quarter.

The Jury found a verdict of accidental death, the foreman remarking that in all probability they would never be able to discover who removed the handrail from the prow, and that it might have been taken away weeks before it came under the notice of the foreman. The Jury added a rider, expressing their conviction that the accident could not have happened but for the removal of the handrail, and that something should be done by the government on behalf of the deceased's widow and children.

1885 – A FATAL MEAL.

The Coroner (T. Bramsdon, Esq.) held an inquest yesterday afternoon at the Old Countryman, Thomas Street, Landport, on the body of Louis John Ockendon, aged 70, of 47, Cottage View, Fratton. The deceased, who had formerly been a labourer in the Dockyard, yesterday went to his brother's, Richard Ockendon's, house in Thomas Street, where he had dinner, of which he ate ravenously. Shortly afterwards he was seized with coughing, and foamed at the mouth. Dr. Crewe attended, but deceased was dead on his arrival. A post mortem examination revealed a piece of un-masticated beef in the windpipe of the deceased, which had caused a stoppage in the air passage and produced death. A verdict of accidental death was returned.

1885 – SUICIDE IN DORSET STREET.

This was held before Portsmouth Coroner (T. A. Bramsdon Esq.), touching the death of Arthur Hudson Burgess aged 31 years; late of 27, Dorset Street, Landport, who was found dead yesterday having hanged himself on his bed post at his residence. The evidence adduced showed deceased was formerly a hammer-man employed in the Dockyard, but had been paralysed during the last nine years. His wife was employed by Messrs. Helby & Co, stay factors, and yesterday morning she left home to go for some material for her work. On her return she found deceased in a crouching position on the floor with a rope tied round his neck, the other end being attached to the bed post. She called a neighbour named Mary Ann Morton, wife of a railway porter, who severed the rope with a pair of scissors. The police were called in, and Dr. Green was sent for. That gentleman, on examining the body, found life extinct, and the external appearances were consistent with death by hanging. Deceased had twice previously attempted suicide, and had a brother in the lunatic asylum. The Jury returned a verdict of suicide while suffering from temporary insanity.

1886 – ATTACK ON PRISON WARDERS.

A serious melee has occurred at the Portsmouth Convict Prison. A number of prisoners were at work in the laundry, when one of them named Greenwood, who is undergoing a sentence of fourteen years' penal servitude, seized a long iron bar belonging to the house, upon which some clothes were being dried, and attacked his warder with the weapon. Another warder, seeing what had happened, drew his sword, and forced Greenwood to act on the defensive, A second convict then joined in the fray by throwing clogs at the officers, but he was soon silenced, and Greenwood, after being knocked about the head a good deal by the warder whom he had first attacked, and who had drawn his baton, was secured and placed in confinement, awaiting the arrival of one of the directors, who will investigate the case. Greenwood had been previously flogged.

1886 – ATTEMPTED SUICIDE WITH A REVOLVER.

On Saturday evening a man, named John Holland, about 21 years of age, attempted to commit suicide by shooting himself with a revolver on the beach between Stamshaw and Tipner. It appears that two men, named Ayland and Cockburn, hearing a pistol shot, proceeded to the beach, and found the defendant bleeding from a bullet wound in the shoulder. In answer to their questions, he said he was an omnibus conductor, and had been accused of stealing a penny, and he wished he had finished himself. Dr. Blackman of Landport, was called, and advised that he should be taken to the Hospital at Mile End. This was at once done, and it was then ascertained that the bullet had lodged in the back part of the left shoulder. He was detained for treatment, and then stated that he had been accused of giving a passenger an old ticket which he picked up from the floor of the bus, and in consequence of which he was suspended from his employment. We believe the bullet has been successfully extracted, and, should he recover, he will be charged with the offence before the Magistrates.

1886 – KILLED ON TRAMWAY.

Herbert Pharoah, aged 6 years, whose parents reside in Cresswell Street Landport, was riding on the foot-board of a tramcar in the Commercial Road, Landport, on Thursday evening when he was ordered off by the conductor, and in getting down he fell, and the front wheel of the car passed over his right leg and foot, crushing them in a shocking manner. He was picked up, and conveyed to the Hospital by P.C.s Lily and Kinchin, where the injured limb was amputated, but the child died early on Friday morning. An inquest has been held and a verdict returned of "Accidental death."

1886 – AN ELEPHANT AT LARGE.

An elephant escaped from a travelling menagerie near Hilsea Barracks, Portsmouth, on Saturday morning and attacked a sentry, throwing him to the ground.

1886 – THE FATAL ACCIDENT AT THE LANDPORT RAILWAY STATION.

An inquest was held at the Portsmouth Hospital yesterday touching the death of Robert Charles Shaw, aged 59 years, a retired carpenter R.N. late of Holly House, Landport Terrace, Southsea, who was found lying on the railway near the Landport station shortly before noon yesterday.

Mr. G. Feltham watched the case on behalf of the deceased's relatives.

The evidence adduced that showed that deceased was invalided from the service ten years ago suffering from gout. He left home at ten o'clock yesterday morning, telling his wife he was going to see the Foreman to Mr. Cooper, builder, of Landport, about a leak which existed in the roof of their house. Later on deceased was seen on the high level platform of Landport Railway station by James Cummins, a signalman on duty there. He walked along the platform several times and, at length, descended the slope to the six foot way. An engine passed, and hearing the driver blow the whistle, Cummins asked deceased what he was doing on the line. He made no reply, but walked past the signal box to the platform.

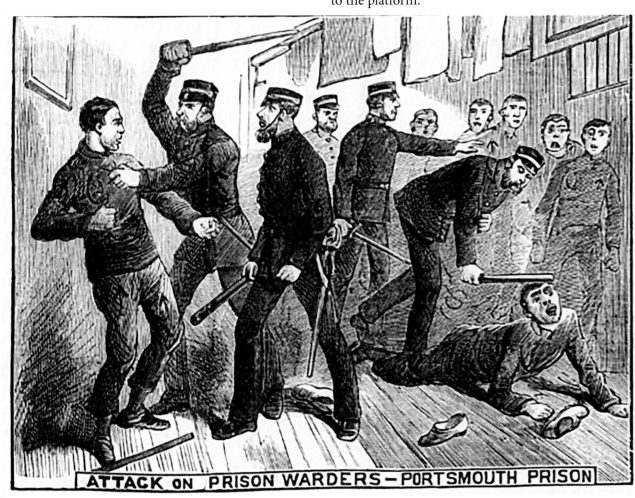
ATTACK ON PRISON WARDERS – PORTSMOUTH PRISON

At 11.45 a.m. Mr. Albert Horsey, stationer, of Queens Street saw deceased's body lying in the four foot way at the extreme end of the platform, and noticed a frightful bruise on the head, from which blood was flowing. Mr. Horsey rushed to the signal box nearby, and told the man in charge to stop the train which was then due. He then gave information to P.S. Moss and Ticket-Inspector Harfield, and deceased was removed to the Hospital.

The House Surgeon, (Dr. J.P.W. Freeman), found that he had sustained a compound fracture of the skull, a scalp wound, and a compound fracture of both bones of the left leg. He never regained consciousness, and died last night at 11.30.

Only one train passed the signal box from the time Cummins spoke to deceased until after the discovery of the body. The driver, (Mr. Jeffreys), said the train was drawing up when passing the spot. He felt no shock, nor did he find any suspicious marks on the engine when he examined it on his return from London at four a.m. today.

Judging from the nature of deceased's injuries, the doctor formed the conclusion that the engine struck the deceased, but the wheels did not pass over him.

The Coroner, in summing up, pointed out the entire absence of any evidence which might lead to the supposition that deceased's death was brought about by any other means than accidental.

The Jury found a verdict of accidental death, adding that they exonerated the railway employees from all blame.

1888 – MILITARY AFFRAY AT PORTSMOUTH.

The feud which has for some short time existed between the 1st Battalion South Lancashire Regiment, stationed at Victoria Barracks, Southsea, and the 2nd Battalion Connaught Rangers, stationed at Cambridge Barracks, Portsmouth broke out into active combat on Wednesday evening and for a time caused much alarm at Portsmouth, Portsea, and Landport.

There had been previous skirmishes, one of which took place in the neighbourhood of Warblington Street Portsmouth, on Monday evening. That, however, seemed to be merely a brush preliminary to the field day which the Connaught Rangers appear to have promised themselves on the following evening; for it was the men of this regiment who, judging from the official version of the affair, were the real aggressors on the occasion. We gather that the origin of the dispute between the younger members of the two regiments is that the Connaught Rangers have been ordered to leave for Aldershot next week, although they have only been in this garrison since August 3rd last, whereas the South Lancashire Regiment will remain here, although having been quartered at Victoria Barracks since February 3rd, 1886, on returning from Aden. This appears to have been regarded as a grievance by the Connaught Rangers, and the younger members aforesaid did not conceal their vexation from those whom they considered their more favoured rivals.

The evening's disturbance seems to have commenced, as did that of Monday night, in Warblington Street, Portsmouth. There was a crowd of soldiers in that thoroughfare about half past eight, and in consequence of their threatening appearance the borough police went to Lieutenant-Colonel C. H. Bunbury, the Commanding Officer of the Connaught Rangers, who at once sent out picquets and himself accompanied them. The picquets proceeded to St. Mary's Street, whither the disturbing soldiers had made their way; and the latter, on seeing them, left the neighbourhood, the street being cleared about half past nine.

Fearing disturbances, some of the shopkeepers, in view of possible damage, had put up their shutters, but when this peaceable result, so far as Portsmouth proper was concerned, had been arrived at, they took them down again. Meanwhile a party of fifty or sixty soldiers, all of whom belonged apparently to the Connaught Rangers, caused considerable excitement by parading through Queen Street, Portsea, about a quarter past eight, accompanied by a large crowd. They sent scouts every now and then into the public houses along that thoroughfare, with the presumed object of searching out any luckless men of the South Lancashire Regiment who might be ensconced within these premises. Their efforts in this direction appear to have been fruitless, and the party made their way along Edinburgh Road to Landport.

It was in this part of the town that the actual conflict occurred which gave rise to so many startling rumours as to the doings of the two regiments. A large party of the Connaught Rangers had assembled in Commercial Road, between Charlotte Street and All Saints' Church, by half past nine, and it seemed that the disturbance commenced by twenty five or thirty of them attacking a man of the South Lancashire as he was coming from the piece of land on which boat-swings, &c., are erected in the manner of a fair, at the corner of Oxford Street. The unfortunate man who was thus set upon was severely maltreated, and he sought refuge in an adjoining grocery shop. His attackers followed, but here the spirit of fair play prompted the civilian bystanders to prevent a continuance of so one-sided a fight. The tables were turned upon the Connaught Rangers, who, concluding that discretion was after all the better part of valour, took to their heels. One of them was followed into a public house where he sought refuge, and the indignant civilians knocked him about pretty considerably.

During this affray the soldiers had used their sticks and belts pretty freely, and one or two of them were in the possession of more formidable weapons; one man, for instance, being armed with a poker and another with the handle of a shovel. The South Lancashire man who was the subject of the attack sustained several cuts on the head, which might have been caused by blows from belts.

While this encounter, which occupied but a few minutes, was in progress the police and the picquets were hurrying to the spot. On hearing at the Central Police station at Landport of what was taking place the Chief Constable (Mr. Cosser) at once despatched all the men on duty in and about the station to the scene, and telephoned to all the other police stations for every available man to be despatched. The response was remarkably prompt, the crowd that had quickly assembled outside the Central Police station audibly expressing its wonder as to where all the police came from. The news reached the Chief Constable at rather a fortunate time for such a muster, the large force of men on duty in the town, between 70 and 80, being for the greater part capable of ready concentration. Messages to the commanding officers at the different barracks, requesting the assistance of picquets, were despatched concurrently with this mustering of civic forces. These messages were quickly and as courteously acted upon, and strong picquets, in charge of officers, and accompanied by members of the military police, were despatched from Anglesea Barracks, where the 2nd Battalion Dorsetshire Regiment is quartered, as well as from Cambridge Barracks.

A large force of military and police, capable of grappling with a disturbance of much greater import than had by that time developed, was consequently soon on the spot. The appearance of this disciplined and composite body over-awed the disturbers of the peace, and after thirteen men of the Connaught Rangers had been taken into custody as being ringleaders in the disturbance, their comrades found it desirable to beat a retreat, and did so. Thanks to the promptitude of the police and of the military officers, a number of whom personally tendered their assistance to the Chief Constable at the central station, the streets soon resumed their normal appearance.

The affair, thus nipped in the bud without much being done by way of wounding or disablement, assumed at one time a very threatening aspect, and caused a great deal of alarm both in the neighbourhood of Commercial Road, where of course a tremendous crowd soon gathered, and in other parts of the town.

The thirteen prisoners were taken to the Central Police station, and detained there for some time as a precautionary measure, although no specific charge was preferred against them by the police. There was no serious fighting with the police against whom the Connaught Rangers had no animosity, their sole quarrel being with the men of the South Lancashire Regiment. They offered practically no opposition to their arrest, and delivered up their belts at the Police station with lamb-like meekness. Some of them were injured about the face and head, having evidently received as well as given severe punishment.

About eleven o'clock the prisoners were handed over to a strong piquet, and were conducted to barracks to be dealt with by the military authorities. By this time things were becoming quieter in the town, many men of the regiments concerned having made their way back to headquarters, some of them accompanying the picquets thither so as to avoid any chance of being dragged into the quarrel. The picquets effectually paraded the town in strong force, and acted as a wholesome deterrent to would-be combatants. One picquet was formed from the guard of the Connaught Rangers on duty at the Tipnor Magazines.

The thirteen men who were arrested were made prisoners at large on arrival at Cambridge Barracks, and allowed to go to their respective rooms for the night. On Thursday the affair was investigated by the officer commanding the Connaught Rangers, who remanded the case, and the circumstances will be brought under the notice of General Sir George Willis in the usual way. The Connaught Rangers will leave Portsmouth for Aldershot on Wednesday next.

1888 – FRIENDSHIP AND FATE.

An awkward accident befell some members of the Park Lane Chapel Choir, Southsea, on Tuesday night. The choir had driven over to Hayling Island to give a concert in the school room there on behalf of the funds of the church carried on by their Non-conformist friends in the island. The entertainment passed off successfully, but the journey home was not so devoid of mishap. Before reaching Havant the horse attached to one of the vehicles reared, breaking the shafts, and throwing the occupants, most of them ladies, into the road. All were naturally alarmed, but none were seriously hurt. The horse bolted, but was promptly stopped by Mr. William Adams, who rendered every assistance to the party whom fate had thus overtaken. They walked to Havant, and reached the Railway station just after the last train had left for Portsmouth. Consequently they remained at Havant for the night, and returned home to their anxious friends on Wednesday morning.

1889 – DEATH FROM HYDROPHOBIA.

The Coroner (T. A. Bramsdon, Esq.) opened an inquiry yesterday afternoon, at the Portsea Island Union Workhouse, Kingston, into the circumstances attending the death of James Percival Belsey, a victim to hydrophobia at 19 years of age, lately living at 3, Smith's Court, North Street, Portsea.

Opening the proceedings, the Coroner detailed the main facts of the case, and said that after the deceased had been bitten at Cosham he was seen by Dr. Heygate, whose request that he should call at his surgery was not complied with. The deceased, however, appeared to have called at Mr. Baker's, chemist, Cosham, and he advised him to call on Dr. Robinson on his way down. That seemed to have been done, although Dr. Robinson was not at home, but when the deceased had reached Kingston cross the wounds were cauterised by Mr. Cooper, chemist.

The Coroner further referred to the deceased being seen at the Landport Hospital subsequently, by Dr. O'Conor, to his treatment afterwards by Dr. Colt (who had consulted in the case with Drs Maybury, McGregor, and Mumby) and to the eventual death of the deceased in excruciating pain at the Infectious Diseases Hospital at Milton. There was, however, he said, one gratifying circumstance in the case, and that was that it was believed that one of two dogs which had been killed by the police at Portsmouth, under the Dogs Act, was the animal who had bitten the deceased; that was certainly gratifying, because it was not pleasant to know that such a dog was abroad in the country. The Jury then viewed the body, which was lying in the mortuary at the Infectious Diseases Hospital.

Formal evidence as to the identification was then given by deceased's sister, Rose Wood, wife of a labourer employed in the Dockyard.

Clara Figgins, a young woman employed as a domestic servant at Argyle House, Southsea, stated that she became acquainted with deceased about three months before Christmas, and in November last walked out with him. On the evening of Friday, November 16th, they walked together to Cosham, and when at Hilsea Lines a black and tan collie dog came out of the fields. It was a stray dog, and it followed them to Cosham. She noticed that the dog looked vicious, and although it did not then snap at them she was afraid of it. They went into a coffee tavern, and coming out found the animal waiting for them. They walked towards Havant, and five minutes afterwards she remarked, "That dog is following us now; I don't like the look of it." She then turned round to look at the animal, which immediately attacked her, seizing her by the jacket. The deceased pushed her back, the dog then flew at him, biting him under the eye and the eyebrow and nose. Deceased did not strike at the dog before it attacked them.

Dr. Heygate, of Cosham, who drove up soon afterwards, advised them to go to Mr. Baker, chemist, of Cosham. The latter, on being consulted, sent them to Dr. Robinson, but that gentleman was not at home, and they proceeded to Kingston Road, where they saw Mr. Cooper, another chemist. Mr. Cooper advised them to see Dr. Green, and they went to that gentleman's house, but he happened to be out, and subsequently deceased's wound was cauterised by the chemist, who recommended him to go home and see a doctor. At first Belsey thought lightly of the injury, which merely looked like a scratch, but subsequently complained of pains in the head, which he attributed to the bite. Dr. William H. Heygate, residing at Cosham, said he recollected that when driving along the Havant Road on the 16th November he saw the deceased with a young woman, when the latter, in an excited manner, exclaimed "That dog will kill us, unless it is stopped." He then saw a dog on the footpath, and on hearing that it had bitten the man, struck at it as it was evidently making for the two persons again. The dog after that came round the witness's side, and as it was about to spring at the cart he struck it and it ran back up the Havant Road. He then told the young man and woman to walk on, and he would keep the dog back, but after going about 20 yards the dog again followed. He afterwards drew the attention of Constable Pearce to the dog, and told him there was something wrong with it.

Constable Pearce, of the Hants Constabulary, stationed at Cosham, said he saw the dog several times, and tried to catch it, but was unable to so do. He last saw it near the railway crossing at about a quarter to ten o'clock. It was a stray dog, and did not belong to anyone living at Cosham. Dr. John O'Conor, the House Surgeon at the Landport Hospital, said he first saw the deceased about ten o'clock on the night of the 16th of November, where he stated that the dog had bitten him after he had slipped down. There were slight abrasions over the right eyebrow, one below the under eyelid, and one on the bridge of the nose. He inquired about the dog, but the deceased said he did not think it was at all rabid. He believed something had been done to the wound previously, and he dressed it with chloride of mercury. The deceased did not seem at all in fear, and he left the hospital. He saw him again afterwards, and he seemed to be getting on all right, having no head symptoms.

Deceased's sister was then recalled, and on reply to the Coroner said that on the 16th Nov. deceased was in good health before he left home to meet Miss Figgins. He continued in good health until about the 9th inst., when he first complained of a headache, which his relatives attributed to a cold. On the 16th, when he returned home from work he complained of feeling very unwell, and went to bed. Next morning he was very ill, and complained that his head was bad. He grew worse as the day wore on, and appeared very strange and wild, and could not drink water although he was thirsty. Dr. Colt was called in, and on Monday that gentleman again attended with Drs Maybury, McGregor, and Mumby. By direction of the last-named, the deceased was afterwards removed to the Infectious Diseases Hospital.

Dr. B. H. Mumby, the Medical Officer, stated that he saw the deceased in company with Dr. Colt on Monday morning last, and he was then very excitable. Any mention or sight of water created a spasm of muscle all over the body, and though he expressed a desire to drink water, as soon as he touched a cup containing milk he was thrown into a violent paroxysm. After two or three attempts, however, he managed to drink a little milk, about a teaspoonful. That also threw him into a strong paroxysm, and caused him a great deal of pain in his chest and difficulty of breathing. Being clearly a case that required a great deal of attention in hospital, the deceased was thus removed to the Infectious Diseases Hospital.

All the symptoms increased afterwards in severity, especially the desire for drink, showing clearly that it was a case of hydrophobia. The deceased was very violent in hospital. Under chloroform a pint and a half of beef tea was administered through a tube. Death took place at ten o'clock on Tuesday morning, and was due to asphyxia. A post mortem examination since made showed that the brain was congested as well as all the other organs, and the spinal cord.

The Coroner: The death was due to hydrophobia? – Yes. Constable Alfred Blake, of the Portsmouth Police Force, said that in consequence of instructions received he went in search of a collie dog, and found one in Fawcett Road. It was a stray animal, and had since been shot.

George William Monckom, an inspector under the Contagious Diseases (Animals) Act, said that the dog destroyed was a mongrel collie, of the ordinary black and tan kind, with a pointed nose and bushy tail, similar to the one which had bitten the deceased. P.C. Warr said that he and P.S. Hood had made inquiries at Cosham, but could find nothing of the dog in question. The Coroner, in summing up, said that the case was one of a very painful nature, but it might allay public fear to know that most likely the dog had been destroyed. The Jury returned a verdict to the effect that the deceased had died from hydrophobia, the result of being bitten by the dog in November last.

1890 – A LUNATIC AT LARGE IN PORTSMOUTH.

On Wednesday, a strange looking individual paid a visit to the office of Mr. G. Feltham, solicitor, Portsea, and recited the particulars of his claim to £100 which he said was withheld from him by the Magistrates at Doncaster. His story was as peculiar as his manner, and when asked his name and address he raved and danced around the office in a manner which showed that he had taken leave of his senses. Nothing but an assurance that he would find the £100 waiting for him if he called on the following morning would pacify him, and he left the office apparently very pleased with the result of his interview with Mr. E. J. T. Webb, Mr. Feltham's representative.

As soon as he had gone the latter telegraphed Fisherton Asylum, and learned that his mysterious client was a criminal lunatic, named George Diamond, who escaped from the establishment a week ago, and who had been convicted at Doncaster for a criminal assault upon the daughter of one of the Magistrates of the town, and had been found to be insane. The police, who had already been supplied with the man's description, were communicated with by Mr. C. S. Macfarlane, and two detectives were waiting to receive him at Mr. Feltham's office at the time appointed for his visit on Thursday.

The lunatic was punctual, and had turned into Union Street when he caught sight of the constable in uniform, who happened to be close to the office, and immediately showed him a clean pair of heels and darted down Catherine Row. He was pursued but his disappearance was sudden and complete and the police are still searching for him. It is pretty certain that he is in hiding somewhere in the borough as the exits both by land and sea have been closely guarded by the police ever since he disappeared. It may be added that a reward of £5 is offered for his apprehension.

Diamond is about 36 years of age, about 5ft 6in. or 7in., is dressed with a peaked cloth cap, corduroy waistcoat and trousers, dark trench coat, thick heavy boots and a kerchief round his neck. In general he appears as though he has been a tramp for some time. He is of full complexion having a full length beard and a moustache. The madman was seen in Union Street on Monday by Mr. H. Edwards, who lives opposite

Mr. Feltham's office. He rang the office bell, but being a holiday Mr. Feltham and his clerks were absent. The man then crossed the street and after looking through the window at Mr. Edwards for some twenty minutes he walked quietly away.

1891 – A PORTSMOUTH CHARACTER IN COURT.

Margaret Devereux, of Portsmouth, wife of a man well known in that town as "Tip-toe Johnny," was summoned by Eliza Gale, of High Street, Somerstown, for committing wilful damage. Mr. Gregory prosecuted. According to the evidence of the complainant, who is the defendant's aunt, the latter drove up to her house in a carriage on May 11th, accompanied by three women. All were drunk. Defendant entered the house, and after the usual salutations, announced her intention of "smashing up everything," saying it all belonged to her. Without more ado, the defendant commenced to smash everything she could lay her hands upon—pictures, china ornaments, and glass—and was only restrained by the appearance of Sergeant Caiger, who found the room full of wreckage. The defendant did not deny the smashing, but said the property was her own. She was ordered to pay 25s., with the alternative of seven days. She loudly announced her intention of "doing" the seven days, and forbade "Johnny," who was in court, to pay. But "Tip-toe Johnny" subsequently paid the fine, and took his spouse away.

1891 – AT THE CORONER'S COURT.

Two inquests were held at the Town Hall, on Monday, before the Portsmouth Coroner, (T.A. Bramsdon, Esq.) The first related to the death of Mabel Florence Maffey, the infant daughter of William George Maffey, a stoker, serving on board H.M.S. *Marathon*. Deceased, who was four months old, was a delicate child, and suffered from a cough. Her mother took her to bed with her at 53, Unicorn Street, Portsea, on Friday night, and at 4.30 next morning Mrs. Maffey awoke to find her baby dead. Dr. Mulvany was called in, from the appearances presented by the body, and the circumstances attending death, that gentleman formed the opinion that the child was suffocated. Death was attributed to overlaying, and the Jury found a verdict to that effect.

In the second case the deceased person was Elizabeth Mary Rees, of 15, King Street, Portsea. Deceased was the widow of a sergeant-major of the Hampshire Artillery Militia and lived with her son, to whom she had complained of frequent bilious attacks and a cough. She was unwell on Thursday, and on Friday remained in bed. She became feverish and while apparently in a deep sleep breathed her last on Saturday morning. Her son said that she was sixty-five years of age, but Mrs. Bamber, the landlady of the house in which they lodged, described her as a strong, active woman of 75. She also said that the lady was a little eccentric, and she believed that she overtaxed her strength when the Queen visited Portsmouth recently. Deceased went into the dockyard to witness the launch, telling her that she had seen Her Majesty riding about at Kensington when a girl, and wished to see whether "there was any difference in her now." Dr. Sutton said he was called after death, and found the body still warm. He was of the opinion that deceased died from syncope, arising from senile decay, and chronic disease of the liver. Verdict, natural causes.

1891 – SHOCKING MURDER AT STAMSHAW.

Disaster has followed disaster at Portsmouth. Hardly had the public excitement cooled down from the heat concerning the fatal fire in Commercial Road, on the 28th ult., when, on Saturday evening last, just a week later, Portsmouth was horrified by the news of a wife murder at Stamshaw. Inquiries proved that the rumour was only too well founded. The terrible occurrence took place at Jubilee House, Twyford Avenue, where, in the presence of her younger brother, a lad of fifteen, and her only surviving child, a boy of five, Esther Watts was shot dead by her husband. Afterwards the wretched man attempted to commit suicide with the same revolver, but only succeeded in inflicting a wound in his wrist. Watts was taken into custody soon afterwards, and conveyed to the Buckland police station, whence he was conveyed to the police court on Monday morning and charged with the murder at the ordinary sitting of the Magistrates.

Edward Henry Fawcett Watts, for such is the murderer's full name, is 38 years of age, and his wife was 32. They were married about fourteen years ago, and have had a family of seven children, only one of whom, the little boy who saw the murder committed, is now living. Watts has been in the Army, having served in the Royal Artillery. Part of that time he spent in India, and it is said that he there received a sunstroke. After leaving the Army he entered the Navy, and served for some years as an able seaman. He was invalided from this service about four years ago, and has since done labouring work, the scene of his last employment being some gasworks in London.

Although his behaviour when sober is described in terms of high praise, Watts has for years past been addicted to drink, and in his cups his whole disposition appeared to have changed, for his manner and conversation were irritating to a degree, though he does not seem to have been openly quarrelsome. Things have gone with him from bad to worse, and as the craving for drink fastened its hold upon him he became less and less inclined for work, until latterly it appeared that he had been living mainly on the earnings of his wife as a laundry woman.

They were lately living in London, but a month ago Mrs. Watts returned to Portsmouth, and went to live at the residence of her father, a bargeman named Hickley, who lives at Jubilee House, Twyford Avenue. She had found it impossible to live with her husband any longer, and so they separated in this way, Mrs. Watts retaining the custody of the child. On her return to Portsmouth she obtained employment at the Brunswick Laundry, North End, where she continued working until the day of her tragic death.

The affairs of the unhappy pair were in this condition when Watts appeared suddenly upon the scene at Portsmouth on Friday evening, having come down from London. He went to the Brunswick Library and had an interview with his wife when she left work at eight o'clock. What transpired is not wholly known, but it is stated that high words passed between them, in the course of which Watts said to his wife, "You have seen this Easter, but you will never see another." After this interview he left her, and he seems to have gone later to the Derby Tavern, Derby Road, where he had two or three glasses of ale, and then asked the landlord (Mr. Hoskins) for a sheet of paper. This was supplied, and Watts wrote a note in pencil, and afterwards folded up the paper and put it in his pocket. In the light of subsequent events this action is supposed to have been indicative of a determination at the time to commit the murder and suicide, it being conjectured that the note contained some explanation of his reasons for the premeditated crime.

This, of course, is a matter that will be cleared up at the inquest or at the police court proceedings. Watts is supposed to have spent the night somewhere in the neighbourhood, but the next that can at present be definitely ascertained in regard to his movements is that at about four o'clock on Saturday afternoon he was seen walking slowly along Twyford Avenue, apparently a little the worse for drink. He went to Jubilee House, and knocked, and the door was opened by Mrs. Watts' brother, a lad of fifteen. Watts asked to see his wife, and walked through the passage into the back sitting room, where she was nursing her child who is down with the measles, having left work at the laundry at one o'clock. "I want to speak to you quietly," said Watts to his wife. Mr. Hickley was in the room, and Mrs. Watts, regarding her husband's remark as a hint for him to leave, replied, "What you have to say you can say before father."

Thinking, as he afterwards explained, that it would be better to leave them to converse alone, Mr. Hickley, however, went out of the room and proceeded into the garden. Two or three minutes later he heard a noise in the room, and thinking his daughter and her husband were quarrelling, he went back. There he saw his daughter seated in a chair, dead, with her head leaning back and bullet wounds on her neck, from which blood was flowing copiously. Near her stood her husband and Mr. Lancaster, another son-in-law of Mr. Hickley's, who had been in an adjoining room, and had rushed in on hearing shots fired. Mr. Lancaster had picked up a revolver from the floor, with which weapon the murderer had apparently attempted to commit suicide. The bullet that he had fired at himself, however, had passed through the flesh of his left wrist, just escaping the main artery, and made its exit an inch or two nearer the hand.

THE VICTIM

ARREST OF THE MURDERER.

Watts was then overpowered, and the deceased's younger brother ran out of the house in search of a policeman. He found Constable Dorey at Kingston cross, who hurried back with him. In the meantime the wretched assassin was held without much difficulty, for violence soon gave way to despair. "She was too good for me," he said. "She would never have lived with me, and I could not ask her to forgive me again." When Constable Dorey entered the house, Watts said, "I'll go quietly; don't put the darbies on." Of course, however, he was handcuffed, and the constable took him to the Buckland police station, where, on being formally charged by Sergeant Hayward with the offence, he made no reply. He remained at the station in the immediate charge of Constables Moth and Murphy, who were relieved later on by other officers.

Watts was quiet in his demeanour, and not very talkative, but he spoke to his custodians during the evening, the purport of his remarks being, of course, not divulged by the police. Soon after the wound in his wrist was inflicted it was temporarily bound up with a handkerchief, and on the prisoner's arrival at the police station Dr. J. McGregor, of St. Mary's Crescent, was summoned to attend to the injury. He went to the station and dressed the wound, which was not of a serious character. The prisoner, who is a native of Maidstone, is 5ft. 7in. in height, and has dark brown hair and grey eyes. He is generally considered to be a good-looking man, and has a heavy dark moustache, the rest of his face being clean shaven.

PRISONER BEFORE THE MAGISTRATES.

At the Portsmouth police court on Monday, before Captain McCoy, Major Greetham, and Messrs. G. S. Lancaster and W. Edmonds, Edward Henry Fawcett Watts, 38, was placed in the dock on a charge of murdering his wife. The Magistrates Clerk (Mr. Addison): Edward Henry Fawcett Watts, you are charged with the wilful murder of your wife, Esther Emily Watts, on the 4th inst. Mr. G. R. King prosecuted on behalf of the police.

STATEMENT BY AN EYE-WITNESS.

William Harding Hickley, a youth of 15, was then placed in the witness box, and examined by Mr. King. Do you live with your parents at Jubilee House, Twyford Avenue, Stamshaw? – Yes, sir. Are you a Labourer? – Yes. Had you a sister named Ethel Emily Watts? – Yes, The wife of the prisoner? – Yes. For the past three weeks had the deceased been residing at Jubilee House? – Yes. And was she there about twenty minutes past four on Saturday last? – Yes. What room was she in? – The back room. And who was there besides? – I, my father, and a little boy, her son. The boy is about four years old? – Yes. Did anyone come to the house at that time? – The prisoner. Who let him in? – I did. A knock came at the door and you answered it? – Yes. What did he say to you? – He said "Is Esther home?" I said "Yes, walk in."

Did he follow you into the room? – He followed me into the passage, and he stayed there. I went into the room and told his wife he was there, and she told me to tell him to come in. I told him to walk in. When he came in, did he say anything to the deceased? – He said to father, "Well, how are you getting on now?" Father said, "Pretty rough and have been all the winter." The prisoner took up the little boy, who said, "I've got the measles." Prisoner said, "It don't matter if your father do catch it." Where was the deceased sitting at this time? – She was sitting in the corner alongside the fire. What did the prisoner do? Did he sit down? – Yes. Where? – He sat opposite in the other corner on a chair. Did he say anything to deceased? – He said "Can I have five minutes conversation with you?" What did she say? – She said, "Say what you have got to say here." Then did he say anything? Father got up and walked out, and prisoner said, "Is this affair going to come to an end?" What did she say? She said, "I have told you," and I didn't properly hear what she said more.

What happened after that? – He said, "You left me in a pretty pickle in London; you left me £6 in debt." Did she make any reply? – Prisoner went on to say that he

THE MURDERER

owed £1 to Mrs. somebody (I didn't catch the name) and £4 to the Loan Club. She said, "You have got the benefit of that, I had none of that. How about the furniture and cups and saucers and plates? You have not brought none of them down with you." What did he say or do then? – He got up and took his pocket-handkerchief out of his pocket. I never seen what he done afterwards. I was sitting back reading a book. But all of a sudden he jumped up and said "Take that," and I heard him fire the first shot.

Did you see him fire it? – No. I jumped up and heard the deceased holloa out "Oh," and then I see the little boy go running out, and he holload out, and my sister hollaoed out. I ran into the street in the rain, and stopped to see if he was coming, and then ran down Twyford Avenue after the police. How many shots could you hear? – Three or four, rather quick. Did you see either of them fired? – No. I could not get a policeman in Twyford Avenue, and ran down Kingston Crescent and got two police and one in private clothes against Smith and Vosper's shop.

At the time that you heard shots fired, was there anyone else in the room but prisoner, deceased, the little boy four years old, and yourself? – No, sir.

THE DOCTOR'S EVIDENCE.

Dr. Josiah George Blackman stated: I am a resident medical practitioner, practising at Kingston Crescent. On Saturday were you called to see the deceased? – Yes, about twenty minutes to five. You went to Jubilee House, Twyford Road, Stamshaw. – Yes. Will you say what you found? – I found in the back room downstairs in a corner near the fire the deceased sitting in a chair, with her head resting on the right side, over the arm of a settee. One arm was also resting on the settee, and the other hanging down on the lap. The left leg was extended and the right was bent. She was quite dead. The body was quite warm.

Of course, you pronounced life to be extinct? – I did. Did you make a post mortem examination yesterday in conjunction with Dr. MacGregar? – I did. Will you briefly detail the result of the post mortem? – There were seven wounds of entrance and exit of the shots. Will you just localise the shots? – On the right hand at the outer side of the wrist I found a contused wound, which, on tracing its track, I found communicated with another wound in the ball of the thumb. The bullet had fractured the metacarpal bone of the thumb. Was it a bullet wound? – Yes. On the right breast, two and a-half inches above the nipple, and one inch to the outer side of the breast bone was a circular hole with clean edges, which was contused and scorched. This ran in an outward direction three and a half inches, at the end of which I found the bullet produced.

Another bullet (produced), I found on the table in the house. In the centre of the neck, immediately upon the left of the middle line, is a wound half an inch over, the scorching extending for an inch and a half around. A probe passed into this wound passes beneath the skin and emerges at another wound two and a half inches distant.

The two wounds were caused by one bullet? – Yes, the track passing upwards and outward. Half an inch behind the middle of the right ear was a wound, on tracing which I found the bullet to have passed through the spine between the first and second bones, splintering the second bone, and severing the spinal cord, and continuing upwards ends at a wound half an inch behind the left ear, slightly below its centre. The wound behind the left ear is much marked with powder.

By the Bench. The bullet entered behind the left ear and came out behind the right ear. There was a large haemorrhage in this wound, and great contusion.

Mr. King: What was the cause of death? – The injury to the spinal cord by the bullet which passed through it. And severed it? – Yes. Were the other organs all healthy? – Yes.

Mr. King, addressing the Bench: That is all the evidence I propose to call today, sir. The Chairman (Captain McCoy): What is your application?

Mr. King: "A remand for a week sir, in order that the Chief Constable may communicate with the Public Prosecutor."

Prisoner was accordingly remanded for one week.

THE PRISONER'S WOUND.

Before the remand was granted Dr. James McGregor was called to speak as to the bullet wound which prisoner had sustained. The witness stated: I am a resident medical practitioner practising at Kingston. Mr. King: Were you called to attend the prisoner on Saturday? – Yes. At what time? – Half past five. Where at? – Buckland police station. What did you find? – He was suffering from a gunshot wound. Where? – In the left hand. Severe? – No. When you say gunshot wound, do you mean bullet wound? – Yes. Is he in a fit condition to be removed to Milton Prison – Yes.

THE INQUEST.

The inquest was opened at the Town Hall on Monday by the Coroner (Mr. T A. Bramsdon).

George Hickley, the father of the deceased, was the first witness. He identified the body, and stated that deceased was 32 years of age in February last. Her husband was invalided from the Navy about five years ago, and was in receipt of a pension. They had been married about fifteen years. Witness had not known them to live unhappily together until lately. They were living at Lewisham last Whitsuntide, and later they resided in New Cross Road, London. Altogether they had lived in the metropolis for eighteen months past. On the 20th ult. deceased came to witness's house, bringing her only surviving child with her. She remained there, getting a living at the Brunswick Laundry, North End, where she obtained employment on the 24th ultimo. Her husband drank very heavily at times. Witness had heard by letter that they quarrelled, but he had not seen them quarrel. About twenty minutes past four on Saturday witness, with deceased, her child and witness' son William, aged 14 years, were together in the back room of the house, downstairs. Witness heard a knock at the door, and it was opened by his son William. Then witness heard Watts' voice as he came up the passage. Witness's son came into the room, and said, "Here's Ted," and Watts then came to the door of the room and said to deceased, "Can I have five minutes' conversation with you?" She said, "If you have anything to say to me, come inside." Watts then entered the room and shut the door. "Well, George." he said, addressing witness, "how are you getting on?" Witness replied, "I'm very rough, Ted, and have been all the winter." Watts then said, "Will you have something to drink?" to which witness answered, "No, thank you; i'm very nearly a teetotaller."

Watts was sober, so far as witness could tell. He sat down on the opposite side of the room to his wife, and took their little boy on his knee. Watts caressed the child and kissed him, and the boy said "I've got the measles, daddy." Watts then looked up, and said to his wife, "Well, are we going to make this affair up? I'm going back tonight." Deceased said "You had my answer last night." Watts asked "Is that your final determination? You won't look over it anymore?" Deceased replied "I have looked over it too many times, and it's no use to. The more I look over it the worse you get; you get worse every time." He said "You left me in a pretty mess in London." Witness then got up and left the room.

The Coroner: Was the conversation of an angry nature? – Witness: There was nothing angry at all in the way the words were spoken. Did your daughter speak sharply to him? – No. She did nothing to aggravate him? – No.

Continuing, witness said he left in the room the deceased, her husband, their child and witness's son William. About two minutes after he had gone from the room he heard some noises in rapid succession, at least two or three, but he could not say how many. Witness did not think at the time that the noises were those of a firearm, although they corresponded to the sound. Witness then heard a scream, and hurried indoors. In the kitchen he saw another of his daughters, Mrs. Lancaster, who exclaimed "He's killed her!" When witness reached the door of the back room he met his son-in-law, William Lancaster, who handed him the revolver produced, saying, "You had better take this."

Witness took the revolver and held it down to the floor. William Lancaster added, "He has killed her." Watts was in the room at the time, and remained there till Constable Dorey came. Witness saw that his daughter was seated in her chair, with her head leaning over a settee close behind. He noticed a wound on the left side of her neck, from which blood was flowing. She appeared to be dead.

Witness sent for a doctor and for the police. When witness entered the room after so hearing the shots fired Watts was half kneeling and half leaning over the deceased. He said, "It's no use sending for a policeman, she's dead, and I shall be dead before a policeman gets here." Witness noticed blood flowing rather extensively from a wound in his left wrist. The blood dropped and formed a pool on the floor. Soon after witness entered the room Watts stood on his feet. "She was my wife and I loved her," he said. "You have no cause to send for a policeman, I shall be dead before the policeman gets here."

Watts had never had a revolver in his possession to witness' knowledge until Saturday last. He was quite cool after firing the shots, and did not make any complaint against his wife. Witness did not know of his own knowledge that Watts saw his wife on Friday night, but had been told that he had gone up to the Brunswick Laundry to see her. Witness had been told that deceased had left her husband on more than one occasion, but he did not know it for a fact.

By the Jury: Deceased had never told them much about her husband. They had learned more about him from other people than she had ever disclosed. She refused to say much concerning him, telling witness that he had enough trouble of his own.

William Handler Lancaster, plasterer, of Jubilee House, said that Hickley, sen., was his father-in-law, and lived with him. His house had six rooms and a washhouse. He had no personal knowledge of deceased's relations with her husband. Witness was in the kitchen on the ground floor about a quarter or twenty minutes past four o'clock on Saturday, when he heard a knock at the front door. The door was opened and someone was admitted. About four minutes afterwards the first witness came out of the back room into the kitchen and passed thence into the yard. A minute elapsed, and witness heard a noise which at the moment he thought was caused by deceased struggling to get away from her husband. He heard two distinct sounds, but he did not recognize the report of firearms. Deceased cried "Oh," and on rushing into the back room he found her seated in a chair between the cupboard and a settee, with her head resting on the latter. He first noticed a wound under the left ear, from which blood was flowing. Watts was in a kneeling position, leaning on her breast, with his right hand on the floor, touching the revolver with outstretched fingers. Witness jumped across the room and snatched up the weapon, whereupon Watts said, "It's done, Bill; I shall not try to get out." Witness said, "I know you won't while I'm here."

Emma Louis Lancaster, wife of the last witness, said that although deceased and her husband had lived in Portsmouth for several years, both in their early married days and prior to their going to London, she had never known them to quarrel.

At this stage the inquiry was adjourned till Wednesday afternoon, when Susan Elizabeth Gay, wife of George Gay, labourer, living at 8, Kent's Cottages, Stamshaw Lane, deposed that at about five-and-twenty minutes past four o'clock on Saturday afternoon her sister, Mrs. Lancaster, came to her. In consequence of what she said witness went to Jubilee House, where she saw deceased sitting in a chair. She was dead, and her head was resting on the end of a settee. Watts was sitting on a chair opposite her, and said to witness, "Hullo mate; how are you getting on?" She said, "Whatever have you done now Ted?" and he replied, "I have killed her this time." Witness said, "She isn't dead, is she?" He said, "Yes, she is, worse luck." Witness rejoined, "I don't think she is; I'll go and get a drop of water." She obtained some from the kitchen and sprinkled it on deceased's forehead and hands, whereupon Watts observed, "It is no good to do that," Witness said, "Do you think she is dead, then?" and he answered, "undo her dress and feel around her heart. That is the place to tell." Witness undid deceased's dress, and told him that she could not feel anything. He said, "Let me try," and putting his hand inside her bodice, said "She's gone right enough." Witness said, "Whatever made you do that, Ted?" to which he replied, "She was mine. She was my wife, and I loved her too well to do without her. It was no good to ask her to look over it again, because she would not."

Witness noticed that blood was dripping from his left wrist, and he asked her for a piece of rag with which to tie up the wound. Then he asked her to give him a drink of water, and thanked her for it. Taking half a sovereign from his pocket, be said, "Take this and get something for yourself and the boy." He also produced a little bag, saying, "You might as well take this; there is half a crown in it, which will get something for the boy." Witness took the coins, and subsequently handed them to Detective Money, by whom they were produced. He seemed quite rational and sober, and when the policeman came, said "All right, Bobby." Witness identified the brooch produced as belonging to deceased, but did not notice it when she undid her dress. She had not the slightest doubt that the dress was fully fastened when she went into the room. The Coroner explained that he pressed the witness closely upon that point, because while the woman was shot in the right side of the breast there was no corresponding mark of the passage of the bullet through her dress bodice. Dr. Blackman, however, intimated that he could throw light upon the matter, and the attention of the Jury was drawn to the fact that the third button from the top was missing.

Esther Hickley, mother of the deceased, stated that deceased was married to Watts fifteen years ago on October 27th last. Watts was at times addicted to drink, and when in that condition he was very excitable and quarrelsome. She had never seen them quarrel; but she knew that they had separated more than once, and her daughter had told her that they had quarrelled. When sober Watts was a very quiet man. A Juror: Witness had never heard Watts threaten deceased, but the latter had told her that he had done so.

Constable Stephen Dorey deposed that at 4.40 p.m. on Saturday he was on duty at Kingston Cross with Constable Thomas Dorey, when the witness William Harding Hickley (deceased's brother) gave them information, which led them to go to Jubilee House. On arrival he saw witness George Hickley (deceased's father) standing at the front door, holding a revolver (produced), which he gave up to witness. He then went into the back sitting room on the ground floor, where he found Watts. Opposite him sat deceased with her head and right hand resting on a settee. On seeing witness, Watts rose and said "Here I am, policeman. Is she dead?" He replied, "I think so" and lifting deceased's head, found that she showed no sign of life. He noticed a wound behind her left ear, and asked if a doctor had been sent for. Mr. Lancaster informed him that Dr. Blackman was coming. Watts then said "Why did she not answer my question? I was drove to it, but I love her like I love my life, and we will both die together." He then noticed that his left arm was bleeding, and lifted the limb, which Watts said had a bullet in it. He asked him to tie it up, and he did so with a piece of rag. He then said to Watts, "I shall arrest you for lawfully shooting this woman." He said "All right policeman, I'll go quietly."

Witness left his brother constable in charge of the room and took Watts to the Buckland police station. Subsequently he charged him with "wilful and maliciously murdering, killing and slaying Esther Emily Watts, his wife, with a loaded five chambered revolver at Jubilee House, Twyford Avenue, Stamshaw, at 4.30 p.m. on the 4th inst." In reply to the charge Watts asked "Is she dead." Prior to charging Watts witness said "I am about to charge you, but before doing so I caution you that any statement you may make will be taken down in writing and may be used for or against you at your trial." On searching him witness found seven ball cartridges in the left pocket of his coat with a receipt relating to a constabulary revolver and fifty cartridges showing that 1s. had been paid on account. The weapon was bought from James Sprunt and Son, 78 Loampit Vale, Lewisham, for 14s. 9d. on March 28th. Prisoner had also in his possession one army and two naval discharge certificates, a letter dated April 3rd, 1891, and the bed ticket give him at the Speedwell. The letter was read by the Coroner's clerk, as follows:

Stamshaw, 3rd April, 1891
Dear Esther,

Will you give me an interview with you outside your own door, that is, where you are living, tonight? I am not drinking and if you will not accept of it, that is, the few shillings I have to spare, let the boy have the same. Answer this "Yes" or "No," as I shall go to London tomorrow by the 8 a.m. train. Answer this at once, and oblige,
Yours etc,
R Watts.

P.S. Give an answer to the bearer, "Yes" or "No." If "Yes," I will come as soon as brings the word. If "No," I shall go to London in the morning on account of my work.

Yours etc,
R Watts.

On the back of the letter was written,

"All lies, no truth in it."
Yours, etc., R.H.F.W.

Watts was sober, and appeared to understand what was taking place. Detective Money said that he visited Jubilee House shortly after six o'clock on Saturday and afterwards examined the back sitting room. On the floor near, and to the right of the deceased, he found a button, which corresponded with those on the dress worn by her. On the floor under the settee, about 18 inches from the body, he discovered a portion of a brooch, bent, and close to her feet he picked up a novelette soaked with blood, and with a hole in it. The letters dated March 21st, 26th, and 28th, and April 1st, he found on the sideboard in the room.

The four letters were read by the Coroner's clerk. The first three were dated from 294, New Cross Road, New Cross. They all commenced, "Dear Esther," and the following is their gist:

In a letter dated March 21st. Watts wrote: "I now send these few lines to inform you I have sent Arthur's things by Parcel Post, You can tell him from me I shall see him soon. I am coming down to Portsmouth during the Easter holidays, and I will then give you something in the form of money. So I will now close, hoping you and the boy are quite well, as it leaves me at present, under the circumstances, and I beg to remain yours as in years gone by, only broken-hearted, E. WATTs.

The letter of March 25th ran: "I am leaving our old home today. I have sold nearly all the things. . . . I am still not drinking. I have not had any since you have gone, and I can assure you this has been a lesson for me this time. I have got a situation on the new line from East London to Shadwell, and my money will be 4s. a day, with one night extra a week, making 28s. a week. I wish to ask you if you will accept the balance of my pension, and I will remain up here all the summer and pay everyone what we owe and save 15s. a week towards what we owe, and at the end of the year I will come to Portsmouth to you. Give me this chance, and I assure you it will never happen again. It never did while we were in Portsmouth before, and if anyone can tell you I am drinking or doing wrong during this year, you can send to me to say so and never look upon my face again,. So think well of this, and let me know as soon as you can. You didn't do a womanly trick in going and leaving me to pay the debts the best way I could, but, God knows, I freely forgive you. From your loving and broken-hearted husband, E. WATTS (Six crosses followed the signature.)

On March 28th Watts wrote: "I now send you these few lines to ask you the reason you have not answered my letters…. I have got to go to work on Tuesday morning next at Humphrey's boiler factory, at 6d. an hour, with half a day overtime every night, with the exception of Saturdays, as they are so very busy. Do try and answer this before next Friday, because when I got my pension if there is no letter from you I shall go to Wales with a steam trial party. I shall be in Portsmouth for the Easter Review on Monday next. I may see you but you won't see me, not if I can help it, not until I have got an answer. Your loving husband, E. WATTS."

The letter of April 1st was dated from 28 Cranbrook Street, Deptford, and read as follows: "I now send these few lines in answer to your letter I received last night, and I am sorry to think you will not look over it on the conditions I mentioned, which I think you have misunderstood. I told you if I was in good work and kept myself as a man should do, and would during the whole of the time send as much money as I could every week, also my pension every quarter, as I got it. Could you look over it then, as living away from you is killing me and I know it is all my own fault. Send a letter in answer to this as soon as you get it so that I may have the answer by Friday morning before I take my pension. If you don't send me word by then you may expect to see me in Landport by Friday evening, as I intend coming to see you and the boy unless you send me word. Your loving and broken-hearted husband, E. WATTS."

Witness had received from Dr. Blackman the clothing worn by deceased, and in the neck of the dress bodice he found the outside rim of a broken brooch. The following letter he took from the dress pocket:-

Kingston Cross, 3rd April, 1891
Dear Esther,
Just a line to tell you that I am in this town, and I wish you to bring the boy, and anyone else you like to me this evening. Meet me if you can, at 8.30 p.m. tonight, at Kingston Cross as I want to see you very much on important business. Send word back by bearer "Yes" or "No," as I shall go to my lodgings if you don't come and see me or tell me when you will come. I shall not be answerable for my actions.
Yours etc. E. WATTS.

P S. Send me word if you can come or not tonight, or when you will come to the same place by the person that brings this to you. I am in lodgings and it is costing me a shilling a night for the same, so answer this as soon as you get it, and let me know the result. Yours, etc, E. WATTS.

Witness went to the Speedwell on the same day, and in the room engaged by prisoner found a box of revolver cartridges wrapped in the sleeve of a woollen jersey.

Dr. Josiah George Blackman having given similar evidence to that given before the Magistrates, the Coroner summed up, and the Jury at once returned a verdict of WILFUL MURDER against Henry Edward Fawcett Watts. The Foreman added "We wish to make a strong recommendation as to the sale of revolvers which at present exits, more especially as this one was bought on the instalment system, the purchaser paying a shilling deposit and taking possession of the weapon. We desire to urge upon the Government the necessity of passing some law whereby licenses for the possession of revolvers should be obtained, and every person holding one should be registered. In this case a man obtained a revolver very easily, and brought it from London to murder a woman in cold blood."

FUNERAL OF THE VICTIM.
On Thursday amidst every demonstration of sympathy, the remains of the victim were laid to rest at the Portsea Cemetery, St. Mary's Kingston. The coffin bore upon it seven beautiful wreaths and a floral cross sent by sympathising friends, including the employees of the Brunswick Laundry Company. In the first carriage were Mr. and Mrs. Hickley, father and mother of the deceased; Mr. John and Mrs. Gay, brother-in-law and sister; and Mr. Joseph and Mrs. Lancaster, brother-in-law, and sister, while in the next were seated Mr. Lancaster and Miss Hickley, Mr. Gay, and Miss Kate Hickley and Mr. Savage and Mrs. Hickley. The procession passed through Winstanley Road, Stamshaw Road, Derby Road, London Road, Buckland Road, and St. Mary's Road, to the Cemetery where it was received by the Rev. W. Matson, the Nonconformist minister of the Cemetery, and conducted to the mortuary chapel when the first portion of the funeral service was read. The progress of the procession from the chapel to the grave on the unconsecrated side of the new ground, a considerable distance away was slow and impressive, large numbers of people joining it on the way. At the grave-side, too, a large number of spectators had assembled, but everything passed off in the quietest possible way, and Mr. Matson having delivered the brief remaining parts of the service the crowd dispersed, and, the mourners having returned to the carriages in waiting, another scene in this terrible tragedy was completed. The whole of the arrangements were carried out by Messrs G. Andrews and Sons.

EXECUTION AT WINCHESTER.
On 26th August, Edward Henry Fawcett Watts, who was sentenced to death at the recent Hampshire Assizes for the murder of his wife Esther Emily at Portsea, was executed at eight o'clock yesterday morning at Winchester Gaol. Berry was the executioner. Only a few reporters were admitted to the execution, but, as usual, a number of persons congregated in the roadway to watch the running up of the black flag.

1891 – SERIOUS FIRE AT PORTSMOUTH.

Late last night a fire broke out in Church Lane, Portsmouth, involving the partial destruction of a long range of workshops and stages. The building, which is very old, contained a large quantity of straw and other highly inflammable material, and the flames quickly broke through the roof, and shooting high up into the air created a lurid glare, which could be seen at a distance of several miles. The summit of St. Thomas's Church and the trees in the churchyard were brilliantly illuminated, and the night being very dark the scene, from a spectacular point of view, was exceedingly fine.

Mr. George Hopkins, whose house, in the Red Lion yard, is within a few feet of the workshop occupied by Messrs. Robert Polton, and Co. builders, plumbers, house decorators, and gasfitters, was one of the first to discover the fire. He had retired to rest shortly before eleven o'clock, and was about to get into bed, when the reflection of the flames arrested his attention, and he then found that Messrs. Polton's premises were on fire. Two horses standing in the stables immediately below the workshop were quickly rescued, and another horse and a goat, in an adjoining stable, were also removed from danger.

At Southsea the position of the conflagration could be easily determined at a glance, and fears being generally entertained for the safety of the old parish church, large numbers flocked through Pembroke Road into High Street, and swelled the crowd already gathered there from the immediate neighbourhood. The spectators, to their credit be it said, were very orderly, and in no way hampered the movements of the firemen. Within a few minutes of the outbreak the hose kept at the fire station in Pembroke Road was on the spot and connected to two hydrants in Church Lane, from which a copious supply of water was poured into the burning building. The alarm was telephoned to the central station at Landport, and the steam engine and other appliances were taken to the scene of the fire without the slightest delay.

The Chief Constable (Mr. A. W. Cosser) assumed command, and under his directions five deliveries, two from the engine and three from hydrants, were brought to bear upon the flames, which were localised and practically extinguished within half an hour. The borough constables were generously assisted by Garrison Sergeant-Major Dillon and a staff of military policemen, and the services of a party of Royal Artillerymen from Cambridge Barracks was also proffered, but the Chief Constable thought it unnecessary to trouble them, and sent a message of thanks for the kind offer. Mrs. Maria Snook, of Hampshire Street, Southsea, is the owner of the property. The origin of the fire is unknown.

1891 – BROTHEL KEEPING.

On Tuesday at the Portsmouth Police court before the Mayor (Sir W. Pink) and G. Curtis and A. S. Blake, Esqs., Robert Desk was charged under information for having on the 13th, 15th, 16th, 17th, 21st, 23rd, 25th, and 28th of September kept the house 7 and 8, Little Charlotte Street, Landport, as a brothel, and Mary Ann Deck, his wife, was charged with assisting in the brothel.

Mr. G. H. King prosecuted, and Mr. Hobbs (Hyde and Hobbs) represented the defendants. Formal evidence having been given by Mr. Kent, a rate collector, as to the premises in question being in the occupation of the male defendant.

P.S. Palmer stated that he visited the house on Sunday, the 13th ult., and saw there three women, who were known as prostitutes. Mr. King: Are they living there? – Witness: Yes, there are six living there. Witness continued by stating that earlier the same evening he had visited the house, and when, by permission, a search was made for a man for whose apprehension they held a warrant. The female defendant on that occasion told them that she had nobody living in No. 8, but that she had five women living in No. 7. Witness saw two men go to the house about twelve o'clock that night. Mr. Hobbs: How do you know these women to be prostitutes? – Witness: They told me so themselves and one of them said she had been "on the old town" for years. Witness also said that he had on later dates seen men and women go to the house.

Chief Inspector Bidgood stated that he was with the previous Witness on the 13th, and at the door he at first saw two little girls. When they were allowed to go over the house one of the women (Sherratt), admitted to him that she obtained her living by prostitution. Later, after he had seen a man enter the house he saw the male defendant, who refused them permission to go over No. 8, adding "You have been here once before tonight; you can go over No. 7, but not over No. 8 without a warrant." Witness afterwards heard the door the shut, and the lights were put out, so that they were prevented from going over any part of the premises.

P.C. Phillips stated that he watched the house between eleven and twelve on the night of the 13th and he saw one prostitute go there.

Mr. Hobbs remarked that Mrs. Deck had let her house to lodgers, and if every lodging house was to be watched in the borough as this had been by the police it would entail great hardship.

Mrs. Deck, the female defendant, after being sworn, said that the woman, Sherratt, never had lived in the house. One of the women was there to look after the (witness's) children, and another occupied a room. She let No. 7 out in rooms, and on Sundays the doors were closed at ten o'clock, and on other nights at eleven. Men never visited the house. By Mr. King: She had taken in a young woman named Steele as a friend, because her father had turned her out of doors. On the 13th there were four women in the house. One of them was the wife of a merchant seaman. Steele slept anywhere, sometimes on the sofa – but why on the sofa, when there are plenty of beds in the house? She slept with the children very often. She denied that Inspector Bidgood had asked any of the women how they obtained their livings, or that any of them had said that they lived by prostitution.

The male defendant also wholly denied the police evidence.

Caroline Wellard, who lived in the house, said she had seen nothing wrong since she had lived there. She was a married woman. Mr. King: How long since you were married? About six years. – What date? – I don't remember, – Where were you married? – At Hythe, in Kent. Witness admitted that she was separated from her husband, and now lived with another man, who was kinder to her than her husband. On being pressed, however, she said it was possible that on 17th and 18th a soldier had gone home with her, as she had visits sometimes from shipmates of her husband.

After some discussion, Mr. Hobbs, at length, consented that the whole of the cases should be taken together, and P.S. Palmer stated that on the 15th and other dates he had seen Wellard and other women go to the house with men, including soldiers and sailors, He also spoke to having seen immorality in the house on looking through the window. Witness continued by saying that the house was one of the worst places in the town. He had seen prostitutes go to both houses, where there were two children, from ten to twelve years of age. The defendants had also quarrelled and had used disgusting language.

Frederick Honeyfield, a neighbour, said it was of daily occurrence that women and men were going in and out of the premises.

After retiring for consideration, the Mayor said the Magistrates felt that there was not a shadow of doubt that the defendants knew that prostitution was going on in the houses. They dismissed the first case, but on that relating to the 15th they fined each defendant £5 including costs, or in default, one month's imprisonment each. On the six remaining cases they fined the defendants 10s. in each, or seven days' imprisonment in each. In all the fine was £16, and in default the imprisonment would run concurrently.

Mr. Hobbs said the fine was rather heavy, and he asked for time on the part of the defendants.

The Bench reluctantly granted until Friday to pay, but said that the proceedings had been greatly aggravated by the conduct of the defendants, it being to them a horrible thing that for the purpose of shielding themselves they should have gone into the box and have perjured themselves as they had.

George Stansfield, of Southsea the owner of the 30 premises, had been summoned under a like number of informations for being a party to the house being kept as a brothel Mr. Killby (Southampton) appeared for the defendant, but on the cases being called Mr. King intimated that he had withdrawn the whole of them.

1891 – SAD DEATH OF A DIVER.

Shortly after nine o'clock this morning a shocking fatality happened in Portsmouth Harbour, near the Portsea Pier, where a party of divers were at work repairing the moorings belonging to the Joint Railway Companies. The operations under the direct superintendence of Mr. Henry Muggridge, master mariner, in the employ of Mr. F. Bevis, contractor, who had with him in an open boat an experienced staff of workmen, who manipulated the diving apparatus. One of the party, a shipwright named Alfred Burton Luke, of 56, Charles Street, Landport, went to the bottom of the harbour in a stout diving dress and after examining the moorings which were dragged out of position during the gale of last week, gave the signal to be pulled up.

He reached the ladder fastened to the side of the boat, but before ascending to the surface returned below, it is believed, for the purpose of clearing one of the pipes which had apparently found some obstruction. Muggridge signalled to him twice to ascertain whether he was all right, but received no reply, and Luke was promptly pulled up into the boat. His helmet was removed, and it was then discovered that he was unconscious and apparently lifeless. The boat was pulled to the pier, and the unfortunate man was carried into one of the rooms in the Railway station, where he was seen by Dr. Colt, who pronounced him dead. The body was then removed to the Borough Mortuary at Landport by Constable Lashley, who took steps to prevent the removal of the diving gear from the boat, in order that the Jury may have an opportunity to inspect it if necessary.

An examination of the diving dress failed to disclose any fracture through which the water could have reached deceased, and the appearance of the corpse indicates death from suffocation. The interior of the dress was quite dry, as was also the plaid scarf taken from deceased's neck when the helmet was removed from his head, and it is believed that while he was endeavouring to secure a free passage to the surface his supply of air was suddenly cut off through the pipe leading from the pump in the boat being completely jammed.

1891 – "TIPTOE JOHNNY" GOES TO PRISON.

John Levi Devereux, of Smiths Lane, Portsea, a well-known character, who goes by the nickname of "Tiptoe Johnny," was summoned for having on the 14th instant assaulted Charlotte Devereux, his daughter-in-law, of 9, Whites Row.

Complainant stated that she was sitting by the bedside of her husband, who was in consumption, when defendant came in. He first jumped on his son's legs, almost breaking them, and when witness's mother said, "Don't do that!" he struck witness a severe blow in the back with his fist, saying "You ___!, That's for getting Mr. Porter to read to my son without my knowledge." Defendant: Oh! Speak the truth.

Witness, continuing, said the blow almost took her breath away. She ran out of the house to Mr. Murphy's shop for protection.

The Assistant Clerk (Mr. Fisk): Has the defendant interfered with you since then?—Witness: Yes, he's always interfering. He has come after me with an open knife up and down Kent Street and threatened to stab me.

Defendant (raising his hands in horror): Oh! (Laughter.) She has been fined in the Chichester Court, gentlemen.

Mary Ann Chandlers, a widow, the mother of the last witness, corroborated, defendant keeping up a running fire of expostulatory comments, such as "Hurt my child!"

The defence was a denial of the assault, and Devereux assured the Bench in tearful tones that all he did was to say he would sooner see his child die in the Union than in a brothel such as that house was, "and so I would, gentlemen," he added.

Two women were called for the defence, but appeared that they were not present at the time of the alleged assault. Defendant said his son was nineteen years of age, and "that woman" (meaning complainant) was forty, and "'most the worst woman in the borough,"

The Chairman said the blow was not a very serious one. Defendant would have to pay a fine of 20s., or go to prison for seven days.

Defendant, exclaiming "I'll do the seven days!" hopped with alacrity up into the dock, whence he was escorted below. "Not a farthing paid," he cheerfully remarked as he went. "Thank you, gentlemen."

1892 – A FATAL FRACTURE.

Yesterday afternoon the Coroner (T. A Bramsdon, Esq.) held an inquest at the Town Hall, on the body of Jane Howe Hart, lately living at 5, Fawcett Terrace, Fawcett Road, Southsea. The deceased was the widow of Edwin Hart, a lawyer's stationer, and she was 71 years of age. On the 30th of October she left home to visit a friend in Buckland, and at ten o'clock at night there a knock at the door, when the deceased's daughter (Mrs. Ellis) found her mother leaning against railings, supported by a strange man and woman. Her hip was greatly injured, and on Dr. Kelso attending found the right thigh fractured at the neck. The deceased afterwards told her daughters that when passing through Nelson Road, Landport, she met a woman, and changing sides they collided, and she was knocked into the road. She rested at Mr. Frampton's, in Commercial Road, but eventually went towards home by tram and bus, though she fell again in Fawcett Road from pain and faintness. Dr. Kelso continued in attendance, but death ensued at a quarter before six in the morning of the 29th ult. He attributed death to blood poisoning from bed sores, brought about by the accident, though she had got over the fracture and the shock. Witness added that the fracture must have been caused by the second fall. The evidence showed that the woman who had knocked the deceased down did not wait to assist her up, but the Coroner said he had no doubt she would see what the result of it was, and that she would be very sorry for what had happened.

The Jury returned a verdict of accidental death.

1892 – A HORRIBLE DISCOVERY AT HILSEA.

Yesterday afternoon a shocking discovery was made at Hilsea. In a field of wheat now being harvested, one of the reapers named Foote, while working near the hedge, saw what appeared to be a man's coat hanging from the bushes. Going closer to the object, he was horrified to discover the decomposed body of a man. The corpse, which was reduced to a skeleton, was in a kneeling position, the legs resting upon the ground, and a thin rope, attached to the branch of a small tree, was tied around the neck. Foote proceeded at once to Cosham Police Station, and gave information to Sergeant Andrews, of the County Constabulary, The officer accompanied the man back to the spot, and the remains were cut down and conveyed to a shed at the back of the Coach and Horses Inn, Hilsea.

Here the sergeant performed the sickening task of searching the clothes for some evidence of identification. The body itself being past all recognition, the flesh was almost entirely eaten away, presumably by vermin; here and there small pieces of skin, tanned to the colour and stiffness of leather, hung upon the blackened bones. Nothing was found in the pockets of the deceased's clothes to establish his identity, but the police sergeant knew that the man was missing from Portsmouth, and, as a result of his inquiries, the clothing was positively identified as that of William Twitchin, a wheelwright, who lived at Castlemans Cottage, Copnor.

The man had been missing for some time, and the discovery of his remains has cleared up the mystery attending his sudden disappearance. The cause which led him to commit the rash act, for it is clear that he hanged himself, is not known, but it may be remembered that at the end of June, Twitchin was arrested, and charged at the Portsmouth Police court with unlawfully wounding Emma O'Neil, his married daughter, by kicking her and breaking her leg. He was admitted to bail, but when the case was called on July 8th, he did not respond.

Mr. Freemantle, of Earnscliffe House, Copnor, and Mr. Emery, of the New Inn, Buckland, the sureties, appeared and said they had kept Twitchin in sight till the previous afternoon, when he suddenly disappeared. They further stated that he was last seen near Portsbridge in the afternoon, walking up and down, very much perturbed. There had been great trouble in the man's house. His wife had attempted suicide, and he was distressed by other worries. These, with the wounding case, had made him very depressed, and the sureties believed that he had committed suicide. They stated their opinion strongly, and their recognisances were discharged by the Bench.

1892 – THEFT AND DESERTION.

A court martial assembled on board H.M.S. *Victory* at Portsmouth this morning for the trial of John Jarvis, leading signalman of the *Iron Duke*, who was charged with deserting from that vessel, and also with stealing the sum of £12 7s. 4d., the property of the members of No.20 mess.

Captain E. Rolfe prosecuted, and the Court was composed as follows: – Captains J. Jones, H.M.S. *Malabar*, (President), A.C. Bromley, *Euphrates*, E. Gissing, *Volage*, Hon. P. C. Predergast Vereker, *Research*, and F. W. Fisher, *St. Vincent*.

Prisoner voluntarily pleaded guilty, and threw himself on the mercy of the Court. The circumstantial letter showed that the prisoner was a caterer of No. 20 mess, and in that capacity received from the paymaster on March 5th, the sum of £12 7s. 4d., "mess savings." He was entrusted with the money to pay the mess bill, and was granted leave of absence from March 5th to 7 a.m. on March 7th. He omitted to discharge the liability of the mess, and failed to return to the *Iron Duke* at the appointed time, but on the 29th ult., he gave himself up to the police at a place in Northumberland.

When brought on board the ship he had nothing to say in answer to the charges preferred against him, and could produce no part of the sum he had taken away when he deserted. Prisoner's certificates showed that he joined the Navy as a boy in board the *Impregnable* in April 1884, and had borne a very good character while serving on various ships.

The Court sentenced him to imprisonment with hard labour for a year and dismissal from Her Majesty's service.

1892 – A MARINE ARTILLERYMAN KILLED AT COSHAM.

An inquest was held yesterday morning at the Station Hospital, Hilsea, before E. Goble, Esq., County Coroner, touching the death of George Penny, a gunner of the Royal Marine Artillery, who was fatally injured at Cosham on Easter Monday by being knocked down and run over by a pleasure vehicle.

Garrison Sergeant-Major Dillon watched the proceedings on behalf of the military authorities, and an officer of the Royal Marine Artillery was also in attendance. The deceased was a married man, and his widow was in attendance at the inquest, but, in consideration of her feelings, the Coroner took the evidence of identification from Gunner J. A. Brooks, R.M.A., who stated that he had known Penny since 1884. He was 38 years of age.

Deceased returned to Eastney Barracks on Sunday from Bermuda, where he had been for three years, and on Monday afternoon witness and a comrade named Harry Gregory accompanied him to Cosham. He was perfectly sober when they left the barracks, and only had a share of two quarts of beer before they got upon a tramcar at Landport, and rode to Cosham. On alighting, they met a second class petty officer of the Royal Navy, who went with them into a public house near the railway station, where they had another quart of beer. He was positive that deceased did not visit the canteen at Eastney Barracks on Easter Monday, nor did he have any beer at dinner.

They were walking gently along the road at Cosham, and witness was in the act of handing a tobacco pouch to Gunner Gregory, when, in turning towards the latter, he saw a brake travelling towards Portsdown Hill. Deceased was then about a yard and a half behind witness, and the brake struck him upon the right hip, knocking him down. The accident occurred about 150 yards from the public house near the railway, and the footpath was crowded with people. Witness did not hear the driver or anyone else call out before deceased was knocked down, but when Penny fell some women screamed.

He heard no singing or shouting on the part of the crowd, and knew of nothing which would tend to drown out the voice of the driver, except perhaps the noise made by the brake, which was drawn by two horses. The animals were trotting when deceased was knocked down, and there were some people in the vehicle. He noticed no one on the right or left of the driver, whose seat was well above the head of the passengers. Deceased was struck by the front wheel of the vehicle and he seemed to spin round before he fell in front of the hind wheel, which passed over the lower part of the abdomen. Witness went to deceased assistance, and finding that he was unconscious, immediately carried him to Dr. Heygate. He was sure that deceased was perfectly sober when the accident happened.

By the Foreman: Deceased slept in barracks on Easter Sunday night. By the Coroner: The driver had a whip in his hand, but witness did not see him strike the horses. He saw some carts standing within four yards of the brake, but the driver, by pulling off, might have cleared them without running into witness and his companions. The driver pulled up from ten to fifteen yards beyond the spot where the accident occurred, and the passengers alighted and ran back to see what had happened to deceased.

Gunner Gregory gave corroborative evidence. He was in the act of taking his tobacco pouch from Brooks when he heard a shout, and looking behind, saw the hind wheel of the brake leaving the prostrate body of Penny. There had been no skylarking between witness and his comrades just before the deceased was knocked down, and witness heard the approach of the horses and the brake. He agreed with Brooks that they were all perfectly sober, and that there was plenty of room for the brake to pass them without accident. The pathway skirting the road was full of people, and for that reason witness and his companions were walking in the road. The horses attached to the brake were going "at a sharp trot."

Mr. Edward Jacobs, of High Street, Cosham, retired butcher and builder, said that he was sitting in his bay window upstairs and had a view of the spot where the accident happened. He saw the artilleryman and others trying to get out of the way of the brake, but could not say whether deceased was struck by the vehicle. He noticed deceased make an attempt to reach the pavement, and believed that in doing so he stumbled and fell between the two wheels, one of which went over him. He was then lying across the road, his feet being within 2ft. of the gutter. He seemed to lie between the wheels for a second or two before he was run over, and had he been a nimble man witness thought he might have got clear.

The brake was travelling at a moderate pace, and the driver had full command over the horses and properly observed "the rule of the road." Had the pedestrians done so there would have been plenty of room for deceased and his comrades to walk upon the pavement. The brake was about ten feet long, and witness thought that deceased had time to drag himself from between the wheels before the hind one reached him, seeing that he fell close to the fore carriage. There were a large number of visitors at Cosham on the afternoon in question, and vehicular traffic was carried on with considerable difficulty. Witness was of the opinion that no blame could be attached to the driver.

Mr. John Carter, a Juryman, observed that 20,678 persons passed Mr. Jacob's house towards the Hill between 12.15 and 5.15 on Easter Monday afternoon.

Andrew Charles Baulf, of 10, Pimlico Place, Church Path, Landport, said that he was the conductor of the brake referred to, which belonged to Mr. William Pannell. They were 25 minutes on the road from the Bedford Hotel to Cosham, and when the accident happened witness was in the body of the brake with three persons, a fourth passenger, named Charles Randall, being on the box with the driver. Randall was sitting on the near side. As the vehicle approached the deceased and his companions, the driver shouted, whereupon Penny reeled round to the right and "caught the side of the brake," which knocked him down. The driver was perfectly sober. Had the man stood still or turned towards the kerb, the vehicle would not have touched deceased.

Charles Randall, licensed victualler, of St. Thomas's Street, Portsmouth, said that he was seated in the body of the brake, close to and behind the driver, when deceased "slewed round" and seemed to stagger and fall. Witness did not believe that the brake struck deceased before the latter "slewed round," The driver was proceeding carefully through the street, in Cosham, and no one was in conversation with him at the time of the accident. He heard the driver shout out, warning pedestrians of the approach of the brake several times after passing the railway crossing, and he estimated the speed of the horses at four miles an hour. Could not say whether the driver shouted to deceased.

Dr. Heygate, of Cosham, said that deceased was brought to his surgery on Easter Monday evening. He was in a semi-conscious state, and evidently in great pain, his knees being drawn up, and his hands clasped across his stomach. His tunic was torn on the left side. Witness had him undressed and examined him, but could find no fracture. Some internal mischief was, however, apparent, and witness advised his immediate removal to the Hospital. A message was sent to Hilsea, but it was found that the only man on duty there could not leave, and a stretcher was obtained from the Police station.

Surgeon-Captain T. Winter, Army Medical Staff, said that he received deceased at the Hospital, and, on examining him, found no external mark of violence other than a slight abrasion on the left thigh. He became worse the next day, and died at 10.10 p.m. On making a post mortem examination, witness found a rupture of the intestines, which had set up inflammation, and caused death.

James Wheeler, the driver of the brake, was then informed by the Coroner that he might give evidence if he desired to do so, but warned that whatever he said would be taken down in writing and might be used against him should the inquest be followed by a criminal prosecution.

The Coroner then summed up, and commenting upon the sad circumstances attending the death of deceased, said that Penny had not seen his wife since his return from the West Indies, where he had been during the past three years, and she was expecting to meet him shortly, when he received his fatal injuries. With respect to the legal aspect of the case, he pointed out that a pedestrian had an equal right with the driver of a vehicle to the use of the road, notwithstanding the provision of a footpath marked by a kerb to give him additional protection from the perils of the street. It was the duty of the Jury, therefore, to determine whether Wheeler had exercised proper care in the management of the horses and the brake, and the question as to whether there had been any contributory negligence on the part of the deceased in walking in the road when the traffic was exceptionally heavy would also form an important element for their consideration. There was not the slightest evidence to indicate that any of the persons concerned in the case were under the influence of drink at the time of the accident.

After a brief deliberation in private, the Jury found a verdict of Accidental Death, exonerating the driver, James Wheeler, from all blame. Through the Foreman, Mr. Matthews, they also expressed their opinion "that greater precaution should be taken by the police or those in authority to prevent drivers of vehicles from halting in the street to feed their horses, turning long brakes in the middle of the street, or obstructing the thoroughfare in any way."

1893 – THE PORTSMOUTH TRAGEDY. THE CASE OF ADA URRY.

Public excitement at Portsmouth concerning the fate of Emma Downton, a child of five years, daughter of a paperhanger and decorator residing at Garnier Street, Fratton, who, as reported, had mysteriously disappeared on the previous Sunday afternoon, was greatly intensified when the police took into custody a girl named Elizabeth Ada Urry, and charged her with lawfully and feloniously enticing her away with intent to deprive Mr. Downton of the custody of his little daughter. The arrest was made on Saturday afternoon.

Elizabeth Ada Urry.

The prisoner, who is said to be about fourteen years of age, lived with her mother at 26, Alver Road, and the attention of the constables engaged in the case was first directed to her on Tuesday week, when she called at the Buckland Police station in company with her mother and Mr. Timpson, an uncle of the missing child, and handed over to Sergeant Brading some pieces of plush, which Mrs. Downton identified as having composed the "Mother Hubbard" bonnet which the missing child was wearing when she left home at a quarter past four o'clock on the Sunday afternoon in question to meet her sister Harriet, aged eleven years, who had gone for a walk with her two little brothers in the direction of Fratton Railway Bridge.

The girl Urry stated that she found the bonnet at about five o'clock on Sunday afternoon, lying between two boats on Southsea Beach, within a few yards of the Clarence Esplanade Pier, and after making inquiries of several persons whom she met in the vicinity of the spot, with a view to discovering the owner, had taken it home and cut it into pieces for the purpose of making dolls' clothes. Her attention had, however, been attracted to the published description of the missing girl, and this had induced her to come forward with the fragments of the bonnet and to tell all she knew concerning it.

Next day she produced a strip of cardinal-coloured ribbon, corresponding to the piece with which Emma Downton's long wavy hair was tied when she left home, and this, she explained, was with the bonnet when

ELIZABETH ADA URRY

she found it on the beach. Meanwhile, the police and others were diligently engaged in seeking a clue to the whereabouts of the missing child, but could find nothing further to indicate that she had reached the beach, nor were they able to discover anyone who had seen the girl Urry there about the time at which she alleged she picked up the bonnet. It transpired, however, that Urry was out on Sunday afternoon wheeling, in a double perambulator, a child about three years of age, who had been entrusted to her care by Mrs. Waters, wife of a greengrocer, carrying on business at 252, Fratton Road.

The girl went away from Mr. Waters' Shop with the perambulator about four o'clock, and did not return until nearly nine, when she left the child at the door, and hurried away before Mrs. Waters had an opportunity of questioning her as to why she had kept her baby out until such a late hour. Presently the police learned from a little girl, named Elizabeth Jane Langridge, who happened to be at Mrs. Urry's house when her daughter returned, that the bonnet was already cut into pieces when the latter first produced it from her pocket shortly after her arrival home; and witnesses also came forward ready to prove that she was near the Dog and Duck, within a short distance of the residence of the Downtons, at 4.20 p.m. She had had with her then a perambulator and one child, but at a quarter to five, when two other witnesses saw her on Fratton Bridge, another child, answering to the description of Emma Downton, was walking by the side of the vehicle.

From this point no further trace of her movements on that afternoon could be ascertained, but Chief Inspector Bidgood, who, during the absence of Mr. A. W. Cosser on sick leave, is acting as Chief Constable, considered the facts of which the police were then in possession sufficient to warrant the arrest of Urry, and, accordingly, a warrant was obtained and she was apprehended at her home on Saturday afternoon by Detective-Sergeant Money, and conveyed in a cab to the Town Hall.

On Monday the Police court was crowded when the prisoner was brought before the Mayor (Alderman R. Barnes) and other Justices, and remanded in custody for a week pending further inquiries. Still no clue to the whereabouts of the missing child could be obtained, and it was not until Tuesday that the mystery was solved. Unfortunately, the worst fears were realised, the lost child being found dead under circumstances which point to a far more serious charge than that of abduction. The shocking discovery was the result of a statement made by the girl Urry, at Kingston Prison, and communicated to Chief Inspector Bidgood, who, accompanied by Mr. Hobbs (Messrs. Hyde and Hobbs), the solicitor acting on behalf of the accused, and by Detective Taylor, and a clerk connected with the prison, proceeded in a cab to the site of some new buildings close to the Cemetery in Highland Road, Southsea, where they found a well about 19 feet deep and containing some four feet of water. Taylor obtained the loan of an implement used by bricklayers' labourers for mixing mortar, and, descending the well, dredged the bottom, with the result that something became entangled in the hooked end of the instrument, and the body of the missing child was drawn to the surface. Mr. Bidgood covered the little corpse with a sack, obtained on the premises, and at once conveyed it to the public mortuary at Landport, where a post mortem examination was conducted, by order of the Coroner (Mr. T. A. Bramsdon, J.P.) by Drs L. Maybury, police surgeon, and J. R. S. Robertson. The well in which the body was found was, on Thursday morning, pumped dry and carefully examined by Detective-Sergeant Money, who could, however, discover nothing tending to throw further light upon the case. Widespread sympathy with the bereaved parents is felt by all classes of the community, and the funeral of their little daughter, which takes place this afternoon at the Kingston Cemetery, will be attended by a large gathering of the teachers and scholars of the school to which the deceased belonged.

INQUEST YESTERDAY. IMPORTANT EVIDENCE. THE CHILD STRANGLED.

The Portsmouth Coroner (T. A. Bramsdon, Esq., J.P.) opened the inquest on the body of the child Emma Downton at half past two yesterday. Owing to the great interest displayed in the proceedings by the public, it was considered desirable to hold the inquiry in the Police court instead of the ordinary Court used by the Coroner, which is a much smaller apartment, and which contains very little accommodation even for an ordinary inquest. Mr. George Hall King watched the proceedings on behalf of the Public Prosecutor, and Mr. Hobbs (of the firm of Hyde and Hobbs) was present in the interest of the accused girl, Elizabeth Ada Urry.

The gallery was crowded by a most respectable audience, and large crowds of people assembled around the entrances. The Coroner took his seat upon the Bench at twenty-five minutes to three, immediately after which his clerk (Mr. Wilson Marsh) proceeded to swear a Jury of fifteen, of whom Mr. Charles Attree was elected foreman.

THE CORONER'S OPENING STATEMENT.

The Coroner then said he thought it would be as well if he give the Jury in a brief form, and in as simple language as possible, the facts and circumstances of this lamentable case. He should take care to do so without the slightest comment which could in any ways affect their minds in coming to a conclusion, but he would simply put before them the particulars with which he had been furnished from official sources to assist him in conducting the investigation. The child, whose death under such painful circumstance they were there for the purpose of investigating, was named Emma Downton, She was five years of age, and lived with her parents at 72, Garnier Street, Fratton. She was last seen alive by her parents in Garnier Street at about a quarter past four on the afternoon of Sunday, the 23rd ultimo. She had just returned home from Sunday school, and when she got indoors took off her jacket, but retained upon her head a "Mother Hubbard" bonnet with a covering of plush. She almost immediately left home, apparently with the object of meeting her sister, who had gone in the direction of Fratton Bridge. From this moment her parents saw nothing more of her alive.

He would now direct their attention to another girl, Elizabeth Ada Urry, who lived in Alver Road, a road running out of Fratton Road, and along the south side of Kingston Churchyard. Before the time mentioned, the girl Urry left home, expressing her intention of going for a walk. She, as it would be shown by the evidence, went to the shop of Mr. Waters, in Fratton Road, about 50 yards away, and asked Mrs. Waters to be allowed to take her little girl Dolly, aged three, out for a walk. The request was granted, and Urry took the child away, returning with her about an hour later. At this time Mrs. Waters was not at home, and Dolly asked her father to allow Urry to take her out in the perambulator. This request was granted, and both Urry and Dolly again left, the perambulator at this time being in good condition.

The next time Urry was seen was about twenty minutes past four, directly opposite the Dog and Duck public house, when she had Dolly Waters with her in the perambulator. He proceeded to describe the locality of this public house as being within a very short distance of the end of Garnier Street, where Mr. and Mrs. Downton resided. She was seen here by a girl named West and by another girl named McInallen, both of whom spoke to her. At this time she was also seen by a girl, named Davies, who was standing at the corner of Penhale Road. Urry was seen to proceed in the direction of Fratton Bridge, and when opposite the Cooperative Stores Davies, who had overtaken her, noticed that she had two children in the perambulator.

When near Fratton Bridge, Urry was again seen with the perambulator and two children, this time by Miss Elizabeth King, who was accompanied by a man named Brewer. These persons would be able to fix the time, and would tell the Jury that the youngest child was in the perambulator and the other walking by its side. From that time nothing was seen of them until 35 minutes past five, when they were seen by a person named Curtis. On this occasion they were sitting on one of the iron seats in the front of Western Parade, Southsea, Curtis being seated on a seat in front of Southsea Terrace. Here they remained until twenty minutes past six.

Next they were seen in the vicinity of Lump's Fort by Mrs. Wise, wife of Captain Wise, who had occasion to speak to Urry, as she was in danger of letting the perambulator fall into the water. The next occasion they were seen was at twenty minutes to eight, when they were observed by a lamplighter named Loveridge near Nazareth Home, in Lawrence Road. His attention was called to them as he was lighting the lamps, by the fact that the deceased had no jacket on. After this nothing was seen of Emma Downton alive. Later in the evening Urry returned to Mr. Waters' with the child Dolly and the perambulator, and then proceeded to her home in Alver Road, where she told her mother she had picked up a child's bonnet between two boats near the Southsea Clarence Esplanade Pier, and in the presence of a Mrs. Langridge produced it.

Later on bills were published announcing the disappearance of the deceased, and on the following Tuesday the pieces of the bonnet were taken by Mrs. Urry to the Downtons, who identified them. Later on the girl Urry was apprehended on a charge of taking the girl away, and she was now under remand on that charge. On Tuesday last, while in the gaol at Kingston, she expressed a wish to make a voluntary statement, whereupon she communicated with her solicitor, who came to the prison, and by his advice and with his concurrence she made a statement which would be produced before them, As a result of this statement the police went to Southsea, and in a well near the Highland Road bridge found the body of the deceased. The well was one used by bricklayers, and was about six feet wide and contained about six feet of water. When taken out of the well she was found to have an ordinary pocket handkerchief round her neck, tied tightly with a double knot at the side of the ear. A post mortem examination had been held, the results of which would of course, be laid before them, but he might say now that the cause of death was strangulation and not drowning.

It would be for the Jury to say how the child got into the well, and further whether any person had been guilty of any crime. He ventured no opinion on the evidence at this stage but he thought he had said enough to enable them to grasp the points as they would be laid before them by the several witnesses who would be called. He had had proper plans prepared to assist them still further in their investigation. He would now ask them to go and view the body in the mortuary, and then they would come back and proceed with the evidence.

VIEWING THE BODY.

The Jury then proceeded to view the body of the unfortunate child, which was lying on a slab in the Public Mortuary in Park Road. A large crowd of people had assembled round the entrance, of course, none but the Jury and members of the Press were allowed inside the building. Mr. Thomas Downton, father of the child, identified the body.

THE PARENTS' EVIDENCE.

Mr. Downton was the first witness called. He stated that he was a painter, plumber, and decorator living at 72, Garnier Street, and deceased, his daughter, was five years of age. He last saw her alive on Sunday week, when she returned home from Sunday school. She was then wearing a "Mother Hubbard" bonnet, pieces of which he now identified, together with a piece of ribbon which was tied around her hair. She went out alone to meet her sister, and when next he saw her she was lying in the post mortem room. She took off her jacket before she left home.

By the Jury: Do you know anything of the handkerchief found around her neck? – No sir, no knowledge of her possessing anything like it. No.

Harriet Downton, the wife of the last witness, said she was the mother of the deceased. She last saw her daughter alive at a quarter past four on the 23rd ult. A quarter of an hour previously she had come home with her sister, who went out again. At the time mentioned deceased put on her bonnet and went out, saying she was going to meet her sister. Witness identified the articles produced as the trimmings of her child's bonnet, and the ribbon as the piece which was tied round her hair. On seeing these things Mrs. Downton broke down, and for a minute or two sobbed quietly.

The Coroner: Do you know the girl Urry? – Witness: I had never seen her before this happened. – And you never gave her any authority to take your child out? – No, none whatever.

Deceased had a cough, and appeared to be rather tight on her chest from the effects of a cold, but otherwise she was in good health. On Tuesday evening, about nine o'clock, Mrs. Urry came to her house, and taking a piece of plush made up into a doll's hat from her pocket, said, "Does this belong to your child's bonnet?" – By the Jury: Had you ever seen Mrs. Urry before, or had you any knowledge of her living in the neighbourhood? – No, she was a complete stranger to me. At what time did deceased's sister return home? – About 20 minutes after Emmie went away.

PRODUCTION OF THE BONNET.

John Timpson, coach-builder, of 50, Sultan Road, Landport, deposed that deceased was his niece. Witness recognised the pieces of material produced as belonging to the bonnet which he had seen her wearing on several occasions. About twenty minutes to ten o'clock on the night of Tuesday week he was in Fratton Road, near Kingston Road, when he met Mrs. Urry and her daughter Elizabeth Ada, in company with Mr. Simeon Downton, brother of the first witness. He (Mr. Timpson) asked whether anything had "turned up" yet, and Mr. Simeon Downton replied "Yes, this person has been to Garnier Street with a bonnet. You had better take charge of it, and come to the Buckland police station with us." On the way to the station witness questioned the girl Urry, and she told him that she picked the bonnet up on the previous Sunday on the Castle side of Clarence Esplanade Pier. Witness said to Mrs. Urry, "Is it not strange that we have heard nothing of this before, ma'am?" to which she replied, "Well, I was away on Monday, or perhaps you might have done."

Part of the plush and trimming produced was handed to witness by Mr. Simeon Downton, and witness asked whether it was not strange that the girl should have cut up the bonnet, to which Mrs. Urry returned an answer to the effect that it was cut up while she was away from home. By that time they had arrived at the Buckland police station. Witness entered first, and told Sergeant Hayward who was outside. They all four subsequently entered the inspector's room, where they saw Sergeant

THE CHILD DOWNTON AND AN ELDER SISTER.

Brading. The latter had just come on duty, and Sergeant Hayward, who was leaving, said to him "A person has just arrived with this part of a bonnet. Will you take their statement?" Sergeant Brading accordingly took a note of the girl's name, address, and age, and questioned her concerning the possession of the bonnet, which she said she had picked up between two boats on the beach near the Pier.

He then asked her if anyone saw her pick it up, and she answered "No." Asked whether she saw anyone about near the spot at the time, she said, "Yes, there was a person close at hand with a child in her arms. I asked her whether it belonged to her or whether she knew anything about it." The woman said that she did not know to whom it belonged. Urry, in reply to further questions, said that she believed the child in the woman's arms to be about two and half years old, and that she had another little doll's bonnet at home which she had made out of the same material as that which she had brought with her.

Sergeant Brading thereupon said, "You had better let us have the whole of what you have got," Witness offered to accompany her to her home to get the other portion, but she said "No, I will run on ahead myself, and if you will come on down, I will meet you at Kingston Church." When witness got to Kingston Church, (the corner of Alver Road) the girl Urry was waiting there, she having another portion of the bonnet, made into a doll's hat with her. She gave this to Mr. S. Downton, who accompanied witness, and took it to the station. Mrs. Urry said she was sorry she had not thought of producing the bonnet before, and hoped they would soon find the missing child. The whole of the time the girl Urry was with them she was very silent, and hardly said a word.

The next day witness was at his brother's house in Garnier Street, when the girl Urry came there, and said she had come to see how Mrs. Downton was. Detectives Money and Digweed were at the time in the house, and at their request they had a private interview with her in the front parlour. After the police had gone, witness asked her if the pieces of bonnet she had produced were all she had. She replied, "I believe so." Mrs. Downton remarked that on there was some lace in the bonnet, and when witness pressed the girl about it she said it must have been the pieces of lace she had burnt. "What right had you to burn them?" witness asked, and the girl replied that they were dirty and of no use to her. He asked her then if she was certain she had nothing else at home, and she informed him that she might perhaps be able to find a few pieces if she looked. He urged her to do so, and she promised to bring back anything she might find, but she did not return to the house. Witness also questioned her as to which way she went to the beach, and she told him that she passed along Fratton Road, returning over Somers Road bridge and through Besant Road at about half past six o'clock. She also said that she passed by the end of Garnier Street on her way home, the bonnet being then in the perambulator. There was nothing in her conduct or demeanour which attracted your attention? – No, sir. I can't say that there was. Did either the mother or the girl Urry say anything to lead to the belief that they had seen the child? – Nothing whatever. Did you ask the girl Urry point blank if she had seen the child? No. I suppose it did not occur to you? – No.

Mary Ann Atkins, wife of William James Atkins, labourer, of 62, Garnier Street, stated that at nine o'clock on Tuesday week she was at the residence of Mrs. Downton, when Mrs. Urry knocked and was admitted. To witness, who opened the door to her, she said that she thought she might be able to throw a little light upon the case, and would like to see the mother of the child. Mrs. Downton exclaimed "I am her mother," and Mrs. Urry, going into the room in which she was sitting said, "Would you know the child's bonnet if you were to see it?" Mrs. Downton replied "Yes, in a moment," and upon Mrs. Urry showing her the doll's hat produced, and asking "Is this anything like it," the mother, without hesitation, said "That is part of my child's bonnet."

Witness took it from Mrs. Urry's hand, and Mrs. Downton then threw herself upon her, exclaiming "If you have brought my daughter's bonnet back, give me back my child." Witness handed the material to Mr. Downton, and proceeded to attend his wife, and was in a fainting condition. Before Mrs. Urry left the house, witness asked her whether that was all she had found; to which she replied "No, the bonnet was cut up in my absence." Witness did not know whether she said she was "out of town" or "had gone to town" at the time the bonnet was taken to pieces.

By the Jury: She saw the girl Urry on Wednesday morning at the Downton's house, and heard her say, in answer to a question by Mrs. Downton, that she found the bonnet lying open with the hair ribbon inside it. Mrs. Downton also questioned her about the lace on the bonnet, and she at first denied that there was any on it. Mrs. Downton, however, persisted that there was, and Urry finally admitted that she had had it, but as it was dirty, she burnt it. The mother then asked her what had become of the shape, and this question seemed to confuse the girl, who, after some hesitation, replied that there was no wire to that.

Simeon Downton, 20, of Cuthbert Road, Kingston, a painter and decorator, stated that, on Tuesday 25th ult, he was at the house of his brother, the first witness, when Mrs. Urry came in. The bonnet produced was handed to him by his brother, and he requested Mrs. Urry to call her daughter and accompany him to the Police station. She did so, meeting Mr. Timpson near

Kingston Church on the way. Mrs. Urry requested him not to let her daughter know that the bonnet belonged to the child, as the girl was hysterical. Witness, after giving up the piece of material first produced by Mrs. Urry, received other fragments of deceased's bonnet from the girl Urry, and took them to the Station, where they were received by P.S. Brading.

Police Sergeant Brading stated that at 10.15 p.m. on Tuesday, the 25th ult., he went into Buckland Police station, and saw in the Inspectors' room, Mr. Timpson, Mr. S. Downton, Mrs. Urry, and her daughter, Elizabeth Ada. Timpson said to him "I think we have some clue in respect to the girl Downton, for this girl, (alluding to Urry), picked up the bonnet on Southsea Beach on Sunday last at five o'clock." He handed witness the doll's bonnet produced, and witness asked, "Is this a portion of the bonnet?" Timpson replied, "Yes." "Has it been identified'?" asked witness, and Timpson answered "Yes, by the little girl's mother and father." Witness asked the girl Urry where she had picked up the bonnet, and she replied on Southsea Beach, about five o'clock on Sunday evening. Witness asked her on what part of the beach, and she said, near the Pier, nearest Portsmouth, Clarence Esplanade Pier. It was lying on the side near the Southsea Castle, and she indicated a distance of about 20 yards. She found it lying between two boats which were the two nearest to the Pier. "Did anyone see you pick it up?" asked witness, and she replied "No." She further said that there was a woman near by with a child about 2 years old, and she asked her if she had lost the bonnet. Witness asked her if she had any more of the bonnet, and she replied that she had some more at home. Witness then said to Mrs. Urry, "We shall require every piece of that bonnet." She replied that she had seen the description of the bonnet that the girl was wearing who was lost from Garnier Street, and thought it answered the description of the bonnet her (Mrs. Urry's) girl picked up on Southsea Beach on Sunday evening. She added "I thought it would throw some light on the case, and I took a portion down to Mrs. Downton for her to see if it was the bonnet. I am anxious that it should be cleared up."

The Coroner: Did you ask the girl if all she had stated was true? – Witness: I did, and she said "Yes, all true." – Did she look confused? – No, not at all. You had no suspicion? – None whatever. She showed no signs of nervousness as far as I could see. Continuing, witness said that Mr. Timpson asked her if she had seen a child near the spot, and she replied "No." The party shortly left the station, and some time later Mr. Downton came back, bringing another portion of the bonnet with him.

By the Jury: Did not ask the girl Urry whether she made any effort to find the child.

THE JOURNEY WITH THE PERAMBULATOR.

Mary Ann Waters, wife of George Waters, a greengrocer, carrying on business at 252, Fratton Road, said that she lived within about 50 yards of the end of Alver Road. At three o'clock on the afternoon of Sunday week Elizabeth Ada Urry, who was known to witness, called at the house and asked if Dolly was in. Receiving an affirmative reply, she requested to be allowed to take her out, whereupon witness dressed her little girl, aged three years and four months, and handed her to Urry, saying, "You won't keep her out long?" She answered, "No. Until four o'clock," to which witness assented.

Witness went out herself at ten minutes to four o'clock, and on going back at 6.30 found that the girl had returned with the child, but had taken her away again. Witness grew very anxious, for Urry did not return again until a quarter to nine o'clock, when witness saw her approaching. She had then only one child in the perambulator. Witness exclaimed, "Wherever have you been with my child?" to which she replied "Out on the Common," or "the beach," witness was not certain which.

The perambulator referred to was the one produced. When asked whether the child had had anything to eat, Urry replied, "Yes," and then, wheeling the perambulator into the shop, said, "Have you sent round to my mother" to which the witnesss answered, "l should think I have, and your mother has been round here." The girl appeared both agitated and confused. Witness saw nothing of the bonnet produced. On the following Wednesday, when the detectives called, witness examined the perambulator, and found that a spring which had been previously damaged and repaired was again broken.

By the Jury: Did the girl Urry say anything about having taken another child with her? – No. Is it customary for her to take your child out? – No, I hardly ever let anyone take her out. The Coroner: Did your child's clothing appear as though it had been disturbed? – No, sir. The child was all right in every way? – She looked very cold, and was fast asleep, but her clothes were all right.

A Juryman: Did you notice any mark of lime upon the perarmbulator when Urry brought it home? – I did not notice the perambulator at all then. The Coroner: Was the perambulator used between that Sunday and the Wednesday following? – No. Did you on the Wednesday notice any lime marks upon it? – No. By the Jury: Had the girl Urry ever taken your child out previously? – No. Did your child say that she had been with another child? – Yes, but not until the detectives told me to question her.

The Coroner: I am afraid, gentlemen, we shall not be able to take too much about that. Did the child appear to be frightened when she came back? – Yes, sir, she spoke about a soldier. Was her clothing damp at all? – No.

Are you on intimate terms with the girl Urry? – No, not extraordinarily intimate. I knew her name, knew where she lived, and had seen her before, of course. The Coroner: You thought you could trust her? – Yes, I thought she was very nice. I knew no harm of her.

Mr. Waters, the husband of the last witness, said that between a quarter to four and four o'clock the girl Urry, who had previously asked his wife's permission to take his daughter out, returned to his house, and his child asked for her perambulator. Urry followed her in, and said, "She wants her pram." Witness let her have it. It was then in good condition. One of the springs had been broken, but was mended. Urry went off pushing his child in the perambulator. He was not present when they came back, but afterwards discovered that one of the springs of the perambulator was broken. By a Juryman: Which way did Urry go with your child? – Down the road, in the direction of Fratton Bridge.

TRACING THE ROUTE.

Mary Ann West, aged 16, living with her parents at 32, Mary Street, Fratton, said that at 4.20 p.m. on the afternoon of Sunday the 23rd, she was standing near the Dog and Duck public house, in Fratton Road. She was in company with Louisa McInallen. While standing there she met the girl Ada, who was wheeling the perambulator produced, which contained one child, little Waters, who was about three years old. Urry said, "Holloa!" and witness replied, "Holloa," and asked her if she was in service. She replied, "Yes." At that time witness noticed a girl named Louisa Davies standing at the corner of Penhale Road. Urry also saw her, for she remarked, "There's a little kid with a long dress on." Witness went on her way through Garnier Street, and Urry moved off in the direction of Fratton Bridge. The Coroner: Did you see any child about five years old with Urry? – Witness: No, sir. You are quite certain she only had the one child? – Yes, quite certain.

Louisa McInallen, of 30, Holloway Street, Landport, said that she was in the company of the last witness at 4.20 p.m. on Sunday week. They were outside the Dog and Duck, when they met Urry, and she heard the latter's remark concerning Davies's dress. Witness went into Garnier Street with West, Urry going away from them, in the direction of Fratton Bridge. Witness was certain that there was only one child with her then. By the Jury: She went straight home, but was at Mary Street when the clock struck five.

TWO CHILDREN IN THE PERAMBULATOR.

Louisa Davies, aged 15, of 48, Lincoln Road, said that on the afternoon of the 23rd ult, she was standing at the corner of Penhale Road, when West and McInallen made a statement to her. She walked down Fratton Road, and when opposite the Co-operative Stores she saw the girl Urry pushing a perambulator with two children in it. The Coroner: Are you perfectly sure of that! – Witness: Yes, sir; I am quite certain. She could not tell what their ages were, nor in what they were dressed. Urry, whom she had known for five years, was going in the direction of Fratton Bridge. By the Jury: She was on the opposite side of the road to Urry, and as she passed her the latter called out "Look at that kid with a long dress on." Besides the two children in the perambulator there was no one else with Urry. Witness was quite positive that the girl pushing the "pram" was Urry, for besides knowing her intimately, the remark she made caused witness to take particular notice of her.

Elizabeth King, a single woman, living at 37, Havant Road, said that at 4.45 on the afternoon of the 23rd, she was in Fratton Road, near Fratton Bridge, walking with a young man named Brewer. She there saw the girl Urry, whom she knew intimately, walking in the same direction as herself, wheeling a perambulator. There was one child in it, and one was walking by the side. One was older than the other, and she should think that the child walking by the side was between four and five years old.

The Coroner: Did you notice the child's bonnet? – Witness: Yes, it projected in front. It was a "Mother Hubbard" bonnet. Was the colour the same as that of those pieces of stuff produced? – Yes, I am sure it was of the same colour. Continuing, she said she drew her companion's attention to the girl, and they watched her and the children go towards Fratton Bridge. She did not notice either of the children particularly, and could not tell the colour of their dresses. Questioned by the Jury, witness said she had Urry in view for several yards, but did not see her speak to the child walking by the side of the "pram."

George Brewer, of 37, Havant Road, Kingston, seaman-gunner R.N, said that about a quarter to five o'clock on the Sunday afternoon in question he had just previously looked at his watch. The last witness called his attention to the girl Urry, who was pushing a perambulator, in which a child was sitting, with its face towards her. Another child, apparently between four and five years of age, was running alongside the perambulator. She was dressed in a red dress, but he could not say if she had on a pinafore or whether her head was covered by a bonnet or a hat. The girl was going over Fratton Bridge, in the direction of the beach. He saw Urry in Court, and identified her.

SEEN ON THE BEACH.

Lydia Wise, wife of Captain Wise, R.N., of Elphinstone House, Livingstone Road, Southsea, said that on the evening of Sunday, the 23rd ult., at about 5 p.m., she was on the beach near Lump's Fort, and saw there a girl, whom she wes certain was Elizabeth Urry, wheeling a perambulator. She did not recognise the perambulator produced as the one she saw, but had an impression that it was a double one of an old-fashioned type. The girl had two children with her, one of whom was the deceased. She identified the latter by her clothing, and parcicularly by the boots, which were somewhat shabby in comparison to her clothes. The child had on a "Mother Hubbard" bonnet made of material like that produced, and was also wearing a red frock with short sleeves.

Witness had not seen the child belonging to Mrs. Waters, and would very much like to do so. The Coroner: That can be arranged? Chief Insepector Bidgood: Oh, yes sir. Witness, continuing her evidence, stated that the girl was hurrying along the edge of the sea wall at a very fast rate, and witness, who noticed that the poor little child walking by her side appeared to be very tired, so tired, indeed, that she was swaying to and fro, rose from her seat and bade Urry be careful that the child did not fall over. The girl did not answer, but, turning to deceased, she exclaimed "Hurry along, or we shall be late home." They were walking in the direction of Eastney, and there was no man with them at that time. Witness had Urry in view for some distance, and saw her dragging the peramubulator up the beach. She was still on the sea wall with the children when witness last saw them. From first to last witness saw no one but the two children with the girl. By the Jury: She fixed the time from the fact that when she spoke to the girl she left the place where she had been sitting for the purpose of keeping an appointment, and it was ten minutes past five o'clock when she reached her destination. By the Jury: When Urry said, "Hurry along or we shall be late home," did the child make any reply? – No, but she looked at me so pitifully. But she made no reply? – No. Would you know the girl Urry again? – Yes, I have identified her.

STARTLING EVIDENCE. A SOLDIER SEEN WITH URRY.

Susan Curtis, cook in the employ of Major Addison, of 14, Cromwell Houses, Nightingale Road, Southsea, said she was sitting on a seat fronting Southsea Terrace on the afternoon of the 23rd ult. On the same seat was a gentleman friend of hers, She did not think he had anything to do with this case, but his name was Bothwell, She thought he was an engineer, but did not know where he lived. There was no one else there, and the time was twenty-five minutes to six by the clock in the officers' quarters at Victoria Barracks. On the seat in front of Western Parade she saw a soldier, a girl, and two little children. There was a "pram" there very much like the one in Court, It was behind the seat. The distance was not far. She went to the next seat, and had a good view. The girl, soldier, and children were on the second seat from the cabstand, and she was quite close to them. She could not say how many feet away they were.

The Coroner: You are not a judge of distance? – Witness: No. She had seen Urry, and had no doubt she was the girl on the seat. One of the children was about five years in old, and the younger about three. The former's dress was red, with a white overall or pinafore. The bonnet was a "poke" bonnet, which meant the same as a "Mother Hubbard" bonnet. Its colour was very similar to that of the fragments produced. The younger child was playing about, and the girl Urry and the soldier were on the seat together. She was not behaving quite as a girl of her age should. Witness thought her "fast." The girl did nothing seriously improper, but "carried on" with the soldier in a "gay" manner, and he "carried on" with her. He was young, about 20 or so. His uniform was red, and his cap was a round one; he had no stripes on his arms, and his trousers were black.

By Mr. Marsh (Coroner's Clerk): She could not say the colour of the band of the cap. She went away at half past six, and they were still there.

By the Jury: She thought the soldier's trousers had a narrow stripe. He had nothing on his shoulders, but his uniform was plain red with white pipings. She thought she would know the dress again. She shifted her seat out of curiosity. She had identified Urry at the gaol on the previous day. On the Sunday she had a short dress and grey cape. The soldier was fair, with a very full face and no moustache. During the time she was there she saw Urry take the youngest child and go, as she thought, into the Castle Hotel, and afterwards came out again and returned to the soldier. The soldier did not go, but stayed with the elder child (Downton). Witness had not positively identified the child at the Mortuary, but the deceased was similar in dress and size to the one she saw.

PRISONER AT THE CASTLE HOTEL.

Maud Amelia Collis, residing at the Castle Hotel, Southsea, said she was in the bar between six and seven o'clock on Sunday, the 23rd, when a girl, having a child with her, came in, and asked if she could go out to the back. Witness had not seen the girl Urry or the child Waters, and the Coroner observed that it would be much better if the police could arrange for the witnesses to see the children. The further examination of this witness was adjourned.

THE PUBLIC PROSECUTOR'S REQUEST.

At this stage of the proceedings, Mr. G. H. King observed that he was acting in this case on the part of the Public Prosecutor. He had been desired by the police to ask the Coroner if, in adjourning the inquest, he would adjourn it for a week, in order to give them every opportunity of making further inquiries. Of course in a case of such a serious character, it was desirable that every shred of evidence that could be obtained should be brought forward, and, in those circumstances, he asked the Coroner, subject to his convenience, to adjourn the case for a week.

The Coroner: I did think that we might be able to complete this investigation today, but I see now that that is impossible. The girl Urry will be brought before the Magistrates again on Monday?

Mr. King: Yes, but of course we shall not be able to complete our case that day. We shall go as far as we can, and then ask for a further adjournment. The Coroner intimated his intention of calling on as much evidence as possible today, and then adjourning.

URRY ANGRY WITH THE DECEASED.

Thomas Bishop, a leading stoker on H.M.S. *Victory*, then entered the witness box. He stated that on Sunday evening, the 23rd ult., he was on the Esplanade, when he saw the girl Urry about 150 or 200 yards this side of the New Pier. She was walking on the asphalt pavement, and was wheeling a perambulator containing a child aged about two or three years. There was another child following behind, and he saw Urry turn round to it, saying in a sharp voice, "Come on, you little ___." He could not catch the last part of her exclamation. A soldier was walking along near the girl, about two yards behind her, but witness did not see him speak to her. He belonged to the Royal Artillery, and he was wearing a blue coat, a white waist-belt, and a forage cap, with a yellow band around it.

The child, who was walking by the side of the girl, had on a red dress and wore a bonnet, the colour of which was similar to the material produced. By a Juryman: At what time did you see the girl Urry? – Witness: Just after sunset, about 7.30. In what direction was the girl going? – Towards Eastney.

URRY IN LAWRENCE ROAD.

Joseph Loveridge, of 61, Eselmont Road, Southsea, a lamp lighter, in the employ of the Gas Company, said that between 7.40 and 7.45 on the evening of the 23rd, he was in Lawrence Road in the act of lighting the lamp which stands opposite the Nazareth Home in Saxe-Weimar Road, when he saw a girl, whom he had identified as Elizabeth Urry, with a perambulator and two children, one in the vehicle and one walking by the side. He had seen the body of the deceased at the moturary, and was certain that the child he saw by the side of the perambulator was wearing the same clothes as the deceased. She had on a bonnet of dark material and no cloak or jacket. As he was passing he heard the child say "Home."

The place where he saw the girl and the children was about 500 yards from the well in which the body was found. When he saw them they were standing still, and Urry was bending over the elder child, as if buttoning something at the back of her neck. The front of the perambulator was pointed towards Albert Road. There was no soldier or anyone else with them at that time. By the Jury: Did you observe anything of the shape of the handkerchief around the child's neck? – I only saw some lace.

URRY'S RETURN HOME.

Helena Elizabeth Jane Langridge, a girl living at 50, Alver Road, Kingston, said that she was at Ada Urry's house at nine o'clock on the evening of Sunday week, whan Ada came home. Mrs. Urry was out at that time. Ada sat down in a chair for a few minutes and then pulled out of her pocket some pieces of plush, with which she tried to make a doll's hat. She went to work with a needle and piece of cotton, telling witness that she had picked up the plush on the beach. Witness left the house shortly afterwards, and knew nothing further of the matter.

PLANS PRODUCED.

Mr. Alfred Henry Bone, architect and surveyor, said he had surveyed the piece of land on the south side of Albert Road, between Exeter and Festing roads.` He produced a plan which showed that eight houses were in course of erection on the ground, and a second plan showing the immediate vicinity of the well in which the body was found, The well, he stated, was close to the rear of the houses, and immediately at the back of the fourth house. It was an ordinary well, such as was prepared by builders for procuring water for their work. It was 6ft. in diameter, and from the top to the water-line measured 13ft. The water, at its deepest point, was 3ft. 2in. A great portion of the upper part of the well was strutted with timber, and then, for a distance of 3ft, 6 in., there was wood cradling, and the remainder was bricked. Eleven feet down was a wooden stage, which enabled one to walk around the well. The top of the well was covered with scaffold boards, a small space of two inches being left between each couple of boards. At the side and on the ground were a tub and a pump used for getting the water from the well. Inside the well were two scaffold poles placed across to strut up the earth. In the condition in which he found the well on Wednesday, it would have been impossible for a child to fall down it without first removing the boards. A sheet of corrugated iron sloped down from the tub to the edge of the well, and a child might possibly crawl under this. Would it have been possible for a child to fall into the well and drop to the bottom without first touching the struts? – Yes. Is there a full view of the well obtainable from the workmen's shed? – Yes. By the Coroner: The width of the staging boards was nine inches, and there was plenty of room for a child to fall without touching them.

THE PRISONER'S STATEMENT.

Mr. Edward Simmons, the Governor of Kingston Prison, said there was at present in that prison a girl by the name of Elizabeth Ada Urry, who was on remand on a charge in connection with the deceased child. On Tuesday last, he learned from her solicitor, Mr. Hobbs, that she wished to make a statement, and she voluntarily, and with the consent of Mr. Hobbs, made the statement which he produced. The writing was that of one of his Clerks, Mr. Bleach, the signature was that of the girl Urry, and the attesting witness was himself. At the time the statement was made there was also present the Matron, Eileen Bertha Warman. The statement was as follows:

"I, Ada Urry, act on the advice of my solicitor, without any threat or promise of favour, wish to state that I saw Emmie Downton on Somers Road bridge, on Sunday, the 23rd April, 1893, somewhere about half past four o'clock in the afternoon. I asked her what was the matter, as she was crying. She said she wanted her sister. I asked her if she would come with me for a walk. She said yes, and I told her to take hold of the handle of the pram. There was in the pram a little child named Dollie Waters. We walked along as far as Clarence Esplanade Pier on Southesa Beach. Emma Downton was sometimes riding in the pram and sometimes walking. We stayed on the beach a little time, playing about, then went back over the Common to Castle Road. While on the beach we broke the spring of the pram by pulling it up with the children in it over the stones. After getting to Castle Road we went through a number of streets, of which I did not know the names. I think we came out by a side street near the Albert Road bridge, and then went over the bridge. When in the side street I missed Emmie Downton. This street runs out of a field, in which there are buttercups and dandelions. She had been walking at the side of the pram, and it was as I was just turning the corner that I missed her. Just before this she complained of being cold round her neck, and I had taken off her hat and put it on the pram and tied my handkerchief round her neck. When I missed her, I searched everywhere for her in the streets and in the field, but could see nothing of her at all, nor could I hear her cry out or make any sound. They were building a good many houses near there. Near the backs at the houses there was a well with a piece of corrugated iron over the top, which partially covered the entrance, leaving an opening large enough for a child to fall through. I looked down it. There was a hole in it, and the water was about as far from the top as from the gas is from the floor in this room (about four feet eight inches.) I could see nothing of Emma Downton anywhere. There were some pits there where the workmen make mortar. I searched round these, but could not find Emmie Downton anywhere. I went back to the pram. Dollie Waters had run to the corner of the street to look for me, I called her, and she came to me and I put her back in the pram. We then went up over the bridge, which I think is Albert Road bridge. We turned round by the iron church, just over the bridges, and then went to Dollie Waters' house in Fratton Road. Her father is a greengrocer. I left her and the pram, and then went home, taking the bonnet with me, and the strings were in it. I was very frightened at having lost the little girl, and was afraid to tell anyone about it, and I was afraid to say what had happened. When I left the beach I walked across the Common, and sat down on a seat where a soldier was sleeping. The children played about the green. He asked me whether I had come to wake him up. He said he belonged to Southsea Barracks. This was before we went to Castle Road. Emma Downton, said she wanted to leave the room, and I went to a public house, which I think is called the Castle Tavern, facing Castle Road, and one side faces the Common. A lady saw us and let us go through to the back."

ANOTHER STATEMENT.

Urry also wrote a letter, which witness initialled, in which she asked Detective Money to come up to the gaol. He came up, with Mr. Hobbs, on Thursday, and had an interview with her, in which she made another statement written by Detective Money. It was as follows:

Kingston Prison, – 4th May, 1893.

"I, Elizabeth Ada Urry, of my own free will, and by the advice and with the consent of my solicitor, desire to say that I am very sorry for the trouble I have given you, and for the stories I have told. But I have told the truth in the statement which I made on 2nd inst. to Mr. Simmons, the Governor of the Prison. (Signed), ELIZABETH ADA URRY."

The letter was attested by witness, and was made by the girl without promise of favour.

THE INQUIRY ADJOURNED.

At this stage of the inquiry the Coroner observed that it would be now most convenient to adjourn until Friday next, and asked Chief-Inspector Bidgood whether he had heard anything concerning the identity of the soldier who had been referred to. Mr. Bidgood said that every endeavour had been made by the police to find him, but without result.

The Coroner: I should think that with this publicity the soldier, assuming that there is no guilty knowledge on his part, will come forward and explain his conduct with regard to the case. Will you please communicate with the commanding officers of the various regiments with a view to finding the man?

Mr. Bidgood: We have already communicated with some of them, sir.

The inquest was then adjourned for a week.

AN IMPRESSIVE FUNERAL. URRY CHARGED WITH MURDER.

The funeral of the hapless child Emma Downton took place on Saturday at the Portsea Cemetery at Kingston, and was witnessed by thousands of sympathisers. The crowd in Garnier Street, where Mr. and Mrs. Downton reside, must have totalled from 3,000 to 4,000. The relatives were gathered in the front parlour. The Rev. L. Railton. Wesleyan minister, first read the 90th Psalm, "Lord, thou hast been our dwelling-place in all generations" He then said that as they were gathered there in a time of great trouble, he would read to them from the 15th chapter of the 1st Corinthians, which gave them that hope which would enable them to dry their tears even in their bitterest sorrow.

Having read this, he offered up an earnest prayer, during which the assembly knelt, the bereaved mother and the aunts of the little one weeping copiously all the while. During the latter portion of the service, and while the few final preparations were being made, the Sunday school children outside sang from their hymn-sheets the hymns, "Death has been here and borne away, A scholar from our side" and "Rock of Ages," being led by Mr. Campbell, the leader of the choir of St. Philip's Mission. Shortly before the starting of the procession the Washington car was decorated inside and out with numerous wreaths, crosses, and bunches of sweetly-perfumed flowers. On each side of the car, also, six girls were arranged, those on the right bearing handsome floral crosses and those on the left beautiful wreaths.

First came a Washington car, containing the little coffin, in which were the remains of poor little Emmie. The casket was of elm, covered with white velvet, embossed with a floral pattern, and was heavily furnished with silver-plated mountings. The plate on the lid bore the following inscription:

EMMA DOWNTON,
Died April 23, 1893,
Aged 6 years.

The plate also contained the text, running along the top and bottom: "Remember now thy Creator in the days of thy youth." The car was full of magnificent floral tributes of sympathy, and many were hung on the outside pillars. The carriages containing the mourners were five in number, and their occupants were:- First carriage: Mr. Downton (father), Mrs. Downton (mother), Mr. Timpson (grandfather), Harriet Downton and her little brother. Second carriage Mr. and Mrs. Atkins (uncle and aunt of the deceased), Mr. and Mrs. George Downton (uncle and aunt), Mr. and Mrs. E. Timpson, and Mrs. Downton (step-grandmother). Third carriage: Mr. and Mrs. Henry Timpson, Mr. and Mrs. John Timpson, Mr. and Mrs. Simeon Downton. Fourth carriage: Mr. and Mrs. W. Downton, Mr. and Mrs. George Tree, Mr. and Mrs. Rutledge. Fifth carriage: Mr. and Mrs. Smith, Master and Miss Atkins (cousins of the deceased), and the Rev. L. Railton.

Following these came other carriages, containing representatives of friendly societies and other bodies, and immediately after the last carriage came the procession of school children, numbering between five and six hundred. At the head of them walked twenty two of the deceased's classmates, little mites with sorrowful faces and carrying beautiful bouquets of sweet-scented flowers. Then there were two hundred or more children belonging to St. Philip's Evangelical Mission, about fifty being boys and the rest girls. There were also about two hundred children from the Wesley Chapel, Arundel Street, thirty from Victoria Road, Southsea, and more than fifty from the Penhale Road Chapel.

The procession, which was augmented on the way to Kingston, was organised by Mr. Sawyer, President of St. Philip's Mission, and the Secretary, Mr. Jeaking, and many teachers of the various schools were engaged in looking after their young charges. The children nearly all bore flowers of some sort, some of the bouquets being quite large and very handsome. Four members of the Penhale Road Ambulance Corps, under Mr. Mockford, were in attendance to act as bearers, and some of the wreaths were borne by other children.

The procession, on turning into Fratton Road, moved very slowly, owing to the densely packed crowds which lined the way on both sides, and which rendered locomotion extremely difficult. The windows, as in Garnier Street, were nearly all thrown up, and on both sides, the pathways were crowded, and it was impossible for the ordinary traffic to proceed. This was the case all the way to the Cemetery, on reaching which the cortege proceeded at once to the graveside, about which an open space had been kept clear for the accommodation of those chiefly concerned in the sad event.

The coffin was lowered, and the remains of the little one were consigned to the earth amid profound silence, broken only by the sobs and muttered prayers of those within reach of the officiating minister's voice. The opening strains of that well-known hymn "Rock of Ages, Cleft for Me," were next heard, and as the singing commenced the crowd began to surge and press forward until the barriers were broken down, and the remainder of the space which had been enclosed, immediately became filled by the general public. After the hymn, Mr. Thomas Hogben offered a short prayer, and as he made touching allusions to the sad fatality, he asked for comfort for the parents in their great sorrow. Mrs. Downton became convulsed with grief and had to be held up by her husband, who was also greatly affected. Following this the Rev. L. Railton recited the Lord's Prayer, in which the spectators joined, and then the well-known hymn, "Safe in the Arms of Jesus," was sung, the verses being read out one by one. "Only a few more trials, – Only a few more tears" sang the vast concourse of people, and as the pathetic notes rang out there were but few who were not deeply moved, and many women sobbed bitterly.

After the hymn the Rev. L. Railton delivered an impressive address, as follows:

"My dear friends, we are met here today under circumstances of no ordinary character. For ten days past, ever since it became known amongst us that a sweet little girl of five years was missing, and that no traces of her could be discovered, the heart of Portsmouth has been terribly moved. He would, indeed, be a skilful interpreter who could analyse and express for us all the various elements of thought and feeling which have been started by this unusual incident. As the days have gone by and the cloud of mystery which covered the disappearance of the little one has been, to some extent, lifted only, alas, to reveal a tragedy too terrible for words, we have all seemed, without reference to social rank and station, to gather round the home which has been so rudely invaded, and to utter our lamentations.

And here, today, we are brought together to commit to the dust the remains of her, who, though unknown to nearly all of us, has exercised such a potent spell over the entire population of the borough. Whatever else we may say at this moment, surely only voice, the deepest sentiment of the entire town when I turn to our stricken and mourning friends, and assure them of our sincere and heartfelt sympathy. Grief like theirs no stranger can interpret, but for the time being we seem to have become one family. Those of us who have children of our own have been especially touched, for might not the same sorrow have been ours? Oh dear friends, is there not something Divine about all this? Is there not a token that amid all the sin and sorrow over which we mourn, there is, as well, a broken shaft which speaks of a brighter past, and tells also of a future of hope? May this pathetic incident draw us all nearer to each other, and thus shall the Scripture be fulfilled, "A little child shall lead them."

During the period of sad uncertainty how much prayer has been called forth on the part of those who are used to pray, aye, and on the part of those who have been slow to pray. How comes this, that when pressing need arises we are so ready to call on God? Is it chance? Alas, that even those of us who profess to believe in prayer should need so much reminding of our privilege! but it is cause for thankfulness that on any ground we are led to make our wants and wishes known to God.

It was on Tuesday evening, when the whole matter was enveloped in mystery, that I was led to call on Mr. and Mrs. Downton, and offer them what consolation I could, and after our conversation, when one felt perfectly helpless effectually to aid, I proposed we should kneel before God, and open the case to Him, and ask Him that some clue might be given. Within an hour of that time the remnants of the little bonnet were brought to the house. Doubtless many others prayed besides those who were in that room, but the great fact is an answer came, and through that incident have followed all the other disclosures. Shall the little child who has led us to prayer lead us still further in the same direction? Shall we all resolve to bring our burdens of every kind to Him who has promised us succour in the hour of need? "Call upon me," said the Lord, "in the day of trouble, and I will deliver thee, and thou shalt glorify Me."

But more. What a shock has come to us to know that a crime so awful as this should have been slumbering in our midst. We are not yet assured of all the circumstances, and although one unhappy girl, who is present to all our thoughts, seems deeply implicated, how relieved we should be to know that upon one so young there does not rest the full incidence of the guilt. But here is the lesson from the old Book again, "Be sure your sins will find you out." Portsmouth's sin is very great. Much of it is secret, and much of it is public. The secret sin will become public soon. There are detectives in God's Kingdom, and everything will be brought to light. Let us not be deceived, "Whatsoever a man soweth, that shall he also reap" and this applies to high and low alike.

Our Sabbath-breakers will be brought to justice, our sweaters, our drunkards, our formalists; nothing is to be hidden; all shall be made manifest. We speak of the keen discernment of our police force, which cannot be too highly praised, but there is an eye which searches into the hearts of the children of man. "All things are naked and open to the eyes of Him with who we have to do." "God will bring every work into judgment, and every secret thing, whether it be good or evil." We shall be arraigned, each one of us, and happy they who have betaken themselves to Jesus the stronghold of hope, for they shall be without condemnation in that great day.

But shall we not follow the little child further? Where is she now? Is she not folded in the Good Shepherd's Arms; in the arms of Him who said, "Of such is the Kingdom of Heaven"? Through the blood of the great sacrifice she has entered into the Eternal Light, Her endless felicity has begun, and the Lamb shall lead her to fountains of living water; all tears are wiped from her eyes. Dear, mourning friends, lift your eyes and hearts Heavenward. Your little one cannot return to you, but you can go to her, And so may we all. But there is no entrance into that lovely Paradise but one. "'There is one God and one Mediator between God and man – the man Christ Jesus." All other mediators are but a grand impertinence. "I am the door," saith He; I am the way. I have the keys of death and of the grave." Through Him we all may have access into the favour and into the Kingdom of our God, We must commit our cause into His hand, for nothing is more clear in the Word of God than this, that "there is none other name given under Heaven among men whereby we might be saved but the name of Jesus."

When the shepherd would have his flock go through some narrow entrance, he not unfrequently sends forward into the fold a little lamb, after whom the mother, yea, and the great family behind, follow, and they find safety and provision abundant. So may it be in this case, Led by this little child, may we all leave our sins, and, being washed in the blood of the Lamb, pass through the gates into the City where all the nations that are saved do walk."

While Mr. Railton was speaking, the great crowd maintained absolute silence, broken only by a low murmur when he mentioned, the unfortunate girl who is connected with the tragedy, and a deep "Amen," solemnly uttered, as he spoke the words of sympathy and comfort to the parents. At the conclusion of his addresses another hymn, "Death has been here and borne, away," was sung, and was followed by a second prayer, delivered by Mr. Sawyer, of St. Philip's Mission, Fratton. The Rev. L. Railton then pronounced the Benediction, and the ceremony came to an end. The whole of the funeral arrangements were in the hands of Mr. Roberts, Sen. of 74 Fratton Street, who, notwithstanding the great difficulties he had to surmount, carried out his work in a way that is deserving of the highest commendation.

AT THE POLICE COURT.

At the Portsmouth Police court, on Monday, before the Mayor (Mr. Alderman Barnes) and Major W. V. Greethem and Messrs. J. H. Corke and G. S. Lancaster, Elizabeth Ada Urry, of 26, Alver Road, Kingston, 14, was charged on warrant, first, that she did feloniously, unlawfully, and by fraud entice away one Emma Downton, then a child under the age of 14 years, to wit, of the age of five years and one day, with intent to deprive Thomas Downton, the father of the said child, of the possession of the child, on the 23rd ult. The second charge was that she feloniously, wilfully, and maliciously, of her malice aforethought, did murder kill and slay one Emma Downton, aged five years and one day, by strangling her with a pocket handkerchief at Southsea, on the 23rd ult.

Mr. George Hall King again appeared for the prosecution on behalf of the Treasury, and Mr. Edward Hobbs, of the firm of Hyde and Hobbs, defended the prisoner.

Mr. George Hall King said he was there on behalf of the Public Prosecutor to prosecute the prisoner on a charge of the wilful murder of Emma Downton. It was well within the recollection of the Magisrates that a week ago he was before them preferring a charge of a different character against her, viz. that of enticing the deceased child with a view to depriving her father of her possession, He then expressed a hope that the evidence which would be forthcoming would tend to an elucidation of the mystery. Since then the mystery had been elucidated, but in an entirely different way to that which was expected, and he was there now to charge the girl Urry, who now stood in the dock, with the most serious, charge known to the law, that of wilful murder.

He then proceeded to repeat the facts and circumstances already well known, such as the prisoner being traced to Southsea and being seen with the deceased and the child Dollie Waters up to twenty minutes to eight on the evening of Sunday the 23rd ult. At this time, said Mr. King, she was seen with two children in Lawrence Road, close to the Nazareth Home. That spot was only about 500 yards from the place where the body of the deceased was found. There was a still stronger piece of evidence against the prisoner which would be forthcoming upon the next occasion, for he should have to ask the Magistrates for a further remand. It was this. About eight o'clook on the night in question the prisoner was seen by a lady named Pickett, near Exeter Road, with two children.

Mrs. Pickett was an invalid, and quite unable to attend the Court that day, but she would be able, according to the statement of her medical adviser, to be present on the next occasion. This lady would tell the Magistrates that she saw the prisoner with the two children at a spot within twelve yards of the well in which the body was discovered. One of the two children, that was to say, the one about 3 years of age, had evidently strayed away and was calling out, as Mrs. Pickett assumed, for its nurse. Mrs. Pickett, called to the child, and almost simultaneously the prisoner called to it. Mrs. Pickett, on looking in the direction from which the prisoner called, distinctly saw her with the deceased child, holding her against her right thigh with both hands. Thus they traced the prisoner with the deceased child up to the very spot where the body was found, and the significance of the fact that she was holding the deceased against her thigh with both hands could not be over-estimated as proof of the prisoners guilt. The exact position would be described when Mrs. Pickett came before them, and it was a grave question whether, at that time, the child was not actually dead, and the reasonable suggestion on the part of the prosecution was that when seen by Mrs. Pickett, the prisoner was going towards the well for the purpose of dealing with the body and so concealing the crime of which she had been guilty. The reason Mrs. Pickett could not trace the prisoner farther than twelve yards from the well was that her vision was obscured by the buildings close by.

Nothing whatever was seen of the prisoner beyond this point until she reached Mr. Waters' with Dollie Waters, at a quarter to nine at night, having been out with both children something like five hours.

When she left, Mr. Waters' home in the afternoon the perambulator was in a perfectly good condition but when she returned at night it had been seriously damaged. He did not lay much stress upon the condition of the perambulator. It was accounted for by the prisoner herself, who, in her statement before the Governor of the Prison, alleged that it was broken while she was drawing the two children in the vehicle up the beach, nor did the prosecution make any suggestion as to a soldier being implicated in the matter.

It was utterly impossible for the prosecution to suggest what answer should be given to the charge now preferred against the prisoner. He had simply to put sufficient evidence before the Magistrates to warrant him in asking them to commit her for trial. So far as he was concerned, he was desirous that not one word of his should strengthen the evidence it was his duty to adduce before them, but he was bound to ask their Worships upon that evidence to send her for trial. Briefly, his grounds were these. He should put witnesses into the box who would trace the prisoner and the two children from a quarter past four in the afternoon of the day in question right up to eight o'clock at night, at which latter hour she was seen still in posession of the two children at a spot only 12 yards from the well in which the body of the deceased was found. The evidence was strong, clear, and incontrovertible, and he was strictly within his prerogative when he asked the Bench to say that the prisoner was accountable for the death of the child.

When the prisoner reached home that night, after having delivered up the Waters' child, she said nothing whatsoever about losing the deceased, and produced the bonnet worn by the deceased, together with a ribbon with which the child's hair had all been tied. She heard the hue and cry about the deceased having been missed, but made no sign, instead taking out of her pocket the material of which the child's bonnet had been made, and proceeding to tear it for the purpose of making a doll's hat.

On the Tuesday following, when the full description of the deceased's clothing, etc., had been published, she called attention to the fact that the material which she had torn up resembled that which had been described in the police notices. An interview was susequently arranged between Mrs. Urry and Mrs. Downton, the mother of the deceased, with the result that the materials were at once identified. Upon this the police were communicated with, and the prisoner was asked to go to the police station, and with all the coolness imaginable she went there and declared that she had found the bonnet on the beach near Clarence Esplanade Pier between two boats. By her own admission since, it was shown that that statement was untrue. Notwithstanding the agony of mind of the parents and the fact that she knew exactly where the child was to be found, she failed to give that clue which was in her possession, and which would have enabled the deceased's whereabouts to have been inmediately discovered.

Mr. King then proceeded to quote from the girl's statement to show that it was inconsistent with her innocence of the graver charge now preferred against her, particularly in reference to the allegation that she had missed the deceased as Mrs. Pickett would distinctly prove seeing the prisoner holding the girl against her thigh with both hands within twelve yards of the well where the body was discovered.

Another strong point against the prisoner was that when the deceased was found, the handkerchief was tied around her neck. Now, Dr. Maybury and Dr. Robertson, by whom the post mortem examination had been made, would prove that the child was strangled before she was put down the well, and strangled, too, by means of the handkerchief which was found tied around her neck.

This evidence against the prisoner was materially strengthened by the fact that the prisoner herself admitted having tied the handkerchief round the child's neck. Clearly the prisoner, when she made this statement at the prison, knew very well where she had been and what she had done, and accounted for the presence of the handkerchief round the child's neck by saying that she had placed it there because the child had complained of being cold. He submitted that if the evideence of the medical witnesses proved, as it would prove, that the child was strangled, then he was entitled to say upon that evidence, and upon the other evidence which would be adduced in the case, that the prisoner's was the hand by which the child was strangled, and her hand which subsequently disposed of the dead body in the well.

He proposed that day to put in sufficient evidence to justify a further remand. He had fifteen witnesses present, and he thought he should have no difficulty in convincing the Magistrates, after they had been heard, that it was impossible to resist his application, and his further application, which would be made at a later stage, for her committal to the assizes on the capital charge, where she would be placed on trial before a Jury, and where a tribunal superior to that would meat out such punishment as the law had laid down, He trusted that no words of his might strain the evidence against the prisoner, but it was his duty, on the part of the prosecution, to place the evidence before them as it stood, and ask their Worships to deal with the case accordingly. He then proceeded to call witnesses.

The evidence given was similar to that adduced at the previous Police court hearing and at the inquest last week. It related to the disappearance of the child, the production of the fragments of her bonnet by the prisoner Urry, and the journey over Fratton Bridge with a perambulator which was taken by Urry on the evening of the disappearance, when the deceased and the younger child, Dollie Waters were seen in her company.

A remand was afterwards granted until Thursday.

THURSDAY'S EVIDENCE.

The Police court at the Portsmouth Town Hall was again very crowded at noon on Thursday, when the hearing of the charge of murder against the girl Urry, was resumed. The Magistrates on the Bench were the Mayor (Alderman R. Barnes), Major W. V. Greetham, and G. S. Lancaster and J. H. Corke, Esq. Mr. G. H. King again appeared for the prosecution, on behalf of the Treasury, and Mr. Hobbs (Hyde and Hobbs) watched the interests of the prisoner.

The prisoner was, on the application of Mr. Hobbs, allowed to be seated. She looked very pale.

The Mayor: I wish to say at this early stage of the proceedings that I feel almost disgusted at seeing in Court persons levelling opera glasses at the prisoner.

URRY AND THE SOLDIER.

Susan Curtis, cook, of 14, Cromwell Houses, Nightingale Road, Southsea, stated that at half past five on Sunday, the 23rd of April, she was seated in front of Western Parade, and saw the prisoner there with a perambulator and two children, one being the child Waters and the other about five years old. The prisoner was sitting on a seat with a soldier in a red coat, and when witness left at half past six the prisoner was still there. Witness saw the prisoner take one of the children to the Castle Hotel.

VISIT TO THE CASTLE HOTEL.

Maud Amelia Collis, at present residing at the Castle Hotel, Southsea, repeated her evidence provided at the inquest as to a girl bringing a child there and going to the back between six and seven o'clock on Sunday, the 23rd of April. She could not identify the prisoner, but the girl was about her height.

GOING TOWARDS EASTNEY.

Thomas Bishop, of 14, Park Street, Southsea, a leading stoker serving on board H.M.S. *Victory*, said about half past seven on the day in question he saw the prisoner between the Castle and the South Parade Pier. She was going towards Eastney and had a perambulator with a child in it. There was a second child following behind, whom he had identified as being the deceased. Mr. King: Was any soldier with her at that time? – Witness: There was an artilleryman about three yards behind her. Should you say he was with the prisoner? – Not to my knowledge; he did not appear to be so. Justices' Clerk: Being an artilleryman, he would have a dark coat on? – Witness: Yes.

THE LAMPLIGHTER'S STORY.

Joseph Loveridge, of 61, Esslemont Road, Southsea, a lamplighter in the service of the Portsea Island Gas Company, said that between 7.30 and 7.40 on the evening in question he was engaged in his occupation in Lawrence Road, and he saw the prisoner there with the perambulator and two children. One of the latter, between three and four years old, was in the perambulator, and the other, about five years old, was standing close by. The latter was the child to whose body he had identified in the mortuary. Mr. King: Did you hear the elder child say anything? – Witness: I heard the child say "Home." Were other words said? – Yes. In what direction was the perambulator going? -Towards Albert Road. How far would it be from there to where the child's body was found? – I should say of about 500 yards.

THE SOLDIER AGAIN.

George Fellingham, of 63, Castle Road, Southsea, an assistant to his brother, a railway carrier, said that at ten minutes after six on the evening in question, when sitting in front of Western Parade, he saw the prisoner and a soldier sitting upon a seat and two children were running about. He saw a perambulator there, and it was similar to the one produced. The elder of the two children was wearing a bonnet of a material and colour similar to that produced. He left the prisoner and the soldier on the seat when he went away.

SEEN NEAR THE WELL.

Mrs. Catherine Eleanor Pickett, living at 1, Rosebery Terrace, Highland Road, Eastney, said she was at home on the evening in question, and being unwell she was sitting in her bedroom. From the window she could see the back of some new houses which faced into Highland Road.

Mr. King: Now tell the Bench, in your own way, what you saw and heard. – Witness: I heard a child cry, and on looking I identify her by the bonnet as being Waters. I did not see the child's face, and though I called to the girl who was there she did not turn her face, but I heard her say "Come along." The girl was stooping and holding a child until the other came back to her.

The Justices' Clerk: Can you give us a better description as to how she was holding the child? – She appeared to be holding it by the arms, but it was too dark for her to see clearly. The girl and the two children afterwards disappeared from the witness's view. The elder girl had a round hat and cape on, and her hair was loose round her shoulders. The clothing which the prisoner was wearing was like that worn by the elder girl she saw.

AWAY FROM THE WELL WITH ONE CHILD.

Louisa Kempstor, domestic servant, living at 33, Worthing Road, Southsea, was in Festing Road at about a quarter after eight on the evening of the 23rd ult., and in going towards the Albert Road railway bridge she saw the prisoner come from behind a pile of bricks on some vacant land with the perambulator and one child, which by its size, she should think was between two and three years old. The child appeared to be asleep. The prisoner was wheeling the perambulator across the vacant land towards Festing Road. Mr. King: Was she going slowly or fast? – Witness: She was hurrying, and she turned her head round several times and looked towards the pile of bricks. Where did you lose sight of the prisoner? – On the vacant land. The Justices' Clerk: The Magistrates would like to know if you saw a second child there at all? – Witness: No, sir.

Mildred Gore, the wife of William Gore, a bathing machine proprietor living at 2, Somerset Villas, Somerset Road, Southsea, said that about 8.10 on the Sunday evening she was on Albert Road bridge. She saw prisoner there with a little child in a perambulator. The little one appeared to be between three and four years old. There was no other child with her. Prisoner asked her (witness) the nearest way to St. Mary's Road. Witness replied that she did not know. The Clerk: In which direction was she coming? – Witness: She was coming from Festing Road and going down Albert Road.

At this point the Court adjourned for a quarter of an hour.

CONCERNING THE WELL.

Mr. A. H. Bone, architect, Cambridge Junction, Portsmouth, formally proved the correctness of a plan of the neighbourhood between Alver and Festing roads, and it showed the positions of the various houses spoken of by the witnesses, and also of the well. He also spoke to the correctness of a model, made upon a scale of 2ft. to 1in., and that also showed the well in which the body was discovered. The well was 14ft. 6in. in depth from the surface, and the water was 3ft. 2in. in depth. The windlass of the well would be visible from either Highland or Festing roads, the land being all open and without fences.

George Powell, living in Leopold Street, Albert Road, a labourer in the employ of Mr. Quick, builder, who is erecting eight houses in Highland Road, said he was employed there on the 22nd ult. There was a well at the rear of one of the houses, and when he left work at one o'clock on that day the well was open and without boards on the top. When he saw the well again at six o'clock on the morning of the 24th it was covered with a nine-inch board and with corrugated iron, the exact positions of which he explained by the moveable model.

John Bennett, of 22, Goodwood Road, Southsea, the watchman employed at the new buildings spoken to by the last witness, said he was on the land on the 23rd from 9.00 a.m, until 8.30 p.m. and walked from back to front occasionally. He was there also on the previous (the Saturday) afternoon, and he then covered up the well with a board and corrugated iron. On the Sunday he was several times out of sight of the well.

BELONGING TO THE DECEASED.

Eleanor Elizabeth Jane Langridge, twelve years old, living at 50, Alver Road, Kingston, proved being at the house of the prisoner's parents at nine o'clock on the night of the 23rd, when the prisoner returned home fully dressed. After a short time the prisoner took from her pocket the bonnet material produced, identified as that of which the deceased child's bonnet was made. The prisoner set about making a hat for herself with the material, and when asked where she had got it she said she had picked it up on the beach.

Ellen Butler, widow, of 1, Sutherland Road, said that on the morning of the 24th ult. she found the wire and lace produced and a piece of lining, which she had since burnt, on a piece of vacant land at the corner of Sutherland Road. She handed the material to Detective Taylor.

Mrs. Downton, the mother of the deceased child, on being called, identified the lace as having formed a portion of the front of the bonnet worn by her daughter. The wire also was about the length of the shape of the bonnet.

Mr. King said that so far as he was concerned that will be the last witness to be called that day. The next witness he proposed calling would be the prisoner's mother, whose evidence would go to some length.

The prisoner was then remanded until one o'clock next Thursday.

THE INQUEST RESUMED, – YESTERDAY'S EVIDENCE.

The adjourned inquest on the body of Emma Downton was resumed yesterday afternoon before the Borough Coroner (T. A. Bramsdon, Esq., J.P) at the Portsmouth Police court. Mr. G. H. King, the prosecuting solicitor, was present, as was also Mr. E. Hobbs, the solicitor for the defence.

The attendance of the general public was not so large as on the previous occasion. Owing to the difficulty experienced by the Jury in hearing the witnesses,

Mr. Attree, the Foreman, requested the Coroner to allow them to sit in the solicitor's seats, and to this Mr. Bramsdon readily assented.

MRS URRY CALLED.

Elizabeth Urry, the mother of the accused girl, was the first witness called. She was attired in black, and appeared to feel her position very keenly. She was accommodated with a seat in the witness box, and gave her evidence in a low tone. She stated that she was a widow, living at 26, Alver Road, Kingston. Her daughter, Elizabeth Ada, who had been mentioned in the course of the proceedings, was 14 years of age on the 9th January last. She left the house about three o'clock on the 23rd ult., with the intention of going to a friend's house at Stamshaw, and witness did not see her again until a quarter past nine that night, when she was standing at the door on her (witness's) return home. Witness asked her where she had been, and she said that she had visited the beach.

The Coroner: You spoke rather harshly to her, did you not? – Witness: Yes; Mrs. Waters had sent round to me to ask where her child was, and I told my daughter that she was very naughty for keeping the child out so late. During supper time (witness continued) her daughter said she had picked a bonnet up on the beach, and witness told her she ought not to pick things up in that way.

On Monday morning witness saw her daughter with the material produced (stated to be part of deceased's bonnet), and she said that she thought it would make Alice (her doll) a nice bonnet. That afternoon witness went to Portsdown Hill, leaving her daughter home with her sisters and some friends. Witness had heard some rumours that night, and on the Tuesday her daughter told her that she had read a description of the missing child's bonnet, and asked witness if the cream coloured material did not correspond with that she had picked up.

In consequence of something said by a neighbour, witness, on the following day went to Mrs. Downton, who identified the bonnet as being that which her daughter had worn. Witness afterwards went with her daughter and some friends to the Buckland Police station where they left the bonnet with Sergt. Brading. Some other material from the house was also given to the police. On the Wednesday witness put her hand into the pocket of the dress worn on the previous Sunday by her daughter, and there found a piece of lining and a piece of cardinal coloured ribbon, both of which the girl said she had picked up with the bonnet. The police afterwards searched the house and found some other pieces of the bonnet.

The Coroner: Now look at that handkerchief; do you identify that as being your daughter's? – Witness said she did not. Do you know if your daughter had a handkerchief like that? – I don't know. By the Jurors: She did not know whether her daughter had a handkerchief on the Sunday, neither could she tell whether her daughter had any handkerchiefs at home now. (The handkerchief was that found round the neck of the deceased child; it was knotted, and was much discoloured.)

Evidence was also called to prove the movements of the prisoner Urry on the evening of the deceased's disappearance, the witnesses being those who were examined at the Police court on Thursday. Other witnesses deposed to the recovery of the deceased's body from the well and to the picking up of a piece of lace which had belonged to her at the corner of Sutherland Road.

THE WELL AND ITS COVERING.

George Powell, of 24, Leopold Street, Albert Road, a labourer in the employ of Mr. Quick, builder, said that on the 22nd and 24th of last month he was at work on some houses in the course of erection in Exeter Road. The well at the rear of the fourth house was used for building purposes. On Saturday, the 22nd ult., he left the place about 1.15, and at that time the well was completely uncovered. He next saw the well at a quarter to six on the Monday morning following, and it was then covered by a nine-inch board and a sheet of corrugated iron, placed between the framework of the windlass.

By the Jury: It would be impossible for a child to fall down the well when the board and iron were in position. It would, however, be very easy to lift the sheet of iron up. The weight of the iron was about 27 or 28 pounds, and it measured 2ft. by 7ft. If the corrugated iron was moved, a child could fall down, for the board did not cover the mouth of the well.

Mr. Hobbs: Was there a tub there? – Witness Yes, at one end of the well. Was one end of the corrugated iron allowed to rest on the end of the tub? – Yes, one end came down to the ground and the other end was raised on to the tub. It was so when I saw it on Monday morning.

In answer to further questions, witness said that there was a tub at one end of the well, and a pump at the other, and the sheet of the iron passed over the well between the uprights of the windlass. The space between the iron and the ground at the tub was about 18 inches. He did not think it would be possible for a child to crawl under it and fall down the well.

John Bennett, living at 22, Goodwood Road, Southsea, the watchman at Mr. Quick's new houses, said that he went on duty there at half past one on Saturday, the 22nd ult., and shortly afterwards he covered up the well with one nine inch board and a sheet of corrugated iron. No child could then fall into the well, nor could one get into the well under the corrugated iron. The iron and wood were in the same position on Monday morning as that in which he placed them on Saturday. He was about the place all day Sunday, leaving soon after eight o'clock. His meals were sent to him, and he did not leave the premises the whole day. He was positive of that. At half past seven he was talking to a friend at the back of the buildings, and was then in full sight of the well. He was there for about twenty minutes, and after that he walked round to the front of the houses, and looked into the windows and front rooms. He left the place altogether at half past eight, but between eight o'clock and that time he went round to the back of the buildings twice. He did not see a girl there, neither did he see a perambulator nor a little child. He heard no one call out. Just before leaving he visited the well, and it was in the same condition as when he first saw it on Saturday. It took him about ten or twelve minutes to walk round the buildings.

By a Juryman: If a child crawled under the corrugated iron, would the frame work of the well prevent it from falling down? – Witness: Yes. The Coroner Did you see a soldier anywhere near the well during the evening? – Witness: There were lots of people on the ground at the back during the evening, but I saw no soldier nor anyone near the vicinity of the well.

WELL WHERE THE BODY WAS FOUND.
(Sketched from a Special Photograph.)

THE MEDICAL EVIDENCE.

Dr. Lysander Maybury, the police surgeon, was next called, and said: I first saw deceased at 5.45 on the evening of the 2nd inst. at the mortuary, Portsmouth. I made then a superficial examination, and at 10 p.m., in conjunction with Dr. Robertson, I made a post mortem examination. Deceased was fully dressed, with the exception of her hat, which was not present. She had on an apron, the waistband of which was untied and loose, a red dress, a linen and flannel petticoat, red drawers, stays, chemise, and under flannel. The drawers were fastened, as also were the clothes. She had on black socks and button-boots. The clothes at the back were covered with mud and grit. The hair was muddy and contained grit, especially at the back, and a piece of wood about three inches long, which I handed to Detective Taylor. There was no blood in the ears. On the right side of the forehead there was an abrasion one inch by three-quarters. There was another one in about the centre of the forehead half an hour by a quarter. There were a number of reddish marks on the forehead and face a quarter of an inch and an eighth of an inch in diameter.

The face was placid, and livid, especially on the left side, and was slightly swollen. The eyelids were closed, and the pupils were moderately dilated. The tip of the nose was not flattened, there was no frothy mucous within the nostrils, and no grit or foreign body. The lips were swollen and livid. There was some frothy mucous between the lips and the teeth. The tip of the tongue protruded about a quarter of an inch between the teeth, which were tightly clenched upon it. The lip was swollen and greatly congested. The gums were livid, especially their dental borders. The tongue was swollen, and there was no grit or foreign body within the cavity of the mouth.

There was a cotton pocket handkerchief (produced) tied tightly round the neck. The knot was at the right side, and a little to the back. It was a "granny's knot," and not a reef knot. There was some hair in the knot. On cutting the handkerchief off from the left side, it showed signs of great pressure. It was not twisted, but folded, and averaged five eighths of an inch wide and half an inch in thickness. There was no hard substance in the handkerchief. The mark caused by it ran horizontally round the neck with a slight obliquity upwards at the back. It was white in colour, and showed elevations and depressions corresponding to the folds of the handkerchief. The mark was one inch wide in front and half an inch at the sides and back. On cutting the mark across in the front and at the sides of the neck there was no glistening membrane beneath the skin, or no bruising or laceration of the muscles, and no extravasation of blood. There was no fracture of the cervical invertebrae or the wind pipe.

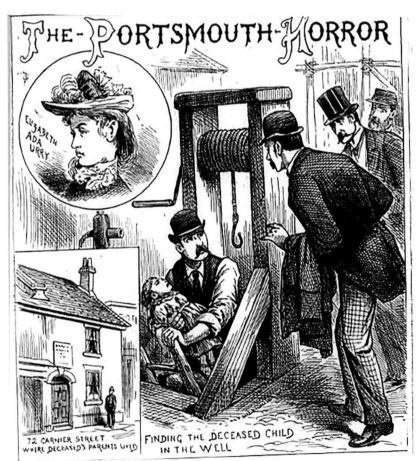

72 CARNIER STREET WHERE DECEASED'S PARENTS LIVED

FINDING THE DECEASED CHILD IN THE WELL

The palms of the hands were wrinkled and white, as though they had been poulticed. The tips of the fingers were white and the nails were livid. There was great indentation on the tips of the thumbs, caused by pressure against the index finger. There was no foreign body within the grasp of the hand or beneath the finger nails. The soles of the feet were white and wrinkled, as though they had been poulticed. The toes and nails were black from lividity. The body was fresh, and showed no signs of decomposition. There was no gooseskin, and no fracture of any of the bones of the body. The anterior edge of the right lung overlapped the left by a quarter of an inch. The lungs were swollen, and there were some old pleuratic adhesions at the upper part of the left lung. They were congested, and when cut the pressure caused dark fluid blood to exude. The bronchi were congested, but contained no water, mud, or grit. The root of the tongue was intensely congested, as also the epiglottis, larynx, and trachea. The mucous membrane of the larynx was swollen. There was no foreign body, grit, mud, or water in the larynx or trachea.

The veins of the heart were prominent, and of a bluish colour. The heart was not contracted. The left ventricle contained about a drachm and a half of dark fluid blood. The right side of the heart was full of dark fluid blood. The stomach contained 5 ounces of fluid and partly digested food. It contained no foreign body, grit, or mud. The liver was congested with dark fluid blood. The spleen was normal, and the bladder was empty. On deflecting the scalp, the abrasion described on the right side of the forehead was found to have extended through in the form of a bruise. There were a number of minute marks on the interior of the scalp. The brain was greatly congested and the interior of the brain substance showed minute red points. The veins in the interior of the skull were greatly congested.

In my opinion deceased died from strangulation caused by the handkerchief round her neck, and when dead or insensible she was placed in the well. She did not die from drowning.

The Coroner: Will you kindly explain what led you to form that opinion? – Witness: By the handkerchief round the neck, by the mark caused by the handkerchief, by the state of the internal organs, by the absence of foreign matter in the mouth, by the absence of water in the trachea, lungs, and stomach.

Must very considerable pressure have been brought to bear to cause that strangulation? – Witness: Considerable pressure. Do you think it possible that under some circumstances the handkerchief might have been tied round the neck, and death might have been brought about accidentally, by strangulation? – Witness: I do.

Do you think that a girl of the age of 14, such as the girl Urry, might have accidentally done such a thing? – She might, yes. Can you tell us a circumstance in which such events would occur? – I would rather not enter into that. Supposing Urry had been in a passion and tied the handkerchief round the child's neck, might that have caused strangulation? – Yes, if she used sufficient force.

Would a child of the age of five years, having been taken about the town from four to seven o'clock, become somewhat weakened in consequence? – It would be fatigued.

Can you form any opinion as to how long the child had been without food? – I cannot say, because fatigue retards digestion. It might have been six or seven hours.

Would not the fact of the child being fatigued and not having had food for so long make her succumb easier to strangulation? – Decidedly.

I take it the deceased child could not have got into the well by any act of her own? – No. Were there any other marks of violence on the body than those you have described? – None others.

If there was great pressure used, would you expect to find laceration of the muscles? – In an adult person, yes; but not so much in a young child, as the muscles are elastic. It depends on the ligature used. A handkerchief is soft.

How were the marks on the face caused? – Either before or after death, by the child falling onto the gravel or by falling into the water and striking the bottom or sides.

A Juryman: Would it be possible for the child to have been strangled without the person committing the act being aware of it? – I think not, although the handkerchief might have been tied so tightly as to prevent the child calling out.

Might the handkerchief have been fairly tied round the neck, and after immersion in water become very tight, and produced strangulation? – It would produce a mark, but could not bring about death. I have experimented, and find that a calico handkerchief does not tighten to any extent by immersion in water.

If the handkerchief had been tied fairly tight round the neck, might not a fit of coughing or crying have caused strangulation? – No.

The Coroner: If the child was not strangled before she was put into the water there would have been some evidence of drowning? – Decidedly so. There would have been water in the lungs.

Could the child have been accidentally strangled without screaming or making some noise? – Yes.

The Foreman: But the girl could not have strangled the child without being aware of it? – It is very unlikely. I cannot say whether it would have been possible or not.

The Coroner: Might the deceased have had some bronchitis? – She might. Would that make strangling easier? – Yes, it would.

The inquest was then adjourned until Tuesday next, at three o'clock.

INQUEST PROCEEDINGS. VERDICT: WILFUL MURDER.

On Tuesday, at the Police court the Portsmouth Coroner (T. A. Bramsdon, Esq., J.P.) resumed the inquiry into the circumstances attending the death of Emma Downton, aged five years, whose dead body was discovered in a well at Eastney on the 2nd. Besides the witnesses and others engaged in the case there were very few persons in Court. Mr. G. H. King, who is prosecuting in the charge of murder against the girl Ada Urry, and Mr. S. Hobbs (Messrs. Hyde and Hobbs), the solicitor for the defence, were both in attendance.

WAS IT AN ACCIDENT?

Dr. Maybury was recalled, and in reply to the Coroner said that if the deceased was standing by the perambulator and Urry was tying the handkerchief around her neck he thought it would be impossible for Urry not to know that the deceased was being strangled. The Coroner: Would it be otherwise if Urry lost her presence of mind? – I think it might be.

Continuing, witness said that deceased would be insensible in about one minute, and dead in from four to five minutes after the handkerchief was held around her neck. It would depend upon how tightly the ligature was placed upon the neck.

If the handkerchief had been loosened, say within four or five minutes, do you think there would have been a fair chance of the deceased recovering? – Yes, in four minutes certainly, and possibly in five minutes.

The Coroner: If the deceased had been in a perambulator, with her face turned towards Urry, do you think it would have been possible for her to have been strangled and for Urry not to have known it? – I do not think so; in my opinion it was impossible.

How would it have been if deceased had been in the perambulator with her back towards Urry? Witness: It would have been possible, but very improbable.

Would a sudden and violent compression of the neck by a handkerchief, render deceased powerless to call out? – Witness: It would. In your former evidence, when you mentioned the word accidental, do I understand you to mean unintentional? – That was the meaning I took.

Have you any additional evidence to offer as to what made you form your opinion that death arose from strangulation and not drowning? – Yes, because of the position of the tongue. In drowning cases it is generally behind the teeth, but in this case it was protruding from the mouth. Witness said he wished to add that he had made experiments with regard to the action of water upon cotton pocket handkerchiefs. He had experimented with old and new ones, and found that there was no shrinking but elongation, varying from an inch and a quarter to two inches. The handkerchiefs were about the same size as the one round deceased's neck. One was immersed for one day, and three others for nearly three days.

By the Jury: If the handkerchief had been tied fairly tight round deceased's neck and she had attempted to run away, and the girl had caught hold of the handkerchief, it might have produced strangulation if she had held it long enough and used sufficient force. Though the handkerchief was so tight as to cause an indentation, I do not think it would have been impossible to have placed a finger inside it, as the neck is pliable, and would give way.

FURTHER MEDICAL EVIDENCE.

Dr. John Robert Stephenson Robertson, of Southsea, deposed that he was present with Dr. Maybury when the post mortem on the body of the deceased was made.

The Coroner: Now I don't want to take you all through this evidence again, but do you agree with Dr. Maybury? – Yes. That death was due to strangulation? – Yes. What was the cause of the strangulation? – From compression of the handkerchief round the neck, When the deceased was put into the well do you think she must have been either dead or dying? – That she must have been either dead or unconscious. And that the deceased could not have got into the well herself? – Quite so.

What marks of violence were there on the body? – There was a large bruise on the right side of the head, another on the left, and several smaller bruises about the face. They were caused by the deceased falling before she was put into the well, or when she got to the bottom. Do you think that under some circumstances strangulation could have been brought about unintentionally? – I do. Do you think that Urry in tying the handkerchief around deceased's neck might have caused strangulation unintentionally without being aware of it? – Witness: That depends upon circumstances. Under what circumstances do you think she would not have known it? – Witness: If deceased had had her back towards the girl, or if she tied the handkerchief tightly and went away from the perambulator.

Do you think that in order to produce strangulation considerable force would have to be used? – Witness: Yes; considerable force. That force would have to be considerably more than would be ordinarily required to tie the handkerchief round deceased's neck? – Witness: Certainly.

You have heard the evidence of Dr. Maybury, do you disagree with him upon any point? – Substantially I agree with him, but if he had said that the child would become insensible in about one minute and dead in about four minutes I think it would have been nearer the fact.

By a Juror: If the child had fallen down the well in a conscious state I should not have expected to have found more bruises or abrasions on the body than there were, owing to the struts.

A Juror: The Jury would like to know what the medical gentlemen mean by considerable force; can they give it in description by weight of pounds? Coroner: I don't think any medical gentleman could say that; that is a matter of evidence, you know.

ADA URRY INTERVIEWED.

Detective Sergeant William Money said that early on the morning of the 26th of April he saw the girl Urry at her home in Alver Road, Kingston. He said to her, "I am a police officer, and I have come to see you respecting a bonnet you found on the beach last Sunday night. I want you to tell me the exact spot and the time, as near as you possibly can." She replied; "I found it between two boats near the Pier shortly before five o'clock." "Why are you able to fix the time?" witness asked. She replied, "After I picked up the bonnet I saw a steamboat come to the Pier, and I went to see what time it was by the clock in front of the Pier. It was then five o'clock."

At about eleven o'clock the same morning witness was at 72, Garnier Street, interviewing Mrs. Downton, when Urry came there, He asked her where she went between the time she left home at three o'clock on Sunday and the time she returned home. At that time there was no suspicion against her. She said "I left home at three o'clock, went to Mrs. Waters' house, and got her little child, and took it straight to a friend of ours, who lives in Sutherland Road, Southsea. She was not home, and I came straight back to Waters' house and got the child's perambulator, and took it on to the Beach." "Which way did you go to the Beach, where you found the bonnet?" asked witness. She replied, "Down Fratton Road, Fratton Street, over Somers Bridge, Somers Road, Cottage Grove, Green Road, Castle Road, across the Common, and straight on to the Beach. I took the child out of the pram, and we sat between two boats. After we had been there a little while, the little child went round to the other side of the boat. I went after it, and there I found the bonnet."

Witness asked her if she had seen the description of the little child that was missing, and she replied "Yes." Witness asked "Did you see her anywhere near where you found the bonnet, or did you see a child like her near the spot that could have dropped it?" She replied," I only saw a lady with a little child, I asked her if the bonnet belonged to her, and she said no. I remained on the beach a little while, and then came home the same way that I went, but I was a long time coming home, as I let the little child walk and play as I came across the Common, and I also stopped at Somers Bridge to let the child see the trains, and I got home at eight o'clock."

Witness added: She then handed me the hair ribbon produced, which she said she had found in the bonnet on the beach. She also said "I think I have some small pieces of the lining at home," and later on she handed me the portions of the lining produced. On the 29th of April I saw her at her home and said to her "I hold the warrant for your apprehension, but before reading it to you I caution you that anything you may say may be used in evidence against you." I read the warrant, to which she made no reply. I then searched the house, and in the back room I found the two small pieces of material produced, and in the front sitting room I found other pieces produced.

On the 8th inst. I saw the prisoner in the police station, and I then said to her, "I am about to charge you with a very serious offence, and I want you to clearly understand that anything you may say in answer to it may be used as evidence against you; do you understand what I mean?" She said "Yes," I then said, "You are charged that you feloniously, wilfully, and maliciously, and of your malice aforethought, did murder, kill, and slay one Emma Downton, aged five years, by strangling her with a pocket-handkerchief at Southsea, on the 23rd of April last." In reply, she said, "No, sir; that is not so."

THE ADMISSIBILITY OF URRY'S STATEMENTS.

The Coroner asked Mr. King if he had anything to say about the statements made by the prisoner.

Mr. King replied that as some legal technicality arose with regarding the statements made by Urry at the Gaol or to Detective Money, he had ccommunicated with the Treasury, and so far as the prosecution was concerned, he could say that those statements would not be put in as evidence by the prosecution. Of course the defence could put them in if they liked. The Coroner asked Mr. Hobbs if he wanted them put in. Mr. Hobbs: So far as this case is concerned they are already put in. The Coroner: That is so, but under the circumstances I shall ask the Jury to disregard them, unless you voluntarily put them in. Mr. Hobbs: No, sir. I shall not put them in. I have not tendered the girl Urry as a witness, and I do not propose to put the statements in as evidence. The Coroner: I asked you previously if you intended to tender the girl as a witness, and you said you did not, or else I should have communicated with the Home Secretary, and taken steps to have had her brought here.

THE SUMMING UP.

The Coroner then proceeded to sum up. He thanked the Jury for the attention they had given to the case. The questions they had put had materially assisted him in the inquiry. The name which was foremost in their minds was, of course, that of the girl Urry, and he asked them to follow him while he recounted the girl's movements on the afternoon of the 23rd of April. He then detailed her movements, as deposed to by witnesses. He advised the Jury, however, not to place too much reliance upon what the witnesses had said about the time, and he also wanted to ask them to dismiss from their minds any question about a soldier. They must be guided only by the evidence and not by any chimerical ideas. It might be that Urry had sat upon a seat with a soldier, but she was seen afterwards without any soldier.

He then particularly noted the very long time which the children must have been dragged about, pointed out that the last time the deceased was seen alive was in Fawcett Road by the lamplighter, and spoke of the movements which were seen by Mrs. Pickett from her house in Highland Road. From that time they would have to deal only with circumstantial evidence, and there came in their great difficulty.

They would, however, remember that one witness had seen Urry going in a hurried manner from the direction of the well. Undoubtedly she had had possession of the child, and if there had been no guilty knowledge on her part one would have thought that if she had missed the child, or if the latter had strayed, she would have appealed to some person whom she met. Yet Urry went home with the greatest coolness and said nothing, and such coolness and cunning one scarcely met with in the greatest criminal, much less in one of so tender an age.

Did Urry put the body in the well, and under what circumstances did it come there? To decide these points he had given them every practical opportunity to readily judge by the questions he had put to the doctor. There were two facts which arose in connection with the matter. One was that the strangulation might have been brought about wilfully with the intention of killing by intentionally tying the handkerchief round her neck so tightly as to kill her. In that case it would be murder. Then there was another way by which death might have been brought about. The child had been dragged about the town for hours, and as far as could be deduced from the witnesses, had been treated kindly.

The question was, did the child annoy Urry in some way, and did she, in a fit of passion or in a fit of gross carelessness, tie the handkerchief around her neck and unintentionally strangle her? If that was the case, then Urry would have been guilty of manslaughter. They had no explanation as to the actual way in which death had been caused. He meant they had no explanation from the girl Urry herself. They would have to consider in their own manner as to what had happened. Then there was the question whether death could have resulted from a pure accident, and one Juryman had asked what actual amount of force would be required to bring about death by accident. That was a very difficult thing to say, and it was a point upon which they would have to judge for themselves.

He asked them whether such a thing appeared to be at all likely, whether under any circumstances death could have been brought about by accident, supposing the girl Urry to have lost her presence of mind. What was the object or motive that the girl could have had to have brought about the death of the little child? She was a stranger to her, and there was no proof of any quarrel with the child, so far as the evidence went. In one case it was shown that she did not treat it with motherly care, but it would not be sufficient to bring about death by a wilful act of murder. These points they must give great consideration to, and they must also exercise a great amount of leniency with regard to the consideration of the point.

He had puzzled his mind as to what the object could have been in committing this serious crime. The only thing that occurred to him was as to whether she wanted to obtain possession of the bonnet. The pieces they had seen in Court showed that the bonnet was a very pretty one, and such a one as a girl of mischievous character might desire to possess herself. But, would she resort to the most serious of all crimes – murder – in order to obtain the bonnet? The history of the case showed that the girl Urry was possessed of a cunning which would have prompted her to have taken possession of the bonnet without resorting to such a terrible end. If Urry had wished to have got possession of the bonnet she might have left the child in some field, some lane, or some building, and run away with the bonnet. This was one way in which she could have secured the bonnet. The other was that she might have carried out the act of murder.

It was only a fair assumption to think that if the girl Urry was guilty of the strangulation she might have been prompted to have got rid of the body by putting it down the well, which, if done by her, must have been performed very quickly. For himself, he must say that he was a little sceptical as to the watchman, whose time he much questioned. He had a doubt whether the watchman was around the buildings at the times he had given, but he had no doubt they would give that and every point which had been brought before them due consideration. They were there for the purpose of pointing to the individual who had been guilty of the strangulation, supposing they could do that, and it would be some consolation to them, in their arduous duties, to know that their responsibilities were not too great as if they had been in another Court.

The Coroner's summing up occupied half an hour.

THE VERDICT.

The Jury retired at seven minutes before five, and the questions which the Coroner required to be answered were replied to as follows:-

1. What was the cause of death? – **Strangulation.**
2. If the deceased was strangled, by whom? – **Elizabeth Ada Urry.**
3. Was such strangulation wilful and intentional? – **Yes.**
4. If not wilful or intentional, was it the result of culpable negligence or carelessness?
5. Was the strangulation due to purely accidental causes?

The two last questions required no answer.

The Coroner: That is a verdict of wilful murder against the girl Elizabeth Ada Urry. The Foremen added that the verdict had been arrived at by 14 out of 15 Jurymen. They were twenty-seven minutes considering their verdict.

The thirty-four witnesses who had given evidence at the inquest were then bound over to appear at the next Winchester Assizes, at which Urry will be tried by virtue of the Coroner's a warrant.

AT THE POLICE COURT.

At the Portsmouth Police court on Thursday, the Magistrates held a special sitting, at which Elizabeth Ada Urry, aged 14, of 26, Alver Road, Kingston, was again brought before them on remand, charged with the murder of Emma Downton, aged five years, the daughter of a paper-hanger, living at 72, Garnier Street, Fratton, and whose dead body was found, it will be remembered, in a well off Highland Road, Southea, more than a week after the child had been missed from home.

The Court was crowded, the public interest in the case being evidently still very great. The Magistrates on the Bench were Major W. V. Greetham, S. Lancaster and J. H. Corks, Esq.

Mr. G. H. King prosecuted, and Mr. Hobbs (Hyde and Hobbs) appeared for the defence. The prisoner, who was attended in the dock by the female searcher, looked pale, but appeared to be completely self-possessed, and after gazing around the crowded Court, devoted her attention to the examination of the several witnesses. When her mother entered the Court and stepped into the witness box she burst into tears and wept bitterly for a considerable time.

The first witness called was Henry Collins, a licensed boatman, of Little Southsea Street, who stated that on the 23rd ult. he was in charge of five boats on the beach close to the pier. Four of the boats were in use at five o'clock, He did not see prisoner there on that afternoon. Had she been at the spot with a perambulator he would have seen her.

Elizabeth Mary Whiting said that prisoner was her daughter, and was born on January 9th, 1879. Both witness and the girl had gone by the name of Urry. On the evening of the 23rd ult., the prisoner told her that she had found a bonnet on the beach. Witness said that she was very naughty to pick up things and bring them home not knowing where they had been, to which she replied that she thought it would make a doll's bonnet for her sister. Witness afterwards saw her making a doll's bonnet, which she placed on her younger child's doll. The material was on the doll when witness and her younger daughter went out for a walk.

On the following Tuesday prisoner drew her attention to the contents of the bill relating to the disappearance of the child Downton, and, after visiting Mrs. Downton's house, witness took the girl to the Buckland Police station, where she made a statement to P.S. Brading. The material produced was then handed to the police, and next day they received another piece, together with a strip of cardinal-coloured ribbon, which witness found in her daughter's dress pocket. Prisoner was arrested on the following Saturday, Detective Money taking possession of two other pieces of the material which he found at her house. Witness could not identify the handkerchief produced, and knew nothing about it.

Detective Charles Taylor said that on Tuesday the 2nd inst., he went to a well at the back of some property in Highland Road, Eastney. He got down on to a circular stage, just above the water, and with the aid of a bricklayer's larry, he dragged the bottom of the well, and pulled the body of the dead child out of the water. It was hoisted, by a rope, to the top of the well and conveyed in a cab to the public mortuary. It was dressed in the clothes produced, and a handkerchief was tied tightly round the neck.

The Magistrates' Clerk (Mr. Addison) read a telegram from the Mayor, stating that he was detained in London.

Dr. Lysander Maybury, the police surgeon, detailed the result of the post mortem examination made by him and Dr. Robertson on the body. He described minutely the condition of the body, the marks and bruises upon it, and the mark made round the neck by the handkerchief, which was folded and tied tightly with a "granny's knot." Death was caused by strangulation through the handkerchief being tied round deceased's neck. She was put in the well when dead or insensible. He was positive that death did not arise from drowning. Considerable force must have been used in tying the handkerchief. In the opinion of witness, the prisoner would possess sufficient strength to tie the handkerchief around deceased's neck in such a way as to cause strangulation. The handkerchief would not tighten in the water, but the marks upon the deceased's neck could have been produced before or after death. If caused after death, however, other appearances which he had described would have been absent. He based his opinion as to the cause of death upon the result of the whole post mortem examination, and not on any one point.

Mr. Addison: And you are of the opinion that the mark was caused before death. – Witness: I am morally certain, or rather scientifically certain as to that.

Detective-Sergeant Money repeated the evidence which he gave at the Coroner's inquest concerning the prisoner's statement as to her movements on the 23rd ult. He also spoke to finding several pieces of the material forming the deceased's bonnet at prisoner's residence, and to arresting her on a warrant charging her with enticing the child away from home. On the 8th inst. he charged her with having murdered Emmie Downton, after administering a caution, the nature of which she said she understood, that anything she might say concerning the matter might be used in evidence against her. In reply to the charge she said, "No, sir, that is not so."

Mr. A. H. Bone, architect (recalled), stated that the space between the corrugated iron, which it had been stated covered the well in which deceased's body was found, and the mouth of the well was 13 inches.

Mr. King, intimated that the case for the prosecution was now complete, and Mr. Hobbs, in reply to the Magistrates' Clerk, said that he would reserve his observations until the Magistrates had given their decision. The accused was then formally charged, in the name of Elizabeth Ada Whiting, that she did feloniously and of malice aforethought kill and murder Emma Downton.

Major Greetham cautioned her that whatever she might say in answer to the charge would be taken down in writing and used in evidence against her at her trial, upon which Mr. Hobbs said that the defence would be reserved, and no witnesses would be called on prisoner's behalf at present.

The prisoner was then committed to take her trial at the Assizes at Winchester.

The girl Elizabeth Ada Urry arrived at Winchester by the eight o'clock train from Portsmouth, on Thursday night, on her committal upon the capital charge. A considerable number of persons had assembled at the station. The girl walked out with tolerable unconcern, carrying a bunch of flowers, and her custodians being in plain clothes, she was not at first noticed. A cab was called, and she was driven to the prison in the Romsey Road.

BEFORE JUDGE AND JURY.

In the Crown Court at the Hampshire Assizes this morning, before Mr. Justice Day, Elizabeth Ada Whiting (better known in Portsmouth as "Ada Urry"), 14, was indicted for feloniously, wilfully, and of her malice aforethought; killing and murdering Emma Downton, aged five years at Portsea, on the 23rd of April.

Mr. Bucknill, Q.C., and Mr. Folkard, (instructed by Mr. G. Hall King, of Portsmouth, on behalf of the Treasury) prosecuted, and prisoner was defended by Mr. C. Matthews (instructed by Messrs Hyde and Hobbs, of Portsmouth).

The Court was crowded, among those present being the Mayor of Portsmouth. The Jury were called punctually at ten o'clock, but it was some time before Mr. Justice Day entered the Court. The reason for the delay in the commencement of the proceedings was, it is understood, that Mr. Bucknill, Q.C., the principal counsel for the Crown, together with Mr. Matthews, who defended, were in consultation with his Lordship to the desirability, under all the circumstances, of abandoning the indictment for the capital offence and accepting a plea on the part of the prisoner on the count for manslaughter.

At twenty minutes past ten order was called and Mr. Justice Day took his seat, immediately after which the prisoner was arraigned, and, in reply to the Clerk of the Assizes as to whether she was guilty or not guilty of the wilful murder of Emma Downton, replied in a firm voice, "Not guilty."

Prisoner, who was very pale, was dressed precisely the same as when before the Magistrates, her dark frock being partially covered by a light drab mantle. She wore a white straw hat, trimmed with ribbons and cream lace. When the Jury were being empanelled, Mr. Matthews engaged in earnest conversation with the prisoner, after which Mr. Bucknill proceeded to open the case on behalf of the Crown. As the charge was read to the Jury, the prisoner burst into tears, and she was then accommodated with a seat in the dock, where a female warder was in attendance with her.

OPENING SPEECH FOR THE PROSECUTION.

Mr. Bucknill said it was his duty, on behalf of the prosecution, to lay before the Jury the facts which would lead them to come to a decision one way or the other to the guilt or innocence of the prisoner. They had heard that the prisoner was charged with the wilful murder of a little girl at Southsea, and he had before him a very painful, though at the same time simple, duty. He was not there as an advocate, but simply as one charged with the duty of laying before the Court and the Jury actual facts of the case as disclosed in the case presented by the prosecution. He would not say one word which might appear to press harshly upon the prisoner, but he had no option but to so arrange the facts that justice might be done.

The learned counsel then proceeded to give a complete history of the case. With the plan of the locality before him, Mr. Bucknill traced prisoner's movements from the time she left Fratton Road with baby Waters in the perambulator on the afternoon of April 23rd, until she returned home late that night and commenced to cut up the deceased's bonnet. Referring to the prisoner being seen on the Common with two children, and in conversation with a soldier, he said he did not suggest that the latter had anything to do with the case, or that he was even known to the prisoner; indeed, it appeared that while sleeping on a seat he was awakened by the children, and spoke to them.

After touching upon the circumstances which led to the arrest of the Prisoner on a charge of decoying the deceased from home, the learned counsel described the manner in which the body was discovered in the well. The doctor's evidence, he said, was most important; indeed, its importance could not be over-estimated, for the doctors felt convinced that the child Downton was dead when placed in the well. He would remind the Jury, however, that he did not say that because the child was dead when placed in the well, it followed that she was murdered. It was possible that the deceased might have been killed by misadventure. In that case it would not be murder.

On the other hand, although he could not place his hand upon any motive for the crime, it was possible that in some unforeseen circumstances, perhaps in a fit of temper, or in a wicked, mad spirit, the prisoner might have killed the child. It was the duty of the Jury to determine whether the prisoner was guilty of manslaughter or wilful murder.

In conclusion, he submitted that the handkerchief found round the neck of the deceased was placed there by the prisoner, and that the child was dead when placed in the well where the body was discovered on May 2nd, in consequence of a statement made by the prisoner.

A WITNESS CALLED.

Thomas Downton, father of the deceased child, was then called into the box. While the witness was being sworn, Mr. Hobbs, prisoner's solicitor, had an interview with his client, at the conclusion of which Mr. Matthews, addressing the Judge, said the accused had expressed a desire to be counselled by him as to the position in which she stood before the Court. He (Mr. Matthews), accepted the responsibility of counselling her, in the hearing of the Judge and Jury, to say that she had been guilty of an act of manslaughter. His learned friend, Mr. Bucknill, to whose fairness he would testify in presenting the case to his Lordship and the Jury, had said that it was one in which no motive was to be found, a case in which it was possible that the girl might have placed the handkerchief round the child's neck without intending to kill her, and having so placed the handkerchief by the application of some unlawful force, brought about the death of the deceased. In the circumstances, he ventured to submit that a fair and proper solution of the case was that it was one of manslaughter. At the proper time he proposed calling witnesses to speak as to prisoner's character. That, however, was a matter for after consideration, but he understood that Mr. Bucknill was ready, on the part of the prosecution, to consent to the acceptance of a plea of manslaughter upon such an admission made by the prisoner in the hearing of the Judge and Jury as he was now able to tell the Court she would make.

Mr. Bucknill said that he had heard with great relief the statement made by his learned friend. If his Lordship thought that in this case, on the facts he had opened— and he had not omitted anything— justice would be met by prisoner pleading guilty to a charge of manslaughter, and admitting that she placed the handkerchief around the child s neck, and that the child was dead when placed in the well, he was ready to accept that plea; because he was not in possession of any facts enabling him to suggest a motive for the murder, he was not in a position to show that the prisoner had any wicked feeling towards the deceased, or that she had ever seen her before the afternoon in question.

Mr. Justice Day said it was not for him to judge as to the weight of the evidence which was available to the learned counsel for the Crown. It was true he had read the depositions, but he had not the advantage which Mr. Bucknill possessed of having the whole of the facts and circumstances brought to his knowledge. Of course, it was competent for the Jury to take a view of the case other than that the prisoner had wilfully murdered the child, and it would, if the case went on, be his duty to tell the Jury that the moment the little girl Emma Downton died by the hands of the prisoner at the bar, wilful murder was *prima facie* proved against her, and such circumstances as would reduce the crime of murder to one of manslaughter would have to be shown by the prisoner. This would be the instruction he would have to give to the Jury.

Mr. Bucknill, however, had the evidence before him, and he also had the circumstances in his mind as given to him by those by whom he had been instructed. If, therefore, he thought, having this knowledge in his possession, that the Jury would not be likely to find a verdict of guilty upon the more serious charge, he (the Judge) thought he would be quite right in assenting to the course proposed by Mr. Matthews on behalf of the prisoner. The circumstances of the case were painful, but if Mr. Bucknill thought there was a probability of the Jury returning a verdict of wilful murder it was the duty of the Court and the Jury to proceed with the indictment upon which the prisoner had been arraigned.

GUILTY OF MANSLAUGHTER.

The Crown accepted a plea of guilty of manslaughter, and "Elizabeth "Ada" Urry" was sentenced to five years' penal servitude.

1893 – THE COPPER STREET FIRE.

An inquest touching the death of John Henry Shea and his three children, who perished in a fire at 17, Copper Street, Southsea, was opened yesterday afternoon, at the Town Hall, before the Portsmouth Coroner (T. A. Bramsdon, Esq., J.P.) and a Jury of fifteen, who appointed Mr. D. Quick as their foreman.

The Coroner, opening the proceedings, observed that the Jury had been called together to inquire to the death of four persons, the circumstances in connection with whose end were of a very serious and painful character. A more lamentable case could hardly be imagined, seeing that the deceased perished in a fire which occurred at a dwelling-house. The deceased man, Shea, with his wife and three children, occupied part of

No. 17, Copper Street, premises belonging to Edward Colley, of 39, Great Southsea Street, and sub-let by a person named King to various others.

The house, which was situated on the corner of Copper Street and Waterloo Passage, contained eight rooms, two of which were in the basement, two on the ground floor, two on the first floor, and two on the second floor. The passage ran at the side of one of the back rooms, from which it was divided simply by match-boarding. The back rooms on the ground and first floors were rented by Shea, who at the time of the fire, was sleeping with his wife and children in the upper apartment. A man named Peter Hardman occupied with his family the front room on the ground floor, while Alfred Windle and his wife were in the front room on the first floor. The other rooms were unoccupied.

Shea, who had just retired from the Cameronians, went home at ten o'clock, and he believed the Jury would be told that he was then under the influence of drink. He appeared to have had some money, the amount of which would probably be given in evidence later on. It seemed that his wife and he had had some words.

Mrs. Shea (interrupting): I beg your pardon, sir, but there were no words; none whatever.

The Coroner, continuing, said that that was an important matter which should receive consideration at the hands of the Jury. At 12.30 a.m. the fire was discovered. The wife detected it and went downstairs to find it so severe as to prevent her from returning to the bedroom. An alarm was at once raised, and the Fire Brigade went with all possible speed to the place, but were unable to save deceased. He did not desire to make any comment at this stage of the inquiry, except to say to the Jury that it was their duty to inquire whether the fire was accidental or arose in consequence of the act of incendiary. He did not suggest that there was any incendiarism in this case, and simply mentioned the matter in order that the Jury might start with a clear understanding as to the nature of their duties. He purposed taking evidence of identification only that afternoon, and would then adjourn the case until next Monday afternoon, at three o'clock, when an omnibus would be in attendance to convey the Jury to the scene of the fire. The ruins would meanwhile be kept as present, assuming, of course, that there was nothing dangerous about them.

VIEWING THE REMAINS.

The Coroner and Jury then proceeded to the mortuary, where the four bodies were lying. All presented a terrible appearance, being partly consumed by the fire and otherwise mutilated by heavy objects which had fallen upon them while the fire was in progress. Mrs. Shea went to the mortuary leaning for support upon two female friends and appearing very ill and well-nigh broken down by shock and intense grief. Before the disfigured remains of her deceased husband and children were exposed to view, the Coroner, in sympathetic terms, begged her to spare herself the ordeal of gazing upon the still forms, which were lying upon the slabs in the dead-house. She, however, requested to be allowed to look upon the bodies, exclaiming in piteous tones "Oh it is cruel! What have I done that you should not allow me to see my husband?"

The Coroner, however, decided that she should not be called upon to identify the remains, and she was gently removed from the mortuary by Chief Inspector Bidgood before the coverings were lifted off from the dead, and the bodies were formally identified by Mr. Pordage, Superintendent of the Fire Brigade, as those found by him after the fire had been extinguished. The first witness was Arthur Pordage, the Superintendent of the Portsmouth Fire Brigade.

He deposed that at 12.42 that morning, then being in bed, he was called through the alarm which was given at headquarters. Three minutes later he was turning into Commercial Road with the fire engine and six men, and at 12.47 they arrived on the scene and found the back part of No. 17 on fire. Flames were coming from each window at the back and through the roof. The house consisted of four rooms at the front and four at the back, the rooms being one over the other. The staircase was a part of the back room of the house, and from each front room there was a door leading out on to the stairs. Witness found that Fireman Batt and P.C.s Starks and Ray had already arrived and were at the front of the building with the jumping sheet and the loose ladders from the fire escape. He was told that there were several children in the home.

The Coroner: How did you know that?— Witness said he was told that by the neighbours. The steamer and a stand-pipe were got into work, and with Firemen Davey and Tanner he proceeded to search the rooms. The flames were then coming through the panels of the doors of the room. He could see that the floorings of the back rooms were burnt right through. They found no traces of the children at the front, but there was a small dog in the first floor front room partially suffocated. The dog he handed out, and it was now alive. They then went to the back, and through the window of the first floor room witness could see the bodies of the father and of the two girls. It was some time after that, however, before they could get into the building to get the bodies out. The body of the boy they found shortly afterwards in a cot on the opposite side of the room. Witness subsequently had the bodies wrapped up and conveyed to the mortuary cart, and the fire was gradually extinguished by the steamer. There were three escapes there, but it was difficult to get the ladder up to the back, as the fire was much advanced when they arrived. The flames were very severe, and there was great difficulty in getting the ladders through Waterloo Passage.

The Coroner: How long do you think it was after you got there before the bodies were seen? Witness thought it was ten minutes. They searched the front rooms, and made attempts to get into the back, but it was impossible for them to do anything there. The flames, as he had said before, were coming out from each window. There was an abundance of water, and the Water Company's turncock went with the engine. The Coroner: You usually search for people as soon as possible? – Witness: Yes. We did so on this occasion at the front, thinking they might have escaped from the back into the front. The Coroner: Did you see Mrs. Shea? – Witness said he saw her in the house of Mrs. King, and she gave him to understand that just before going to bed she saw her husband strike a match to light his pipe, and that he dropped the match upon the floor. She was, of course, greatly excited.

The Coroner: Did she tell you anything about her husband? – Witness: She said he was under the influence of drink, and that she had remonstrated with him for being in that condition, but that after a few words with him she went to bed. Did she say where she left her husband? – She said she had left him in the back room downstairs, but that he afterwards came upstairs, sat upon a chair bedstead, and fell asleep. She also said that about half past 12, as nearly as she could say she awoke and found the room full of smoke, to which she called the attention of her husband. He told her to open the window, and she did so, when she found the stairs also full of smoke, when the kitchen door was opened the flames shot up the stairs. Owing to that she was unable to get back to her children, and she then said that she went into Waterloo Passage and gave an alarm to Mrs. King and the police.

As far as witness could ascertain he believed that match-boarding formed the divisions between the rooms and the staircase. The wall was not more than 4 inches thick. The front door of the house was Copper Street, and the passage went through to the back. The Coroner: So that if the match-boarding caught it would rapidly communicate with the staircase? — Witness: Yes, more especially as the door and the window were open. Did the roof fall in?— Yes, at the back, —Witness further detailed the position of the bodies in the house. The two girls were on the bedstead, which had partly fallen through the floor, and one of those bodies fell into the room below, where it was found by Sergeant Vassie, of the Fire Brigade. He first saw the body of the man with the limbs projecting through the flooring, lying across what was the bottom step of the staircase, face downwards. Witness had the joist sawn through, so that the body might be lowered through to the first floor without any dismemberment. The body of the boy was found in the cot at the back part of the room.

The Coroner: You had plenty of assistance? – We had five hose-reels, three escapes, and one steamer, with eight men of the Fire Brigade, and many constables. Everything that was possible was done to get into the building, and there was no disorganisation among the crowd. There was nothing of a suspicious nature? — Witness, replied in the negative. The premises were very old, and he believed the fire originated in the back room on the ground floor, as there was a hole in the floor there. The front rooms were not seriously damaged. Witness, in further examination, said that the premises might be better described as having a front room and back room on each floor, with basement cellars and ground, first, and second floors.

Mary Jane Shea, who was dressed in deep mourning, deposed that the bodies viewed in the mortuary were those of her husband, John Henry Shea, aged 33, lately a private in the Scottish Rifles (Cameronian), and had taken his discharge, after 17 years' service, with a pension of 9d. a day; Johanna Shea, aged eight years; Mary Emma Shea, aged six years and George Shea, aged four years. Witness is now living with Mrs. King, at No. 35, Gold Street.

At this stage the Coroner adjourned the inquiry to three o'clock on Monday afternoon next.

An "Eye Witness," resident in Gold Street, writes testifying to the promptness and efficiency shown by the borough Fire Brigade in dealing with the conflagration in Copper Street. "Directly the poor woman (Mrs. Shea) screamed out in the street I saw from my window that the back part of her house was filled with a mass of flames. Had all the fire brigades in London been present, even at that time, no mortal man could have reached the room in which the deceased man and his children were."

RESUMED INQUEST. INSPECTING THE RUINS.

The adjourned inquiry touching the death of John Henry Shea, aged 33 years, and his three children, Johannah, aged eight years, Mary Ellen, aged six years, and George, aged four years, who perished in the fire which occurred at No. 17, Copper Street, Southsea, early Friday morning, was resumed on Monday at the Town Hall, before the Portsmouth Coroner (T. A. Bramsdon, Esq.).

Immediately the Jury panel had been called over, the Coroner observed that there was an omnibus waiting to convey them to the scene of the fire, in order that they might inspect the ruins. Accompanied by the Chief Constable (Mr. H. Le Mesurier) and the Superintendent of the Borough Fire Brigade (Mr. A. Pordage), the Coroner and the Jury then proceeded to Copper Street, where the positions which the bodies of deceased were found were pointed out, and several firemen experimented with the fire escape in order that the Court might clearly understand the difficulty experienced making use of the apparatus owing to the peculiar construction of the premises and the narrowness of the passage which they are approached from Gold Street.

On the return of the Coroner and the Jury to the Town Hall, Superintendent Pordage produced three plans of the premises which he had prepared for the information of the Court.

Mrs. Shea, who was attired in deep mourning, was then recalled. She said she had lived at No. 17, Copper Street since the 6th of last month. She and her family occupied the back bedroom on the ground floor and the back room on the first floor. Her husband took his discharge from the Army last Wednesday, and received £42 12s. 5d. as deferred pay. Of this, £30 was placed in the bank, and he retained £12, 12s. 5d., giving to witness £6 4s. 9d. He went out after dinner on Thursday last, and was brought home at half past eight by a man named Rogers. Witness could see that he had been drinking, and remonstrated with him for taking so much. Her husband replied that this would be the last drop of drink he would ever take, as he was going home to see his dear mother. Witness and her husband had supper in the room on the ground floor, deceased then drank another pint of beer. After supper Shea sent Johanna to Mr. Cartwright's shop for half-an-ounce of tobacco, and when she brought it back he filled his pipe and lighted it, throwing the match on the floor near the fireplace. There was a stuffed rug near the hearth and a bundle of firewood in the fireplace. Witness told him to be careful with his matches, and he had put his foot on the match and said it was all right.

The Coroner: Are you sure that he put the match out? – Witness: Yes, sir; I am positive. This was at about half past nine. There was a small fire in the grate, and a paraffin oil lamp was alight on the table. The table was placed against the wall, facing the fireplace, and near the staircase. About ten o'clock witness went to bed, turning the lamp out before she left the room. The Coroner: Are you sure you put it out? – Witness: I am positive. I turned it down and waited until the light died right out. Continuing, witness said that the children went to bed with her, and her husband followed her upstairs immediately. He placed his pipe on the mantelpiece, but she could not say whether he put it out or not. There was a fringe round the mantelpiece. Her husband and the boy George slept in a bed-chair, and witness and her two daughters slept in the large bed. Witness soon went to sleep and after a little while she awoke with a choking sensation. She found the room full of smoke, and called out to her husband, "Oh John, the room is full of smoke." "Open the window," replied he, and she did so. The smoke, however, seemed to grow in density, and witness ran into the passage and opened the window which looked out into the yard. Looking through the window, she saw the flames coming out of the window on the ground floor. She cried out "Fire, Fire, John, save the children," and ran downstairs for help. She opened the yard door to call Mr. King.

But why did you not see your children safe first? – I had nobody to come to me then, and thought I must get help. I meant to go back directly, but when I opened the back door again I found everything was in flames. But you had your husband in the house, and you had called him when you found the house on fire? – Yes, but he gave me no answer. He was the worse for drink? – Yes. And you were very much frightened? – I was quite excited, and did not know where I was. But why did you not go back for your children in the first place? – It did not strike my mind to do so. I only thought I must get help.

In reply to further questions, witness stated that when she ran downstairs, not only was the back window looking out into the yard on fire, but the inner door was also burst open by the flames, In fact, the whole room was a mass of fire. She knocked repeatedly at King's house, and broke a window before her screams for help were heard. Then she shouted, "For God's sake make haste! The house is on fire. Save my children. Oh, my children!" She tried twice to get back into the house, but the stairs were then gone, and she could not get near the room in which she had left her husband and children. It was about this time that witness fainted, and she knew no more until she found herself in Mr. King's kitchen. Mr. King went for the Fire Brigade.

The Coroner: When you went to bed, were there any clothes round the fire? – Witness: No, sir. Have you any idea what time you woke up? – It must have been about half past twelve. Then, as you went to bed at ten o'clock you were asleep at least two hours? – Yes, sir.

By the Jury: My husband put the matchbox on the mantelpiece near his pipe when he went to bed.

Elizabeth Hardman, wife of Peter Hardman, bugler of the Cameronians, stated that she was in the house at half past eight o'clock when the deceased man came home under the influence of drink. Later on she again saw him, and advised him to go to bed, but he refused, saying that he was "all right." Shea then appeared to have somewhat recovered from the effects of the drink he had consumed. Witness heard Mr. and Mrs. Shea going upstairs to bed shortly after ten o'clock, and noticed that the man stumbled as he ascended. Witness retired to rest at about 10.30 p.m., and slept until aroused by the cries of Mrs. Shea. Her husband opened the door of their room, and she saw that the staircase and some articles in the passage, including a perambulator, were in flames. She escaped with her husband and two children through the window of the room which they occupied. She heard Mrs. Shea's little girl crying, "Oh! mammy!" but at that time it was impossible for anyone to reach the children from the passage. Witness's husband went back into their room in order to go to them, but was unable to get through the passage. Mr. and Mrs. Shea were on friendly terms, witness heard no quarrelling between them on the night of the fire.

Bugler Peter Hardman, of the Cameronians, said that he opened the door of his room, but could not reach the front door. The back of the house was full of fire. When he heard Mrs. Shea crying, "Save the children!" he had escaped with his family through the window, but he returned to the room, opened the door, and crawled on his hands and knees towards the staircase. The stairs, however, were then crackling, and in the act of falling, and he was compelled to retreat. He saw a man named Windle and his wife at the window of their room upstairs, and, with other men, held out some of his bedding for them to jump out upon. He thought that not more than three minutes elapsed between the time he got out of the house and the arrival of Fireman Batt with the escape. He was greatly excited, and could give no information concerning the arrival of the Brigade. In fact, he did not see the engine at all.

Minnie Windle, the wife of a lance-corporal in the Cameronians, said she and her husband had occupied a room on the first floor of 17, Copper Street. She went into the Shea's kitchen on Thursday evening, and saw the deceased man and Rogers there. The former was under the influence of drink. The Sheas went to bed about ten o'clock, and she did not hear any quarrelling. Witness and her husband went to bed at half past ten, and at about half past twelve she was awakened by someone screaming. She roused her husband, and opened their room door, but had to close it again, as the flames burst into the room. The back part of the house was on fire, and in a minute or two the door of her room began to blaze. She and her husband escaped by jumping into a sheet held by some men in the street, and she was taken in by Mrs. Cartwright.

Alfred Windle, husband of the last witness, corroborated his wife's evidence. About a quarter of an hour after he was awakened he saw the fire escape from the Victoria Barracks arrive. He did not know that three escapes were brought to the fire.

Henry Rogers, a private of the Cameronians, said that he knew the deceased man, when Shea was sergeant, since when he had been reduced first to corporal and then to the ranks. Witness met him at the Casino, in Warblington Street, between 8 o'clock and 8.30 on Thursday evening, and seeing that he was much the worse for drink, persuaded him to go home with him. Witness saw him home, and after staying to supper left the house at 9.15 to return to barracks. Deceased had no drink while witness was with him at 17, Copper Street. The whole family of Sheas were in the back room downstairs while he was there, but just before he took his departure the elder girl took the baby to bed.

Thomas Henry Nancarrow, landlord of a public house, Gold Street, said that the back part of his premises abutted on to the yards in Copper Street, At about twenty minutes to one on Friday morning last he was roused by hearing a woman scream out "Mrs. King! God! My children!" Witness looked out of the window, and saw that it was a woman in her nightdress who was screaming. Looking through the window at the back of his house, he saw a solid sheet of flame coming from the first floor window of 17, Copper Street. Witness dressed himself and went into the street. The flames had then a complete hold on the house, and it was impossible to rescue anyone. He asked if anyone had gone for the Fire Brigade, and was told no. However, someone immediately started off for the Brigade. Witness went round to the front of the house, and saw a man, who was pushed up by two other men, get into the window of the first floor front room, and search about. He was unable to find anyone. However, in a very short time, the fire engine arrived, and he was really astonished in the manner which the Brigade worked. Witness had seen a great many fires, but had never seen one at which the firemen worked more quickly and efficiently than on this occasion.

Edward Parrett, of 1, Waterloo Passage, almost opposite 17, Copper Street, labourer at the dockyard, stated that he was aroused at 12.35 on Friday morning by someone shouting in the passage, and on looking out of his bedroom window he heard the fire crackling. He dressed himself and went into the street to find Bugler Hardman trying to break open the door of 17, Copper Street. Constable Ray then arrived, and witness went with him in search of a ladder. They went to the Victoria Barracks and brought back the fire escape, kept at the main guard, and on arrival found that another escape had already arrived in King's Road. Those in charge of it could not, however, take it through Waterloo Passage, and a ladder from it was quickly carried round to the front of the burning house. When witness first saw the fire, he was of the opinion that the flames had obtained such a hold upon the premises as to prevent anyone from entering at the back.

By the Jury: They asked for help at the main guard. The sergeant there said he had only two men with him and could spare one, but witness did not see him leave the barracks. However, witness and Constable Ray were able to manage the escape which belonged to the borough.

Charles Joseph Triggs, naval pensioner, living at 13, Copper Street, said he was roused by the fire, and saw the back part of No. 17 in blaze. No one could get near the back. He heard Mrs. Shea calling out "Save my children," and witness, getting a "leg up" from two men got into the front room on the first floor, but could find nothing. It was quite impossible for him to get into the backroom. The fire engine arrived promptly, and the Brigade worked very cooly.

Mary Ann King, wife of a refreshment-house keeper, of 35, Gold Street, a house situated at the corner of Waterloo Passage, stated that she rented 17, Copper Street, from the owner, Mr. Colley, of Great Southsea Street, and having furnished it, let it to married soldiers and their families. The basement was used in common by the lodgers for washing purposes. Deceased rented the back room on the ground floor and the apartment above it. The lamp referred to by Mrs. Shea, was an ordinary reading lamp filled with paraffin, and cost when new some time ago, 3s. 9d., she believed. The same kind of lamp was now sold at 2s. 2d. There had been no fire under the copper in the basement on Thursday.

Constable Ray said that at about 12.30 on Friday morning he was in Kings Road, near the Goat, with P.S. Price and Fireman Batt. They heard screams coming, they thought, from Landport Terrace. They went in different directions and in a few minutes came in view of the fire. Witness went to the scene of the fire and saw Mrs. Shea, who told him her children were in the house. He went to the backyard door and tried to get entrance, but the flames were so fierce that he could not do so. Windle and his wife jumped into the blanket which witness and other spectators held. Witness got through the window of the front room downstairs and tried to get into the passage, but could not do so, as the staircase was almost burnt away. He and witness then went for the fire escape outside the Victoria Barracks. Witness asked a soldier on the gate for assistance, as there was a fire and people were being burnt to death. The soldier replied, "I cannot. I have only two men here, and cannot spare them." When they got back with the escape they found that Fireman Batt had got a ladder against the front wall of the house, and he and witness went up and got into the window of the front room on the first floor. Batt fainted, through the smoke, and witness had to pull him out. When witness first arrived on the scene the flames were so fierce as to make it impossible for any person to get into the yard at the back of the house.

Fireman William Batt deposed that he was on duty in Kings Road with the fire escape, and was standing at the corner of Stone Street with the last witness and P. S. Price, when they heard a woman screaming. Immediately afterwards a cry of "Fire" was raised, and witness, after blowing his whistle thrice, met Constable Stares, who assisted him to take the fire escape to Flint Street and thence into Gold Street. Mr. Lever, tobacconist, also lent aid. Finding that the escape would not go through the passage, and learning that several persons had been left in the house, witness, with the help of Starks, lowered the escape, disconnected the extension ladder, carried the latter to the front of the house, and, breaking the window, entered one of the upper rooms. Finding no one there and seeing the fire creeping up through the back, he descended, and next got through the window of the room on the first floor. Mr. Pordage had by this time arrived on the scene, and was entering the first floor window with scaling ladders. When witness reached the fire it was impossible for anyone to enter the back, owing to the flames which were leaping from the windows and doors.

Dr. Maybury, the police surgeon, said that at 1.45 a.m. Friday last he was called to the fire in Copper Street. Arriving there he was shown the dead bodies of Shea and his two daughters, the body of the boy was found while he was there. The remains were removed to the mortuary, and the following day witness made superficial examination of each of the deceased. Shea and the girl Mary Ellen were completely charred. The other girl and boy were not so much burnt except about the head. In his opinion each of the deceased died from suffocation and not from burning, the charring of the bodies occurring subsequent to death.

In summing up, the Coroner observed that they had thrashed out all the evidence in the case, and had before them information sufficient to enable them to arrive at a verdict. There was not the slightest doubt that the unfortunate victims succumbed to suffocation, the result of the fire. As compared with death from burning, their end was a painless one, a circumstance which might be a source of consolation to the widow. Never had he (the Coroner) experienced a case which a fire in such a small place burned with such amazing rapidity in this instance. Deceased was drunk when he went to bed, and when the alarm was given probably became stupefied, and consequently unable to extricate himself from the bedclothes. It was to be regretted that Mrs. Shea lost her head, but they could all fully understand and appreciate the position in which she was placed. He did not think anyone could speak but in praise of the neighbours, the police, and the Fire Brigade. He commented severely on the construction of the house, and said that only a partition and match-boarding divided some of the rooms. In a house constructed in this manner, no one in the upper rooms had any chance of escape if fire broke out below.

He was sure that the Corporation would see that in modern houses the construction was such to make such fires as this impossible.

The Jury returned a verdict of accidental death, They awarded their fees to the widow. The Coroner announced that he had received from Mr. Gill, of Osborne Road, a cheque for half-a-guinea for Mrs. Shea.

1893 – POINT DROWNING CASE.

The body of a man found floating at the mouth of the Portsmouth Camber, and picked up by a waterman named Barron, last Saturday morning, still lies at the public mortuary unidentified. A full description of the deceased has been circulated throughout the country by the police, who, however, have not yet been able to glean any information tending to throw light upon the matter. The pockets of deceased's overcoat were weighted with pieces of brick and heavy stones, and it is believed, that the case is one of suicide.

1893 – MYSTERIOUS OCCURRENCE AT SOUTHSEA.

At his Court in the Portsmouth Town Hall, yesterday afternoon, the Borough Coroner (T. A. Bramsdon, Esq., J.P.) held an inquiry into the death of James Wallace, aged 34 years, a gunner in the Royal Artillery, stationed at Cambridge Barracks, Portsmouth.

William Rafferty, a gunner in No. 1 Company, Southern Division Royal Artillery, stationed at Cambridge Barracks, Portsmouth, gave evidence of identification of deceased. Wallace, he said, was a widower and was a shoemaker by trade. He was usually a sober man and popular amongst his comrades. Witness last saw him alive on the evening of the 26th inst. Deceased then complained of feeling tired, and said he was going out that night and would be dead the next day. Witness endeavoured to cheer him up, and at deceased's request went to the canteen with him and had some beer. At that time deceased was under the influence of drink. Soon after that they parted company, and that was the last time the witness saw him alive.

Susanna Gilbert, the wife of a Bath-chair proprietor, who carries on a greengrocery business at 70, Castle Road, under the name of Yates, said that about 9.30 on the evening of the 26th, deceased, whom she had since identified, came into her shop and purchased six pennyworth of oranges. He looked very pale and staggered slightly as he went out of the shop. She recognised the paper bag and orange produced as those she had sold deceased.

Annie Dove, cook in the employ of Mr. Hastings, of Bayfield, Kent Road, Southsea said she had been out with deceased about a dozen times during the last month. She last saw him alive on Sunday night, when he went for a walk with her. On Tuesday night she went to bed at ten o'clock and did not hear anyone walking about in the front garden. When she raised the kitchen window-blind at eight o'clock the next morning she saw deceased lying in the front garden. She told the housemaid and a boy named Pither what she had seen, and the boy went for a constable.

The Coroner: I believe that since then you have received a postcard from deceased? – Witness: Yes sir. – Where is it? – I burnt it; the housemaid told me to do so. – Did you not know that an inquiry would be held into the matter, and that every bit of information would be needed! I cannot believe that a woman of your age did not know it was a most improper thing to do. What did the postcard say? – "When shall I see you? J.W." – Is that all? – Yes sir. Answering a question by a Juryman, witness said she knew the man lying in the garden was deceased, because she could recognise his face from the kitchen window. There were bars against the kitchen window and also against her bedroom window, which adjoined the kitchen.

Harriet Angell, housemaid at Bayfield, corroborated. She was sure Dove did not go out on Tuesday evening, because she (witness) locked the back door at six o'clock and gave the key to Miss Hastings. She advised Dove to burn the postcard. The Coroner: What business had you to ask her to do that? Did you not know that there would be an inquest? – Witness: Yes, sir. I had no reason in asking her to burn it. I did it without a thought.

Mr. Hugh Hastings, who resides at Bayfield, said that he was at home on Tuesday evening, but did not hear any noise in the garden. When I went to bed at twelve o'clock he fancied he heard footsteps going past his window. The next day he found some footprints near the kitchen window, and after inspecting the deceased man's boots he thought the soil on them might be the same as that on which the footprints were made. He could not recognise the deceased, but remembered that on Sunday and Monday evenings last a soldier in a dark uniform, who was the worse for liquor, came to his back door and he (witness) turned him out. He had the impression that the man and the deceased were the same person.

Constable Foyle said that on Wednesday morning, at a quarter past eight, he went to Bayfield, and found deceased lying on his back in the back garden. His head was against the wall, and bent forward, and his cap was off, being on the ground beside him. He had a bag with six oranges in his hand. He was dead, and witness sent for Dr. Alexander, The body was afterwards removed to the mortuary.

Dr. S. P. Alexander said he saw deceased when he was lying in the back garden at Bayfield, and made a post mortem examination of the remains at the mortuary. Blood was trickling from the left ear, and there was a circular contused wound at the back of the head. There was also a fracture at the base of the skull, which, with haemorrhage, had caused the death. From the position in which he found deceased, witness was of the opinion that he must have fallen heavily backwards and struck his head against the wall, so causing the injury, which produced instantaneous death.

The Coroner: Could he have met with that injury merely by falling back while in a drunken condition? Witness: I think so. – Could the injury have been produced by a blow from a blunt instrument? – It is possible, but I don't think probable. If he had been struck I should have expected to have found some depression of the skull at the seat of the injury, but there was none.

In summing up the Coroner said he first regarded the case as a very suspicious one. He had ordered the fullest inquiry to be made, and the circumstances led to the conclusion in which had been arrived at by the doctor. He could not help saying that the two girls, Dove and Angell, could tell them something more of the case if they would open their mouths, It was clear that the deceased man must have had some communication with them, either by talking to them or by rapping on the window, because the marks of footsteps were found near the window. He did not mean to infer that they had anything to do with the man's death.

The Jury returned a verdict of accidental death.

1893 – A SHOCKING AFFAIR AT SOUTHSEA.

At about half past two o'clock yesterday a painful sensation was created at Southsea by a shocking incident which happened on the Common in front of Western Parade. The sharp report of firearms arrested the attention of several persons who happened to be in the vicinity of one of the garden seats placed for the convenience of the public on the Common, upon which was reclining the body of a young fellow having the appearance of a working man, and apparently about 28 years of age. It was at once seen that the man was seriously injured, and he was bleeding profusely from the head when Dr. Robertson, who was called to give surgical assistance, arrived on the scene and ascertained that the contents of a revolver had been discharged into his mouth.

The weapon was lying near the sufferer, and appearances indicated that the wound was self-inflicted. The man was unconscious, but life was not extinct, and a cab was procured, in which he was conveyed to the Hospital at Mile End with the greatest possible expedition. His removal was superintended by Constable Foyle, and on arrival at the institution he was at once attended by the House Surgeon and admitted for treatment. It has since transpired that the wound sustained by the unfortunate man is not as dangerous as was at first feared, the bullet having passed through his cheek. The patient's name is F. C. Beale, and he is stated to reside at 162, Fratton Street, Landport.

1893 – DEATH FROM ALCOHOLISM AT BUCKLAND.

The circumstances attending the death of Laura Jane Simons, aged 40, of 26, Dumbarton Street, Buckland, formed the subject of an inquiry before the Portsmouth Coroner (T. A. Bramsdon, Esq.), at the Town Hall, on Monday.

William J. J. Simons, a writer in the Dockyard, and the husband of the deceased, stated that some five years ago she became addicted to drink. They took the pledge together, but the deceased gradually broke out again, and had since been at times addicted to drink. She generally enjoyed excellent health, but when under the influence of drink complained of shortness of breath and weakness in her limbs. On Saturday last deceased was drinking more or less throughout the day, and appeared somewhat excited. On retiring to bed about 12 o'clock she fell down 'all of a heap" while undressing and never spoke again. He at once rushed downstairs, and sent a neighbour for his sister and a doctor.

By a Juror: At times, when excited, my wife complained of pains in her side.

Dr. J. G. Blackman, who was called in, and who afterwards examined the deceased, attributed death to alcoholism, the immediate cause being syncope, resulting from the diseased condition of the heart and other organs.

The Jury returned a verdict to the effect that death had been caused by heart disease brought about by alcoholism.

1893 – THE SCENE ON SOUTHSEA ESPLANADE.

This afternoon at the Portsmouth Police court, James Hutcheson Magill Potter, 28, was brought on remand, charged with assaulting Colonel H. Lachlan Young, and also with attempting to obtain money by menace, by writing a threatening postcard to Colonel Young.

The assault, it was alleged, took place last Saturday week, and was deposed to when prisoner was first before the Magistrates. He was then remanded in order that the medical officer at the Gaol might observe the state of his mind. Dr. J. MacGregor now sent in a statement saying he had had the prisoner under his observation, and was of the opinion that he was of sound mind.

Mr. G. Hall King appeared for the prosecution, and said that the prisoner was the son of the Rev. Dr. Potter, and brother-in-law to Colonel Young. On Saturday week the prisoner met the prosecutor and his wife on the Southsea Esplanade, and after using abusive language he struck Colonel Young. He then seemed to have gone to the Southsea Post office and despatched a postcard, which read as follows: "After what has happened today, I tell you once more, and once and for all, that unless you contribute towards my support, I will do something you will be sorry for. I will so worry your wretched life that you will be glad to pay me to keep away, James. There is not much to live for, God knows, but I will have my revenge, but not before the worst happens."

Mr. King observed that the prisoner had been kept by his friends, who allowed him 15s. a week. He had acquired habits of laziness, and was determined not to work. He had resorted to the method of extorting money from his friends, and Mr. King asked the Magistrates to commit him for trial at the Assizes.

Colonel Young said he lived at Montague House, Granada Road, and was a retired Lieutenant-Colonel of the Indian Army. Prisoner was his brother-in-law.

Prisoner: "I wish to God I was out of this blessed world. You come here to worst me, so as to try and put me in prison for two years. You inhuman wretch. May the God who created me judge you as well. I was only singing the hymn, "My God, my Father, while I stray," and I am sure those words went to my Father as I sang them. This world is hard enough, God knows. What is there to live for?" During the delivery of the above the prisoner became very impassioned, and had to be held by two constables.

Colonel Young, continuing, said that on Saturday, the 8th inst., he was walking with his wife, who was in a bath chair, on the Esplanade, when he saw the prisoner looking into the sea.

Prisoner (excitedly): "I wish to God I was under it. What are we born for? Nothing but misery."

The Magistrates' Clerk told him to compose himself, and said he was only making matters worse.

Prisoner: "I don't care. Put me to gaol for ten thousand years. My life is lost, gone! Let me die in gaol, for what I care. If God created this world, He created a wretched, miserable hole. I have often thought, "Is there a God?" The world does not care for me. God knows you won't, but you will be judged someday."

Continuing, Colonel Young said that immediately the prisoner caught sight of him he ran and commenced using horrible language. He was in a very excited condition, and catching him (witness) by the shoulder, pushed him down the bank. He also picked up a stone, and threatened to dash his brains out with it, besides attempting to strike him with a cane. As witness walked along, the prisoner followed him, calling out, "You have stopped my allowance and I must have money. I am starving, and you must give me money."

Prisoner: "No, you will not. You try to hound me down."

Witness, continuing, said that he afterwards applied for a warrant for the prisoner's arrest. The same evening he was at home, when he received the threatening postcard by post. He could swear that it was written and directed in the prisoner's handwriting.

Asked if he had any questions to put, the prisoner said, in a loud voice: "How did I assault you? Can you show any scar where I hit you? As regards the postcard, I wrote it, but I didn't send it. It was in my coat pocket at the time they took me up. I believe it was sent by the people at the police station."

David Spencer, postman, said he remembered delivering the postcard to the prosecutor's house on the evening of the 8th inst.

Charles Wilford, chief warder at Kingston Prison, said he saw the prisoner writing the letter produced. The missive, which was addressed to Colonel Young, was read by the Clerk, and in it the prisoner asked Colonel and Mrs. Young to forgive him for his nasty temper. He meant no harm, and to hurt nobody. He asked also that his allowance might be raised to £1 a week, as he could not keep himself on 15s. He wanted to go to Ireland, for he liked the climate and the people, and thought he could get work there.

Constable Ralph said he arrested the prisoner on Southsea Common on Saturday evening. On charging him the prisoner said, "That reads very well, but I did not assault him. I did not lay my hand on him." He denied sending the postcard.

Prisoner: It was in my pocket when you apprehended me, and it was taken out and sent by you or someone else.

The constable contradicted this.

Catching sight of Colonel Young in Court, the prisoner exclaimed, "Don't you gloat over me. Wouldn't you like to kill me, you hard-hearted wretch!"

Prisoner was requested to sit down, but he replied, "Sit down; I can't sit down. I have some hot Irish blood in me, and I can't sit like a mummy, I have got some life in me. We are all going to the grave, and good job when we get there."

James Hennen, Inspector of Postmen at Portsmouth, said the postcard produced reached the head office between 5.15 and 5.40 on the night of the 8th. It was delivered in the seven o'clock delivery.

The usual caution was administered to the prisoner, who replied, "I wrote the postcard, but I did not send it. I call no witnesses, as I have no friends in this place."

Major Greetham: We now commit you to take your trial at the next Winchester Assizes, which take place in August or July.

Prisoner: Are you going to keep me in prison all that time?

Mr. King: I oppose bail. Prisoner is a most dangerous man.

Prisoner: "No sir, I am not, if people will only leave me to myself, and not come after me, as this man does." Turning to Colonel Young, he shouted out, "Yes, I mean you. I am no fool. How glad you are in your wretched heart that I am going to be tried."

The Magistrates decided to grant bail, prisoner in £100 and two sureties of £50. Prisoner was removed in custody, and as he was going below he turned to the occupants of the gallery and exclaimed, "If you want to do some good in your lives, will you find the money to bail me out with?"

At the Hants Assizes in July, Colonel Young once again took the stand and said that he had once assisted the prisoner with money, and that since the latter had been in gaol he (prosecutor) had received a letter from him regretting his conduct, saying it had arisen through his "beastly temper," that his conscience had punished him sufficiently without any other punishment, and that it was not himself, but "the Devil that was within him."

The prisoner handed up a lengthy document, wishing that it "might be read before the world," but the Judge refused to have it read, as it contained matters altogether irrelevant to the charge.

The prisoner then said that on the day in question he had taken cider, and before that he was not aware that cider was an intoxicant. He accused his friends of turning their backs upon him, instead of receiving him as a "prodigal son," when he returned from Sydney. He denied that he had said anything with an ill motive, and declared that he did not remember anything after he got home. He had been shipwrecked, and had lost all the clothes which his brother-in-law had given him off Newfoundland, "below the cruel waves," but he assured his Lordship that if he had acted wrongly it was entirely owing to the cider. (Laughter).

He pleaded with the Judge not to send him again to gaol, where he had been for three months, and said that he was willing to go to Ireland and earn his living somehow.

The Jury convicted, but recommended him to mercy on account of his infirmity of stuttering.

The Judge said he could not see the slightest grounds for mercy on that account. He had been convicted at Portsmouth two or three times, and he was not going to make the mistake of binding him over to keep the peace. He would certainly go to prison, but he should reserve his judgment until he had made full inquiries about him.

Detective-Sergeant Money said that the prisoner had been well educated at Christ Church, Oxford, but he had been a serious trouble to his friends. He was the son of the Rev. Dr. Potter.

The Judge said that names should not be mentioned, as the prisoner had given his friends trouble enough already.

The Foreman said they did not know all that.

The Judge said the prisoner had had abundant opportunities of doing well.

Detective-Sergeant Money added that the prisoner had in 1889 shot at his father's house with a revolver.

Sentence postponed.

Two days later, James Hutcheson Magill Potter was sentenced to 18 months' imprisonment with hard labour.

1893 – DROWNED IN DESERTING.

An inquest was held on Monday, at the Town Hall, before the Borough Coroner (T. A. Bramsdon, Esq., J.P.), concerning the death of William R. Cowdrey, a stoker belonging to H.M.S. *Seagull*. Mr. E. J. Harvey, agent to the Treasury Solicitor, watched the case on behalf of the Admiralty.

Thos. Cowdrey, an able seaman, serving on board the *Fusce*, a War Department vessel, lying at the Gunwharf, identified the body as that of his brother whose age was 24 years, by tattooing on the arms, and by his hair and clothing. Witness last saw deceased alive on the 16th of June. Frederick Stockman, ship's corporal, of H.M.S. *Vernon*, also identified the deceased, whose ship was attached to the *Vernon* as a tender. The deceased and two others tried to break out of the ship some time ago, but the boat upset when they got some distance from the vessel, and Cowdrey was lost, the others were recaptured, and being afterwards charged with attempting to break out of the ship were sentenced to 92 days' imprisonment.

Thuckston Crafts, captain of a pilot cutter, stated that he found the body of the deceased floating in mid-channel off the Victoria Pier, at five o'clock, on Sunday morning, and towed it ashore, where he handed it over to Constable Dighton.

James Henry Dawe, surgeon on board H.M.S. *Vernon*, who afterwards examined the body, said that in his opinion the corpse had been in the water for several days. There were no marks of violence beyond a few unimportant abrasions, and appearances pointed to death by drowning.

fetch the teapot she would tell his fortune by the tealeaves. (Laughter.)

The Magistrates sentenced her to seven days' hard labour.

1894 – THE TALE OF THE TEA LEAVES.

At the Portsmouth police Court, Sarah Mann (54), has been charged with pretending to tell the fortune of Alice Mary Tribbeck, a cook.

The prosecutrix told how the woman called and asked for sixpence.

The Clerk: Did she say what it was for?—She said, "The dragon's blood to put on the paper costs 6d." (Laughter). The Clerk: What did she say the dragon's blood was for?—To draw the young men on the wish paper. (Loud laughter.) She also said she should want some more money for the loving cup. She had been to the house four times before. I refused to give her any money, and she became very abusive and called me bad names.

The Clerk: Did she tell you your fortune?—She told me I should have three husbands. (Laughter.) Detective Arthur Peet proved apprehending the prisoner, who in the reserve room said if he would

1894 – OUTRAGE AND SUICIDE NEAR PORTSMOUTH.

A Portsmouth telegram states that at Titchfield, on Thursday night, a farmer named Walker attacked a lad with an axe while the lad was attending to the cattle, inflicting a dangerous wound on his head. Walker, who is believed to have been insane, was subsequently found in a stable, where he had cut his throat, and he died soon afterwards from the self-inflicted injuries.

1894 – PORTSMOUTH FOOTBALL FATALITY.

Mr. E. Goble, County Coroner, held an inquest on Tuesday afternoon at Hasler Hospital concerning the death of Arthur William Richmond, naval

sub-lieutenant, who was fatally injured on Friday last in a football match at Portsmouth. Mr. E. Harvey represented the Admiralty.

Dr. Sylvester Richmond, of Greenhithe, Kent, identified the deceased as his son, aged 20, who was stationed at the Royal Naval College, Portsmouth Dockyard. Deceased had sprained his ankle in a football match some week or two ago, but had recovered from that. The first intimation witness had of the accident was a telegram from the captain of the *Excellent,* and he and Mrs. Richmond came down at once to Haslar, where witness arrived at 10.30 on Saturday evening. Deceased was then dying, and was but half-conscious.

Sub-Lieutenant John C. Kennedy said he was one of the team from the Royal Naval College playing against the Cameronians on the Men's Recreation Ground, Portsmouth, on Friday. They were one man short, and deceased was a goalkeeper, which was his usual post. It was an Association game. During play the College had two or three penalty kicks for "fouls."

The Coroner: Was the knee used at all in those fouls? – Witness: I don't remember, I think so for tripping. Witness also said that only elbows and shoulders should be used in charging. In describing the accident he said that the ball had been shot at the goal and deceased had kicked it. One of the Cameronians was running to try and get the ball through, and just after it had been kicked he and deceased collided, and deceased fell. The two were both going for the ball, and kicked very nearly at the same time. The Cameronian missed, and at the moment of the collision still had one knee up. The two men were only two feet apart when they kicked. Witness was a little behind the Cameronian, and so could not see whether deceased came in to contact with the Cameronian's knee, but that was his impression.

The game was stopped and deceased was helped up, when he said he was all right and was only winded. The game then went on, and deceased went to his post again, but was replaced a few minutes afterwards. The game was not a very rough one. Deceased was not charged from behind, and no penalty kick was claimed for the occurrence. By Mr. Harvey: In witness's opinion nothing could have been claimed, as it was a perfectly fair charge.

Mrs. Richmond, deceased's stepmother, deposed that deceased made no complaint about anyone to her, but told her the injury was done by the knee of a man of the opposite side, who had been very kind to him, and had helped to rub him.

A discussion then ensued as to whether the man who collided with deceased was to be called next or last. The Coroner put it to the Jury, and they decided by show of hands to hear the man's evidence next.

The Coroner cautioned the witness, who said he was willing to give evidence. He deposed that his name was William Rowe. He was a private, and aged 23. He and deceased both kicked the ball, and he really believed that his knee must have caught the deceased when they collided. Deceased stood between the posts for ten minutes, and walked away to the dressing, room.

Sub-Lieutenant Martin F. Stapleton, who also played in the match, bore out the statements of the other eye-witnesses, and said that he had been told that deceased was taken from the dressing-room to the College in a cab in much pain.

Sergeant C. J. Eynott, R.E., who was the referee in the match, said the fouls were two for tripping, and one for holding, both against the Cameronians. He was 20 yards off when the accident occurred, and merely saw the collision and one player on the ground. On being told the player was hurt he stopped the game, and when deceased stood up, renewed it. Players colliding was a very common thing. The affair was purely an accident, and no foul was claimed, and he did not give one.

Surgeon Frederick James Burns, one of the Hospital staff, who first attended deceased on Saturday evening, said that deceased grew suddenly worse, and died on Sunday morning at 1.10. The post mortem examination revealed perforation of the small intestines and extravasation of the contents. Death was due to syncope from traumatic peritonitis, caused by the rupture of the bowel.

The Coroner said it was an accident to be very much deplored, and that a large amount of caution should be used when teams met for games of football. Because of such accidents it did not follow that they were to expunge football from the list of sports, but it was a caution to be careful and to carry out the rules of the game, after having studied them closely.

The Jury returned a verdict of accidental death, and added expression of sympathy with the deceased's father and Mrs. Richmond.

1894 – DARING ROBBERY IN SOUTHSEA.

It has transpired that an extremely daring burglary took place on Monday morning at the residence of Mr. Frank Aylen who lives in cottage No. 23, Cottage Grove, standing back a little distance from the building line. Mr. and Mrs. Aylen were sleeping in the back bedroom with their little son, a child of about three years of age, who occupies a cot in the corner of the room. The parents had gone to bed about ten o'clock on Sunday night, closing the bedroom door after but between four and five o'clock the following morning, Mrs. Aylen was alarmed to see a man standing in the bedroom. She only caught a momentary glimpse of the intruder, who, on seeing that he was discovered, hastily made his way out of the room. She could not see him sufficiently well to identify him, all that she was able to notice being that he was a short, thick-set man. She roused her husband, who jumped out of bed and ran downstairs just in time to see the man escaping through the open window by which, as a subsequent examination showed, he must have gained admission to the house.

A search of the premises showed that the burglar had succeeded in forcing the button of the front window downstairs, a task by no means difficult, and involving little risk of his being overlooked, inasmuch as the street door and window are at the side of the house, looking out on a somewhat dark passage leading from Cottage Grove. The unwelcome visitor had ransacked the front room, but finding nothing there, had gone upstairs, and turning the handle of the door of the bedroom in which the inmates of the house were sleeping, had entered, first of all searching the chest of drawers that stood by the window. Then he crossed over to the foot of the bed, and turned out some drawers in the washstand, but failing to secure any valuable booty, he proceeded to the farther side of the room, when he lighted upon Mrs. Aylen's purse which was lying on the top of another chest of drawers. He secured the purse, but in doing so dislodged a bunch of keys that had been placed on it, and the keys falling to the floor gave the alarm. The purse contained the sum of £4. 10s in gold and silver.

The police have been communicated with, but so far neither the burglar, nor the purse, nor the money has been recovered. The same night an attempt would appear to have been made to enter the adjoining cottage, which is occupied by a widow, for on going downstairs in the morning she could not for some time open the street door, which had evidently been tampered with, but had resisted the efforts of the would-be marauder, who, moreover, was much more exposed to the view of passers-by while on that door, which faces the thoroughfare.

There are a number of house breakings in the area currently being investigated by the police.

1894 – ANOTHER HUMAN OSTRICH – DEATH AT THE MILTON ASYLUM.

The Portsmouth Coroner has been acquainted with the death at the Milton Lunatic Asylum of Sarah Brookman, 51 years of age, which occurred two days ago. It is believed, pending a post mortem examination, that the deceased woman's death was brought about by the many articles she was in the habit of tearing and swallowing. The inquest was held this afternoon.

Deceased was 51 years of age, and was admitted into the Asylum as a pauper patient from Southampton in 1881.

Dr. Walter Brunton, the Assistant Medical Officer, said that she would swallow all sorts of rubbish and stuff that she might come across. At times she had also torn up her dress and swallowed pieces of it. Notwithstanding these peculiar habits, she enjoyed fairly good health until last Tuesday, when she complained of pains in the stomach and vomiting. Dr. Brunton saw her, but did not think she was seriously ill. He did not see her again, and at six o'clock the same evening it was reported to him that she was dead. She was not at all a tractable woman, and could understand but very little.

Ellen Bulger, charge nurse of the ward to which deceased belonged, spoke to having seen her swallow pieces of her dress and underclothing. She was well cared for, and had plenty of food.

Eva Longland, an attendant, said that deceased continued vomiting all Tuesday afternoon, although some medicine was given to her with a view to stop it. At six o'clock witness noticed serious symptoms setting in, and at once sent for the doctor. Before he arrived, however, deceased expired.

A post mortem examination was made by Dr. Charles Arthur Kent, acting assistant medical officer. He found that the intestines were matted together by an old disease, and in one was lodged a piece of cabbage-stump, two and half inches long, and about the thickness of the little finger. The state of these organs prevented the obstacle from passing, and ulceration and stoppage in the bowels were set up. Several of the other organs, including the heart, were diseased, and death had resulted from syncope, following heart disease and stoppage in bowels. The doctor added that an operation might have saved a healthy person's life, but in the case of the deceased it was utterly impossible.

The Jury returned a verdict of accidental death.

1894 – RESCUED FROM THE MOAT AT HILSEA.

At a quarter past four p.m. on Monday, the attention of a thatcher named King was attracted by a floating object in the fresh water moat outside the Hilsea lines. Suspecting that what he saw was a human body, King went into the moat and succeeded in bringing ashore a woman between thirty and forty years of age, who was in an unconscious condition. She was taken to the Coach and Horses Inn, and after some brandy had been poured down her throat, and Dr. Heygate was sent for. On his arrival the doctor used means of artificial respiration, with the happy result that the woman was restored to consciousness, and declared to be out of danger. It was gleaned from her that she was unmarried, and that she lived in Regent Street, Southsea whither she was taken. Her name has not transpired, and it seems that she gave no account of how she got into the water.

1894 – THE ALLEGED KIDNAPPING OF A PORTSMOUTH BOY.

Today, Thomas Cannon and Florence Cannon were charged with leaving James Leach, aged 10, a child in their custody, without visible means of subsistence.

The boy stated that while he was playing on Portsdown Hill the prisoners came and forced him to accompany them. The man seized his wrist and threatened to cut his throat if he raised an alarm. They tramped to London and afterwards to Rochester. Prisoners sent him out with matches, but in reality he had to beg for money. If he did not take back threepence daily he was thrashed. He had often been beaten cruelly. When a School Board officer came about him, the prisoners took him out at night and deserted him. He slept all night in a cart.

Medical evidence was given to the effect that the boys' body was covered with bruises (probably caused with a poker or stick) and wounds.

The prisoners were remanded pending the arrival of the boy's parents. It is stated that the reason for the charge being framed as recorded above is that the alleged kidnapping was committed in another jurisdiction.

The Chatham Stipendiary Magistrate (Mr. E. J. Athawes) had the case of alleged kidnapping before him again on Thursday. Thomas Cannon, a travelling tinker, and his wife, Florence, were charged with taking away from his home at Landport, Portsmouth, a boy of ten years of age, named James Leach, and also with abandoning him in such a manner as to cause him unnecessary suffering. The prosecution was undertaken by the Society for the Prevention of Cruelty to Children.

The boy's mother and father now gave evidence, stating that their son had been missing since July 18, when he had been sent from home at Landport to a neighbouring shop to purchase the groceries. Other evidence went to show that the boy was met by the prisoners in the vicinity of Portsdown Hill. The male prisoner caught hold of his wrist and told him to accompany them, at the same time threatening to cut his throat if he made a noise or told anyone that the prisoners were not his parents.

Since then the boy had travelled the country with the prisoners begging. They had lived in Rochester for some time past, and during that period the boy was sent out begging, and if he did not return home he was beaten. The boy was seen on several occasions by the local Inspector of the Society and had been taken home. On the night of November 25th the boy was deserted by the prisoners at Gillingham and discovered the next morning, in a half-frozen condition, sleeping under a cart. The prisoners denied that they kidnapped the boy or treated him badly. They found him ten miles from Portsmouth in a neglected condition and took pity on him.

The Stipendiary Magistrate sentenced the prisoners to three months hard labour each for employing the lad for begging purposes. He also said that the prisoners should be handed over to the Portsmouth police at the expiration of their sentence to answer the charge of kidnapping. The prisoners both wept copiously on being removed to the cells, and the man said he considered he had done the boy a good turn, not a bad one.

Today, at the Bench in Fareham, before Mr. J. C. Garnier and other Justices, Thomas Cannon, 29, and Florence Cannon 21, described as tramps, were brought up from Maidstone Gaol on the charge of having decoyed and taken away James Leach, ten years of age, with the intent to deprive Richard Leach, father, of his lawful custody at Portsmouth.

A letter had been received from the Public Prosecutor's Department, Treasury, Whitehall, to the effect that the Public Prosecutor did not intend to proceed further with the prosecution. It was, however, thought necessary to take a short deposition as an addition to the depositions which had already been taken in Kent.

The lad Leach, a sharp-looking boy, was then sworn, and he stated that his father lived at 37 Durham Street, Landport, and that at ten o'clock on a Friday morning, about five months ago, he was sent out by his mother to buy bread and milk. He, however, walked to Portsdown

Hill, where he saw the prisoner. They told him to come with them, and that if he made any alarm and told his parents they would cut his throat.

In cross-examination by the prisoner, the lad stated that he and his wife took hold of his hands and dragged him away, but he was afraid to call out, though people were not far away.

The male prisoner said he would like to make a complaint of the treatment which they had received. The Justices Clerk: 'You can, of course, take your own course, but you will have to abide by the result.'

The Chairman: "We have nothing to do with trying the case here, though you might have suffered. You are sent here to be discharged."

The male prisoner (to the boy): How were you dressed?—The lad: I had my clothes on.—Had you boots and stockings? No.— Had you a coat on? One arm was out of the sleeve.—Didn't I tear the lining out of your trousers because they were running with vermin? No.—You had on a very old pair of trousers? Yes.—What had you in your hands? Fourpence and a milk jug. The female prisoner said she had no questions to ask the boy. She had, however, been a good mother to him all the time she had had him—she had been too good, in fact, to him. The Chairman then discharged the prisoners, and in ordering the boy back to the custody of his father he expressed the hope that nothing of the kind would occur again.

The father said he hoped not as he had had five months of anxiety over the matter. An aunt of the boy, living in Southampton, who had consented to take charge of him, said she would not have minded seeing the prisoners get five years for what they had done.

1894 – A RUNAWAY HORSE.

John Martin, of Cosham, was driving away from the Cosham Railway Station on Saturday afternoon, when his horse was frightened by a passing engine, and bolting, threw Martin out of the cart and over the hedge. The unfortunate driver sustained a severe fracture above the left elbow, besides several more or less serious wounds about the head. He was taken with all despatch to the Royal Portsmouth and Gosport Hospital, where he was attended by the Assistant House Surgeon, Dr. Morley, who reported this morning that the sufferer was progressing favourably. The horse was fortunately stopped before any further damage was done.

1895 – AFTER THE CRAB TEA WAS OVER.

On the 17th July the employees of the Portsmouth Dairy Company held their annual excursion, going, in a number of brakes to Warsash for a crab tea. Subscriptions towards the expenses had been solicited from the various farmers dealing with the Company, among whom is Mr. Henry Bone, who also holds the license of the New Inn, Drayton. He said that he could not give them any money but would give them a supper on their return, and it was arranged that they should all eat at the tavern at 10.30 on their homeward journey. However, they were delayed, and did not get back to the New Inn till between 11 and 11.30. Bone had then retired to rest, but was awakened, but as the party could not stay to partake of supper, which was laid out in the tap-room, many having to meet the milk train at 12 a.m. next day, he served them in the bar with beer, spirits, and bread and cheese etc. While they were there, Sergeant Bloomer and Constable Appleton came in, asked the landlord if he had an extension, and finding that was not the case, took the names and addresses of those present, and Mr. Bone was, in consequence, charged, at Havant Police court on Saturday, before Major C. P. Boyd, General Williams, and Messrs Rawson and Mosdell, with a breach of the licensing laws, in having opened his premises after 11 p.m. to serve persons who were not bone fide travellers or lodgers in the house. Mr. M. Hyde defended. The Bench, having some doubt as to whether the fourteen men found in the house, five of whom were not employees of the company, were the bone fide guests of Mr. Bone, reserved judgment on the whole case for a fortnight.

1895 – STARVING A FAMILY. SAD CASE AT LANDPORT.

John Wiggins, of 7, School Lane, Landport, was summoned before the Portsmouth Magistrates on Tuesday for neglecting his children. The case, said Mr. E. King, who prosecuted, was out of the ordinary run altogether. Defendant would not work and his wife and children had been nearly starved to death. Inspector Barker said defendant was a bricklayer's labourer with six children. On one occasion witness visited the house and found it absolutely empty save for a small mattress some three feet by eighteen inches, forming the only sleeping accommodation for the whole of the children. They were entirely destitute. On another occasion witness went to the house and found Wiggins "mad drunk." Declaring he would burn the house and die in it, defendant piled up what little furniture there was and set fire to it. However, on the police being sent for he put the fire out. At that his wife and family were turned out of doors.

Other witnesses supported the charge, one saying that all defendant had done during the last five months was to join the Militia.

Mr. Curtis said the Bench would be failing in their duty if they did not give defendant the full penalty the law allowed. He would have to go to prison for six months with hard labour.

1895 – ALLEGED BRUTAL ASSAULT.

Frederick Lincoln, 20, a Lance-Corporal in the Northumberland Fusiliers, was charged on a warrant with assaulting Edith Nash, of 37, Highbury Street, Portsmouth, on the 8th inst. The prisoner pleaded not guilty.

The prosecutrix, a single woman, appeared in Court with her head bandaged up, two black eyes, and sundry bruises on her right cheek and jaw. She stated that at 6.30 p.m. on Tuesday she met the prisoner in the Colewort Arms and had a pot of beer with him, for which he paid. Her sister and a girl named Maude were in the bar at the time. She left in about ten minutes, but returned shortly after seven o'clock and had another glass. She was in and out all the evening till 9.15, when the prisoner and she went to her apartments. There the prisoner seized her round the neck and tried to take her purse out of her pocket. She prevented him, and he then struck her in the right eye with his fist. She fell, striking her left eye against a chair, and as she lay on the ground he kicked her on the side of the face near her right ear.

By the Court: Nothing improper had taken place, and the prisoner had given her no money. She saw the prisoner once before on Sunday evening, when he was on guard. She became insensible, and the prisoner made off.

Louisa Nash, sister of the prosecutrix, said that she saw the prisoner leave the Colewort Arms with her sister, but never saw him afterwards.

Several witnesses gave evidence as to the prisoner being in the company of the prosecutrix on Tuesday night, among them being Rebecca Clancy, of 48, Highbury Street, who said that she let lodgings at No. 37. About 9.30 on the night in question, the prisoner and the prosecutrix passed her in Highbury Street.

About 9.45 she saw the prisoner leave the court and go towards the Casino. Prosecutrix came down about an hour afterwards, covered with blood and with her eyes so swollen that she could not see. She had been drinking, but was not drunk. The prisoner did not seem to be drunk.

Dr. Bishop, House Surgeon at the Hospital, said that the woman's injuries might have been caused as described. Considerable violence must have been used. When arrested the following day by Detective Moth, the prisoner said, "I'm innocent. I can prove an alibi."

Detective Moth said that they had been unable to obtain any evidence as to the alleged larceny; so did not proceed with that charge.

The prisoner now said that he went into barracks at 8 o'clock on the night in question, and that at 9.30 he was in bed. He would call the Sergeant of the Guard, the Orderly Sergeant, and others to prove his statement.

Sergeant Wells said that he was the Orderly Sergeant on the night in question. He called the roll at 9.30, but did not see Lance-Corporal Lincoln there.

Alderman Marvin: You have called the wrong witness.
Prisoner: I was there and in bed at the time.
Witness: No, sir: he was not there. His bed was vacant, but it was occupied at reveille the next morning.

Lance-Corporal George Holthue stated that he went round with the last witness in the barracks on the night of the 8th inst., but he could not say the prisoner was in his bed.

Private Winfield, also of the Northumberland Fusiliers, was called by the prisoner, but he said he did not see the prisoner at all in the barrack room that night. He could not say whether the prisoner was in bed.

Sergeant-Major Redhead deposed that from half past nine on the night of the 8th inst., to six the next morning the prisoner was in barracks.

The Assistant Clerk: How do you know that? – The book contains the report. – But did you see him? – No. – Who made that report? – Orderly-Sergeant Wells.

Alderman Marvin: It is a serious thing, I suppose, to make a false return? – Yes.

The Magistrates said that they had not the slightest hesitation in believing the prosecutrix's statement. They, however, ascertained that the prisoner had been in the regiment for two years, and that he had an excellent character, and taking the circumstances into account they merely sentenced him to two calendar months' imprisonment with hard labour. He had been guilty of a brutal and aggravated assault.

They commended Detective Moth for the manner in which he had placed the case before the Court.

1895 – A DEFIANT HAWKER.

Arthur Eames was summoned for selling watercress by outcry on Sunday, the 25th ult., in Constitution Place, Fratton. He did not appear, but P.S. Bulbeck said that the defendant had given his name and address six times that morning. There were three previous convictions, and a fine of 5s. was imposed, or five days' imprisonment. A week was allowed for payment.

1895 – A QUESTION OF AGE.

Messrs. Hawkes and Jenkins, bakers, of Crown Street, Portsmouth, were summoned under the Factory and Workshops Act for employing Frederick Watkins, aged 17, before six o'clock on the morning of the 5th ult. Mr. John Edward Harston (Factory Inspector) prosecuted. It appeared that on August 6th Mr. Charles Edward Whitelaw (Factory Inspector) visited the place, when Watkins told him, in defendant's presence, that he had been at work from midnight on Sunday, the 4th ult., to ten o'clock on the morning in question. Mr. Jenkins said that he did not know Watkins was there. Watkins said that he did not know, and Mr. Jenkins discharged him on the spot. Watkins was summoned as a witness, but did not appear, the police not having been able to serve the summons.

Mr. Jenkins said that when Watkins entered his employ he said emphatically that he was over 18 years of age, and had since joined the Navy as a cook's mate, to do which he would have to make a sworn declaration that he was over 18 years age.

On the Sunday previous to Bank Holiday he started work at ten o'clock at night, and continued, with intervals for meals, until ten o'clock the following morning. Mr. Jenkins said that Watkins distinctly told him he was over 18.

On the day in question he did not come to work until twelve o'clock, and went off at nine o'clock the next morning. This was done at the boy's own request, as he wanted to get off for the holiday. Defendant's foreman said he always thought the boy was over 18, and Frederick William Bailey, master-at-arms in the Navy, said that when Watkins entered the Service on August 10th he stated that he was born on Oct. 30th, 1875.

The Magistrates thought that Mr. Jenkins had employed the boy under a misapprehension, and consequently they fined him only 5s. towards the costs. Mr. Harston, who appeared for the Authorities, said that if employers would only insist on the production of a birth certificate when they employed young lads the matter would be settled.

1895 – SHOPKEEPERS AT VARIANCE.

Mrs. Griffiths and May Griffiths, her daughter, who live at 21, Lake Road. Landport, appeared to answer separate informations charging them with using abusive language towards Charlotte Maud Barton. Mr. E.J.T. Webb appeared for Barton, and Mr. B. Kent for the Griffiths. The parties are neighbours, Miss Barton and her father keeping a fish shop, and the defendants a fruit shop next door. For some years the Bartons, according to their account, had been annoyed by the Griffiths. On the 4th inst. the two defendants commenced a fresh series of provocations, by dancing in front of the shop and swinging the tails of their dresses, at the same time screaming out "Stinking fish" and "Go and fry your stinking fish." Provocation was denied. [Proceeding.]

1895 – ATTEMPTED SUICIDE. RESCUE AT PORTSEA.

At the Portsmouth Police court, today, Cicely Harris, 41, of 52, Hanover Street, Portsea, was charged with attempting to commit suicide off the Hard on Monday night.

Paul Johnson, of 5, Forbury Road, Southsea, employed in the Dockyard, said that just after ten p.m. he saw the prisoner rush on to the Hard, crying, "God help me. Save me. I'm going." She ran down the slope and threw herself into the water. A younger woman followed her on to the Hard, screaming for "Help." Witness at once jumped into the water and took hold of the prisoner. The water was about four and a half feet deep. With the help of a Naval bandsman, witness dragged prisoner, who was then in an unconscious condition, out of the water, and in ten minutes succeeded in partially restoring animation. Dr. J. H. F. Way was immediately sent for, and the woman was removed to the warmer atmosphere of the police station.

Inspector Moss said that earlier in the morning prisoner told him that her husband had received his quarter's pension last week, and had spent the whole of the money. It was owing to a quarrel arising out of this matter that she tried to take her life.

Her husband, however, declared that this statement was untrue.

Prisoner was remanded for a week, and Mr. Johnson was thanked for his services. The Magistrates offered to compensate him for his loss of time, but he asked them to put the money into the poor-box.

1896 – THE CHILD MURDER NEAR PORTSMOUTH.

At Hants Assizes at Winchester on Friday before Mr. Justice Day, Philip Matthews, late groom and coachman, of Teignmouth, was indicted for the wilful murder of his daughter, Elsie Gertrude, aged 5, at Copnor, near Portsmouth, on Easter Tuesday morning.

Mr. Temple-Cooke and Mr. Gill prosecuted Mr. Barnes defended.

Mr. Temple-Cooke recapitulated the facts as they have already appeared. Prisoner was a coachman in the employ of Dr. Piggott, Teignmouth, and bore good character. Last year Charlotte Malony came to Teignmouth and an attachment sprang up between prisoner and her. Then commenced disputes between prisoner and his wife and prisoner left the latter and went to Portsmouth with Maloney. Prisoner after living there in adultery with Maloney returned to Teignmouth and on the 6th April took away the deceased child, and next day she was found throttled at Baffin's Pond, Copnor, near Portsmouth. The motive for the act advanced by the prosecution was that the prisoner, who was in a penniless condition, was unable to keep the child —who was by his first wife—and provide also for Maloney.

Dr. Piggott, in his evidence, said prisoner was greatly affected by the loss of his first wife, and since he had been in prison he had noticed a strangeness in his demeanour. There was evidently a serious nervous disorder.

J. Westcott, of Teign Street, Teignmouth, at whose house prisoner lived with his wife and child, deposed warning the prisoner against letting the child come to harm when he took it away from Teignmouth on Easter Monday. Prisoner said he was taking it where it would be well cared for.

Charlotte Maloney, the young woman with whom the prisoner eloped said she believed him to be a free man. He told her that Mrs. Matthews was a wife only in name and he introduced himself to her mother in March as witness's lover and eventually as her husband. They had wedding cards printed, and stayed at a hotel together as man and wife, prisoner stating that his real name was Burt. She was now *enceinte*.

Evidence was further called to the discovery of the body of the child in a field near Portsmouth and to prisoner's having called at Mrs. Maloney's house at four o'clock in the morning of Easter Tuesday looking worried.

Doctors Maybury and Macgregor stated their opinion that death was the result of strangulation by throttling and not of fright. The marks on the throat were not the result of accidental pressure.

In defence. Mr. Barnes urged that the death of the deceased was accidental, being due to the prisoner having laid down to sleep in the field with the child in his arms. Prisoner was not responsible for his actions at the time of the occurrence. The prisoner had always been kind to the child and there was no motive of murder.

The Judge, summing up, rather discounted this theory, and the Jury retired to consider their verdict. After fifteen minutes consulting they found prisoner "guilty," and the judge passed sentence of death in the usual manner. Matthews remarked, "I am glad to go where my child has gone." The Press Association says that the judge held out no hope of mercy in this world. Matthews remarked that he was innocent.

1898 – AN UNNATURAL FATHER.

Edward Wild, 46, upholsterer, was charged with wilfully and cruelly neglecting his five children, Cordelia Clara aged 13, Arthur Ernest, aged 10, Mabel Annie, aged 5, Gerald William, aged 4; and Helena Violet Wild aged 1 year and 4 months. Mr. Temple-Cooke, (instructed by Mr. G. Hall King) prosecuted.

The prisoner, he said, could earn from £2 to £3 a week if he liked, and the neglect with which he was charged was the result of the prisoner's drunken and lazy habits. He had been married for twenty years, and had nine children, and during that time he had bought no clothes for them, and had only bought two pairs of the boots for the lot. Mrs. Wild, the wife of the prisoner corroborated.

The prisoner could earn good money if he would work, but he allowed her only 5s. to 6s., a week for household expenses, and never anything for boots or clothes. The two pairs of boots mentioned he had bought since she first brought him to Court. She had had to work to support herself and the children, but was now broken down in health, and her eyesight was affected. The eldest girl, out of service, and the eldest son, a bus conductor, corroborated. They had done their best to help their mother, and neighbours had also given her food for the children.

Mr. Pulling, journeyman butcher, of 38, Catherine Street, Southsea, a next door neighbour of the prisoner, said that he had frequently given Mrs. Wild food for the children when they cried for bread. She was a very hard-working woman, and had worked night and day for the children. He had heard the machine going.

Inspector Barker of the National Society for the prevention of Cruelty to Children, also gave evidence.

Dr. Marwood, of Campbell Road, Southsea, said that he had examined the children in February last and found them in a bad state of health, owing to neglect and insufficient food. There was no organic disease to account for the condition of the children. They were partially starved, all of them.

Wild, who elected to give evidence on oath, said that for the last five to six years, his wife had been very jealous of him, and accused him to his customers of being unfaithful to her. As a result, he had lost his business, and could not earn anything like as much money as he had used to.

The Recorder summed up at length and after a few minutes deliberation the Jury returned a verdict of guilty. The Recorder sentenced Wild to twelve calendar months with hard labour, saying that even the beasts of the earth took care of their young instead of neglecting them as he had done.

When before the Magistrates, who could have sentenced him to six months hard labour at the outside, the prisoner declined to have the case summarily disposed of and elected to go before the Recorder.

1897 – SUDDEN DEATH AT COSHAM.

The County Coroner (Mr. E. Goble) held an inquest at the Railway Hotel, Cosham, on Thursday afternoon, touching the death of Ann Champion, who lived with her daughter at 2, Windsor Terrace, Cosham.

Miss Champion said that her mother and she had lived there for three years. Deceased was 90 years of age and subject to epileptic fits. On Sunday evening she died in her chair while witness was administering brandy. Until last February a young lady lived with them as help. Witness admitted refusing admittance to the police, and added that her relations were medical people, and she could get a certificate of death. Witness alleged that she had been boycotted and cruelly treated by her neighbours.

Miss Monckton stated that for months she was a lady's help to the deceased, but left last February. She had never seen the old woman have a fit, but had heard her scream once in the night.

Mrs. Ash, who formerly was a neighbour, said that she had heard the deceased scream, and also exclaim, "Don't hit me again; don't hurt me." Both witnesses said that Miss Champion was addicted to drink.

Mr. Scullard, a retired Constructor, also a neighbour, gave evidence of hearing screams proceeding from the deceased's house. He, too, had heard the exclamation, "Don't hit me, don't hurt me again."

Dr. W. H. Heygate next gave evidence. He produced a letter which he had received from Miss Champion asking him to give a certificate of death. The letter was a long one—six pages. In it she spoke of their affluence, and made mention of an insurance into which they had paid £150. Witness said that he had never attended the deceased before. When he went to the house he found the deceased on a bed, dead. The place was in a filthy state, and the body was very emaciated and dirty. He made a post mortem examination. The heart showed signs of an old standing disease, which was sufficient to produce sudden death. The stomach was empty and there were no signs of brandy or acid poisoning. He could not definitely state the cause of death. The end might have been accelerated by insufficient food, shock or excitement.

After deliberation in private the Jury returned a verdict of "Death from senile decay," adding as a rider that the Jury were of the opinion that the deceased should have had somebody to look after her, as they considered that her daughter was totally incapable of doing so.

1897 – A SIAMESE SAILOR'S SOVEREIGN.

At the Portsmouth Police court today before Mr. J. Read and Mr. J. Byrne, Benjamin Grant, 41, and Frederick Taylor, 36, were charged with stealing, by a trick, £1, the property of a quartermaster on the Prince of Siam's Yacht, now lying in Portsmouth harbour. An interpreter was sworn. The interpreter asked the witness how he wished to be sworn, and with considerable difficulty elicited that he would not be sworn, but if he did not tell the truth his god (Buddha) would cut his throat. The master, who gave his name as "Yacht," no christian name, said that he met the prisoners at the "Golden Fleece" in Ordnance Row, Portsea. He had with him a bag containing a watch and some money.

Grant asked to see what was in the bag, and he showed him. Grant took the watch out to look at it, and at the same time abstracted the sovereign, which he pressed behind his back, he made signs that he had lost the money, but Taylor signified that he had not got it, and witness went for constable.

"Been," another Siamese quartermaster, corroborated.

Constable Wolstenholme also gave evidence. He was applied to by the prosecutor, and went with him to the "Golden Fleece," when "Yacht" pointed the prisoners out to him. Both prisoners denied the charge. The Siamese were sober, but the prisoners had had a drop to drink. The sovereign was not found on either of the prisoners.

Prisoners pleaded not guilty, and called the landlord, James Richard Perrin, as witness on their behalf. He saw nothing suspicious in the prisoners' conduct. The Magistrates dismissed the case, saying that it was one of suspicion, but there was not evidence enough to convict the prisoners.

1897 – THREE SUDDEN DEATHS.

Three sudden deaths occupied the attention of the Portsmouth Coroner (Mr. T. A. Bramsdon) at his Court in the Town Hall, on Friday.

ACCIDENT AT THE TOWN QUAY.

The death of Joseph Henry Appleton, aged 56, a labourer, who lived at 25, Plymouth Street, Southsea, a house occupied by his married daughter, Mrs. Price, first occupied attention. Three days before Christmas day the deceased was injured on the Town Quay, being thrown from one ship to another by a "monkey box," which fell on him while working in a coal brig. His head and left shoulder were badly hurt, and for a fortnight he was treated at the Portsmouth Hospital. He never properly recovered from the accident, and died suddenly on Tuesday night. Dr. Cashin, of Southsea, described the results of a post mortem examination, from which it appeared that death was due to the rupture of an aneurism. The accident might have aggravated the condition of the chest, but in witness's opinion death was entirely due to natural causes. A verdict in accordance with the medical evidence was returned by the Jury.

FATAL PLAY.

The second inquiry was relative to the death of Sidney William Harding, aged one year and ten months, whose parents live at 31, Maitland Street, Landport. It appeared that on the 5th instant another little boy, aged three years and five months, was playing with a Burmese dah, a long knife, something like those used by butchers. This child, who had been amusing himself by throwing bits of wood at his father, threw the knife also, and the point stuck in the deceased's head. A neighbour, named Mrs. Hope, dressed the wound, and the child was subsequently conveyed to the Hospital, death taking place at that institution. The weapon was brought from Burma by the father, who had been soldier.

In reply to questions from the Coroner, the mother said she took away the boy from the Hospital on the 17th because the nurse said the wound was well. Witness, however, did not think the child was well, it did nothing but cry, and the wound, which had healed, began to look inflamed, she took the child back again to the Hospital, where it died. Dr. Slocock, assistant house-surgeon at the Hospital, said the wound appeared to be a very slight one, and by the 17th it had quite healed up. On the 21st the child was again admitted, but gradually sank and died. A big abscess had formed beneath the skull cap and apparently inflammation had been caused by the blow. Exhaustion was the cause of death. "Death by misadventure" was the verdict returned by the Jury.

THE CAMBER FATALITY.

The death of Joseph Jewell, the man who met with his death in the Camber, also came before the Jury. Edward Cole, master mariner, living in Southampton, stated that the deceased, who was a coal porter, lived at Longcroft Street, Southampton, and came to Portsmouth on a pleasure trip with him in the barge *Baby*. On Thursday they went out together, and had 2s. worth of whiskey between them. About ten o'clock witness left deceased to go aboard the barge, and did not again see him alive. The deceased knew his way about Portsmouth. At this point the Coroner announced that at present the case was incomplete, and an adjournment would therefore be necessary until Friday next.

1898 – FINED FOR ASSISTING DESERTERS.

Edward and George Johnson were charged at Portsea with being in possession of the uniform of two gunners of the Royal Artillery; stationed in the Isle of Wight, who had deserted. The police found the gunners in the Johnsons' house in a court at Portsea, wearing civilian clothes, but the regulation boots by which they were detected and their uniforms were concealed. In evidence, the gunners stated that they paid George 3s. to assist them. Edward Johnson was discharged, but

George Johnson was fined £5 or two months' imprisonment, the police stating that a fraternity existed at Portsea to assist men to desert.

1898 – HILSEA BARRACKS POISONING.

A Court of Inquiry is to assemble at Hilsea Barracks, Portsmouth today, to investigate a case of wholesale poisoning of soldiers which has just occurred there. Some days ago half a dozen Artillerymen were suddenly taken ill just after dinner, and developed such alarming symptoms that they were at once removed to Hilsea Station Hospital. Upon arriving there they told the medical officer in charge that all the other men in the barrack-rooms they had just left were ill also. Altogether thirty men, all exhibiting serious symptoms of arsenical poisoning, had to be sent to the Hospital. None of the cases proved fatal, although many of the men were in a serious condition. Investigations were set on foot, with the result that some vinegar which the men had used at dinner was suspected to have caused the mischief. A sample taken and submitted to analysis was found to contain arsenic in poisonous quantities.

1899 – A VALUABLE STAMP ALBUM. CURIOUS CASE AT PORTSMOUTH.

At the Portsmouth Police Court, on Thursday, before Alderman T. King and Mr. J. Read, Alexander Leopold Croyle, 37, was charged with stealing a stamp album and stamps valued at £280, from Stanfield House, Clarence Parade, Southsea, the property of Major Frank Fraser.

Mr. E. J. Harvey appeared to prosecute on behalf of Major Fraser, and at the outset complained that although he had produced an order to prosecute to the Police, he had not been due afforded the slightest information regarding the case, even the name of the man in custody having been refused.

Mr. King said he had been instructed to prosecute on behalf of Messrs. Curtiss and Sons, Limited. It appeared that Major Fraser had in the first instance instructed Messrs. Maple and Co., of London, to move certain goods from Portsmouth. They thereupon instructed Messrs. Dartnall of Brighton, who, in their turn, instructed Messrs. Curtiss and Co., of Portsmouth, to provide a van and horses. Prisoner was in the employ of Messrs. Curtiss. He (Mr. King) was perfectly willing to hand over the prosecution to Mr. Harvey, as it would relieve his clients of the responsibility. Mr. King then handed the notes of evidence with which he had been supplied by the police to Mr. Harvey, and the Bench adjourned the case for an hour to enable Mr. Harvey to peruse them, and for the attendance of Major Fraser.

Major Fraser stated that "he was formerly in the 3rd East Yorkshire Regiment but was now retired, and now resided at 16, Maddock Street, Hanover Square, London. He was lately residing at Stanfield House, Clarence Parade in Southsea. He last saw the albums, which was really the property of his son, aged 13 years, in the safe at Stanfield House on the 18th June. The stamps were collected by the boy's grandfather and although he did not know the value of the book himself he believed the collection was valuable. He was willing, however, to put the album at a nominal value say £6 or £10. Mr. Fisk: Shall we say £4 10s. – Witness: Yes. The value was therefore amended accordingly.

Mr. Lothian Bonham-Carter, brewer, of 19 High Street, Portsmouth, stated that at 1.30pm on the 24th he was in a shop kept by Miss Norkett, who dealt amongst other things in stamps. The prisoner came in and offered the album for sale for 10s. Witness looked at the album, and thinking it was worth more than the price named offered to give the prisoner a sovereign for it. He took the prisoner's name and address and intended to send him some more money if upon inspection he found the book was really worth it. He asked the prisoner how long he had been collecting and he replied "Ever since I was a boy." In looking through the album that night witness found an envelope pasted down and upon unsticking it he saw the prosecutor's name and address. His suspicions were aroused and he wrote to the prosecutor the same night and subsequently forwarded the album in the condition he had found it. He thought £4 10s. was a fair value for the book.

Detective-Sergeant Warr stated that he arrested the prisoner in Broad Street, Portsmouth. Prisoner said, "I am very sorry, sir, if I did anything wrong; I saw the book on one of the room floors, and picked it up with some other paper, which I took home. That was on the last day we were employed there, I sold it the following Saturday, I know I was not aware it was of any value, or I should not have taken it. I am very sorry I did it."

Prisoner now pleaded guilty, and added that he did not think the book was of any value. It was stated that the prisoner had been in the employ of Messrs. Curtiss about six weeks, and had always done his work satisfactorily.

Inspector Munt said the prisoner had hitherto borne a very good character. After a brief deliberation in private, the Bench ordered prisoner to undergo 14 days' imprisonment, but without hard labour.

1899 – ALL THROUGH POVERTY.

At the Portsmouth police court on Wednesday, Elizabeth Burke, 36, of 46, Central Street, Landport was charged with having attempted to commit suicide by taking a quantity of oxalic acid, on the 26th.

Benjamin Newton, a waiter, stated that about 12.30 on the day in question he was called in by the prisoner's husband and upon going into the house he saw the prisoner sitting in a chair vomiting. She had taken some oxalic acid, and he mixed her some salt and water, which, however, she refused to take. She said, "I have done it through poverty. Let me die." He believed she was in a state of great poverty, her husband having done no work for eight years.

Another neighbour said that prisoner stated she had taken two pennyworth of poison and wished to die. Asked why she had done it, she replied "Worry, worry, worry, worry." The poison, was purchased by the prisoner at Mr. Blackadar's, she informing the assistant who served her that she wanted it for cleaning straw hats.

Dr. Robinson (Assistant House Surgeon) stated that he admitted the prisoner to the Hospital. She was in a collapsed condition and was still very weak, although she was in no danger. Superintendent Moss said that the prisoner's surroundings were very bad and some kind people were making efforts to do something for her and her family. While these arrangements were being completed it was desired to have a remand for a week. It would be entirely for the prisoner's good. The Bench accordingly remanded the prisoner.

1899 – ROUGHS AT SOUTHSEA.

At the Portsmouth Police court, on Wednesday, Michael Enwright, 22, was charged with being disorderly while drunk in Alexandra Road, Portsmouth, on Tuesday afternoon. The prisoner, who was said to be a tramp staying in a common lodging-house, was alleged to have been very drunk and behaved very badly, using filthy language. Evidence was given to the effect that when arrested by Constable McGrail, he became exceedingly violent and behaved like a madman. First he struck McGrail on the left cheek, then kicked him on the thigh, arm, and in the back, and eventually laid on his back and kicked him in the stomach with both feet. The help of several gentlemen near Government House had to be requisitioned, but the prisoner behaved so violently that it was with considerable difficulty that he was overpowered. Ultimately McGrail had to handcuff him with his arms behind his back. He continued kicking and struggling and had to be carried the whole way to the station. When in the cells he again kicked McGrail. Inspector Moss said the prisoner was one of a gang of roughs who infested Southsea at this time of the year, got drunk, and molested everyone. The Bench sentenced him to a month's hard labour.

1899 – THE DESERTER AND THE SCARECROW.

The Marine Artilleryman who some time since broke out of Eastney Barracks while under Military arrest, has been sentenced to twelve months' hard labour and dismissed from H.M. service. Dressed only in a shirt and trousers the deserter climbed over the barrack wall and completed his attire by appropriating the clothes of a scarecrow in a field. He tramped as far as Wiltshire, where a policeman found him sleeping in a haystack, and arrested him as a vagrant. It was then noticed that he had the appearance of a deserter, and he was sent back to Eastney to be dealt with by the Military authorities.

1899 – DEATH OF A KINGSTON NONOGENARIAN.

The death took place last Monday of a well-known resident of Kingston in the person of Mrs. Mary Mills, of 12, Kingston Crescent, who had lived there for 31 years, and kept a small twine shop. Her age was 92. She was married in 1834 to Mr. David Mills, of Totnes, Devonshire, who died four years ago. Mrs. Mills preserved all her faculties, and had never had a day's illness in her life. The funeral took place on Thursday at Kingston Cemetery. Many interesting reminiscences used to be related by Mrs. Mills, whose memory was very good. When a girl of eight summers, whilst residing in Totnes, and before the advent of steam locomotion, the soldiers returning from Waterloo, halted whilst passing through the village on their march to London, depositing their kits and baggage in front of the house in which she attended school. She had to clamber over the baggage before she could gain entrance to the house. Her memory carried her far back very vividly to the celebration of George the Third's jubilee, in which she took part, marching in the procession, and partaking of tea in the meadows, with games, etc.

1899 – "MONTE CARLO DAMSELS."

At the Portsmouth police court on Monday, before Mr. T. Cousins, Mr. W. Payne, and Col. A. R. Holbrook, John Patrick Hurley, 21, was charged under the Vagrancy Act with exhibiting indecent pictures by means of a machine called the "Kailoscop," in Charlotte Street, Landport, on Saturday night. The Chief Constable (Mr. A. T. Frickett) prosecuted, and Mr. B. Kent appeared for the defence.

Detective Matthews said that on Saturday night, about 9.30, he was passing through Charlotte Street, in company with Detective Moth and Constable Jenkins, and saw the prisoner standing on a truck in the street. On the truck were eight machines (produced), and the prisoner had a gong, and was shouting out "Come and see the Monte Carlo Damsels," etc. Witness saw several boys and girls, whose ages ranged from 12 to 16, put their pennies in the slot. Witness put a penny in the slot and saw the pictures. He considered them indecent, and he asked Detective Moth to look at them. He came to the same conclusion; and they arrested the prisoner and took him to the Town Hall.

At the request of Mr. Kent, witness pointed out those pictures that he considered indecent, and suggested to the Magistrates that if the prisoner undertook not to expose them again the justice of the case would be met. Mr. Cousins said that they had seen the pictures, and were unanimous in their decision. They would hear the whole of the evidence. Detective Moth corroborated Matthews' evidence, adding that in his opinion the pictures were obscene. Constable Jenkins also gave confirmatory evidence. He added that the prisoner made indecent remarks. Mr. Kent put the prisoner in the box, and he denied that the pictures were indecent or obscene. He was only a paid servant, and the pictures were not his property. He travelled from one town to another and had only been here a week. The Mayor of Gravesend had looked at the pictures. The pictures were the property of a Mr. Morley. He would give an undertaking that he would not exhibit the pictures which the Magistrates objected to.

After deliberating in private, the Chairman said that they had seen the pictures and were clearly of the opinion that some of them were indecent. What made the case worse was the mode in which they were indiscriminately exhibited in one of the public thoroughfares of the borough. They adjudged the prisoner to be a rogue and vagabond under the Act, and taking into consideration the prisoner's undertaking, should impose a penalty of £5 and the costs, 5s. They had power to give him three months' imprisonment. Mr. Kent made an application for the restoration of the machines, but Mr. Cousins explained that they had no power to do so. A charge against Henry Staunton Morley and the owner of the machines, was withdrawn on the application of the Chief Constable.

1899 – A LUNATIC'S SUICIDE. EXCITING SCENE AT MILTON ASYLUM.

MADMAN CHASED BY ATTENDANTS.
Considerable excitement was caused at the Portsmouth Lunatic Asylum at Milton this morning by a tragic incident, the suicide of one of the inmates, a man named Thomas Hardwick, aged 23, an ex-Army man, who killed himself in an outburst of frenzy by cutting his throat.

Hardwick, it appears, had served in Egypt in the Irish Rifles, but was invalided home for enteric fever. He is not a Portsmouth man, having only come to the town four or five months ago. He was living in Highbury Street, Portsmouth, with his wife and children, and about a fortnight ago became violent in his behaviour towards them, repeatedly threatening to "do for" them, that he was removed to the Asylum. By some means or other he became possessed of a knife, with which, it is said, he rushed through the corridor followed by the attendants, and, before he could be seized, cut his throat, inflicting a wound which speedily proved fatal.

STEALTHILY SNATCHED KNIFE.
From inquires made, it appears that Hardwick was admitted to the Asylum on Monday last. He was not then in a violent mood, but seemed to be in a sort of stupor, and could not, or would not, give any account

of himself. While in the breakfast room with the other inmates this morning Hardwick seems to have been attacked by a sudden violent fit, for while one of the attendants was cutting up the bread, he stealthily approached the table, and seized a knife that was lying there. The knife was lying within reach of the attendant's hand, and if he had seen what Hardwick was up to he could readily have prevented his seizing it. Unfortunately, however, his attention was at the moment directed elsewhere, and the madman's movements were very quiet.

TRAGIC END OF THE PURSUIT.
The hubbub that arose as soon as the other inmates saw that Hardwick had got the knife soon apprised the attendant of what had happened, and with one bound he made after the madman, followed by other attendants, who quickly came onto the scene. Hardwick, however, had got a start of some yards, and before he could be seized and disarmed, had reached the dormitory door, ten or fifteen yards away, where, seeing that escape was impossible, he hastily drew the knife across his throat. He fell down in a heap, and the attendants found that he had inflicted mortal injuries.

When the news was conveyed to Mrs. Hardwick, she was greatly affected. She went up to the Asylum this morning to see her husband's body and created a painful scene, being almost hysterical with grief.

"I'M MAD, I'M MAD."
Inquiries made in the neighbourhood show that Hardwick was a steady, sober, hardworking man. He came from Brighton between three and four months ago, and since then has been lodging in one room at 47, Highbury Street, a private house let in furnished apartments by the landlady of the "Blue Anchor." He was employed by Mr. Bramble on some works at Southsea Castle, and was at work on Saturday the 29th ult. Previous to that, his wife had not noticed anything peculiar in his manner, nor had he ever used any threats towards her. In fact, he seems to have been very fond of his wife and two children, of whom the eldest is only two years. On the day in question he returned home as usual. During the evening he complained to his wife of pains in his head. She asked him to describe them, on which he suddenly exclaimed, "I'm mad, I'm mad. I have got a feeling that I must murder my wife and the children. Something tells me that I must do it." He then burst into tears and begged his wife to take him somewhere.

Hearing this, the poor woman was naturally alarmed. Her husband was, however, perfectly quiet and quite docile. He made no objection to seeing a medical man, and the husband and wife walked together to Dr. Morley's, in the High Street. Here Mrs. Hardwick informed Mr. Morley, jun. of what had occurred. Mr. Morley asked Hardwick what was the matter with him, and the latter repeated the strange statement he had made to his wife.

Mr. Morley asked him, "But what makes you think you are mad?" and the unfortunate man replied, "something tells me I must murder my wife and children. I don't want to do it." He was much agitated and the doctor's opinion was that he was not right in his head.

ENTICED TO THE POLICE STATION.
At his suggestion, the wife enticed him round to the Police Station in Pembroke Road, Dr. Morley following. Here a similar scene occurred, and Sergeant Harvey sent for Mr. Coward, the Relieving Officer by whom Hardwick was removed to the Imbecile Ward of the Workhouse. Here he was detained for a week and was then removed to the Lunatic Asylum.

All the neighbours speak in high terms of both Mr. and Mrs. Hardwick.

FURTHER DETAILS.
It would seem that Hardwick was a very quiet patient, never speaking unless spoken to, and had manifested no suicidal tendencies. About 7.40 this morning, the

The Sorry-go-Round

charge attendant, Arthur Himmens, was cutting up the bread while another attendant, named Tobin, was buttering it.

A spare knife, with which Himmens was going to assist Tobin in buttering the bread, was lying on the table near at hand. The deceased and the other patients were walking up and down the ward at the time, and the deceased walked down from the east end of the ward towards the table and suddenly snatched up the knife and ran towards the dormitory door. Himmens and Tobin ran after him, but before anything could be done the deceased, who had gained the door, drew the knife across his throat and ran off again through the dormitory. In the dormitory he again drew the knife across his throat, and throwing the weapon away fell back into the arms of Himmens, who was close behind him. Himmens laid him on the floor, and endeavoured to staunch the wound with a pillow case, while Tobin went for the doctor. Dr. Blackwood was the first to attend to the man, and Drs Elliott and Mumby afterwards arrived. The wound was a very bad one and two or three times the deceased nearly chocked from the haemorrhage. Everything that could be thought of was done to save the unfortunate man's life but he gradually sank and died just before eight o'clock.

It appears that this is the first suicide at the asylum since it was opened.

1899 – SIDELIGHTS ON CONVICT LIFE.

There are not many more impressive lessons in practical morality than a visit to such an establishment as Her Majesty's prison, Kingston, near Portsmouth, on a fine spring morning. It is an experience which brings forcibly home to the mind of the average citizen the truth that it is a good thing to be as true and just in all one's dealings as the exigencies of business permit, to make money as honestly as possible, to pay one's debts when ordered to do so by one of Her Majesty's judges, and also to pay such of Her Majesty's taxes as cannot be evaded by impunity.

It is, of course, the same light that shines on bond and free, the same blue sky over the green field and the grey prison yard; but somehow, when the iron gate clashes to behind you, and the bolt of the lock clicks back into its place, the sun does not seem quite so bright and the blue heaven looks a good deal farther off. The high walls cast long, dark shadows, and whichever way you look the field of vision is bounded by straight, hard lines, clear cut against the sky – in a word, you have entered the House of Bondage where men move by other wills than their own, where they might think but may not utter their thoughts to each other, where they may not take a step or make a movement without permission, or in obedience to some regulation; where, in short, they have ceased to be men and have become passive, volitionless units of a huge machine with which they must grind on for their allotted span, or be broken into pieces by it.

There are two or three reasons why such a prison as Kingston should be included. In the first place it differs considerably from the English Convict Establishment proper, such as Portland, Dartmoor, or Parkhurst, in that it is what is technically termed a "local" prison; that is to say, it receives prisoners only from a given district, whereas a convict may be sent to the others from any part of the country.

The chief difference, however, between Kingston and the Convict Prison proper is practically the difference between penal servitude and hard labour. To most people there is no distinction between these two terms, but in reality there is a very great difference. A man cannot be sent to penal servitude for less than three years, nor to hard labour for more than two. The experienced malefactor much prefers three or even four years' penal servitude to two years hard labour. These are his chief reasons for the preference:

In penal servitude the work is lighter, the food better and rather more plentiful; the privileges which may be won are greater; and absolutely good conduct is rewarded by a maximum remission of one-fourth of the sentence.

There was a time when hard labour for a given time meant hard labour to the last hour of that period. The tendency, however, of all our prison management is now towards leniency. This leniency may be wise or otherwise from the moral point of view; but it is the Law, and there is an end to the matter. Since the new regulations came into force on the 1st May last it is possible for a prisoner undergoing a term of hard labour to work off a portion of his sentence just as a criminal doing a term of penal servitude may do, provided that his sentence is over six calendar months. These regulations have, in fact, been made retrospective, and any prisoner undergoing a term of more than six months' hard labour on the 1st May is entitled to this privilege.

The comparative effects of penal servitude and hard labour on the health of the prisoner are the subject of some difference of opinion. I have questioned those who have done both forms of "time," and invariably I have been told that penal servitude as a rule is good for the health, granted always that the prisoner has a sound constitution to begin with; while hard labour for any period over nine months breaks a man up. On the other hand, however, it is only fair to state that the Governor of Kingston tells me that he has frequently released prisoners after a term of hard labour in much better health than he received them.

As far as my own observation enables me to judge, I would certainly prefer three years' penal servitude to eighteen months' hard labour, even under the new and more merciful regulations. In all the Convict Prisons I have visited saving, of course, the Convalescent Home at Parkhurst, the prisoners, apart from that undefinable something which distinguishes the Bond from the Free, appeared to be strong, healthy, and to a certain extent, content with their lot. I cannot say that this was the case at Kingston. It seemed to me that there was a good deal of truth in what I had heard from those who had done various terms of hard labour.

For instance, a considerable proportion of the prisoners at Kingston are soldiers and sailors who have been convicted of offences by court-martial, and handed over to the civil authorities for punishment. Now, while I was standing with the Governor in the central hall from which the galleries radiate, a prisoner coming from the upper tier of the cells on to the landing, from which the iron staircase leads to the lower floor, caught sight of us. Instantly he drew himself up, squared his shoulders, pulled his drab, arrow-marked jacket down, ran down the stairs with a light, springy step, and marched along the hall as though he was on parade. There was no mistaking the drilled soldier, even in the uniform of the felon. He had only been in a week or so, and the deadly machine had not got its work in on him yet.

I had not, however, been very long in the prison before I saw how great a difference there was between the men who had only just got into the grip of this machine and those who had descended from the level of the drilled soldier or sailor, or of the free civilian, to that of the mere felon "doing time," and this difference was perhaps most noticeable in the exercise yard, where the prisoners were doing their hour's tramp, some ten paces apart, round a big circle on a narrow path paved with flagstones. It only need a glance at the gait and carriage of a man as he passed on his way round the endless path to tell what he had been, and what he was, and how long he had been enduring the just punishment of his evil doings.

But this is recreation; for, even behind prison walls, all things go by contract, just as they do outside them, and this is the recreation from hard labour. There is a little building, built of red brick instead of blue-grey Devon stone like the rest of the prison, standing somewhat apart from the main building in a corner of the exercise ground and prison garden. On the chocolate coloured door are painted in white letters the two words "Wheel House." As the Governor's master key will open it, we will go in and see hard labour as it is.

As the door opens, the dull, grinding sound that we heard outside grows a little louder and clearer. The door closes behind us with the inevitable clash and click of the returning bolt. The "house" is an apartment some thirty feet long and fifteen feet wide. On the left hand side are the wheels, four of them in two tiers, divided by a gallery running the whole length of the house and communicating with the floor by a staircase at the opposite end. On the right hand side there is another lower and shorter gallery on which stands the warder in charge. The wheels are separated, as will be seen in the photograph, by a section of brick wall.

Each wheel is divided into compartments, cutting off each prisoner from the other. The object of this is to prevent the prisoners from seeing or hearing each other, though I have heard from casual acquaintances who have "been there," that conversation in a low voice pitched in a different key to that of "the music of the wheel" is perfectly easy and intelligible, and that newcomers who understand the trick can in a very short time send the latest news of the outside world all through the prison while climbing up "the endless staircase."

At the farther end of the house from the door there is a gong fixed against the wall, and near this is a brass disc swung like the pendulum of a clock. Every fifteen minutes this swings back and strikes the bell. Then you hear the officer in charge sing out something like this, "A1, B1, C1, D1."

The Governor, standing in the central hall from which the galleries radiate.

And as each letter and number is called out a prisoner steps from the wheel on to the stilt-like steps behind his compartment, and goes thankfully to take his place on the seat, which at the same moment is vacated by another man, whose turn to take another climb has come. The regulations prescribe fifteen minutes on the wheel and five minutes off.

Not the least interesting feature of this depressing House of the Everlasting Stairs is the difference between the way in which the work is tackled by the old hands and the new ones. Just opposite to the gallery on which we were standing was a compartment occupied by a cleanly built young fellow of about twenty two. Saving for the monotony of the exercise, the wheel apparently troubled him very little. As each step of the "staircase" came under the edge of the wooden partition on which the hand-bars are fixed, his foot slipped up on it and rested there with no apparent effort, until it was time to move it up again.

On either side of him were men, pretty nearly twice his weight and a fourth as tall again, who were labouring at the same work in a style that made one's knees and thighs ache to look at them. They were making the mistake of putting their feet on too late. The result was that they were no sooner on than they had to be off again, for the tread wheel has a way of its own with laggards. If the foot remains an instant too long on the step it moves away from under; so the foot slips off, and the next step scrapes the ankle and instep in no gentle fashion. The resulting attitude is undignified even for a felon, added to which the officer in charge generally has something pungently unpleasant to say on the subject.

The difference in the amount of labour done in the same time was very noticeable when the periods of rest came around. The young old-hand stepped down cool and calm, and looked about him with a smiling air of superiority; with the air, in short, of a man who knows his work and can do it with the least possible effort. The new hands, possessing twice his strength, climbed bunglingly down, limped towards the seats of rest, and sat gasping and sweating, elbows on knees and head hanging forward between their hands, from which it follows that even on the tread wheel there is scope for practised skill and natural aptitude.

The energy spent in the forced labour of the tread wheel, (tread mill by the way is quite incorrect), is not wasted at Kingston. The wheel is geared on to mill stones which grind corn into flour supplied to several prisons. With its full complement, the wheel accommodates forty men, but, as there are often a less number on it,

The tread-wheel.

the difficulty of turning it is regulated by increasing or diminishing the supply of grain.

One of the hardships of hard labour consists in the fact that the diet is of the lightest and the labour the heaviest at the beginning. There are three classes of diet, increasing in generosity as period after period of imprisonment passes. According to the new scale, "as modified by Rule 313," prisoners doing seven days or under have eight ounces of bread and a pint of gruel for breakfast and supper. On Sunday they have for dinner bread and suet pudding, eight ounces each; on Monday the same quantities of bread and potatoes; on Tuesday eight ounces of bread and a pint of porridge. Wednesday's dinner is like Sunday's; Thursday's like Tuesday's, Friday's like Monday's; and Saturday's like Tuesday's.

A good illustration of the increasing leniency with which the authorities, doubtless in deference to a more or less mistaken public opinion, are treating the scoundrels committed to their care is to be found in the fact that "Juvenile offenders under the age of sixteen years of age may, in addition to any of the diets to which they are entitled under the rules, be allowed milk not exceeding one pint per diem at the discretion of the Medical Officer." It is thus that a paternal Government seeks to build up the constitutions of those undergraduates in crime who, in nineteen cases out of twenty, will complete their course at the public expense.

A month's "hard" means a Class A diet as above for the first seven days, and then No. 3, which consists of bread and gruel for breakfast and supper; bread, potatoes, and suet pudding on Sundays and Wednesdays, bread, potatoes, and cooked beef (three ounces, weighed after cooking and without bones), Mondays and Fridays; bread, potatoes and soup on Tuesdays, Thursdays and Saturdays.

Before the New Regulations came into force, a prisoner did not taste solid meat until he had done a month. To this diet, as to the other, a pint of milk a day can be added for the juvenile offenders. After four months the diet becomes more liberal. The quantity of meat is increased from three to four ounces, of suet pudding from eight to twelve, and of potatoes from eight to twelve. Beans and bacon may be substituted for the beef, and three days a week a pint of cocoa and two ounces extra bread may, at the prisoner's option, be substituted for a pint of porridge or gruel at breakfast. Under these new rules, the first day's diet for all classes of prisoners, irrespective of age or sex is for breakfast. Eight ounces of bread and a pint of cocoa; for dinner, twelve ounces of bread, a quarter of a pound of "Colonial or American beef or mutton, preserved by heat," and for supper half a pound of bread and a pint of porridge.

Men serving longer sentences have No.3 diet for four months, and are then promoted to No.4 or full diet. They then have eight ounces of bread and a pint of porridge for breakfast; six ounces of bread, eight ounces of potatoes, and twelve ounces of suet pudding for dinner on Sundays and Wednesdays, the same quantities of bread and potatoes with four ounces of cooked beef without bone on Mondays and Fridays, eight ounces of bread, eight ounces of potatoes, and a pint of soup on Tuesdays, Thursdays and Saturdays. Supper is the same as breakfast.

Serving out dinner to the prisoners.

After nine months, however, a pint of cocoa and two more ounces of bread may be chosen two days a week instead of the porridge or gruel, while slightly larger quantities of Colonial beef or mutton, and fresh or salt fish, may be substituted for English beef, and other vegetables for the potatoes if the prison authorities consider it advisable. The hospital, (Convict Convalescent Home), dietary is totally distinct from this. It is far more generous, and a list of extras that may be ordered, at the discretion of the Medical Officer, begins with ale, ends with wine, and includes beef tea, cake, eggs, ice, poultry, spirits, mineral waters and jelly. The common dietary for men without hard labour is the same as that for women and boys under sixteen, and is slightly lighter than the hard labour diet.

I have gone into the subject of diet rather fully because it bears closely upon what I said with regard to the present condition of hard labour. The longer the period of his term a man serves the better he is fed and the more lightly he may be worked; but it is quite within the discretion of the governor to move idle or badly behaved prisoners back a class or so – that it is to say, to lighter food and harder work. To the average well fed citizen these dietaries will not seem to contain many luxuries, but luxuries, after all, are a comparative term, and to a man who has lived and worked seven days on bread and water and gruel, and has been a month without tasting meat, a plate of beef and potatoes may be what a Hotel Cecil dinner would be to a half-starved tramp.

Of course there are other punishments – the bread and water diet, solitary confinement, the birch, and the dreaded "cat," but these are very seldom necessary in hard labour. Reduction in class is usually enough. In the vast majority of cases even the fear of this suffices. For instance, the Governor tells me that out of 1551 male and 289 female prisoners received at Kingston in a year, only thirty men and three women were punished even in the slightest degree. As regards the men, this low average is no doubt accounted for by the fact that some 50 percent of them are, or have been, either soldiers or sailors, and their instinct of discipline makes them, in prison parlance, "excellent prisoners."

It may here be interesting to note the stages by which the soldier or sailor who has forgotten alike his own honour and that of the Service makes "the Rogue's March" back to civil life. Men tried by court martial may, according to their offence, be sent either to a military prison, or they may be handed over for punishment to the civil authority.

Now the sentence sometimes includes these words; "and to be dismissed with ignominy from the Service." In this case the culprit is adjudged unworthy to wear the Queen's uniform, so he is handed over to the civil power as a civilian, and as such is released when he has served his time. In other cases he is conducted to the prison door by an escort and enters the prison gates in uniform.

Then comes the inevitable bath; his regimentals are rolled up into a neat package and put away into a compartment in the storeroom, while he dons the drab livery of crime. I saw several of these bundles at Kingston, everything brushed and neat, the gold-braided forage cap on top of the bundle, and the natty little cane stuck through it.

If the term is not a long one, and the man's prison reports are good, he is released in his uniform and handed over to an escort at the gate; probably to hear something on the way that will be good for his soul. On the other hand, in the case of long sentences at the end of which the broken felon will be of little or no use as soldier or sailor, or when the reports are bad, an intimation comes from the War Office or the Admiralty to the effect that there is no longer a place for him in Her Majesty's Service. Then the uniform is sent back, and a suit of civilian clothes is required pending his release.

It would hardly be believed that a British soldier or sailor would deliberately place upon himself the indelible brand of the felon in order to get out of the service of his country, and yet, strange as a statement may sound, it is absolutely true.

The visiting room.

There were men at Kingston, both soldiers and sailors, who had deliberately committed a crime of one sort or another merely because they were not satisfied with the conditions of their service. One man, a sailor with a previously good record, had incurred a penalty of eighteen month's hard labour with his eyes open, just because he had been set to work in a depot when he wanted to go on foreign service. To the credit of the Services, however, it ought to be added that such instances are very rare indeed.

Then again, while some men were doing time to get out of the army, others were doing it for trying to get in again, that is to say, for "fraudulent enlistment," a crime mostly manufactured by the iniquitous system of deferred pay. But others were there for trying to re-enlist under false names after having been dismissed from the Service for crime or insubordination, which, of course, is a very different matter. It was somewhat curious to see men in the same prison undergoing the same penalties, some for getting out of Her Majesty's Services, and some for trying to get in again by the back door.

There are respects in which the prison at Kingston differs from the regular convict establishment, which may be of some interest to the average citizen of the world, since we most of us have debts and all of us have taxes to pay.

A portion of the prison building is set apart for the accommodation of three classes of prisoners who are not criminals – Offenders of the 1st Division; Prisoners on Remand or awaiting trial; and Debtors. The difference between these three classes and the other prisoners consists mainly in this: They do not work in the prison sense of the term, and, with certain restrictions, the "offenders" may feed themselves or have their food sent in by their friends.

I will take that the third class is the one in which the average citizen takes the most sympathetic interest, and conclude by describing as possible the daily life of a debtor in a modern prison. Imprisonment for debt is, of course, technically done away with. If you are skilful and unscrupulous enough to induce a usually too easily convinced judge that you cannot pay your just debts, you go free, with the possibility of a pleasing consciousness that you have forced the man you have defrauded to throw good money after bad; but should you fail in this, the judge will make an order that you shall pay in certain instalments, and if you disobey this order it is possible that you may get arrested – several weeks after the order has been made – and if you do not pay then you will be imprisoned for Contempt of Court.

Before the passing of the New Regulations, debtors and offenders of the first division were not required to work, and during certain hours of the day they had the privilege of associating together in what was called the Day Room, that is to say, a sort of Common Room very plainly furnished, but still a pleasant change from the cell. Now, however, the first of the New Rules reads, "A debtor prisoner shall at all times, except when at chapel or exercise, occupy the cell assigned to him." In other words, the Common Room is abolished, and the condition of the debtor is brought a little nearer to that of the convicted prisoner.

Then again, instead of passing his time reading or conversing, or in lonely meditation in his cell, he is obliged to work, "at his own trade or profession, provided his employment does not interfere with the regulations of the prison, or at work of an industrial or manufacturing nature, and he shall be allowed to receive the whole of his earnings subject to a reduction of the cost of his maintenance and for the use of implements when furnished by the prison".

The Regulation has already led to some rather amusing dilemmas. For instance, a young governess was committed for debt, but the judge could not send her to prison without finding her something to do. She bravely volunteered to do "something in the painting line," but as there was no scope for her abilities in this direction, he compromised by giving her fourteen days to pay in. After her came a company promoter, whose talents, as the judge remarked, might have been exercised in the Day Room in promoting

Outside view of Kingston Prison and the Governor's residence.

a company for the payment of his and his fellow prisoners' debts; but the cleverest of financiers could not do much at his "trade or profession," while locked in a cell.

After him came a circus proprietor, and it was immediately seen that it was just as impossible to run a circus while sitting alone in a cell as to promote companies. Of course, under the old rules they could have sat in the Day Room, put their heads together, and turned the circus into a limited liability concern, and discharged their debts out of the profits. Instead of this, they were each allowed fourteen days to get together the wherewithal to purchase their liberty.

Debtors are fed on the same scale as "Offenders of the 1st Division who do not maintain themselves," that is to say, Class 3 diet, as described above, with the exception of the substitution of half a pint of cocoa for gruel at breakfast and supper. Previous to the 1st May, debtors, like Offenders of the 1st Division, were allowed, if they could, to maintain themselves and to receive either a pint of malt liquor or half a pint of wine during the twenty four hours. They will now be obliged to content themselves with the prison diet.

There is no doubt that the change is a wise and a just one, for under the old rules it was possible for a debtor who had defrauded his creditors, by making his money over to his wife or relations, to live in comparative luxury for a week or so and come out with a clean slate.

For instance, there was one gentlemen in Kingston who was doing seven days for £2 17s. 6d. Seeing that board and lodging of a sort were thrown in, and that he knew that his creditor had spent a good deal more than the amount of his debt to get him there, he would probably come out with the consciousness that he had spent a fairly profitable, if not agreeable week.

1900 – EXTRAORDINARY CASE OF FRAUD ON A PORTSMOUTH TRADESMAN.

An extraordinary case of imposture, of which a Portsmouth victualler was the victim, came before the Portsmouth Magistrates.

Jennie Martin, alias Broadhurst, aged fifty four, was nominally charged with obtaining by false pretences food to the value of 5s. 6d. from Stephen Blackman, landlord of the Foresters' Arms, North Street, Portsea. On February 8 the prisoner, a fairly well-dressed and well-spoken person, called at prosecutor's house, and engaged a bed there for five nights. In the course of conversation she said she had come to Portsmouth to search for her husband, who had deserted her, but she desired first to see the Rev. Mr. Clegg, one of the clergy attached to St. Jude's Church, Portsea. Next day she said she had seen Mr. Clegg, that he had taken her case up, that he would assist her in her search, and would make himself responsible for her maintenance whilst she remained in the prosecutor's house. She added that Mr. Clegg would write to the prosecutor to that effect, and subsequently the prosecutor received such a letter, and from time to time others, purporting to come from the Rev. Mr. Clegg.

Believing these representations, he continued to supply her with food and lodgings until May 26th. During that interval she told him they had discovered her husband, but only to find that he was dead, and she went into mourning for him, after first persuading the prosecutor's wife to furnish her with the outfit. Then she introduced into the story a Lord St. Clair, who she informed them would, within a reasonable time of her husband's death, marry her, and letters began to come from "Lord St. Clair," which, like those purporting to be from Mr. Clegg, were forgeries. She told the prosecutor that when Lord St. Clair married her she would make him rich in return for all that he had done for her, but, she said, his lordship would not care for her to remain living at a public house, and so he took private lodgings for her, and early in May furnished her with a wedding outfit, and on the 25th she left to be married, but he saw no more of her until she was in custody.

Altogether she had defrauded him of about £90. Both Mr. Clegg and Lord St. Clair were mythical individuals. The prisoner was sentenced to two months' hard labour.

1900 – MURDER BY HYPNOTISM.

The Portsmouth Coroner (Mr. T. A. Bramsdon) sat at the Town Hall this afternoon to inquire into the circumstances attending the death of William Coombs, formerly a horse feeder at the Corporation Stables, and, at the time of his death, an inmate at the Borough Lunatic Asylum, Milton. On Friday last the deceased, in company with a number of patients, was taken out for a walk on Southsea Beach, and when near Eastney Barracks he suddenly fell forward and died almost immediately. The deceased had not complained of illness, and was apparently a very healthy man.

After the evidence of two attendants had been taken bearing out the above facts, the inquiry took a startling turn. A patient named John Shelley was placed in the box. Dr. Mumby, the Superintendent at the Asylum, stating that he believed the man was in a fit state to give evidence. A letter which this patient had written to the Coroner was then read. It was to the effect that the witness desired to give evidence, as he was intimately acquainted with the deceased, who, he asserted, was continually complaining of what was done to him. The witness then replied to questions in a rambling and strange manner, and after he had made some remarks about hypnotism the Coroner observed that this matter was not relevant. The witness thereupon replied that the deceased had complained of it. He was always complaining of hypnotism himself. Hypnotic influence, he asserted, was the cause of the deceased's death. "I maintain that he has been murdered by hypnotic influence," said the witness, who, however, admitted that his treatment at the Asylum was satisfactory. The witness was requested to stand down.

Dr. Mumby, the Medical Superintendent at the Asylum, was then called, and attributed death to heart disease.

The Jury returned a verdict of "Death from natural causes," whereupon the patient expressed himself dissatisfied with the finding, complaining that he had not been heard properly with reference to this important matter.

The wife of the deceased man stated, when identifying the body, that she was quite satisfied with the manner in which her husband had been treated at the Asylum.

1900 – A BIG FIRE AT PORTSEA.

A serious and destructive fire has been raging all night in St. George's Square. Portsea, the premises attacked being a large forage store in the occupation of Messrs. Ashdowne and Co., corn factors and Government contractors.

The Fire Brigade received notification of the outbreak at 6.19 on Monday evening and the horse escape and a steamer were soon on the scene in the charge of Superintendent Vassie. On their arrival they found the place well alight. There were ten tons of straw and 14 tons of hay in the building, and the flames, which apparently originated in the loft, soon travelled downwards to the material below. The steamer was got to work with three deliveries, but little progress was made, and the deliveries were subsequently transferred to the hydrant.

The outbreak proved a most difficult one to deal with, for it was impossible to locate it properly while the firemen were greatly inconvenienced by the dense and pungent smoke thrown out by the sodden smouldering forage. During the night, the chief efforts of the Brigade were devoted to preventing the flames spreading to the buildings on either side, and in this they were attended with complete success. When daylight came, the burning stuff was gradually removed from the building, the operation proving an extremely lengthy one. Indeed, the outbreak was not completely extinguished by ten o'clock this morning.

The origin of the fire is at present unknown. The foreman (Mr. Ware) thinks that the discharge of fireworks by boys may be responsible, while Mr. Vassie, the Superintendent of the Fire Brigade, favours the theory of spontaneous combustion. Of course, the entire amount of fodder has been destroyed, for that which escaped the flames was completely saturated with water, but the building itself—although the roof was partly destroyed—is not so very badly damaged.

The damage, of course, is of a very extensive nature, and, it is stated, is not covered by insurance. Great excitement was created in Portsea by the conflagration, and the operations of the Brigade were watched by thousands of spectators.

This morning, at ten o'clock, Sergeant Ogburn and four firemen were still on duty at the scene of the fire, and the volumes of smoke which issued from the stores demonstrated that their services might still be required. The store is a two-storied building extending 60 feet back from St. George's Square, in the centre of a block of buildings between Britain Street on the right and back and Little Britain Street on the left. The contents of the stores, about 23 tons of hay and straw, were completely destroyed by fire and water, while a quantity of specially prepared fodder intended for shipment to South Africa was burnt. The roof was burnt off and the building, which is practically only a shell, was burnt through in places.

The fact that surrounding buildings were not destroyed reflects the greatest credit on the Brigade, who worked with great zeal from the time of their arrival until four o'clock this morning, when they began to get the fire under control.

The Royal Standard public house, which is next to the store, at the corner of Little Britain Street, did not escape injury, as the water poured through the roof and deluged two of the back bedrooms. The effects of the fire were apparent through the wall, which, fortunately, is exceptionally thick, or the whole premises would undoubtedly have gone. Next door to the public house is an oil and coal store, but the oil was got out in time, and averted disaster in that direction.

As soon as the fire was got under control, a large number of men were set to work to clear out from the store the still smouldering hay and straw, which was piled up in a great heap in St. George's Square.